THE MAKING OF OUR URBAN LANDSCAPE

THE
MAKING OF
OUR URBAN
LANDSCAPE

GEOFFREY TYACK

OXFORD
UNIVERSITY PRESS

OXFORD

UNIVERSITY PRESS

Great Clarendon Street, Oxford, OX2 6DP,
United Kingdom

Oxford University Press is a department of the University of Oxford.
It furthers the University's objective of excellence in research, scholarship,
and education by publishing worldwide. Oxford is a registered trade mark of
Oxford University Press in the UK and in certain other countries

Published in the United States of America by Oxford University Press
198 Madison Avenue, New York, NY 10016, United States of America

British Library Cataloguing in Publication Data

Data available

Library of Congress Control Number: 2021952847

ISBN 978–0–19–879263–5

Printed and bound in Great Britain by
Clays Ltd, Elcograf S.p.A.

Preface

Over half the world's population currently live in towns or cities, and by 2050 the number is expected to rise to two thirds. The vast majority of the British people are town-dwellers, and urban agglomerations account for some ten per cent of our land use. Towns and cities are the background against which we live our lives, and if we try to understand their history we can go some way towards understanding ourselves. Most of our towns can trace their origin back to the Middle Ages, some even to the Roman Empire, and more or less substantial traces of the past can still be seen in their streets, their buildings and their public spaces. Few visitors can be unaware of the influence of the past on the appearance of Edinburgh or Bath, but the past has also shaped the public faces of Manchester, Birmingham, Glasgow, Cardiff and other towns and cities across our island. 'Place-making' has become something of a vogue word among urban planners in recent years, and this book has been written with the aim of explaining the processes by which the places that we often take for granted have been created over the past millennium or more.

I have been interested in the history of the urban landscape ever since my childhood in South London. My father worked as a civil servant in a former warehouse complex next to Tower Bridge, and my mother grew up in the East End; my grandmother never left it. I started exploring central London as a teenager, and on foot—still the only way to properly understand towns and cities. My first paid employment involved writing the histories of North London suburbs, and since then my interests have taken me to towns throughout the British Isles, Europe and the wider world, especially the United States. A large part of the fascination of urban history lies in its variety; each town, each suburb even, has its own unique history. If the reader can share some of my enjoyment in getting to understand these places better, I will have achieved a large part of my aim.

All historians stand on the shoulders of their predecessors, and for a historian of the urban landscape those shoulders are both broad and numerous.

I am indebted to early chroniclers and topographers such as John Leland in the sixteenth century and Celia Fiennes in the seventeenth, and to more recent writers such as W. G. Hoskins, the doyen of English local and land-scape history (though not a lover of large cities), to the compilers of the invaluable *Cambridge Urban History of Britain* (2000), and to the authors of the many excellent town and city histories that have come out in recent years. I have made extensive use of multi-volume works such as the *Victoria County History* for those parts of England that have been covered; the *Historic Towns* atlas, still flourishing and expanding; and Nikolaus Pevsner's *Buildings of England* series (especially in its second, revised incarnation), and the com-panion volumes on Scotland and Wales. Our understanding of urban history has been profoundly enhanced in recent years by the research of archaeolo-gists and urban geographers, and I have also done my best to incorporate their insights into my narrative. I am grateful to Malcolm Airs, John Blair, David Clark, Perry Gauci, Trevor Rowley, Otto Saumarez-Smith, Robert Thorne and Steven Ward, who have read and commented on drafts of the chapters, but above all to my wife Penny for her companionship and her astute comments on the manuscript as it evolved. I also owe a debt of grati-tude to Matthew Cotton at the Oxford University Press for encouraging me to write the book, and to Kizzy Taylor-Richelieu, Cathryn Steele and Gayathri Venkatesan for seeing it through the publication process.

This book inevitably reflects my own interests. I share William Blake's belief that 'art and science cannot exist but in minutely organized particu-lars', and I find the histories of individual places more enlightening than theories of urban development, useful though they can sometimes be. I have a special interest in buildings, both for themselves and for what they tell us about the past. I make no apology in giving more emphasis than some other writers to developments over the last two centuries. These were, after all, the years that did most to shape the urban landscapes that we experience in our daily lives—the urban population of Britain only surpassed that of rural areas in the middle of the nineteenth century. Change is, and always has been, an essential feature of urban life. I vividly remember visiting Milton Keynes, now a thriving city of some 250,000 people, when it was little more than a gleam in the eyes of planners and architects, and I finished writing this book just before the coronavirus pandemic of 2020-21, which tempor-arily emptied town and city centres with long-term results that still remain to be seen. To fully understand today's urban landscapes, we need to try and understand change, unearthing the layers that lie beneath the surface of what we now see and experience, and attempting to make sense of the often piecemeal, un-coordinated processes that have created the world that we now inhabit. I hope that this book will help readers do this for themselves, and to take pleasure in the process.

Geoffrey Tyack
Oxford
November 2021

Contents

List of Illustrations and Maps

I

Creating an Urban Landscape

Before towns existed, the British landscape had been shaped by millennia of geological activity and by generations of human intervention. These factors helped determine the siting of our towns, and they have influenced the ways in which they developed down to modern times. Towns and cities already existed in Mesopotamia as early as the fourth millennium BCE, and they grew up later in Egypt, China, northern India, and eventually Mediterranean Europe. But they did not emerge in Britain, at least in a recognizable sense, until the Romans extended their control over southern parts of the island in the first century CE.

The First Towns

Much of what has been called 'lowland' Britain—the south and the east—was already intensively farmed in pre-Roman times, and some of the towns founded by the Romans occupied the sites of existing 'tribal' capitals or *oppida*. They included *Verulamium*, adjacent to the modern St Albans, and *Durovernum Cantiacorum* (Canterbury). Starting in the mid first century, the Romans imposed a colonial government on the indigenous population of the areas that they conquered, guaranteed by the presence of an occupying army that in time guaranteed the settled circumstances within which trade could flourish. The towns of Roman Britain were a means of controlling the native population and spreading Roman cultural values to what in time became a Romano-British elite. They sheltered permanent and relatively dense populations made up of tradesmen, craftsmen and some agricultural workers. They were places where goods were regularly exchanged in markets. And, most important of all, they possessed a sense of civic identity expressed in monumental buildings, public spaces and clearly defined boundaries that sharply distinguished them from settlements in their rural hinterland. Linked by a network of roads, they played an essential part in promoting an integrated economy throughout Romanized Britain and across the English Channel, allowing communication to take place, and goods to be traded, over long distances.[1]

At the height of the Roman Empire in the second and third centuries there were twenty or so fairly substantial towns in Britain and another fifty or so smaller settlements with urban characteristics, most of them in the south, middle and east of the island: there were few towns in what became Wales or in the north-west of England, and none in Scotland.[2] Britain was a peripheral part of the Roman Empire, and none of its towns was very large. Few had populations of more than about 5,000, even in their heyday, or areas of more than a hundred or so acres: the average size of regional capitals such as *Ratae Corieltauvorum*, within whose walls the town we now call Leicester later grew up.[3] A handful of towns, notably London, with an estimated population of 60,000, were larger than this, combining both military and civilian functions. But they paled into insignificance in comparison with Chang'an (the modern Xian) in China, which may have housed some 250,000 people in the second century CE, and even more with imperial Rome, with its million or so inhabitants.

Roman towns contributed to the later development of the urban landscape through their siting, their fortifications, and to some extent through their street patterns. London and Gloucester, to take two examples, grew up at places where the new road system crossed important rivers; they were built on higher ground above flood plains, which were crossed by causeways like the one over the River Severn that was clearly shown in Samuel and Nathaniel Buck's panorama of Gloucester in 1734 (Fig. 1.1). London was built on a gravel terrace on the north bank of the Thames, and there is still a noticeable rise in the ground from the river to the heart of the modern financial centre by the Bank of England; the south bank, by contrast, was marshy—there is still a street called Lower Marsh near Waterloo Station—and it remained relatively poor and unpopulated until quite recent times.

Many towns were sited on or near the borders between regions with differing economies, where goods could be exchanged. *Deva* (Chester) began as a legionary fortress strategically placed at the point where the River Dee (then navigable) could be bridged; here the agricultural Cheshire

Fig. 1.1 A Panorama of Gloucester in 1734. The city is seen from the west, with the River Severn in front and a causeway crossing the flood plain to the West Gate. The Cotswold hills are in the background.

Plain meets the hills and mountains of North Wales. At York (*Eboracum*) the Romans' military fortress was established above a flood plain on one side of the River Ouse, which was navigable for sea-going vessels. A civilian settlement or *colonia* was laid out on the other side of the river, and this helps explain the complicated street plan of the modern city. *Lindum* (Lincoln) was sited more dramatically at the southern end of a limestone ridge high above the River Witham, which gave access to the North Sea, and the town was subsequently extended 200 feet downhill towards the river.[4] *Isca Dumnoniorum*, the Roman town on the site of modern Exeter, was likewise established at the end of a ridge, at the south-western end of the road known as the Fosse Way leading from Lincoln; it overlooked the flood plain of the River Exe,[5] as is obvious to anyone climbing from the quayside to the city centre today. *Aquae Sulis* (Bath), by contrast, owed its origin to hot springs, dedicated to the goddess Sul (the Celtic equivalent of Minerva) and situated within a loop of the River Avon surrounded by an amphitheatre of limestone hills. It was already the site of a popular cult before the Romans arrived, and under the Romans it became a pleasure resort, centred on the baths which gave the town its present name and reputation.

Fortifications were an essential feature of Roman towns from the late second century onwards, as they were for towns worldwide. Walls were constructed partly for defence, but they also demarcated boundaries and controlled access through their gates. The circuit of walls was sometimes rectangular, as at Lincoln and Chester, sometimes oval-shaped, as at Canterbury and Bath, sometimes irregular, as in London. Their presence sometimes helped determine important elements of the modern street plan, as is still obvious even when the walls themselves have gone. The streets called Upper and Lower Borough Walls in Bath follow the boundaries of the Roman town and of the medieval city that grew up on its site, and at Winchester (*Venta Belgarum*) the footprint of the Roman walls was used in subsequent Anglo-Saxon and later defences. Town walls were originally of earth and timber, but many were later rebuilt in stone, and stone walling of the Roman period still survives, albeit with many later alterations and restorations, in the fragmentary remnants of London's fortifications. The walls at Canterbury, partially built of hard lumps of flint taken from the surrounding chalk hills, can be clearly seen from the southern ring road, and a twenty ft.-high stretch is incorporated into the former church of St Mary Northgate (Fig. 1.2). At York a 'multangular' tower of the local white limestone

Fig. 1.2 The Roman walls of Canterbury were rebuilt in flint after 1363, with rounded bastions, and have been much restored since then. The Dane John earthwork, heightened and landscaped in 1790, is in the background.

from the Roman legionary fortress survives in a corner of the Yorkshire Museum gardens,[6] and the foundations of the east gate of Gloucester can be dimly seen through a transparent panel on the pavement outside a 1950s shopping complex. But the only Roman gateway to survive above ground is at Lincoln, where the Newport Arch, north of the cathedral, has precariously survived for the best part of two millennia, infuriating bus and lorry drivers who have sometimes got stuck underneath it.

Roman towns were sometimes laid out in grid fashion—a pattern that can be taken back to fifth century BCE Greece—with the major streets intersecting at a central point, often at, or close to, the main public space or forum. They were usually straight, like those of Pompeii or of abandoned British towns such as Silchester (Hampshire), which had a chequer-board pattern. Some modern towns on Roman sites retain elements of this arrangement. The main east-west and north-south streets of Chester and Chichester still follow the lines of their Roman predecessors, and at York the streets now called Stonegate and Petergate approximate to the lines of streets within the legionary fortress. But that is quite unusual, and in London, Canterbury and

Cirencester—to take three of the larger towns of late Roman Britain—the modern street pattern dates from long after the Romans left.

Little survives of Roman town buildings, at least above ground, but archaeology has revealed much that lies hidden underground. The remains of the amphitheatre of Roman London can now be seen underneath the Guildhall Museum, and a Mithraic temple of the third century CE on the banks of Walbrook (a tributary of the Thames) was unearthed in 1954 and has recently been restored to its original position under a modern office block. The wall of a bath complex (Jewry Wall) can still be seen at Leicester, another town where the Roman street pattern has vanished, and a fragment of the amphitheatre at Chester survives outside the walls. The Norman castle at Colchester stands on the substructure of a temple built soon after the death of the Emperor Claudius in 54 CE, and mosaic pavements have been unearthed at Cirencester and at Dorchester (Dorset), a smaller provincial capital, where some are now displayed within the foundations of a house built in about 300 CE. The artificial hill known as Dane John at Canterbury, part of a public garden since 1790, was a burial mound in Roman times, and was later used as the motte of the Norman castle. But at places like Manchester and Doncaster all we have is the Old English name element *ceaster*, derived from the Latin *castrum*, meaning a fortified place.

The patchy urbanization of Roman Britain was a false start. Urban life and civilization as we would recognize it disappeared within the century after the legions left at the beginning of the fifth century. Towns were gradually abandoned, though not immediately or all at the same time.[7] Central government vanished, and the economic networks that sustained urban life withered. With the veneer of urbanity removed, Britain became once more an overwhelmingly rural island, politically fragmented among chieftains and their followers, many of them immigrants from northern Europe and from across the Irish Sea; their territories eventually coalesced into the kingdoms and principalities that made up what we now call England, Wales and Scotland. In some places elements of urban life lingered on, in however distorted a form. The walls of some Roman towns survived, as at Caerwent (Monmouthshire) and Silchester, two of the most evocative sites in southern Britain, echoing Ovid's 'Iam seges est ubi Troia fuit' ('Now there is a corn field where Troy once was'). *Verulamium*, one of the most important towns of Roman Britain, was also abandoned,[8] but a town (St Albans) later grew up outside its walls on, or close to, the burial place of England's first Christian martyr. And it was chiefly through the presence of the Church—the main communicator of Roman civilization, especially through the Latin language—that this memory and, arguably, the very idea of urban life, was communicated to later generations.

With the first conversion of Anglo-Saxon immigrants to Christianity, starting in the 590s, churches began to be built within, and sometimes outside, the walls of some former Roman towns, or what remained of them. The seventh century, or even earlier, church of St Martin, outside the walls of Canterbury, contains re-used Roman masonry and brickwork, and the remains of other churches of similar date have been found on the site of the ruined monastery of St Augustine. But it took a very long time before there was any evidence of what we would now understand as urban life connected with such churches, or of the minsters (large churches served by communities of priests or monks) that were described by the Venerable Bede in his *History of the English Church and People*, written in 731. By then long-distance trade with the Continent had revived, leading to the establishment of *wics* or trading settlements on the banks or mouths of navigable rivers. This happened in the area to the north of the Strand—meaning shore—leading west out of the walls of Roman London towards Westminster, where a royal church was later founded on or near the site of the present Abbey. Recent archaeology has unearthed a substantial settlement on the site of the modern Covent Garden, and the name of the busy street called Aldwych (old *wic*), further east, perpetuates its memory.[9] The *wic* suffix also appears at Ipswich (Suffolk) and Sandwich (Kent) on the east coast. And between two and four thousand people may have been living at *Hamwic*, laid out on a rudimentary grid plan by the early eighth century on a site near the mouth of the River Itchen at the head of Southampton Water.[10] Settlements of this kind traded with Continental ports such as the now lost *Dorestad* in Holland, but most were no larger than modern villages, and none has left any visible trace.

Internal trade also revived in seventh-century England, some of it making use of roads, including the Roman Ermine and Watling Streets. But the most profitable internal trade was, and remained, water-borne, both along the coast and along rivers. Nowhere in Britain is more than seventy or so miles from the sea, and many inland areas could be reached by ships, which had much shallower draughts than those of today.

York

The development of water-borne trade goes a long way towards explaining the revival of York. The Anglo-Saxon King of Northumbria founded a minster church on the site of the legionary fortress of the Roman *Eboracum* in 627, and it became the seat of an archdiocese a century later in 735. During the eighth century the town became an important 'emporium' or entrepot for goods, with trading settlements growing up on three distinct sites: one to close to the present York Minster; another on the site of the Roman *colonia* on the opposite side of the river; and a third close to the present street called Fishergate, near the confluence of the Ouse and its tributary the River Foss (Fig. 1.3).[11] In about 780 the poet Alcuin described York as:

'A haven for the ships from distant ports
Across the ocean, where the sailor hastes
To cast his rope ashore and stay to rest.
The city is watered by the fish-rich Ouse
Which flows past flowery plains on every side;
And hills and forests beautify the earth
And make a lovely dwelling-place, whose health
And richness soon will fill it full of men.
The best of realms and people round came there
In hope of gain, to seek in that rich earth
For riches, there to make both home and gain.'

Massive Danish (Viking) raids came in the 830s, followed by the Scandinavian takeover of much of the north and east of Britain. They had a devastating effect at first, but York, the *de facto* capital of northern England, reaped the advantage of new trade across the North Sea.[12] A commercial area grew up on the relatively high ground to the south of the Minster, between the floodplains of the Ouse and the Foss; it was centred upon a market place which still flourishes, bounded roughly by the present Parliament Street, Shambles and Pavement. There was also an industrial quarter around Coppergate further south, where the 'Jorvik' excavations of 1976–81 have revealed much about the everyday life of the town in the tenth century. A route—Coney Street, now the city's main shopping street—ran south from the Minster area towards the market, parallel to the wharves that went up on the lower ground along the east bank of the Ouse. Finally, in about 980, a new bridge was built on the site of the present Ouse Bridge, leading from Micklegate, within the settlement on the site of the Roman *colonia*, to the market. The present, seemingly haphazard, street plan embodies these changes, the street names, mostly ending in the word 'gate' (*gata*, meaning 'road'), also perpetuating the Scandinavian influence on the city's development.[13]

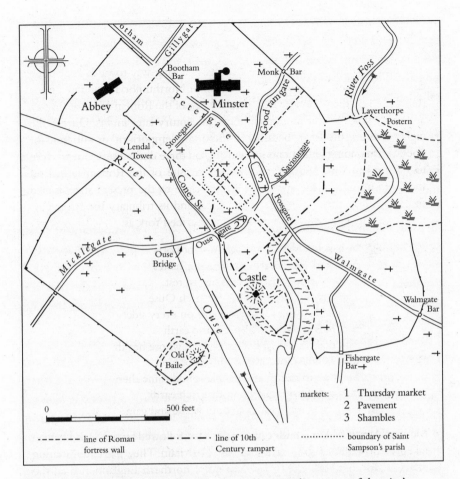

Fig. 1.3 The complex plan of York reflects the episodic nature of the city's development. The Minster (at the top) stands within the site of the Roman fort (*praetorium*), and Petergate and Stonegate follow the lines of Roman streets. The Anglo-Saxon town grew up on rising ground further south with a bridge across the River Ouse. The Normans built castles on either side of the river, and the walls were later rebuilt and extended to enclose the enlarged city, as shown here.

When the Anglo-Saxon kingdom of Wessex revived after the defeat of the Danish army at Edington (Wiltshire) in 878, King Alfred (d.899) and his successors established fortified enclosures or *burhs* near the boundaries of the Danelaw, the part of the country that remained under Scandinavian control. More went up on strategic sites within the midland kingdom of Mercia, which had been swallowed up by the Scandinavians; they included the so-called 'Five Boroughs' of Derby, Nottingham, Stamford, Lincoln, and Leicester, the last two on Roman sites. The southern part of Mercia came under the control of Wessex during the reign of Alfred's successor Edward the Elder (d.924), and in the reign of Edward's son Athelstan (d.939) the Wessex kingdom extended its control over most of what we now call England. The first *burhs* were military encampments—part of what has been called a 'defensive system of fortified centres'—and most encompassed the sites of existing minsters.[14] But, as a more sophisticated market economy developed, and political conditions settled down in the later tenth and eleventh centuries, some, especially in southern England, became the nuclei of towns. They provided the later Anglo-Saxon kings with revenue from tolls and market dues. Some contained mints, and others, such as Derby and Stafford, became, and have remained, centres of the county administration that was established at about the same time.[15] The most important of these new foundations was London, where, during Alfred's reign, an urban settlement was re-established within the Roman walls, close to St Paul's Cathedral (founded in 604); its loose grid of streets—still recognizable in the modern street plan—stretched from the river front to Cheapside (*ceap* being the Old English word for market) (Fig. 1.4).[16]

In some respects, *burhs* developed in a similar fashion to Roman towns. Those that became towns had gates and fortifications—at first of earth, not stone—and some at least had grid-like street plans. The Anglo-Saxon earth banks around Wallingford (Berkshire, now Oxfordshire), a riverside *burh* on the banks of the Thames, are still clearly visible in the area called Kinecroft to the south-west of the market place, depopulated after the Black Death of the 1340s and still a public open space (Fig. 1.5).[17] The two main streets, probably existing by the year 1000, still follow a roughly rectilinear pattern, one running east-west from the river crossing, the other crossing it at the town centre, to the south of which was, and still is, a wide market place.[18] Siting was critical to the success of any town: it was essential to be close to rivers, but it was important not to be too close, because of the risk of flooding. That is why Oxford, which also began life as a *burh*, occupies a gravel terrace or promontory some way to the north of the main river crossing over the Thames.[19] The street plan here, like that of Wallingford, is organized around two thoroughfares (Cornmarket Street and the High Street), crossing at a central market place from which the market stalls could spill out into the surrounding streets.

The late tenth century saw what has been called a 'rapid and sustained economic expansion' in England.[20] That helps explain the revival of Chester, where a *burh* was established in or about 907 by Alfred's daughter Aethelflaed,

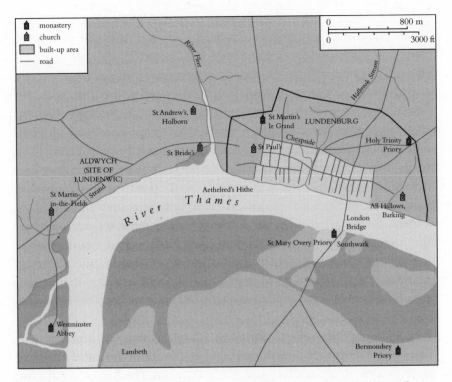

Fig. 1.4 A map of late Anglo-Saxon London. The walled city is on the north bank of the Thames, the light shading indicating the built-up area as it was in the tenth century. The Strand leads west across the Fleet river towards Westminster, passing the site of the earlier Anglo-Saxon *Lundenwic*. There is a suburban settlement at Southwark, at the southern end of London Bridge, but otherwise the marshy south bank remained largely undeveloped until the 18th century.

'Lady of the Mercians', within the walls of the former Roman fortress. The two main streets followed the Roman lines, as they still do, save for a kink at the central crossroads where the alignment was deflected by the building of a church; Lucian, a monk at St Werburgh's Abbey (now the Cathedral) mentioned 'two excellent straight streets in the form of the blessed Cross, which through meeting and crossing themselves, then make four out of two'.[21] At some stage in the tenth century the walls were extended south towards the River Dee, and here a port grew up from which ships could sail to Ireland and France.[22]

Given the paucity of extant buildings and the relative lack of documentation, it is difficult to pinpoint precisely when the 'proto-urban' settlements of the Anglo-Saxon period became towns. Norwich, not mentioned by

Fig. 1.5 Wallingford was laid out grid-fashion in the 10th or the 11th century and was protected by earth ramparts, which still survive. The open space called Kine Croft (upper left) was depopulated after the Black Death of the 1340s, and the castle, fragments of which survive, was built by Normans to command the Thames crossing by the present bridge.

name until the 980s, was one of several developed in a piecemeal, episodic way, its modern street plan only emerging after several false starts. There was no Roman settlement on the site alongside the navigable River Wensum as it meandered between Mousehold Heath—immortalized by the Norwich School of early nineteenth-century artists—and a lower ridge on the opposite side of the river. A settlement or *wic* was founded in the eighth century on the north side of the river, near the present Fishergate, and it was later enclosed within a defensive bank, recently discovered and possibly dating from after the Viking takeover in the ninth century.[23] The town prospered in the eleventh century because of its location in what was then one of the wealthiest parts of England, with a thriving local trade in wool and grain and contacts with ports across the North Sea. As it grew it swallowed up outlying settlements, and it gradually expanded onto the south bank—the centre of the present city—with a new market at Tombland (meaning an empty space) and a quay near the church of St Martin-at-Palace, where Anglo-Saxon masonry can still be seen. By 1086 Norwich was one of the largest towns in England, with an estimated population of between 5,000 and 10,000.

Successive changes often created complex street patterns which must be disentangled before today's urban landscapes can be fully understood. Stamford in Lincolnshire, one of the 'five boroughs' of the Danelaw, is a case in point. Here a *burh* was established in the late ninth or early tenth century on an important strategic site on rising ground to the north of the River Welland at the last point at which it could be easily crossed as it flowed eastwards towards the Wash. The fortified enclosure was roughly rectangular in shape and was bisected by an east-west street (the present High Street). Then in 918, following the expulsion of the Danes, a second *burh* was created by King Edward the Elder on the south (Northamptonshire) side of the river. The main road from London to Lincoln and York—the Roman Ermine Street—was diverted to run through it, descending to cross the river at the point where the valley could be most easily bridged. It then followed the south-western boundary of the Danish *burh,* resulting in two right-angled bends in the centre of the town that vexed motorists until the building of a modern bypass. The main street of the Anglo-Saxon settlement still forms the southern entrance into the town, which gained prosperity from the growing trade in wool and cloth and spilled out of the Danish fortifications. New market-places were laid out to the west of the *burh* boundary, and in Broad Street to the north, still the site of a flourishing street market.[24] The town reached its peak of prosperity in the twelfth and thirteenth centuries, with a Norman castle guarding its western border, seven parish churches, and a circuit of fortifications—of which only a single bastion survives—to mark its expanded boundary (Fig. 1.6).

The street plan of modern St Albans, the successor town to the Roman *Verulamium*, was also determined by a decision to divert a major road. The Abbey, containing the remains of the Romano-British Christian convert Alban (d.304 CE), was refounded, probably in the 960s, and a market place subsequently grew up at its gate. Watling Street—the Roman road leading north-west from London—was then diverted to cross the valley of the River Ver, proceeding steeply uphill to the Abbey before meandering down to another river crossing close to the abandoned Roman forum, where it rejoined the original route.[25] The Abbey (now the cathedral) was rebuilt on a vast scale after the Norman Conquest, using brick from the abandoned Roman town, and the town flourished thanks to the presence of the saint's shrine, and to its position on one of the most important roads in medieval England.[26]

Fig. 1.6 Stamford was built on rising ground on the north side of the River Welland, the towers and spires of its medieval parish churches still defining its skyline. The meadows in the foreground were and are liable to flooding, and have remained undeveloped.

Today's urban landscapes do not give much sense of what Anglo-Saxon towns looked like. Defences were usually of heaped-up earth, but a massive stone tower by the western wall of Oxford, now dated to around 1050, and later incorporated into the castle, points to substantial strengthening in the years preceding the Norman Conquest, and this may have been matched elsewhere.[27] Street frontages were not continuously built up,[28] and, at least before the early eleventh century, houses were not expected to last very long.[29] They were usually built either of planks supported by piles driven into the ground, or of hardened mud mixed with straw (cob); it was common, as the excavations at Viking York have shown,[30] for the living quarters to be raised over sunken basements. Small houses were intermingled with larger ones, some of them belonging to the secular and ecclesiastical owners of what have been called 'urban manors'; Frewin Hall in Oxford, the vaulted basement of which survives beneath a building now used for student accommodation, and set well back from the main streets, may have been an example of this kind of elite residence.[31]

Many of the smaller churches that proliferated in the longest-established medieval towns have Anglo-Saxon origins.[32] There were 25 churches in Norwich before the Norman Conquest, some of them originating as private chapels attached to large houses before being incorporated into the parish system when it was established during the eleventh and twelfth centuries.[33] Holy Trinity Goodramgate in York, set well back behind the street frontage, may also have begun in this way. Other churches were built near

town gates, like St Michael's in Cornmarket Street, Oxford; it adjoined the
north gate, and the upper storey of the surviving stone tower of *c.*1050 gave
direct access to the walkway on top of the town's fortifications.[34] Some
churches were placed at street intersections, at intervals along the most
important streets, or even, like St Clement Danes in London, in the middle
of streets.[35] In Cambridge, an inland port which grew up in the late eighth
century under Danish rule, there are churches at fairly regular intervals
along, or close to, the two main streets; one (St Bene't) still retains its sturdy
eleventh-century tower of flint.[36] Usually rebuilt and enlarged by later
generations, such churches were the focal points of townspeople's spiritual
and, to some extent, their community lives, and their churchyards became
their final resting places; many have remained valuable open spaces in
densely-built urban agglomerations, not least in the City of London, where
they still provide oases of greenery among the towering office blocks that
surround them.

Winchester

Anglo-Saxon monarchs were peripatetic, but in so far as England had a
capital it was Winchester. The city occupies a Roman site, sloping down eastwards from chalk downs to a crossing over the River Itchen, beyond which
the ground rises steeply to St Giles Hill, later the site of a fair. The first known
post-Roman settlement grew up around the Old Minster, founded in 648 by
Cenwalh, King of Wessex, close to the site of the present Cathedral. Its presence helped determine the later configuration of the south-eastern part of
the town, but the present 'purposely rectilinear framework of streets', as it has
been called, was not finally laid out until the ninth century. A High Street
runs east to west, and is crossed by a grid of streets running north to south at
roughly regular intervals, though not precisely following the line of the
long-disused streets of the Roman town (Fig. 1.7).[37] Other streets followed
the line of the walls just inside their perimeter; they included the present
St Swithun Street on the south side and the busier North Walls and Eastgate
Street, now part of the city's inner ring road.

Anglo-Saxon Winchester was, in the words of a modern historian, part
of 'a deliberate policy of urban formation in response to the military situation' at the end of Alfred's reign.[38] The High Street contained the main
market, with gates at each end, specialized trades such as tanners and butchers
later clustering together in the lesser streets, as they still do in many Middle-
Eastern towns.[39] Some of the property boundaries within the walls go

(continued)

Continued

back to pre-Norman times. A tract of land on the north side of the High Street known as Godbegot ('good bargain') was granted to the cathedral priory in 1012 and remained in the possession of the Dean and Chapter until 1866;[40] the land was later subdivided, and fifteenth-century timber houses (one of them now a restaurant) occupy the eastern part of the site, extending back from the street frontage between a side alley and a street formerly called the Fleshmarket. Some Anglo-Saxon masonry survives in the city's West Gate, the only one to survive; rebuilt in the twelfth century, it was remodelled in the following century and rebuilt again in the late fourteenth, with typically late-medieval machicolation on its outer side. There were other gates in Southgate Street—originally Goldsmiths' Street—and at the northern end of the present Jewry Street, and lesser ones elsewhere, including a narrow postern gate in the south wall; the church of St Swithun, patron saint of the city, was built above it. As in many towns, the walls themselves were rebuilt in stone and flint in the thirteenth century, and they still survive in part, some of the stretches containing Roman brick and tile. And, as in all of the larger Anglo-Saxon towns, suburbs grew up along the streets leading out of the city, some of them, like that on the hilly ground to the east of the Itchen, still retaining a semi-rural character.

The south-eastern quarter of Anglo-Saxon Winchester was dominated by churches whose presence, or former presence, has helped determine its present leafy, secluded character.[41] The Cathedral stands on the site of the New Minster, founded next to the existing Old Minster by King Edward the Elder in 901;[42] nearby was a royal palace, later expanded by William the Conqueror, and the 'Nunnaminster' (St Mary's Abbey), founded by King Alfred's widow (d.902) but suppressed at the Dissolution of the Monasteries.[43] Benedictine monks were introduced into the New Minster in 964, and at about the same time its precinct—now the Cathedral's inner courtyard (Close)—reached its present extent, with a wall built around it by King Edgar (d.975), creating what became an independent 'liberty' with its own water supply, later recycled as the town drain; a similar walled precinct also surrounded the Bishop's Palace at Wolvesey—'wolf's [or Wulf's] island'—to the south of St Mary's Abbey. The Normans began the present cathedral in 1079, and, starting in 1067, they also transformed the western part of the city by building a castle on the high ground by the west gate. Subsequently enlarged and strengthened, it has all but vanished, but the magnificent hall of 1222–36 survived as Hampshire's county court house, around which the later council offices have clustered.[44]

Medieval towns could not flourish without substantial infrastructural improvements, the most important of which were connected with drainage and the supply of water. Winchester's drainage was improved towards the end of the ninth century by restoring channels that had existed in Roman times on the eastern side of the city, prone to flooding from the River

Itchen.[45] The river was also essential for the powering of mills. A mill was mentioned in 940, and one still survives, though much rebuilt, on the bridge over the river, beyond the site of the East Gate; others along the river banks were used mainly for cleaning (fulling) the wool from the local downland, the most profitable aspect of the city's medieval economy.

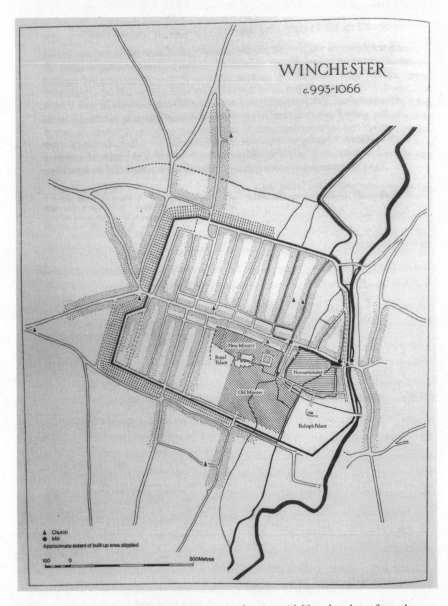

WINCHESTER
c.993-1066

New Minster

Royal
Palace

Nunnaminster

Old Minster

Bishop's Palace

▲ Church
● Mill
Approximate extent of built-up area stippled

100   0   500 Metres

Fig. 1.7 Winchester stands on a Roman site, but its grid-like plan dates from the 9th century. The main east–west street contains the market area, and lesser streets run north and south. Most of the south-eastern area of the city (shaded) was occupied by churches and by the palaces of the Bishop and the late Anglo-Saxon kings.

The Normans and After

The urban growth that helped transform medieval Europe was a response to large-scale economic and population expansion. The last major Viking raids in Britain occurred in the first quarter of the eleventh century, and the population of England may have doubled between the reigns of Alfred and William the Conqueror (d. 1087). By the end of the eleventh century an estimated ten per cent of the English population lived in towns;[46] by 1300 that proportion may have doubled, largely because of an expansion of the rural economy and the need for the marketing and processing of goods.[47] Most medieval towns were small by modern standards. London had an population that may have numbered about 60,000 by the end of the thirteenth century: roughly the same as it had been in Roman times but substantially smaller than the 100,000 or so of thirteenth-century Florence or the estimated 220,000 of Paris. Some 22,000 people lived in York and Norwich, the second and third largest towns in thirteenth-century England, but at least half of British town-dwellers lived in much smaller places with populations of 2,000 or so: the size of a largeish village today. But medieval towns differed from villages in three main respects. Their inhabitants held their property by free, not servile, tenure, meaning that they did not have to do unpaid work on their lords' land; there were regular markets; and most, though not all, of the inhabitants were involved primarily in non-agricultural pursuits.[48] With the granting of charters, starting in the twelfth century, many towns, including most of the larger ones, were self-governing. Towns were valuable to kings and powerful landlords, both lay and ecclesiastical, because of the income deriving from market tolls, and also because their inhabitants were easily identifiable and could pay taxes. That helps explain why there were so many new foundations in the twelfth and thirteenth centuries.

When the Normans invaded England in 1066 there was already a network of towns that had to be subdued before they could properly control the country. Their chief means of achieving that aim was through castle-building, a process that usually entailed the demolition of existing houses.[49] Castles contained disparate buildings grouped within a fortified enclosure: housing for the lord and his entourage, accommodation for his dependents, prisons, court houses and churches with their own communities of priests. Their impact on the urban landscape was, and in some cases still is, overwhelming. Some castles were dominated by tall residential stone towers or

keeps, such as the White Tower at the Tower of London, probably begun
c.1075-9 and 'unparalleled north of the Alps',[50] or the formidable tower at
Rochester, a much smaller town commanding the crossing of the Roman
Watling Street over the River Medway in Kent. Sometimes the strong point
was a tall artificial earth mound or motte with a wooden stockade at the top,
usually rebuilt later in stone as a 'shell keep'. The castle at York was of this
type. It occupied a strategic position at the junction of the city's two rivers,
the Foss and the Ouse, the latter guarded on its far side by a second fortification, of which only the tree-covered mound (Baile Hill) survives. The castle
motte, with its shell-keep ('Clifford's Tower', begun c.1245), overlooks a
courtyard or bailey, which became the administrative centre for England's
largest county, impressively rebuilt with a new court-room and prisons in
the eighteenth century (Fig. 5.3). The motte at Leicester Castle was levelled
to form a bowling green at the beginning of the nineteenth century, but the
twelfth-century hall, the castle's ceremonial centre, survived as the county
court room, cased in brick in the late seventeenth century and functioning
till recently; it is now used by de Montfort University. Even where castle
towers and mottes have vanished, as they have at Southampton—the site is
now occupied by a block of flats—their presence can still usually be traced
within the landscape, often by deviations in the street plan.

Sometimes the building of a Norman castle gave rise to the planned
extension of an existing town. Nottingham, on its sandstone cliff overlooking the flood-plain of the River Trent, started life as one of the five Danelaw
burhs, with defences that existed by 921. A castle went up after the Norman
Conquest, and a 'French borough' with its own independent jurisdiction
was laid out on an 88-acre site between it and the burh, with a church of its
own and a spacious market place on its northern side; there is still a noticeable dip in the ground between the two settlements, clearly seen at the
point where the street called High Pavement, on the southern edge of the
older town, drops down at its western end before continuing up towards
the castle.[51] At Lincoln, another of the Danelaw burhs, the castle was built
within the walls of the Roman colonia at the top of a promontory overlooking the River Witham; the new buildings took up half the site, with a new
cathedral accounting for much of the rest. 166 houses were demolished, and
the market was moved, together with a substantial proportion of the population, to a site outside the south gate of the Roman site. From here a steep
hill stretches down to a 'lower town' by the river—something more commonly found in the hill towns of Continental Europe—on the far side of

which a suburb (Wigford) stretched out alongside the Roman Ermine Street. Two eleventh-century churches survive here, along with a twelfth-century stone building known as St Mary's Guildhall, now thought to be a remnant of a royal residence.

Norwich was likewise transformed by the building of a Norman castle and cathedral. The castle, with its massive square stone tower begun in around 1094, was strategically placed between the existing market at Tombland and a newly-established market in a 'French borough' laid out to the west. Meanwhile, as part of the Norman policy of siting cathedrals in major centres of population, the Norfolk bishopric was removed to Norwich from rural North Elmham. The cathedral was begun, like the castle, in 1094, and involved the destruction of a substantial part of the Anglo-Saxon town; the ecclesiastical precinct that resulted helps shape the character of the modern city. At Durham the Norman castle and cathedral still preside over a kind of Acropolis on an almost impregnable site within a loop high above the River Wear: one of the most spectacular urban sites in Britain (Fig. 1.8). It was first occupied in 995, after the Benedictine monks of Lindisfarne, an island off the coast of Northumberland, had fled Viking raids, carrying with them the bones of St Cuthbert, the seventh-century apostle of Northumbria. The cathedral was rebuilt on a massive scale, starting in 1093, twenty years after the Bishop's castle had gone up, its motte and shell-keep now occupied by the University of Durham. At first the city's market occupied a site between the castle and the cathedral, but in the early twelfth century the Bishop, Ranulf Flambard (d. 1128), moved it to a 'lower town' at the bottom of the steep hill. It was he, according to the chronicler William of Malmesbury, who 'joined the two banks of the River Wear with a stone bridge [Framwellgate Bridge], a major construction supported on arches.' A second bridge, Elvet Bridge, was built by Bishop Hugh du Puiset after 1225, giving access to another suburb on the far side of the river, and further stimulating the town's economy.

Some castles gave rise to the foundation of new towns. The present town of Windsor (Berkshire) was established as an adjunct to the royal castle founded by William the Conqueror two and a half miles away from the previous settlement of Old Windsor. Towns were also established next to castles in contested areas near, and beyond, the Scottish and Welsh borders. Newcastle, on the English side of the Scottish border, originated in 1080 with the building of a castle by William the Conqueror's son Robert on the site of a Roman fort near the eastern end of Hadrian's Wall, overlooking the

Fig. 1.8 Durham grew up within a loop of the River Wear following the foundation of the Cathedral, with its relics of St. Cuthbert, one of the apostles of Northumbria. The cathedral still dominates the surrounding landscape, and has been complemented since the late 11th century by the Norman castle, facing it across Palace Green. Most of the houses shown in this air view are now occupied by departments of the University, incorporated in 1837.

steeply sloping banks of the River Tyne. And not long afterwards, in about 1130, Edinburgh was founded by King David I of Scotland on an even more impregnable site on a ridge south of the Firth of Forth. It was protected by its castle, 350 feet above sea level; for Thomas Tucker, a customs officer under Oliver Cromwell, it gave 'both rise and growth to that city inviting people to plant and settle there for sheltering themselves'.[52] From here the main street descends by 120 feet to Holyrood, where an Abbey was founded in 1128 (Fig. 1.9). Now usually called the Royal Mile, it has been described as 'an enormous elongated market place' flanked by residential plots going steeply downhill on either side, like a 'double wooden comb, the great street the wood in the middle and the teeth of each side the lanes.'[53]

Scottish towns were useful instruments of state-formation, especially during the reign of King David I (1124–53), who founded the first chartered burghs in the south and east of his kingdom; there were no towns in the Highlands until the eighteenth century. Stirling and Edinburgh were important seats of royal power, growing up under the shelter of their castles, and Edinburgh became a major trading town which benefited from its position near (though not on) the Firth of Forth. Berwick-on-Tweed, founded by a royal charter of 1120 and a Scottish town until the early thirteenth century, guarded the fiercely contested border with England as it was becoming solidified. Some Scottish towns grew up on sites that already possessed the rudiments of urban life; they included Perth and Dundee, two of what were later known as the 'four great towns of Scotland.'[54] Others, such as Glasgow, started as adjuncts to churches. The church here was founded by St Kentigern (Mungo) in the sixth century and became the seat of a bishop in 1115. The small town at its gate became self-governing from 1175, its single street snaking down to the River Clyde from the Cathedral—since its thirteenth-century rebuilding the finest medieval church in Scotland—with a market cross where it crossed an east-west route (the modern Trongate) running parallel to the river.[55] Old Aberdeen, as it is still called, grew up in a similar way on a hillside site overlooking the valley of the River Don, next to the cathedral of St Machar, with a single street leading south from the church. A larger commercial centre (New Aberdeen) developed at about the same time a mile or so away, to the north of a better harbour on the estuary of the Dee, and this became the heart of the modern city. But Old Aberdeen remained a separately governed ecclesiastical and educational enclave, with one of Britain's oldest universities, and it still retains its distinctive identity.[56]

Towns could be a means of quasi-colonial control, as they had been in Roman Britain, and were to become in Latin America in the sixteenth and seventeenth centuries. Wales had resisted Anglo-Saxon penetration, and there was no upsurge of town formation there in the ninth and tenth centuries. The first identifiable towns were established in the twelfth century by

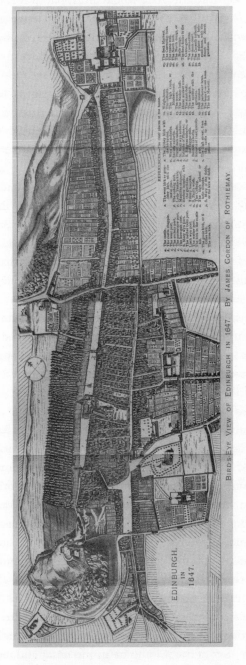

Fig. 1.9 This bird's-eye panorama of Edinburgh in 1637, by James Gordon of Rothiemay, highlights its distinctive topography. The main street runs along the top of a ridge, with the medieval castle on hill to the left and the royal palace of Holyrood on lower ground a mile to the east. The parish church (subsequently cathedral) of St Giles stands in Lawnmarket (left) and most of the houses are densely packed along narrow plots running steeply downhill towards the North Loch. The eastern part of the main street (Canongate) is lined with noblemen's houses with their long gardens.

Anglo-Norman landlords, who encouraged English immigration. That explains the foundation of Cardiff, where Robert FitzHamon built a castle in 1081 on the site of a Roman fort, followed in 1120-47 by the granting of a borough charter; Newport, Cardigan, and Swansea followed later in the twelfth century.[57] There was another phase of town formation in the thirteenth century, when thirty new towns were founded.[58] By 1300 an estimated fifteen per cent of the Welsh population was living in towns, of which Cardiff was already the largest, with over 400 taxpaying burgesses.[59] Some, such as Denbigh, Wrexham and Welshpool, were founded by Welsh lords.[60] But the most impressive Welsh towns were founded in 1283-92 by an English king, Edward I, as part of his campaign to subdue the last of the independent Welsh princes in their mountainous Snowdonia redoubt. These towns were strategically placed close to navigable estuaries in low-lying grain-producing areas on the edge of the stock-rearing uplands. Behind their high walls, they were in effect fortified extensions of castles, as is still obvious at Conwy and Caernarfon,[61] where the walls demarcated the English enclave from the surrounding Welsh-speaking population of the rural hinterland (Fig. 1.14).

Cathedrals and monasteries, like castles, were 'little towns in microcosm':[62] legally independent 'liberties' subject to a Bishop's or Abbot's jurisdiction, occupying spacious sites surrounded by fortified walls, with gateways that were sometimes elaborated and heightened in later years. Some monasteries took the initiative in planning and promoting the towns at their gates. Bury St Edmunds (Suffolk) was founded in the eleventh century outside the walls of its Benedictine monastery, one of the richest and most powerful in England, housing the shrine of the martyred Anglo-Saxon King Edmund (d.869) and acting as a magnet for pilgrims. It was substantially enlarged after the Norman Conquest, when the Abbots laid out a grid of streets to the west of the monastic precinct, with its two impressive gatehouses (see p. 66), and a new and much larger market place. The compilers of Domesday Book recorded in 1086 that the enlarged town contained 342 houses built on formerly agricultural land, and housed seventy-five bakers, ale-brewers, tailors, washerwomen, shoemakers, robemakers, cooks, porters and 'agents', as well as thirty priests.[63] At Reading too the Abbey, founded by Henry I in 1121, transformed the small market settlement that had grown up next to a probable minster church (now St Mary's Butts) in Anglo-Saxon times. Following its foundation, a new market place was laid out outside the monastic enclosure—now a public park—and in the following years Reading overtook Wallingford as the largest and most important town in Berkshire.[64]

The arrival of the mendicant orders (initially the Franciscans and Dominicans) in 1221 and 1224 led to a new wave of monastic building. Most towns of any size, at least in England, were already quite densely built up by then, and the first friars usually had to find sites on the urban fringe, like the Franciscans (Greyfriars) in Reading, whose much-rebuilt church survives alongside what is now a busy road. At Canterbury the Dominicans (Blackfriars) took over a five-acre site, including orchards, on marshy ground next to a branch of the River Stour to the north-west of the city centre; their church did not survive the Reformation, but fragments of their domestic buildings can still be seen.[65] From sites of this kind the friars carried out their mission to the urban population.

The many smaller towns founded in the late twelfth and early thirteenth centuries were first and foremost trading entrepots for the surrounding countryside. The initiative for founding them usually came from aristocratic or ecclesiastical landlords eager to take advantage of the increase in road and river traffic generated by a growing population and a burgeoning economy. Some, like Chipping Campden (Gloucestershire), probably founded in the 1170s, or Melbourne (Derbyshire), where a market was granted in 1230, were grafted onto pre-existing agricultural settlements, sometimes identifiable nowadays by a church standing some distance away from a market place. Others were laid out on virgin sites, often determined by river crossings, as at Henley-on-Thames (Oxfordshire).[66] Others, at a time when large quantities of goods were carried by packhorses, were founded at road junctions; they included Baldock—a corruption of Baghdad, a name given by the Knights Templar—in Hertfordshire.[67] The initiative was often taken by aristocratic landlords such as William FitzAlan (d. 1210), the lord of the small castle at Chipping Norton (Oxfordshire) and probable founder of the town that was laid out on a sloping site above it in the late twelfth century.[68] Other small towns, such as Northleach and Stow-on-the-Wold in the Gloucestershire Cotswolds, were founded by ecclesiastical landlords. At Newark (meaning 'New Work' or fortification) in Nottinghamshire the initiative came from Alexander, Bishop of Lincoln, from 1123 to 1148. He built a castle by the crossing over the River Trent and laid out the town with a central market place overlooked by a parish church, magnificently rebuilt in the fifteenth century. A new bridge went up in around 1170 to take the recently realigned Great North Road through the town; a bypass—still part of the street pattern—for east-west traffic along the ancient Fosse Way from Leicester to Lincoln was constructed later.[69]

Important though internal trade was, the greatest profits were made by exploiting long-distance networks of production and exchange. As early as the tenth century, London's waterfront was being extended by digging piles into the bed of the Thames in front of the Roman embankment and filling the reclaimed space with clay and stone.[70] Other towns followed suit. Southampton was founded in the eleventh century on a gravel ridge by the estuary of the River Test, some distance to the west of the abandoned *Hamwic* settlement. It prospered through the sale of wool from the Hampshire chalk downs and the import of goods from France, especially wine. Southampton was also a port of embarkation, favoured by royalty after the Norman Conquest because of its closeness to Winchester, and a Town Quay was later built on reclaimed land alongside the Solent. Another town that profited from the wool trade was King's Lynn (Norfolk), founded in the late eleventh century by the Bishops of Norwich on a dried-up lake between two tributaries feeding into the Little Ouse, close to the point where it enters the Wash. Well placed as an entrepot for wool and cloth from the east Midlands, with salt workings nearby, it had become so successful by the middle of the twelfth century that it was extended north of the tributary known as the Purfleet stream—since built over—with a second (Tuesday) market place to supplement the original (Saturday) market next to the monastic church of St Margaret, and a church of its own, St Nicholas, magnificently rebuilt in the fifteenth century. And, as the economy grew, and the draughts of ships grew greater, new wharves were created, initially by dumping waste on land reclaimed from the river.[71]

Overseas trade tripled in volume during the late twelfth and thirteenth centuries, leading to the founding and expansion of more ports along the North Sea and Channel coasts. They supplemented, and in some cases supplanted, the trade of older inland ports such as York. The export of wool ensured that, as early as 1206, the customs duties levied at Boston (Lincolnshire) were already surpassed only by those of London. Great Yarmouth (Norfolk), built at the mouth of the River Yare, was another town that profited from the North Sea trade. So too was Hull, founded on an existing site and extended by King Edward I in 1293, when it was fortified on the landward side and supplied with wharves laid out alongside the River Hull (Fig. 1.10), a tributary of the Humber. West coast ports sprang up meanwhile as formerly marginal areas began to be exploited for their

Fig. 1.10 Hull (technically Kingston-upon-Hull) derived its name from a tributary of the River Humber, shown here. The city's medieval prosperity depended on the North Sea trade in wool and other commodities. As in many port towns, a main street (High Street) followed the line of the river, closely packed with merchants' houses. Their back plots, leading down to wharves along the river, contained warehouses for the storage of goods, many of them rebuilt in brick and now, following the decline of the river trade, mostly turned into flats.

mineral wealth. Fowey (Cornwall) was founded in the late thirteenth century by a local Benedictine priory alongside a drowned river valley, mainly for the export of locally mined tin.[72] New ports were also founded further east, but not all were successful. New Romney, on the Kent coast, was intended to benefit from cross-Channel trade, replacing Old Romney, further inland, but it was left isolated when a storm diverted the course of the River Rother to Rye in 1287, and today it is little more than a village.[73] Winchelsea, a more ambitious foundation not far away on the coast of East Sussex, was laid out on a grid plan in 1288, but was never fully built up, mainly because the estuary on which it was built silted up; by the beginning of the eighteenth century Daniel Defoe could describe it as 'rather the Skeleton of an Ancient City than a real town.'[74]

Plans and Layouts

Most medieval towns did not grow 'organically'. They usually started off
with a plan, however rudimentary, to which additions could be made as
economic conditions dictated. Many smaller, and some larger, towns consisted of no more than a widened thoroughfare in which the market was
held, sometimes bisected by a cross street, as shown in an early plan of
Ashbourne (Derbyshire) in the National Archives, dated 1547. Cardiff was
planned in a similar way, with a single main street, parallel to the River
Taf, stretching south from the castle with a couple of rudimentary cross-
streets, the most important of which ran parallel to the castle wall: a layout
that scarcely changed until the phenomenal expansion of the town in the
nineteenth century. This type of layout can also be found at Olney
(Buckinghamshire),[75] St Ives (Huntingdonshire: now Cambridgeshire),[76]
Hungerford (Berkshire) and Brackley (Northants). At Chipping Campden
and Winchcombe, both in Gloucestershire, the main street follows the con-
tour of a river valley; at Warkworth (Northumberland) it ascends from a
crossing over the River Coquet to a castle built c.1200 and rebuilt by the
powerful Percy family in the fourteenth and fifteenth centuries.

The layout of medieval towns was inevitably influenced by the lie of the
land. Tewkesbury (Gloucestershire) grew up on slightly raised ground
between the River Severn, England's longest river, and the Swilgate, a tributary of the Avon. King William I established a market here, and 66 inhabitants were recorded in Domesday Book. Then, in or around 1087, Robert
FitzHamon founded a Benedictine abbey to the north of the bridge over
the Severn, and the monks moved in in 1102; the massive Romanesque
tower of the church still dominates the town.[77] The river was diverted in the
twelfth century to run closer to the Abbey and its mill, cutting off a tract of
common land (Severn Ham) in the process; it was often flooded, and was
subsequently used for grazing by the townspeople (it is still an open space
today). Surrounded to the south and west by a flood plain, and to the east
by common land (Oldbury Field), the town grew on a confined site, with
the High Street running north from the Abbey to a triangular market place.
Here the road forks, with one arm continuing northwards to a bridge over
the Avon,[78] the other leading eastwards, roughly parallel to the Swilgate.
Following its recovery from post-Black Death depopulation in the fifteenth
century and afterwards, there was a very (though not uniquely) high density
of housing on the narrow street fronts and the alleys which followed the

boundaries of the long, narrow plots behind them. Geographical constraints also explain the even denser layout of Great Yarmouth, laid out on a sand-bank enclosing a sheltered harbour at the mouth of the River Yare.[79] Here two curving streets follow the sinuous curve of the river, linked by densely packed housing along narrow plots ('rows') and a quay fronting the river; the market place and church lie at the northern end of the town.

Water supply, and the control of water, has always been a crucial pre-requisite for urban life. The intra-mural landscape of some medieval towns was broken up by streams, nearly all of which later disappeared under-ground as streets were built over them. Walbrook, in the financial heart of the City of London, preserves the name of one of these streams, as does The Strand in the middle of Derby, built over a stream shown in early maps but driven underground when the town expanded in the nineteenth century. River crossings were made at first by fords and later by wooden bridges, most of them later replaced in stone. Oxford was approached across the Thames from the south by Folly Bridge, the earliest documented stone-arched bridge in Britain, dating in its original form from just after the Norman Conquest. A raised causeway (the present Abingdon Road) led to it across the marshy flood plain south of the river, resting on forty stone arches that still survive underneath the road surface; some of them are visible beside the southern approach to the bridge, which was rebuilt in 1825-7.

The siting of towns was also heavily influenced by the presence of springs and wells, and, as populations grew, the supply began to be supplemented from outside sources. Canterbury Cathedral priory had its own water sup-ply in the twelfth century, partly still functioning, and in London the first water main was laid in 1237. At Exeter a system of conduits, shown to mod-ern visitors as 'underground passages', was created in the early thirteenth century to bring water from outside the city, supplementing the springs that had encouraged the Romans to establish a town there in the first place, and possibly compensating for a fall in the water table.[80] Exeter was a major centre of the medieval cloth trade, and the artificial channel or leet that powered the mills by the River Exe, possibly dating back to Anglo-Saxon times, was improved in the twelfth century, leading to the draining of the marshes by the river and the creation of 'Exeter island' on land belonging to the Earls of Devon. This became the city's industrial quarter, with a wharf built in the fifteenth century and a stone bridge, first mentioned in 1196, crossing the river from the gateway at the bottom of the slope lead-ing up to the city centre.[81]

The boundaries of medieval towns were demarcated by walls or earth-works. The walls of Totnes (Devon), an Anglo-Saxon *burh* at the head of the River Dart, were rebuilt in stone following the building of the Norman castle that overlooks the town; they have gone, and by the fifteenth century half the inhabitants were living outside them, but their line is still clearly traceable in the street plan.[82] Many English, and most Scottish, towns had defensive banks or ditches instead of costly walls. The 'King's Ditch' on the south side of Cambridge may have been dug in the early tenth century, and its former presence helps explain the alignment of what are now Pembroke Street and Mill Lane, close to the point where the ditch met the River Cam.[83] Ditches were also built along the outer perimeter of town fortifica-tions where they existed, creating 'fringe belts' that ambiguously straddled the urban and the rural environment.[84] They were usually filled in or built over at a later date, but their former presence is still evident in Broad Street, Oxford, which retains the original width of the town's northern ditch.

Markets were essential to urban prosperity, and they became more so in the twelfth and thirteenth centuries with the relative decline of fairs (less frequent gatherings of traders), where much long-distance trade had previ-ously been focused. Market places still help shape the visual identity of towns like Boston, where the main street curves to follow the bend of the River Witham near its confluence with the North Sea, widening out to form an irregularly shaped space for the stalls next to the bridge; as the town became more prosperous a second, funnel-shaped, market place (Bargate) was built to the north-east, just inside the town wall.[85] Some market places, like those of Cambridge, Norwich (Fig. 1.11), Bury St Edmunds, and Northampton,[86] were square or rectangular. Others were triangular, like that at Alnwick (Northumberland) laid out in the second half of the twelfth century to the south of a Norman castle alongside the Great North Road (the present A1) where it crossed the River Aln, 30 miles south of the Scottish border. The presence of the castle and its extensive precinct ensured that future development was concentrated to the south of the formidable outer defences, and it was here that the market place was situated, possibly on the site of an existing rural settlement, with plots extending behind the three streets leading into it, and back lanes at the far end of the plots (Fig. 1.15). The walls which protected the town have all but vanished, but modern streets still follow their line along the southern and western sides of the town centre, and two medieval gateways survive.[87] Some markets were established inside castle fortifications. The semicircular shape of the market

Fig. 1.11 The Market Place at Norwich, shown in a drawing of 1806 by the Norfolk-born artist John Sell Cotman, was laid out as part of a 'French borough' established by the Norman kings in the late 11th century to the west of the Castle and the Anglo-Saxon town. It is still filled with market stalls, but the houses on the west (right-hand) side were replaced in the 1930s with a handsome new City Hall.

place at Richmond (Yorkshire) was determined by that of the outer bailey of the castle,[88] and at Devizes (Wiltshire) the whole town was enclosed within the castle's outer bailey, its curved streets forming a semicircle within which a market place was formed at the castle's gate in the mid to late twelfth century.

Some market places became overcrowded as the economy expanded. The Normans relocated the market at Hereford to a more spacious site outside the walls of the original Anglo-Saxon *burh*,[89] and in due course it acquired permanent stalls reached by narrow alleys. Encroachments of this kind were usually sanctioned by civic authorities, emboldened by the limited powers of self-government granted in royal charters from the late twelfth century onwards. The Bishop of Lincoln was already putting up permanent structures in the market place at Thame (Oxfordshire) in 1221 in order to increase his rents, and eighteen more stalls were erected by another bishop thirty years later; a block of buildings, including a Victorian town hall, still stands in the middle of the wide main street. Successive encroachments have ensured that the modern market place in Wantage (Berkshire, now

Oxfordshire), now presided over by a statue of King Alfred, the putative founder of the town, is probably less than half its original size.[90] Such changes continued through the succeeding centuries, permanently changing the landscape of many town centres.

Towns laid out on a grid of streets, like Bury St Edmunds or the *bastides* of south-western France, were relatively uncommon. One example is Stratford-upon-Avon, a new town founded by the Bishop of Worcester in 1196, established at a river crossing to the north of an existing village and its church. The streets follow a loose grid plan, with a wide market street leading west from the bridge, which was rebuilt in stone in the 1480s, a gently curving north–south street, and lesser streets following the lines of strips of the former common fields.[91] Salisbury, the best-known example of a new town laid out on a grid plan—though not on a strictly rectilinear grid like those of many American, or ancient Chinese, cities—was founded on a flat, riverside site by the Bishop, starting in 1217, after the existing town, within the nearby Old Sarum hill-fort, had become desperately overcrowded (Fig. 1.12).[92] Old Sarum lacked a decent water supply, and water played an important part in the layout of the new town, with channels running down the middle of the main streets until the early nineteenth century.[93]

Some of Edward I's new towns in Wales were also laid out in grid fashion. The walls at Conwy, founded in 1283, enclose a triangular site with the castle placed by the strategically crucial river crossing and the walls—among the most impressive town defences of the time—rising up towards an Upper Gate and watchtower. The streets follow a loose grid, with a High Street leading from the quayside to a market place and to other streets running parallel to the walls (Fig. 1.13).

Many towns grew through planned additions to the original core, designed to attract more inhabitants and thus to increase the potential economic benefit. Street names such as 'Newland', as in Witney (Oxfordshire), or New Street, as in Henley-on-Thames and Birmingham, are a reminder of such extensions. At Bridgnorth (Shropshire), begun in the early twelfth century on a defensible promontory high above the River Severn, the former outer bailey of the castle is demarcated by two streets (East and West Castle Street), the former closed at its southern end by the castle chapel, since rebuilt as the parish church of St Mary. At a later stage a new market place was laid out along the present High Street to the north of the castle precinct, and, as the economy continued to flourish, three new streets went up at right angles to the High Street, and a second church (St Leonard) was established just inside the expanded defences.[94] Perth, an inland port on the

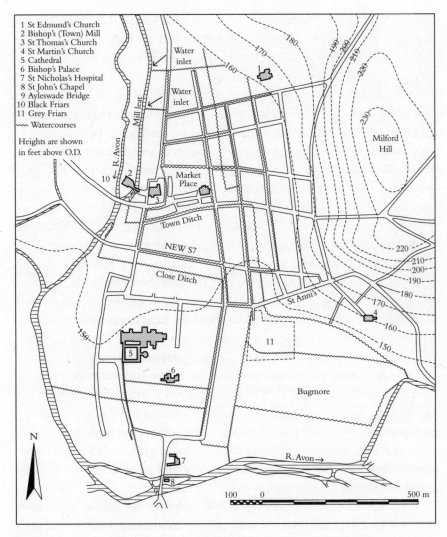

1 St Edmund's Church
2 Bishop's (Town) Mill
3 St Thomas's Church
4 St Martin's Church
5 Cathedral
6 Bishop's Palace
7 St Nicholas's Hospital
8 St John's Chapel
9 Ayleswade Bridge
10 Black Friars
11 Grey Friars
∼∼∼ Watercourses

Heights are shown
in feet above O.D.

Fig. 1.12 Salisbury is a excellent example of 13th-century urban planning. Its streets are laid out on a grid plan, with water from the River Avon running through them (shown as wavy lines on the map). The market place, close to the river, was the original commercial centre; the Cathedral, shown at the bottom left, was isolated within a walled ecclesiastical precinct, as it still is, with riverside meadows to the south.

River Tay in Scotland, grew up in a similarly additive fashion, starting in the mid-twelfth century with a street leading south from the castle to the church of St John and crossed by another street (the High Street) leading east from the bridge. A second, parallel, east-west street (South Street) was laid out in the thirteenth century, and in the early fourteenth century the

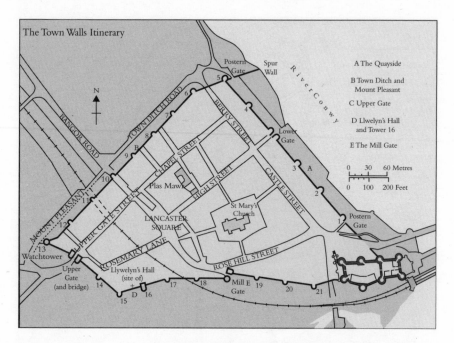

The Town Walls Itinerary

A The Quayside

B Town Ditch and
Mount Pleasant

C Upper Gate

D Llwelyn's Hall
and Tower 16

E The Mill Gate

Fig. 1.13 Conwy is one of the fortress towns established by the English king, Edward I, as an important part of his campaign to bring North Wales under his control. The town is still enclosed within its high stone walls, punctuated by semicircular towers. It is dominated by its castle, next to the river crossing and the riverside wharves. The street layout was determined by the exigencies of the triangular site, sloping uphill from the castle to the parish church and market place.

town was enclosed by earth walls and a ditch whose alignment still influences the street plan as we see it today.[95]

Bristol, one of the most important towns in medieval England, also grew through a series of planned additions (Fig. 1.14). The original *burh* occupied a raised and easily defensible site within a loop enclosed by the River Avon, through which sea-going ships could pass through a gorge to the Severn estuary, and its tributary the River Frome. The Normans built a castle and walls to enclose a main street (Corn St) running along the ridge between the two rivers; it was crossed by another street (Broad Street and High Street) extending down to a quay along the Avon.[96] The market spilled out in the usual way from the central crossing, but further economic expansion depended on making substantial improvements to the town's infrastructure. The River Frome was diverted in the 1240s to join the Avon at a point well to the south of the town, allowing for the creation of a larger quay, partially

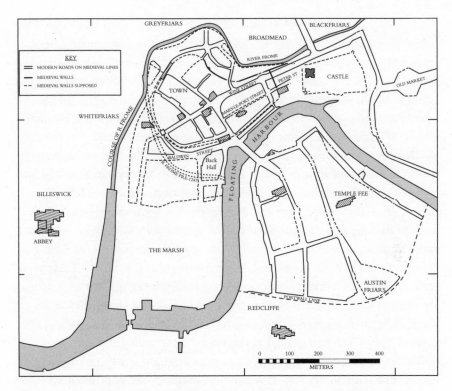

Fig. 1.14 A map of medieval Bristol. The city began life as an Anglo-Saxon *burh* on a defensible site between two rivers, the Avon and the Frome, with a market spilling out from a central crossroads. The Normans built a castle to the east, and growing prosperity in the early 13th century led to planned expansions to the south, and across the River Avon to the south-east. The suburb of Redcliffe was laid out here, and is still dominated by the magnificent parish church of St Mary.

covered over in the twentieth century and now a busy crossroads at the heart of the modern city. A second quay (Welsh Back), for ships of smaller draught, was also created along the Avon waterfront, downstream of a new bridge (Bristol Bridge), which gave access to a suburb (Redcliffe) on the far side of the river, where the new streets were surrounded by an extended town wall.[97] Yet more expansion took place on the meadow land in Lewin's Mead, to the north of the River Frome, where the Franciscans established a monastery in *c.*1250, its site now hidden by a massive office block, and at Broadmead, further east, now part of the city's main shopping centre. Here the Dominican friars established a religious house in 1227–8, which still partially survives within a modern shopping precinct.

Streets are among the most resilient features of the urban landscape. The main streets of medieval towns were wider than we sometimes imagine; some of the very narrow streets often thought of as typical, like the much-visited Shambles in York, were created as a result of market encroachments, or were alleys alongside house plots. The main market street of Stratford-upon-Avon was 90 feet wide, the other main streets 50 feet,[98] and the main streets of Bristol, according to the town's fifteenth-century chronicler William Worcester, were of similar dimensions.[99] The more important streets, like those of Roman towns, had hard surfaces; recent archaeology has revealed evidence of flint cobbles in the streets of Anglo-Saxon Winchester, Lincoln and elsewhere.[100] By the thirteenth century local authorities were making use of paving grants from central government in order to improve surfaces, though these were limited to the main thoroughfares, and the sur-faces were rarely well-maintained; lesser streets generally remained unpaved until the late eighteenth or nineteenth centuries. Drainage was an import-ant consideration, water usually being carried away by an open channel in the middle of the street, like that which still survives in Brasenose Lane, Oxford, and which had existed in the High Street in Anglo-Saxon times.[101] Sidewalks or pavements did not exist, and pedestrians—the vast majority of users—risked drenching by rain from waterspouts or slops from upstairs windows.

Along with the street pattern, and sometimes the line of fortifications, property boundaries are the most enduring aspect of medieval urban lay-outs. In Canterbury, for instance, a plot belonging c.1200 to Solomon the Mercer at the south-eastern corner of Mercery Lane, just outside the Cathedral precinct, still has the same dimensions as it had in the late twelfth century, though the house on the site was rebuilt in the fifteenth century and given its present neo-Tudor façade in the twentieth.[102] Long, narrow 'burgage' plots became common in the second half of eleventh century, and by 1200 they were being laid out fishbone-fashion on either side of streets of most towns, sometimes as a result of subdivision in larger plots. They were usually reached from behind by back lanes, often on the sites of mod-ern streets, or, in low-lying towns such as King's Lynn, by drainage ditches or 'fleets'.[103] Tenants of burgages were exempted from the labour services exacted by feudal lords elsewhere, and their plots became a major token of urban identity. Their presence helps explain the modern topography of places like Kendal (Cumbria), where the pattern of long plots on either side of a wide main street is particularly clear (Fig. 3.9); they can be traced even in the centre of Leeds, where the plots leading off Briggate, now one of the city's main shopping streets, were first laid out in 1207.[104]

Plot sizes varied from one town to another. 60 by 200 feet was the norm at Stratford-upon-Avon, 70 by 400 at Burton-on-Trent (Staffordshire), and even longer at Alnwick (Fig.1.15).[105] In York and some other towns the standard width was a perch (between 40 and 60 feet);[106] in the new towns of Wales most plots measured 80 by 60 feet.[107] Long plots enabled crops to be grown, and animals kept, behind houses, and in smaller towns like Henley-on-Thames or Warkworth some plots are still gardens. But in larger towns they have usually been built over, creating dense urban landscapes that still survive though the boundaries have sometimes, been swept away for new buildings or car parks. As pressure for space increased in the later twelfth and thirteenth centuries, and agricultural production within towns became less necessary—the inevitable result of a growing market economy— plot sizes became shorter, and many were subdivided, as they already had been in Banbury (Oxfordshire) by 1225.[108] The results of such subdivision can be seen in the varying width of the houses along the street frontages, and facing the market places, of many towns. And in ports, where streets ran close to a river front, narrow alleyways usually led between the plots to the wharves on the waterfront, as they still do in towns such as Newcastle, Hull and King's Lynn.

The continuous urban street frontages that we now take for granted do not seem to have emerged until the twelfth and thirteenth centuries. They were then developed piecemeal by different owners at different times, with little attempt being made to impose visual uniformity. Where plots were narrow or subdivided, especially in town centres, it was common for houses to be built with a narrow frontage to the street, but most streets had a mixture of wide and narrow frontages, contributing to the visual variety which has always characterized the landscape of our older towns. Some richer towns-people built their houses of stone, like the builder of the 'Norman House' at the top of the aptly named Steep Hill at Lincoln (Fig. 1.16). It was aligned along the width of its plot, and a similar layout was adopted at the so-called 'Jew's House' further down the hill, also of stone construction, and built c.1150–75, with the ground floor used as a workshop and the living quarters upstairs; in 1290, when the Jews were expelled from England by King Edward I, it was the home of Belaset, daughter of a man called Aaron who came from Wallingford.[109] A handful of high-status twelfth- and thirteenth-century stone houses survive in other towns such as Norwich (the 'Music

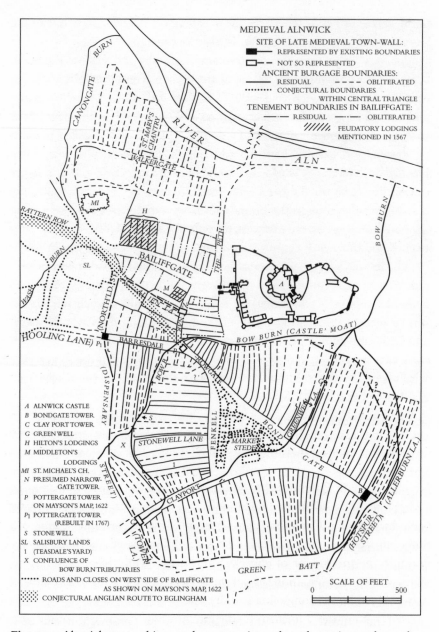

MEDIEVAL ALNWICK

SITE OF LATE MEDIEVAL TOWN-WALL:
■———— REPRESENTED BY EXISTING BOUNDARIES
□—-— NOT SO REPRESENTED
ANCIENT BURGAGE BOUNDARIES:
———— RESIDUAL   -- -- OBLITERATED
·········· CONJECTURAL BOUNDARIES
WITHIN CENTRAL TRIANGLE
TENEMENT BOUNDARIES IN BAILIFFGATE:
——·—— RESIDUAL   ——·—— OBLITERATED
////// FEUDATORY LODGINGS
MENTIONED IN 1567

A ALNWICK CASTLE
B BONDGATE TOWER
C CLAY PORT TOWER
G GREEN WELL
H HILTON'S LODGINGS
M MIDDLETON'S
        LODGINGS
MI ST. MICHAEL'S CH.
N PRESUMED NARROW-
        GATE TOWER
P POTTERGATE TOWER
        ON MAYSON'S MAP, 1622
P₁ POTTERGATE TOWER
        (REBUILT IN 1767)
S STONE WELL
SL SALISBURY LANDS
1 (TEASDALE'S YARD)
X CONFLUENCE OF
        BOW BURN TRIBUTARIES
······ ROADS AND CLOSES ON WEST SIDE OF BAILIFFGATE
        AS SHOWN ON MAYSON'S MAP, 1622
∷∷∷ CONJECTURAL ANGLIAN ROUTE TO EGLINGHAM

SCALE OF FEET
0   500

Fig. 1.15 Alnwick was and is a market town, situated on the main north-south route from Edinburgh to London. It is dominated by its castle, rebuilt by successive members of the Percy family and still the home of their descendant the Duke of Northumberland. Its presence influenced the layout of the town with its triangular-shaped market place, shown at the bottom of the map, and gradually filled with temporary stalls which eventually become permanent. Long, narrow burgage plots stretch behind the houses, their layout indicating successive phases in the expansion of the town down to the mid 14th century.

Fig. 1.16 This 12th century stone house stands near the top of the steep hill rising up from the River Witham to the medieval cathedral at Lincoln. Built of locally quarried rubble stone, the main living accommodation was upstairs, and there was a workshop on the ground floor. The wealth and prestige of the unknown merchant who built it is indicated by the carved Romanesque doorway and the much-restored round-arched window on the upper floor. The roof, of overlapping brick pantiles, replaces the original thatch.

House'), Bury St Edmunds (Moyses Hall), Oxford, York and Southampton ('King John's House'); the foundations of more than thirty such houses have been discovered at Canterbury.[110] But many town houses, at least until the thirteenth century, were still being built of timber planks attached to posts dug into the ground, or of cob. Such modest dwellings were never more than two storeys high, those of cob just one, and in smaller towns one-or two-storeyed houses long remained the norm.

Even before the Norman Conquest, housing extended outside the boundaries of most towns of any size. Spreading out as ribbons of dwellings alongside roads, medieval suburbs formed part of a town's fringe belt, initially attracting craftsmen and poorer people, many of them closely connected with the agricultural economy of the surrounding countryside. Sometimes, though, such suburban streets were later colonized by members

Fig. 1.17 Frenchgate, Richmond, Yorkshire. Frenchgate is an example of the ribbons of housing that extended outside the boundaries of medieval towns when their populations increased in the 13th and early 14th centuries. The width of the street suggests that it was laid out in a spacious fashion in order to attract prosperous citizens. The houses have all been rebuilt, mostly of locally quarried stone, and the cobbled street surface is a survival from the 18th or the 19th century, when local highway authorities improved street surfaces to cater for wheeled traffic.

of the urban elite seeking more spacious housing outside the town centre (Fig. 1.17). Markets outside town walls, many of them for livestock, also became the nuclei of later urban development. Smithfield, on the north-western edge of London, started life as an extramural market-place, as did Gloucester Green, just outside the northern walls of Oxford, supplementing the somewhat constricted market at the central crossroads. And since the late eighteenth century St Giles, the wide main street leading north from Oxford's city centre has accommodated a lively and noisy fair each September.[111] Between and beyond these suburban tentacles were fields and commons, some of them preserved as public or semi-public open spaces, like the North and South Inches at Perth, or Christ Church Meadow and Port Meadow on the flood plain to the south and west of Oxford. Here towns came face to face with the countryside on which they ultimately depended for their prosperity.

2

Building the Late Medieval Town, 1300–1540

The landscape of the small Cotswold town of Burford (Oxfordshire) has not changed fundamentally since the seventeenth century, save for the traffic that often clogs its main street (Fig. 2.1). It rises up to a plateau carrying the modern A40 road from a crossing over the River Windrush near the parish church, which probably occupies the site of an Anglo-Saxon minster. A market existed by the beginning of the twelfth century, and the town subsequently grew through a series of planned extensions,[1] before losing much of its population as a result of fourteenth-century epidemics. It prospered later from the trade in raw wool from the Cotswolds through Southampton, but the population, judging by the chantry returns of 1545, was no more than about 800, and even today it only takes a few minutes to walk from the town centre into unspoiled countryside. Yet, despite Burford's modest size, the wealth accumulated by its late-medieval wool merchants financed a large-scale expansion of the church and the rebuilding of many of the houses, some of which had storage space for bales of wool, others serving as inns for merchants travelling by road. They have survived because of the subsequent decline of the Cotswold wool and cloth trade and the rediscovery, and to some extent re-invention, of the town in the late nine-teenth century by new residents in search of a pre-industrial arcadia.

Most towns in modern Britain already existed in one form or another by 1300, but, apart from churches and castles, few of their earliest buildings survive above ground. That changed in the next two centuries, when many towns began to assume something of their present aspect; in some, especially in the south of England and in East Anglia, there have been few fundamen-tal changes since the sixteenth century. Around a fifth of the population of

Fig. 2.1 Burford was laid out on a hillside, with the main street, where markets were held, leading down to a crossing over the River Windrush. The clock on the left projects from the Tolsey (town hall), built c.1525. The view has changed little since the photograph was taken in the early 20th century, save for the vast increase in car traffic.

England and Wales lived in towns of some sort, however small, by 1300,[2] and by then urbanization was also well under way in Scotland. But by the early fourteenth century the population was beginning to outstrip the food supply, forcing up prices and threatening a subsistence crisis; then in the late 1340s bubonic plague (the Black Death) decimated urban and rural populations throughout Europe. British towns lost about a third of their inhabitants, sometimes more, and many shrank to become little more than villages, like New Radnor in Wales, where a mere handful of houses lined the street grid when John Speed published his map in 1610. Other towns were abandoned altogether following lengthy periods of decline. They include Newtown in the Isle of Wight, a Parliamentary borough sending two members to the House of Commons until 1832; its pretty town hall of 1699 still stands isolated beside a reedy river estuary. Wales suffered grievously from the Owain Glyndwr rebellion at the beginning of the fifteenth century, and a hundred years later it still had only three or four towns whose populations topped an estimated 2,000 people; Scotland likewise had only four.[3] Some towns took years to recover from the fourteenth-century demographic crisis; in Lincoln, formerly one of the most important towns in England, the suburbs were depopulated, and by 1546 all but nine of the city's 46 churches had been abandoned.[4] A petition of c.1450 mentioned ten deserted streets in Winchester,[5] where the population did not regain its pre-Black Death population level until the nineteenth century. The north-eastern quarter of Leicester, now housing the city's main shopping district, was abandoned in the late fourteenth century and given over to orchards; it was not fully built up again for some five hundred years.[6] Other towns such as Stamford and Coventry did well from growing specialization in the wool and cloth trade in the fourteenth century, only to go into decline in the next 200 years, when exports fell.[7]

Urban decline should not be exaggerated. Some towns, like Reading,[8] grew, and others continued to prosper despite—and to some extent because of—the overall fall in their population, which benefited survivors by reducing the pressure on the means of subsistence. Towns continued to market agricultural goods, their main streets filled regularly with animals being bought and sold—a common sight until well into the twentieth century—and their inhabitants providing goods and services for the surrounding countryside. Leicester's High Street was once called Swinesmarket, the nearby Silver Street Sheepmarket, both supplementing the Wednesday market place at the intersection of the present High Street and Highcross Street, now a public open space; a weekday market continues to thrive in the Saturday market place in the south-eastern corner of the town. Religious and pilgrimage sites also remained important, ensuring that urban life continued in places that had lost much of their economic *raison d'être*. A specialized, if transitory, population was attracted to Oxford, to Cambridge and to the three Scottish university towns (St Andrews, Glasgow and Aberdeen),[9] all of which developed service-based economies that compensated to some extent for a decline in manufacturing. Thaxted (Essex), a well-preserved small town with many late medieval buildings, flourished through the manufacture of cutlery, Henley-on-Thames and Faversham (Kent) through the export of grain to London. And St Ives (Cornwall), a rare example of a town newly established in this period, grew through the export of minerals, the initiative coming from a local landowner, Sir Robert Willoughby, following the silting up of the port at Lelant, a short distance to the south.[10] Here, as in many coastal ports, the layout was determined by the local geography, with the main street following the semicircular line of the harbour and the market place hugging the shore.

The most important cause of urban prosperity was the growth in the textile industry. Large tracts of agricultural land in the West Country, the Cotswolds, the Midlands, East Anglia and Yorkshire were converted into sheep ranches after the Black Death and became famous for the quality of their wool, much of it exported. Fuelled by the wool and cloth trades, Salisbury, to take one example, prospered in the fifteenth century, when it was the third largest provincial town in England.[11] Small towns like Chipping Campden, Tavistock (Devon) and Lavenham (Suffolk) became thriving centres of high-quality cloth manufacture, the result to some extent of government-sponsored 'import substitution' at the time of the Hundred Years War (1337–1453).[12] The resulting prosperity helps explain the building of their magnificent late-medieval churches and the handsome houses of their leading citizens; a third of all occupations mentioned in a Muster Roll (military survey) of Lavenham in 1522 were connected with the textile industry.[13] But the place that benefited most from the cloth trade was London, which accounted for 61 per cent of all English cloth exports in the late fifteenth century, compared with a mere seventeen per cent in the early 1300s. Its growing economic importance had a negative effect on other port towns like Boston, which saw its share of cloth exports plummet from 29 to 2.8 per cent in the same period, though this did not deter the leading citizens from constructing the lighthouse-like 'stump' or west tower of the parish church, still a commanding landmark in the flat surrounding countryside.[14] A similar process of economic concentration contributed to the growth of Edinburgh, which, together with its adjacent port of Leith, was handling ninety per cent of Scotland's wool exports by the 1530s, reinforcing its position as the nation's most important town. The Scottish government and Court settled there in the 1530s, and by 1560 Edinburgh had a estimated population of about 12,500, perhaps a little less than that of England's second largest town, Norwich.[15]

Transport improvements were often the key to success. Heavy goods went by river and sea, but roads were essential for local trade and for the delivery of commodities such as wool and metal. The Lavenham cloth industry depended on the import of high-quality wool from Norfolk, Lincolnshire and elsewhere, and bequests for improving the roads leading to it figure in several sixteenth-century wills. River crossings were crucial.

Bewdley (Worcestershire), an inland port on the River Severn, flourished after the construction of a bridge in 1447; John Leland, who travelled the country in the 1530s and 1540s, wrote in 1539 that 'the whole town glittereth, being all of new building'.[16] Most earlier bridges were made of timber, sometimes supported on stone piers, but by the fourteenth century many were being built of stone. Some, like the Bishop's Bridge at Norwich (c.1340) on the main route (now a footpath) leading out of the city to the east, were financed by religious houses. Lay members of religious fraternities could also take the initiative. Abingdon (Berkshire, now Oxfordshire) flourished after the building of a stone bridge diverting traffic away from Wallingford, a few miles downstream; it was built in 1446 by the Guild of the Holy Cross, which also paid for a priest to say masses for the souls of the contributors in St Helen's church (see below, p. 70).[17] At Stratford-upon-Avon the fourteen-arched bridge of the 1480s still carries traffic from the south; it was funded by a successful merchant, Hugh Clopton, former Lord Mayor of London, and he also paid for the building of a causeway across the marshy and frequently flooded approach.[18] The close connection between bridges and chantries sometimes led to the building of chapels on, or alongside, bridges. Most of these have gone, but there is a surviving example beside the bridge over the Derwent at Derby and another of 1426 on the bridge itself at St Ives (Cambridgeshire), a river port on the Ouse; other bridge chapels can be seen at Wakefield (a replica of the c.1348 original), at Rotherham (1483) and at Bradford-on-Avon (Wiltshire), where a tiny oratory was rebuilt in the seventeenth century.

Defences

The first thing seen by a traveller to a late medieval town was its skyline, punctuated by the towers and spires of churches and sometimes by the turrets of a castle. But before entering many towns it was necessary to pass through the defences. Murage grants, starting in 1220, allowed newly independent town councils, already empowered by royal charters, to build fortifications on their own initiative, and many rebuilt their walls in the fourteenth or, less often, the fifteenth centuries. Some, including Bristol and Lincoln, had already expanded their walls to incorporate suburbs, but elsewhere, as at Coventry, the walls were not even begun until the fourteenth century; here the first of twelve gates went up in around 1355.[19] Except in contested coastal or border areas, walls were constructed as much for show as for strictly practical reasons; rebuilding could assert the self-image of the community and its wealthier citizens, who in most cases paid for them themselves and benefited from the tolls paid at the gates.[20]

Medieval town defences were encircled by ditches, which have usually been filled in. Oxford's northern ditch (Canditch) became Broad Street, and houses later went up along its southern side, hiding the wall behind. Holywell Street and Longwall Street follow the outer line of the ditch eastwards and south to the site of the East Gate; the much-frequented Turf Tavern, approached down a slope from Holywell Street, was built within the ditch next to the wall, the full height of which is visible from the pub garden. The construction and appearance of town walls varied greatly from one place to another. Sections of Roman masonry are incorporated within the walls of Chester, surmounted by late-thirteenth or early-fourteenth century blocks of the local red sandstone, and punctuated with towers that served as bastions or lookouts.[21] Semicircular bastions also project from the much-rebuilt Roman and later walling on the southern side of Colchester, and can be seen from a nearby car park (often a good place from which to view urban fortifications). Here, as in other towns with well-preserved walls such as Newcastle and Winchester, small postern gates give access to the narrow intra-mural streets which follow the circuit on the inside.

Town walls were pierced by gateways, some of them as impressive as the castles which they in many respects resembled. Sometimes, as at Warwick and Bristol, gates were surmounted by churches or chapels; elsewhere they could house prisons, as happened at Winchester, where people were incarcerated in the West Gate as late as the Napoleonic Wars. More than any other secular buildings in late medieval Britain, gateways proclaimed a town's identity and prestige, and even today they can tangibly demarcate the central districts. Bondgate—sometimes called Hotspur Gate—licensed in 1434, still holds up traffic entering Alnwick from the south, and the North Bar at Beverley (Yorkshire), built in 1409-10 of brick—a material that became widely used in the eastern counties of England from the fourteenth century onwards—acts in a similar manner (Fig. 2.2). In both towns the street widens inside the gate, contributing to a sense of arrival and enclosure which must have been even more evident in the Middle Ages.

Fig. 2.2 Beverley prospered from the wool trade in the late 14th century, its merchants trading across the North Sea to the Continent. The town was walled, and North Bar, a crenellated, brick-built gateway of 1409, still holds up traffic proceeding towards the two market places. The brick houses to the right of the gate date from the 18th century, when the town experienced a growth in prosperity as a market and administrative centre for the surrounding countryside.

The late-medieval walls at Newcastle, close to the Scottish border, and at Great Yarmouth, on the east coast, still had a defensive, or at least a deterrent, purpose. At Yarmouth they defended the town from potential attackers arriving by sea, and they still encircle the rather neglected fringe of the town centre; work was completed in 1393 with the building of a formidable half-cylindrical south-eastern tower of stone and flint (Fig. 2.3). The coasts of southern England were especially vulnerable to French raids in the early years of the Hundred Years War. The walls at Canterbury (Fig. 1.2) were largely rebuilt in flint after 1363, for fear of a French invasion, and the town is still entered from the London direction through the West Gate of *c.*1378-80, financed by the Archbishop and probably designed by the master-mason Henry Yevele, who was also responsible for the rebuilding of the cathedral nave; the passageway through the gate is squeezed

Fig. 2.3 Great Yarmouth, a thriving river port in the later Middle Ages, has one of the most complete set of medieval fortifications in any British town. They faced east across marshes towards the North Sea, with its lucrative fisheries and its seaborne trade. The section shown here, dating from the 14th century, was built of flint pebbles and random blocks of stone, but it has lost its crenellated top. The upper stages of the semicircular tower incorporate some medieval brickwork and a later gabled roof.

between two massive cylindrical towers reminiscent of contemporary castle architecture.[22]

The small port of Tenby, on the Bristol Channel in south-west Wales, started life as an Anglo-Norman outpost in hostile territory, and a murage grant of 1338 allowed the construction or reconstruction of a west wall cutting off the town, on its peninsula, from the surrounding countryside. Rebuilt after 1457 on the order of Jasper Tudor, earl of Pembroke and uncle of King Henry VII, it is still largely intact, with an unusual gateway enclosed within a large, rounded bastion or barbican.[23] And at Edinburgh the King's Wall, begun in 1427, was explicitly designed, in the words of a 1450 charter, to protect the citizens from 'the evil and injury of our enemies of England'. It ran to the south of the High Street (Royal Mile), but was subsequently superseded by the Flodden Wall, begun in 1514 as a defence against further English incursions, and not finished till 1560.[24]

The Walls of York and Southampton

York owed much of its medieval importance to its role in securing the north of England for the monarchy, and in defending it from the Scots. But the rebuilding of the fortifications in the late-thirteenth and fourteenth centuries seems mainly to have been an assertion of pride in what was still in many ways England's second most important city. The stone walls of local white magnesian limestone—one of the most complete sets of urban fortifications in Britain, and one of the finest in Europe—rest on earth banks which were reared up, probably in the mid twelfth century, in order to cover the surviving Roman fortifications and to enclose districts newly settled in late Anglo-Saxon times. The walls were completed in their present form by the 1380s, along with their almost complete walkway, a feature of most town walls in the Middle Ages, allowing panoramic views of the city, especially on the western side—there was a gap to the east, where an artificial pond (the King's Fishpool) had been created on the flood-plain of the River Foss, since drained and now an amorphous landscape of roads and warehouses. The four main gates were all rebuilt in a showy fashion, probably in the late fourteenth century. The oldest part of Micklegate Bar, the first to be seen when arriving from the south, dates from the twelfth century, but the upper storeys with their crenellated bartizans date from the fourteenth century. Bootham Bar, on the site of the north gate of the Roman legionary fortress, was heightened at about the same time, as was Monk Bar, the main eastern gate. Walmgate Bar, most complete of all, at the far end of what had once been an extramural suburb, still preserves its outer gateway or barbican.

At Southampton (Fig. 2.4) the existing walls were strengthened in response to a French raid of 1338. It precipitated the building of new fortifications alongside a widened quay on reclaimed land by the River Test on the western side of the town. The houses—some of which still survive— were concealed behind blind Gothic arches (the Arcades) that carry a crenellated walkway, still accessible to pedestrians.[25] New walls and another quay, the Town Quay—now the site of a busy road—were also laid out facing the Solent to the south. The usual extramural ditch is still visible outside the east wall, as is the 'Back of Walls' street that runs along the inside. The fortifications incorporated towers and gun-ports; God's House Tower, on the south side facing the Solent, even had an artillery platform, and a sluice gate which could be opened to let water in. Most of the circuit can still be seen, punctuated by gates, the most important of which is Bargate, at the northern entrance to the town. It was enlarged in the 1280s, and the north front was rebuilt again at the beginning of the fifteenth century, with the town's Guildhall on the upper floor and a prison below.

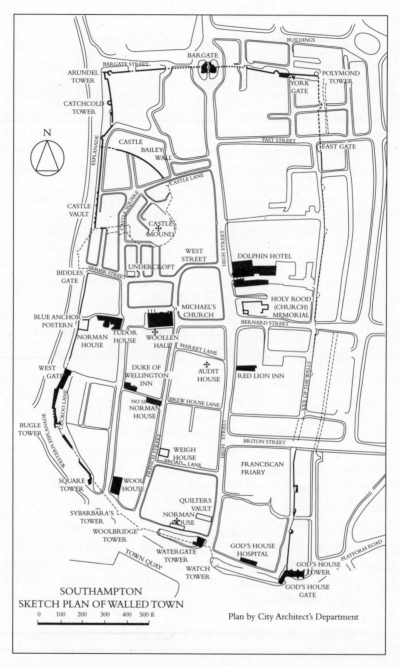

Fig. 2.4 A map of Southampton in the later Middle Ages. Southampton was one of the most important ports of late medieval England. Its walls and towers, most of which still survive, were rebuilt in rubble stone after a French raid of 1338. They enclose the remains of many medieval buildings, some of them with vaulted cellars in which goods for the cross-channel trade were stored.

Homes and Workplaces

Most towns did not expand significantly in the fourteenth or fifteenth centuries, and, apart from market infill, there were relatively few major changes
to their street plans.[26] But that does not mean that there were no alterations
to the urban fabric or infrastructure. The streets of Southampton were
improved under a paving grant of 1384,[27] and a water supply was provided
by Franciscan friars who built a lead water-pipe in 1310, taken over by town
authorities a hundred years later; it was mentioned by John Leland, who also
drew attention to the conduits from which the piped water could be drawn
by the citizens.[28] Such incremental improvements can be matched in other
towns; at King's Lynn seven conduits and nine common privies were listed
in a survey undertaken by the town's Chamberlain in about 1557.[29]

The largest houses in medieval towns were the castles of royalty and aristocracy and the palaces of important churchmen, protected by their encircling outer walls. The great age of urban castle building was over by 1300, but
some castles were rebuilt and refortified by their aristocratic owners in the
often-unstable centuries that followed, though more for show and bravado
than for serious warfare. The Percy Earls of Northumberland built a new
gatehouse and barbican at Alnwick Castle in about 1310-20 (Fig. 1.15) and they
later went on renew the walls and towers, finally turning their attention to
the central shell-keep which contained a set of apartments, made all the
more magnificent when they were remodelled by Anthony Salvin for a later
Earl, starting in 1854. The massive bulk of the castle and its outbuildings still
dominates the northern approach to the town, which remained in some
respects an appendage to it. The two great royal castles in Scotland, at
Edinburgh and Stirling, were also rebuilt within their strongly fortified hilltop enclosures, starting in the late fifteenth century. King James IV, who was
also active at Edinburgh Castle, built a new gatehouse and Hall at Stirling in
about 1500, and his son James V, who succeeded him after his death at the
Battle of Flodden in 1513, completed the conversion of the castle into a
palace when he added a sumptuous suite of state rooms, richly embellished
in the style of Renaissance-inspired buildings on the Continent: a foretaste
of later developments throughout Britain.

Rising standards of living encouraged successful merchants and craftsmen
to rebuild their houses, usually, but not exclusively, of timber framing instead
of the piles and planks used previously. Improved framing techniques made

multi-storey living possible by enabling the upper floors of timber houses to be cantilevered ('jettied') over the lower ones,[30] allowing more space for the upstairs rooms and—according to one line of argument—reducing the weight on the corner posts at ground level. The basic constructional elements were an oak frame, usually resting on a stone (or in some areas brick) base, with a wattle-and daub infill, wooden floors, and a roof covered in turf or thatch, usually replaced later by stone slabs or brick tiles.[31] By the early fourteenth century merchants in the larger towns were building houses of three or even more storeys. One group of four three-storeyed houses in York (Nos. 54-60 Stonegate) has been dated to around 1320,[32] and there are others dating from the fifteenth and early sixteenth centuries in Coney Street (Nos. 16-22) (Fig. 2.5), in Petergate, and elsewhere in the city. Most contained shops or workshops on the ground floor,[33] and many were just one room deep, with a living room above the shop, and an unheated chamber or bedroom at the top.[34] This type of layout could be found throughout Britain, and remained in use well into the nineteenth century.

Fig. 2.5 Coney Street, one of York's main shopping streets, follows the curving east bank of the River Ouse, through which goods were chanelled to the River Humber and the North Sea. The narrow-fronted houses shown here were built of timber in the 15th or early 16th centuries, their upper floors projecting ('jettied') over those below.

The frames of many late-medieval timber houses were strengthened by curved braces to ensure stability and their wattle-and-daub infill covered in plaster, sometimes whitened but often replaced nowadays in a more authentic ochre. Starting in the early fifteenth century, higher-status houses began to feature closely-placed (close-studded) non-structural uprights on their facades. This was a gesture of conspicuous display, seen in buildings like the so-called Henry Tudor house at Wyle Cop, Shrewsbury (Shropshire), dating from the 1430s,[35] and in the so-called Abbot's House of 1459 in Butcher Row in the same town; it was built as a speculation by the nearby Lilleshall Abbey, and contained shops on the ground floor with rentable accommodation above. Several contemporary cloth merchants' houses in East Anglia also have close-studded facades. At Paycockes, a house now belonging to the National Trust on the edge of the small town of Coggeshall (Essex), and recently dated by its tree rings to 1509, the infill is of brick, a practice that became increasingly common in the sixteenth century.

Stone was an increasingly common building material, at least for larger houses, in the towns of the limestone belt that crosses England north-easterly from Dorset to Lincolnshire, and in the 'Highland belt' of the far west and north-west. It was also used in Wales and Scotland, though initially only for high-status houses. The so-called Tudor Merchant's House at Tenby, dating from the late fifteenth century, is built entirely of stone, and Aberconwy House, Conwy, another merchant's house dating from after 1420, has a ground floor of rubble stone and a jettied first floor of timber. Most of the few surviving Scottish town houses of this period are also stone-built, including some much-rebuilt examples in South and North Streets at St Andrews.[36] They were usually only two storeys high, with a 'laigh' (low) floor or basement and an external staircase leading to the first floor with an attic above it. 'John Knox's house' at the eastern end of the High Street in Edinburgh is an almost complete survival, built of stone and heightened to three storeys, with timber jetties and attics, in the early sixteenth century.[37] In 1508, in response to the housing shortage on the confined sites on either side of the 'Royal Mile' linking the castle at Edinburgh to the abbey and palace of Holyrood, the town council encouraged owners to extend their houses forward, but by then people were also beginning to build upwards, especially along the steep slopes leading downhill on either side of the ridge, encouraging a system of multi-storey living in flats which long remained a distinctive feature of Scottish urban architecture.[38]

The houses of the mercantile elite usually grew in a piecemeal manner. None, even in London, matched those of Continental cities like Florence,

Siena or Venice, at least in architectural ambition. Strangers Hall in Norwich, now a museum, occupies the site of a fourteenth-century house set back from Charing Cross, the main street leading west out of the city centre. Reached through an inconspicuous gateway leading between shops into a small courtyard, the most important room was the Hall, built of flint over an earlier undercroft in the mid fifteenth century by a wealthy merchant, William Barley, and remodelled in around 1530 by Nicholas Sotherton, a grocer (dealer in spices); it is open to the roof, with a louvre at the apex to take the smoke from the central hearth. Everyday life took place in parlours and chambers which were extended in the sixteenth and seventeenth centuries, and there is a spacious garden behind. An even more impressive merchant's hall survives in Salisbury, with a rebuilt frontage to the street now called New Canal after the watercourse that originally ran down the middle of the street. It was built towards the end of the fifteenth century by John Hall, three times mayor of the city, whose wealth derived from the profits of wool exports and wine imports, and was heated by a fireplace along one of the walls. The rest of his house has been demolished, but the hall now serves, improbably but effectively, as a cinema foyer.[39]

Some merchants placed their halls at the centre of the street façade. The stone house built, probably by the rich wool merchant William Grevel (d. 1401), in the main street of Chipping Campden has the entrance and service area at one end of the hall and the other important rooms—a parlour at ground level and a chamber above—at the other, lit by a bay window; a passage from the entrance led alongside the 'lower' end of the hall to an open space behind, probably devoted to workshops and storage. A similar arrangement can be seen at the timber-framed house misleadingly called Greyfriars in Friar Street, Worcester, built, probably for a brewer, Thomas Grene, in the late fifteenth century.[40] But the hall at the 'Tudor House' in Southampton (now a museum), built in 1491 by Sir John Dawtrey, Henry VII's Controller of Customs, is now hidden behind a three-gabled, close-studded range along the street front, with what was originally a row of shops at ground level, and a long back wing added later.

Medieval town houses were workplaces as well as homes. The word shop implied a workshop as well as a place where goods were retailed, and in many houses the shop was on the ground floor of the street frontage, an arrangement that has persisted to modern times. There were 270 shops in Chester by 1300, and a comparable number in Salisbury, several of which survive, such as the three-gabled 'Old Bookshop' (now a restaurant), built in the fourteenth century near the gateway to the Cathedral Close, and the mid fifteenth-century No. 8 Queen St, with its two-gabled facade.[41] Many medieval houses were built over cellars or undercrofts, which could function as taverns for the sale of wine and food, as lock-up shops, or as storage space; No. 109 High St, Burford, a three-storeyed timber-framed house of c.1485 (now an antique shop), is built over a stone-vaulted undercroft, perhaps originally leased out as a tavern.[42] Sometimes shops encroached upon the street by means of pentices: lean-tos extending forward from the main living and working spaces.[43] The upper floors Nos. 30-41 High St, Winchester, dating from the 1340s, were extended forward over a covered walkway in the mid fifteenth century,[44] leading to a noticeable narrowing of the street that can be paralleled in other late-medieval towns. And in Chester, starting in the thirteenth century, possibly following a fire of 1278,[45] covered walkways or 'Rows' were built over the undercrofts lining the four main streets, giving access to a second storey of upstairs shops and houses reached by pedestrian passages at first-floor level (Fig. 2.6): a unique arrangement which gives the city much of its character.

Fig. 2.6 One of the Rows in Watergate Street, Chester. Dating originally from the late 13th century, the Rows anticipated some 20th-century shopping developments in their two-storeyed layout, with covered access to the upper-floor shops and balconies overlooking the street.

Lavenham

Lavenham, in the deep agricultural countryside of west Suffolk, was one of the fifteen wealthiest towns in England in the 1520s, despite its population of only some 1,100 people.[46] Its market was established in 1257 and was held in a market place east of the High Street, running roughly parallel to a valley to the east. Manufacturing developed in the fourteenth and fifteenth centuries, supported by an expanding cloth trade; by the 1460s Lavenham was producing the second largest amount of cloth in any Suffolk town, much of it exported to London. Its prosperity is demonstrated by its magnificent church, rebuilt between 1485 and 1540, partly with money from two generations of the Spring family, wealthy capitalist clothiers who 'put out' the wool to domestic weavers, and had their own chantry in the church; fifty other donors contributed to the rebuilding, thirty-five of whom were clothiers. As the town prospered it expanded to the east of its original core, with streets sloping down to a brook, its water supply useful for dying cloth; the aptly-named Water Street has a culverted channel underneath it. The streets of the town were, and to a large extent still are, lined with two-storeyed timber houses, many of them with close-studded facades. Nearly all are laid out along the street frontage of the plots, with entrances for carts on the ground floor; in some there are also openings in the upper floor through which bales of wool could be lifted up or down. Corner sites were especially favoured, allowing for richly carved corner posts supporting projecting 'dragon beams'. Downstairs windows were used to display samples, with wooden flaps that could be drawn up for security at night, as can still be seen at Nos. 10–11 Lady Street (Fig. 2.7). There were also two halls for religious guilds, one of them, for the guild of Corpus Christi, occupying a prominent site in the market place.[47] Wool was bought and sold in purpose-built halls, one of which, with a central open-roofed hall and two-storeyed cross-wings on either side, survives at the back of the Swan Hotel.

Lavenham's cloth trade was badly hit by changes in fashion in the second half of the sixteenth century, and the town, reached only by minor roads and later a branch railway (since closed), has scarcely expanded outside its medieval boundaries. Some houses were hidden behind decorative plasterwork (pargetting) in the seventeenth century, and the facades of others were later rebuilt in brick. New industries such as straw plaiting and horsehair weaving arrived in the nineteenth century, but they did little to change the visual character of the town, whose population in the 1930s was not much larger than it had been in early Tudor times. Many of the houses as we see them today owe much of their character to late nineteenth- and early twentieth-century restoration, when 'unspoiled' places like Lavenham and Burford were discovered by new owners. One example is the 'Grange' in Shilling Street, named after a wealthy clothier who built the house in the fifteenth century. Given a Georgian brick front in the eighteenth century, and subsequently divided up, it was restored to an approximation of its original appearance in the early twentieth century. Today, like many of Lavenham's houses, it is as much a monument to the modern taste for picturesque old towns and their buildings as it is to the aspirations of the family who built it.

Fig. 2.7 A 15th-century house and shop at the corner of Lady Street and Water Street, Lavenham. The façade, of close-studded timber framing, indicates that it was built for a prosperous citizen, probably one of the clothiers whose wealth funded the rebuilding of the magnificent church. Three ground-floor windows (originally unglazed and closed at night by hinged wooden flaps) lit the shop in which samples were displayed. The upper floor is jettied, and the hipped roof is of brick tiles.

Few medieval artisans' houses survive in anything like their original state,[48] and the housing of the desperately poor—a large component of urban populations at all times and everywhere—has disappeared without trace. Probate inventories from the sixteenth and seventeenth centuries suggest that most working peoples' houses consisted of just two, or at the most three, rooms, placed next to each other or one above the other; a house of this type from Taunton (Somerset) has been reconstructed in the grounds of the County Museum there.[49] Some artisans' houses seem to have started as market booths like those that can still be seen in Middle Eastern towns, usually just one room deep, protected by wooden shutters that could be pulled up at night, with residential accommodation above but no garden or plot at the back. A similar kind of arrangement may have prevailed in a group of closely-packed buildings in the middle of Saffron Walden (Essex), where rows of shops now take up most of the original thirteenth-century market

Fig. 2.8 These early 15th-century houses in Tewkesbury were built as part of a speculation by the monks of the Benedictine Abbey, whose churchyard lay behind them. The occupants were craftspeople who leased their houses from the monks. Each had a shop on the ground floor and a room (or two rooms) above. Food was prepared in a room behind, originally heated by an open fire.

place.[50] Small late-medieval houses sometimes survive in what were once the less-favoured outer areas of towns, such as in Walmgate in York,[51] or Spon Street, a suburban street outside the walls of Coventry that is now a virtual open-air museum of smaller late-medieval and early-modern domestic buildings.[52] By the fourteenth century large ecclesiastical institutions were building speculative developments of small houses and shops in town centres. A row of houses in Goodramgate, York,[53] was built in about 1316 on the edge of Holy Trinity churchyard to provide income for a chantry, and a similar row, tree-ring dated to 1410, was built alongside the Abbey churchyard at Tewkesbury (Fig. 2.8); each house has a hall behind the workshop on the street front and a narrow garden behind.[54] Such developments anticipated the ubiquitous working-class terraces of eighteenth- and nineteenth-century towns.

Most manufacturing in medieval towns took place within, or behind, houses, but specialized buildings were needed for the storage of large quantities of goods, especially, as in Lavenham, the wool and cloth which made an essential contribution to the prosperity of many townspeople. Wool could also be stored next to merchants' houses, as may have been the case at No. 25 Sheep Street, Burford, a stone house with a close-studded first floor, tree-ring dated to 1473 and facing the road leading west from Oxford towards Gloucester and the Welsh border.[55] Warehouses for the export of cloth were also built along waterfronts. The late fourteenth-century stone-built, two-storeyed Wool House (now a pub-restaurant) in Southampton looks out onto the Solent on the south side of the walled town, and a fifteenth-century timber-framed warehouse complex, long turned over to domestic use, survives near the bridge at Henley-on-Thames, an inland port. Three larger warehouse groups of similar date can still be seen close to the quayside at Kings Lynn: Hampton Court, built of brick around a courtyard on reclaimed land at the mouth of the Ouse; the 'Hanseatic' (Marriott's) warehouse of brick and stone (Fig. 2.9); and the 'Hanseatic Steelyard' with two rows of warehouses of brick and timber on either side of a narrow courtyard, close to the Saturday Market.[56] Such buildings anticipate the much larger storage buildings that were later to transform the river fronts of many towns.

Urban inns proliferated as road traffic, much of it borne on packhorses, increased in the fourteenth and fifteenth centuries. The White Hart at Newark on the Great North Road was built of timber some time after 1460, with almost continuous glazing along its upper floor; at the late fifteenth-century Angel further south at Grantham (Lincolnshire) the gatehouse-like stone façade is pierced by a central archway with an oriel window above it

Fig. 2.9 The Hanseatic warehouse at Kings Lynn. The South Quay was formed on reclaimed land alongside the River Ouse, close to the original town centre. Ships trading with the Continent docked here, and goods were stored in warehouses, of which this is an impressive, though much rebuilt, example. Built of stone and brick in the early 16th century, it forms part of a quadrangle begun by the merchants of the Hanseatic League and subsequently leased to local merchants.

and canted bays on either side. Inns like these were usually built around courtyards containing accommodation for travellers. The courtyard at the Golden Cross in Oxford, another important thoroughfare town, was entered from Cornmarket Street, leading north out of the city centre, as was the New Inn of the 1390s, just inside the North Gate, its ground and first floors now housing a hat shop and a sandwich bar, the upstairs rooms converted to student accommodation.[57] Inns were also an essential feature of pilgrimage towns. The 'Checker of the Hope' at the corner of the High Street and Mercery Lane in Canterbury, five minutes' walk from the Cathedral, was a massive three-storeyed timber structure built over a still-surviving stone arcade let out as shops; the Bull Inn in Burgate nearby (c.1449–68), had no fewer than 38 rooms.[58] Pilgrims also flocked to the tomb of the murdered, though never canonized, King Edward II at Gloucester. The former Fleece

Fig. 2.10 The courtyard of the New Inn at Gloucester in 1893. Gloucester Abbey (now the Cathedral) attracted pilgrims after the burial of King Edward II in 1327, murdered at the nearby Berkeley Castle. The Inn was built in the mid 15th century around a courtyard, with accommodation for travellers accessed from an open gallery at first-floor level. The buildings, close to the town's central crossroads, have remained substantially unchanged, save for the removal of the ivy shown in the photograph.

in Westgate Street was built in the fifteenth century over an earlier vaulted cellar which till recently was the downstairs bar, and the still-thriving New Inn (*c*.1432) in Northgate Street (Fig. 2.10), close to the central crossroads, retains its courtyard plan almost intact, with galleried hotel accommodation at first-floor level.

Public Buildings and Public Spaces

Market places were the main focal points for social and commercial activity in towns, their importance sometimes marked by the presence of a stone Market Cross. The late fifteenth-century stone cross at Salisbury still survives on its original site (Fig. 2.11), as does a similar one at Chichester, a splendid Gothic structure of stone, octagonal in plan, with an open space underneath surmounted a lantern supported on flying buttresses. It was

Fig. 2.11 Butcher Row and the Poultry Cross at Salisbury. The much-rebuilt Poultry Cross, with its covered space for market stalls, went up in the late 15th century at the corner of Butcher Row, one of the encroachments within the city's Market Place. The surrounding timber-framed houses, some of them subsequently clad in tiles or brickwork, also date from the later Middle Ages.

built by the Bishop in 1501 for the 'succour and benefit of the poor people', who were allowed to sell their goods there without 'toll nor other duties'.[59] Markets were regulated by local government, with different trades being allotted specific sections, and in some towns wooden stalls were constructed for particular trades, often supplanted by permanent buildings. The dimensions of market areas were not sacrosanct. The large rectangular market place at Salisbury was, and still is, the main public open space, but, starting in about 1300, permanent buildings began supplanting earlier stalls at its southern end; the street names such as Fisher Row, mentioned in 1314 and Butcher Row (1380) indicate their original purpose and function.[60] The Shambles (former butchers' market) in York was first mentioned in 1086, and booths were already in existence elsewhere on the edge of the market place as early as 1100;[61] they were rebuilt in the fifteenth and sixteenth centuries as two rows of three-storeyed houses facing each other across a narrow street, their wooden framework clearly visible and their upper storeys almost meeting.[62] Houses had started encroaching onto the open market area of Winchester's High Street by the end of the thirteenth century, resulting in a permanent narrowing of this part of the street.[63] And at Alnwick a survey of 1527 records encroachments that went on to take over most of the spacious market place, leaving a much smaller open area bounded on two sides by the town hall and market hall (formerly the Shambles),[64] with shops on the other sides (Fig. 1.15).

Once a town acquired the freedom to govern itself, it needed a meeting place to serve as an office for setting tolls, a court house for the resolution of disputes, and a location for civic celebrations. Some early town authorities recycled existing buildings, such as the Toll House at Great Yarmouth, a flint-built twelfth-century house that was turned into a warehouse before being taken over for public use in the thirteenth century; it was later used as a prison, a police station, a library and a museum.[65] The civic authorities of Lincoln and Southampton met in rooms over the town gates, those of Cirencester in a room on the upper floor of the magnificent church porch, for which money was bequeathed in 1501. Purpose-built civic buildings, most of them containing a large multi-purpose hall, did not start appearing until the late fourteenth century. Unlike some of their Continental counterparts (e.g. the Palazzo Pubblico in Siena), they were usually squeezed into sites between existing buildings. London's Guildhall, first built c.1270–90, had no street frontage of its own, its vast hall, rebuilt over the pre-existing undercroft in 1411–40, and reconstructed following the Second World War, hides away behind relatively minor thoroughfares.[66] St Mary's Guildhall in Coventry, one of the finest surviving medieval civic buildings in England, likewise occupies a confined site along a narrow street, from which it is reached through an inconspicuous gateway. First built by the city's merchant guild in the early 1340s, it was enlarged to its present size, starting in 1394, with a magnificent Hall of the locally-quarried red sandstone placed at first-floor level over an undercroft.[67] The building has remained in civic ownership, and as the city has expanded new civic buildings have gone up

Fig. 2.12 The Guildhall at Leicester. This relatively modest timber-framed building was put up in the 1340s by a religious guild served by chantry priests of the neighbouring church of St Martin. It was enlarged after being taken over by the town's Corporation, but it retains its domestic character, in sharp contrast to the grand Victorian town hall not far away, built to cater for the needs of the much-expanded 19th-century city.

behind it. In some smaller towns the governing body met in an upstairs room above covered space for market stalls. The timber-framed Guildhall at Thaxted (Essex), dating from the third quarter of the fifteenth century, stands at the top of the wide market place which opens out to the east of the parish church, its two upper floors jettied out above the market area.

Civic buildings were sometimes shared with religious guilds. The timber-framed Guildhall at Leicester (Fig. 2.12) was built in about 1343 by the Corpus Christi guild, which maintained four chantry priests to say masses for the souls of departed members in a chapel at the adjacent St Martin's church (now the cathedral). The timber-framed Hall, with its roof of base-cruck construction, stands along a narrow street, and was twice enlarged in the fifteenth century, when the building began to be used by the town's governing Corporation. Cross-wings were then added at each end, one of which was later remodelled to include a Mayor's Parlour and Jury Room, the other to accommodate prison cells at ground level and a room for the

Town Library above. Other rooms were added later around a small court-yard, creating an intact enclave in the heart of the busy, much-rebuilt modern city. The Guildhall at King's Lynn (1422–8), facing the Saturday market place, was also built by a religious guild; it has a splendid façade of chequered flint and stone, with a Hall upstairs and a warehouse below, used at first for storing wine before becoming a prison after the building was taken over by the civic authorities after the Reformation.[68]

Halls were also built, or taken over, by the trade guilds that played an important part in the economic and cultural life of the larger late medieval towns. The Merchant Adventurers' Hall in York was built by a religious guild in 1357–68 on a site to the west of Fossgate, not far from the city's main market area. Timber-framed, with two aisles, it rests on a stone and brick undercroft which doubled up as an almshouse after the guild was absorbed in 1430 into the Guild of Mercers and Merchants; like its London counterparts, the guild later evolved into a business and charitable organization, initially for overseas traders, which still flourishes.[69] The externally remodelled early fifteenth-century hall of the York Merchant Taylors also survives on a site in Aldwark, next to the city wall, as does the first-floor hall of the former religious guild of St Anthony (1446–53) a short distance away in Peasholme Green, overlooking the former wool market.

The Public Face of Religion

Religion played an inescapable part in the lives of late medieval towns-people. Births, marriages and deaths all came within the purview of the Church, and religious institutions were intimately involved in the provision of welfare, education and the public festivities that punctuated everyday life. The Church owned swathes of urban property, and its buildings, enlarged and beautified down to the very eve of the Reformation, were the most prominent features of many urban landscapes. The imposing central towers and spires of the cathedrals at Durham, Canterbury, Salisbury, York, Lincoln and Glasgow all date from the later Middle Ages, when many cathedrals, like that at Winchester, were expanded and refitted to provide more space for an increasingly elaborate liturgy and for the provision of chantry chapels set aside for intercessory masses for the dead. So too were many of the larger Benedictine abbeys in important towns, such as those at Tewkesbury, Selby (Yorkshire) and Gloucester (now the cathedral).

The English and Welsh (though not all of the Scottish) cathedrals survived the Reformation, and most have retained their churches along with some at least of their extensive precincts, entered through defensive walls and gateways through which many town-dwellers never ventured. Wells (Somerset), now a small market town of about 10,000 inhabitants, prospered in the later Middle Ages from the marketing of wool, but its visual identity still depends on the presence of its Cathedral, rebuilt on the site of an Anglo-Saxon minster from the late twelfth to the early fourteenth centuries, with a massive central tower that went up over a hundred years later. By then Wells had sealed its primacy over Bath Abbey as the mother church of the Somerset diocese, its market place laid out immediately outside the cathedral precinct with two gateways: one, of c.1451, giving access to the cathedral church and its precinct (Close), the other, of the mid fourteenth century, to the Bishop's Palace. The cathedral precinct is ringed by late-medieval buildings for the clergy, including the Deanery, enlarged in the late fifteenth century and entered through its own crenellated gateway, and the Vicars' Close: two terraces of 'one up, one down' stone houses, each with its own stone chimneystack, built in 1348 to house the Vicars Choral who conducted the daily services in the cathedral (Fig. 2.13). The houses face each other across a straight street—a virtually unaltered, though hardly typical, example of late-medieval urban design—entered through a gateway with a Hall next to it and a Chapel and Library of c.1424–30 at the far end. South of the Cathedral and entered from the Market Place by its own gateway, is the Bishop's Palace, a thirteenth-century building, moated, with a gateway of its own over the moat, a Hall (now ruined) of baronial dimensions, and an encircling wall of c.1330–40.[70]

The walls and gateways of late medieval ecclesiastical precincts were a powerful statement of institutional wealth and prestige. They could also act as defences against resentful townspeople. The Benedictine abbey at Bury St Edmunds, one of the richest and most powerful religious houses in England, was, and still is, surrounded by a wall with a massive gateway of 1120–48 that served as the main entrance to the church from the town. To the north, facing the original market place (now Angel Hill), is a second gateway giving access to the 'Great Court'.[71] It was rebuilt on an equally magnificent scale c.1346–53 following riots in 1327, and it now serves as the entrance to gardens laid out on the site of the Abbey after its almost complete destruction after the Reformation. The older gateway to the south now gives access to the modern Cathedral, established in 1914 within the

Fig. 2.13 Built in 1348 of local stone from Mendip Hills, the Vicars' Close at Wells was a planned residential development for clergy who took the services at the Cathedral, seen at the far end. They lived in separate houses, each with its own chimney, anticipating later terraced housing in urban streets.

former parish church of St James's, built in the early sixteenth century to the north of the approach to the Abbey church, and enlarged eastwards in 1964–2005 with a splendid crossing tower (by Stephen Dykes-Bower) that recalls the magnificence of the long-lost medieval Abbey.

The spiritual focus of most late medieval town-dwellers' lives was the parish church. Like mosques in Islamic countries (and in parts of urban Britain) today, parish churches were public buildings as well as places of worship, announcing their presence to townspeople by their towers, from which bells called the faithful to prayer or to the burial of the dead. They punctuated the distant view of towns in the first urban panoramas, drawn in the sixteenth century, and they remained prominent local landmarks at a time when relatively few buildings still rose above two storeys. Most towns were already well supplied with places of worship by 1300, but, despite the dramatic fall in population following the 1340s, and the demolition of churches in some of the less prosperous towns, many others were rebuilt

Fig. 2.14 Originally called the 'town chapel', the parish church at Launceston (Cornwall) was completed shortly before the Reformation. Richly carved externally in locally-quarried granite, it has three parallel aisles, the outer ones largely given over originally to chantry chapels. The porch projects into the street, next to the tall crenellated tower.

over the next 200 years, usually on a much larger scale, and in the ubiquitous 'Perpendicular' Gothic style. Churches of this date and type can be found in towns across the country.

Nearly all the 56 churches within the walls of Norwich were rebuilt in this period, wealthy citizens contributing generously to their construction. St Peter Mancroft, founded in the eleventh century next to the new market place, was rebuilt on a lavish scale between 1430 and 1455, with a richly-decorated west tower and a rectangular hall-like nave, suited for sermons: a fashion pioneered in the churches of the Franciscan and Dominican friars, and therefore easily adapted for Protestant worship after the Reformation. The celebrated west tower or 'stump' of the parish church at Boston (Lincolnshire), begun in the 1420s and finished about a century later, is as much an emblem of the town over which it presides as the towers of the civic halls of Continental cities like Bruges and Siena are of theirs. The tower of Louth parish church, also in Lincolnshire, is equally impressive, built in the 1440s and surmounted by a spire of 1501–15, financed out the profits of the wool trade. St Giles, the parish church in the High Street of Edinburgh (subsequently, and briefly a cathedral), was likewise rebuilt c.1370–1420, and was later enlarged, with a distinctive late fifteenth-century central tower surmounted by a miniature spire supported on flying buttresses; there were forty altars inside the church by the time of the Reformation.[72]

Many parish churches grew by accretion, gradually expanding over their churchyards up to the surrounding streets. Rebuilding could allow the Mass to be celebrated in a more elaborate and dignified form in the chancel, now divided from the rest of the church by a carved rood screen. Rebuilding also catered for a growing demand for private requiem masses for the souls of the departed, many of whom were buried inside the church: an important preoccupation, especially following the official promulgation of the doctrine of purgatory in 1274.[73] Such services were usually celebrated in side chapels closed off from the body of the building behind wooden screens. Rebuilt naves, usually with aisles, and financed by the townspeople themselves, provided spaces for processions and preaching. The need for more altars helps explain the addition of aisles and chapels to churches like All Saints, North Street in York, first founded in the eleventh century. Side chapels were added here, starting in 1325, and by the middle of the fifteenth century both nave and chancel were flanked by north and south aisles, with an octagonal tower and spire to the west and a three-gabled street façade to the east. With its almost complete set of fifteenth-century stained-glass windows given by local donors, it gives as good a sense of what a medium-sized late-medieval town church looked like as any in Britain.

The proliferation of churches in late-medieval towns can sometimes be explained by the peculiarities of land tenure. The lordship of Coventry, one of the most flourishing towns of the period, was split between the Earls of Chester and the Bishops of the joint diocese of Coventry and Lichfield, and this tenurial division explains the presence of two huge parish churches close to each other in the city centre. Holy Trinity, next to the long-vanished Benedictine cathedral priory,[74] was rebuilt in cruciform fashion after a fire in 1257, but in its present form it dates from the late fourteenth century (the chancel was begun in 1391); outer aisles were later added to accommodate

The Churches of Medieval Abingdon

Abingdon, on the River Thames in Berkshire (now Oxfordshire) was a small town dominated by a powerful Benedictine abbey. One of the most important religious houses in medieval England, it was founded in about 953–6 by Aethelwold, one of the standard-bearers of the reforms that transformed monastic life in Anglo-Saxon Britain.[75] There were frequent conflicts with the townspeople, which may help explain why, as at Bury St Edmunds, the church was razed after the Reformation. But the gatehouse, of *c.*1450, survives at the entrance from the market place which grew up outside the Abbey gates. So too does the church of St Nicholas—the *capella ante portam* (chapel in front of the gate)—along with a scattering of residential and administrative buildings including the so-called Exchequer or 'Checker' of *c.*1250 and what might have been a mid-fifteenth-century guest wing overlooking the Abbey's own mill-stream and mill. Most of the townspeople worshipped in the parish church of St Helen, which stands some distance away from the Abbey, possibly on the site of an earlier minster. It is reached from the market place by a sinuous thoroughfare (East St Helen's) leading to the church porch at the foot of the thirteenth-century tower and spire. The church was enlarged incrementally, with new aisles being added one by one to the south of the nave, expansion to the north and east being precluded by the presence of the churchyard and roadway. These additions were funded, at least in part, by two religious guilds, dedicated to Our Lady and to the Holy Cross, and in 1539 an outer south aisle was added by the widow of the Abbey's steward.

As in many towns with wealthy monasteries, the townspeople seem to have shed few tears when the Abbey was demolished without trace. But St Helen's church survived, as did the Long Alley Almshouse (Fig. 2.15), founded alongside the extensive churchyard by the Fraternity of the Holy Cross, founded for seven men and six women in 1446–7; its governing body met in the room above the north porch. The almshouse was remodelled in 1604–5 by the Fraternity's successor, the Christ's Hospital charity, beneficiary of a substantial portion of the Abbey's lands,[76] and more almshouses went up around the churchyard in the late seventeenth and eighteenth centuries, giving it a distinctive, almost collegiate, character that it still retains.

Fig. 2.15 Long Alley almshouses at Abingdon. Built in 1446–7 by a religious fraternity in the churchyard of St Helen's parish church, this row of cottages (left) originally housed thirteen aged male and female inmates. The covered walkway was added in 1604–5 by a local charity which took over many of the Abbey's substantial land holdings following the Reformation.

chantry chapels for religious and trade guilds (mercers, tanners and butchers). The church of St Michael, next to St Mary's Guildhall, was in the 'Earl's half' of the city, and it grew to similar dimensions in the fifteenth century before being raised to cathedral status in 1918. Today its spire, along with those of Holy Trinity and the former Franciscan church (Greyfriars), gives the city centre a distinctive skyline that has to some extent survived the destruction wrought during World War II and the subsequent rebuilding of the city centre (see Chapter 9, pp. 277–8).

Charitable Foundations

Medieval charity was inextricably bound up with religion. There were already over four hundred almshouses and hospitals in Britain by the middle of the thirteenth century,[77] many of them supplying hospitality to strangers and pilgrims as well as care for the sick and elderly. One example is the hospital of St Giles (the Great Hospital) at Norwich, founded in 1249 on a site within a bend of the River Wensum, to the north of the Cathedral precinct. There was a church here already, and it became the hospital chapel, with an infirmary in the nave that allowed the inmates a view of the chancel: a common pattern throughout western Europe. Next to it is a miniature cloister with a communal dining hall, lodgings for the Master of the institution, which still flourishes, and what was originally a dormitory for the chaplains.[78] St Mary's Hospital at Chichester (1269–85), another still-functioning medieval almshouse, all but invisible from the street, also has a hall and screened-off aisles containing the inmates' beds, with a chancel at the east end. And the same layout was adopted at Trinity Hospital in the Newarke ('new work') on what was originally the edge of Leicester. It was, founded in 1331 by Henry, Earl of Lancaster, grandson of King Henry III for twenty (later forty) people within an enclave to the south of the castle. The Earl also established a collegiate church of 1354 which was demolished after Henry VIII's Dissolution of the Chantries, but the much-rebuilt almshouse survives as part of De Montfort University, which now occupies much of the site, along with the outer gatehouse and a pair of houses (now part of one of the city's museums), built 1513 for two of the chantry priests.

Some almshouses were founded by successful merchants. The founder of Brown's Hospital in Broad Street, Stamford (1475–6), housing ten poor men and two women, was a merchant described by Leland as being 'of very wonderful richness'. Here the accommodation was placed upstairs in a stone-built range reached by a staircase and porch, with the inmates' cubicles on either side of a corridor, allowing a view of the chapel at the far end; behind is a cloister giving access to a communal hall, since rebuilt.[79] At Ford's Hospital in Coventry (1509, enlarged 1517), founded by a wool merchant and former mayor of the city, the two timber-framed ranges containing the inmates' rooms face each other across an open courtyard, with a narrow entrance from the street. Their survival in a city which has undergone more than its fair share of twentieth-century devastation and rebuilding is a testimony to the resilience of medieval charitable institutions.

Social services, notably education for the young and care for the poor and sick, were sometimes supplied by religious guilds. The Guild of the Holy Cross at Stratford-upon-Avon, dating back at least to the 1260s, joined forces with two other guilds in 1403 to become the town's governing body, and it put up a two-storeyed Guildhall (meeting room) in about 1417, followed ten years later by a schoolroom. Then, some time after 1502, a row of timber-framed almshouses was added, with a close-studded façade extending along Church Street, the thoroughfare leading from the town centre to the parish church. The Guild's aisleless Chapel, also rebuilt in the late fifteenth century, was completed with funds supplied by Hugh Clopton (d.1496), who took up residence at the end of his life at New Place opposite; the house was later bought by a more famous Stratford-born Londoner, William Shakespeare. The low, pinnacled and crenellated tower of the Guild Chapel punctuates the curving street, while the body of the building flanks Chapel Lane, leading down to the river, with the courtyard between the Guildhall and schoolroom (later the master's house) hidden away behind it.[80]

Some late-medieval town churches were served by 'colleges' of priests who, like the clergy associated with Anglo-Saxon minsters, lived communally but did not take monastic vows. One such body was founded in 1342 by the Guild of St John the Baptist in Coventry at Bablake, just inside the western town wall. The funds came from King Edward II's widow who stipulated that two priests should sing mass for the royal family in perpetuity. By the fifteenth century, when the church was lavishly rebuilt, there were twelve priests who lived in an adjacent quadrangle of mainly timber-framed buildings, two ranges of which survive; they were turned into a grammar school and an almshouse (Bond's Hospital) after the Reformation.[81] The complex of buildings now known as Chetham's Hospital in the centre of Manchester is even more complete. A college of priests, comprising a Warden, eight Fellows, four clerks (clergy) and six choristers, was founded in 1421 in order to serve the parish church of St Mary (now the Cathedral), one of the finest town churches of its date in Britain. The buildings, of local red sandstone, went up on the site of the manor house just to the north of the church, on an eminence above the River Irwell, and are entered through a gatehouse linked by a long service wing to a quadrangle and cloister containing a Hall, lodging for the Warden, and tiny bedrooms for the priests. Manchester was described by Leland in the 1530s as the 'finest and busiest town in the whole of Lancashire, with the best buildings and the greatest population',[82] and, long after the Reformation, the Hospital buildings were turned into a school and Free Library with money left by a wealthy merchant, Humphrey Chetham (d.1653).[83]

The word college was also applied to places of education. Winchester College was established by the Bishop, William of Wykeham, one of the leading figures in King Edward III's England, as a boys' grammar school in a largely undeveloped area just outside the south wall of the city, opposite the Bishop's Palace. Its late fourteenth-century buildings are entered through a gate tower—always a symbol of prestige and authority in late-medieval England—and are arranged around two courtyards, one containing shared rooms for the students, the other with a communal Hall and kitchen and a magnificent Chapel with its own cloister.[84] The school survived the Reformation and has since expanded to the south, creating an educational enclave that still exerts a decisive influence on a substantial part of the modern city. Wykeham saw his school as a 'feeder' for his new residential college (New College) at Oxford University. Medieval universities were founded in order to educate and train professionals: lawyers, physicians and above all the clergy, some of whom became administrators of the church and state. Starting in the late thirteenth century, increasing numbers of the students in the two English universities began to be housed in independently-endowed colleges which have maintained their jealously-guarded identity ever since. The depopulation of much of the north-eastern corner of Oxford after the Black Death gave Wykeham and his master-mason William Wynford—who also worked at Winchester College and Cathedral—the opportunity to construct his college, which was founded in 1379, on a vacant site and on an unprecedentedly lavish scale.[85] The buildings went up inside the town walls, a substantial section of which survive within the College's precinct. Streets, denuded of their residents after the Black Death, were blocked in order to build the quadrangle, with its Hall, Chapel and residential accommodation, and the cloister, initially enclosing a burial ground, that adjoins it to the west. The gate tower (Fig. 2.16), embellished with statues of the kneeling Bishop and of the Virgin Mary, is framed within a virtually intact late-medieval townscape made up of the south wall of the cloister on one side and the Warden's Barn, built to house produce from the College's extensive estates in north Oxfordshire, on the other. And anyone following New College Lane in a south-easterly direction towards Oxford's High Street is still forced to make a series of right-angled bends around Wykeham's buildings: a direct result of decisions made in the fourteenth century.

The landscape of the other ancient English university town—Cambridge—was changed equally radically as colleges, including King Henry VI's foundation of King's College, appropriated much of the land, formerly used as wharves, on the east bank of the River Cam; colleges also acquired sites along the two main streets, swallowing up large numbers of houses in the process.[86] In Scotland the colleges of the University of St

Fig. 2.16 New College Lane looking towards the gateway of New College, Oxford. The college was founded by William of Wykeham, Bishop of Winchester, in a part of the city that saw a drastic fall in population after the Black Death. Begun in 1379, it occupied the site of 51 abandoned houses. The south wall of the cloister is behind the blank wall on the left of the picture, and the right-hand wall marks the boundary of the Warden's lodgings and outbuildings.

Andrews (founded in 1410), and King's College in Old Aberdeen, where the first buildings were begun in 1500, are still important components of the relatively modest urban landscapes within which they were founded.[87] And in London the Inns of Court[88]—quasi-collegiate establishments for the study and practice of the common law, sometimes called 'England's third university'[89]—have left a permanent mark on the area immediately to the west of the City, still the capital's main legal quarter: another instance of the impact of the later Middle Ages on the towns and cities that we inhabit today.

3

Reformation and Rebuilding, 1540–1660

S t Andrews is a small, stone-built town of some 16,000 people on the east coast of Scotland. It is best known today for its university, Scotland's old-est, and for its golf course, but in the Middle Ages it was the most important pilgrimage site in the country. The town's three main streets converged in front of the cathedral, begun *c.*1162 and containing a shrine with relics of the apostle Andrew. But the church was abandoned after the Scottish Reformation in 1560, reformed services taking place instead in the parish church of Holy Trinity. The cathedral was already being used as a quarry by 1577, and further depredations took place after 1649, when the town was fortified against an English army after the execution of King Charles I. Today all that remains above ground is the ruined east wall, parts of the west front and south nave arcade, and parts of an eleventh-century church that preceded the building of the cathedral, surrounded by a vast graveyard (Fig. 3.1).[1] The ruins still dominate the town as seen from the seaward approach, and they stand as a graphic reminder of the often devastating impact of sixteenth-century religious change on towns throughout Britain.

The Reformation, and the Dissolution of the Monasteries that accom-panied it, left a permanent imprint upon almost every British town. The survival of the diocesan system in England and Wales meant that cathedrals, along with their extensive precincts, remained for the most part intact. Some of the larger monastic churches became cathedrals of new dioceses created by King Henry VIII;[2] Westminster Abbey, with its associated school, survived because of its royal connections. The Scottish Reformation occurred later, and it had a more radical effect by imposing a non-episcopal Presbyterian system of church government. Some of the Scottish cathedrals

Fig. 3.1 The ruins of St Andrews cathedral. Parts of the 11th-century church of St Rule, seen in the foreground, survived the Reformation, together with east front of the cathedral itself, of *c.* 1200, and some of its outer walls. Otherwise the site, as with many former cathedral and monastic churches in Scotland, was appropriated by the town authorities and used as a graveyard.

and abbeys became parish churches, but others, like that the cathedral at St Andrews, fell into ruin. Some former monastic churches in England and Wales were likewise turned over to parochial use, though shorn of their ancillary buildings; they include the Benedictine Abbey at Bath, rebuilt as recently as 1499-1533, its former cloister area and outer courtyard becoming public open spaces.[3] The parishioners of Malmesbury (Wiltshire) and Wymondham (Norfolk) were content to use the naves of the former abbey churches for worship, leaving the chancels and transepts to fall into ruin. The reverse happened at the former Augustinian priory of St Bartholomew, Smithfield, on the north-western fringe of the City of London. Here the chancel survived as a parish church for its rapidly expanding district, the ruined nave becoming the churchyard, and houses gradually taking over the site of the monastic buildings.[4] At Reading the Abbey church fell into ruin, but the gatehouse survived and the monastic *hospitium* or guest-house was recycled as a school. The Forbury meanwhile—the area in front of the church—continued to be a public open space before being landscaped as a park in the nineteenth century. But the remains of the sanctuary and Lady Chapel were demolished, and they made way in 1842-4 for the grim gaol in which Oscar Wilde was later incarcerated, leaving only the ruined nave and transepts as reminders of what had been one of England's richest churches.[5]

Other long-established medieval monasteries, such as the Benedictine abbeys at Coventry and Leicester, vanished virtually without trace. So too did most of the buildings of the mendicant orders, though some survived. The Dominican (Blackfriars) church in Norwich, rebuilt after a fire in 1440-70, was taken over by the city authorities and used as public hall, the chancel eventually becoming a church for Dutch Protestant immigrants; the preaching yard in front of the church survived as a public open space, but the original buildings around the cloister have largely vanished. In Edinburgh the Greyfriars' church was pulled down, but a new Protestant church took its place in 1620 and the rest of the site became a burial ground for the city; it now contains one of the finest collections of churchyard memorials in Britain. The residential buildings of the Dominican friars at Bristol and Newcastle were leased by the city authorities to local trade guilds, and have survived, though the churches have gone. More commonly the mendicants' buildings were privatized, like those of the Gloucester Blackfriars. They were acquired in 1539 by a local clothmaker, Thomas Bell, three times mayor of the city; he turned part of the church into a house, which can still be seen, and the buildings around the cloister were gradually given over to other, more mundane, uses.

As the Tudor State became more powerful, tightening its grip over local jurisdictions, urban fortifications in England and Wales became increasingly redundant, though most survived for some time in an increasing state of disrepair. New fortifications only went up when military considerations dictated, and where central government was prepared to foot the bill. This happened at Portsmouth, founded in the late twelfth century on an island site with a sheltered harbour and a waterfront facing the Solent, through which ships could reach the English Channel. Overshadowed by nearby Southampton in the Middle Ages, Portsmouth became an important component of England's defences in the sixteenth century. The existing walls along the waterfront were strengthened in 1538-40 and again towards the end of the century, and more walls went up on the landward side, with a gate (the Landport) protecting the road leading north out of the town;[6] the landward defences were further strengthened by the military engineer

Bernard de Gomme, starting in 1665 (See Fig. 5.12). An equally ambitious scheme of fortification took place in the border town of Berwick-on-Tweed (Fig. 3.2). Here the medieval walls (Quay Walls) were retained along the river front, but massive Continental-style bastions for artillery went up on the landward and seaward sides to defend the town from the Scots, who threatened invasion after Queen Mary's loss of Calais in 1558. They were maintained until the Union of Crowns in 1603, later becoming a public recreational walk enclosing what was until recently a military garrison, incorporating barracks built by the Board of Ordnance in 1717-21, after the Jacobite rebellion of 1715, for 36 officers and 600 men.[7]

The rapid spread of heavy artillery made medieval town walls redundant from a military point of view, at least until the English Civil War broke out in 1642. Supplementary earth fortifications were then put up around some towns, traces of which can sometimes be seen. Despite this, the suburbs of Exeter, the third largest provincial town in England, were deliberately devastated by Royalist troops, making a third of the population homeless; the city's population did not reach its pre-Civil War level until the eighteenth century.[8] Artillery also put paid to the military function of castles. Some survived as royal residences, others as prisons, still more, like those at Warwick

Fig. 3.2 Berwick-upon-Tweed, on the Anglo-Scottish border, was fortified in the Middle Ages, but English fears of invasion in 1558 led to a massive programme of refortification designed to protect the town from artillery attack. The strengthened walls and projecting bastions, completed in 1569, can be seen on the right of this air view. The bridge across the Tweed (left) was built in 1611-c.1626.

and Alnwick, as aristocrats' houses. But many fell into ruin, a process sometimes exacerbated by damage during and after the Civil War of the 1640s; the castle at Bristol was levelled by the Parliamentarian government in 1655 and its site subsequently occupied by seventy houses on two new streets laid out by the city Corporation (see Fig. 1.14). They too were destroyed in the Second World War, since when the site has remained empty.

Rebuilding and Expansion

Most people in sixteenth- and seventeenth-century Britain still lived in the countryside. A third or more of the population lived in towns of some kind,[9] most of which were still very small by modern standards. Only six English towns had populations of over 10,000 by the end of the seventeenth century,[10] a figure roughly equivalent to that of a small town like Henley-on-Thames today (11,619 in 2011). Important regional centres such as Gloucester, Leicester, Nottingham and Hull were only half or two thirds that size, and the multitude of small market towns were still tiny by modern standards, with no more than 2,000 or so residents apiece:[11] the size of a large village now. The urban population in Scotland was even smaller. Only one in twenty Scots lived in towns of over 10,000 people in 1700, and many Scottish towns were—and some still are—much smaller than that.[12] Even London, by far the largest city in Britain, was quite small by modern standards in the mid-sixteenth century, with an estimated population of some 75,000:[13] half that of contemporary Paris or Venice, and roughly equivalent to that of Shrewsbury today. But it was Britain's largest port and, crucially, the seat of government of the largest and wealthiest part of what eventually became the United Kingdom. And as Britain's wealth and overseas trade burgeoned it soon expanded to become one of the largest cities in Europe and, eventually, in the world.

The political and economic disruption of the post-Reformation years affected all towns, and had a catastrophic effect on some. William Lambarde, author of *A Perambulation of Kent* (1576), lamented that Canterbury had become 'in a manner waste, having come suddenly from great wealth and multitudes of beautiful buildings to extreme poverty, nakedness and decay'.[14] But towns in southern and eastern Britain eventually recovered as the economy expanded in the second half of the century, and a measure of prosperity eventually spread too to towns in the 'highland zone' of the north and west. By 1600 the urban population had regained its pre–Black Death level, largely as a result of growing economic opportunities and immigration from the countryside. This in turn led to large-scale domestic rebuilding that permanently changed the face of many towns in lowland England, spreading later to the upland areas of the north and west, and to Wales and Scotland: a process that lasted well into the eighteenth century.

Rebuilt houses offered the spacious and comfortable domestic environ-ment that was increasingly craved by those who could afford it. Glass pro-duction increased in the sixteenth century, making it possible to introduce larger windows. The growing availability of brick and stone also presented an attractive and durable alternative to timber or cob in the design of facades. Chimneys of brick or stone became important external features as hearths were introduced and open halls floored over, giving extra living space and allowing the addition of extra storeys on confined central sites. Glazed windows—a relative novelty—enabled rooms to be better lit, and personal possessions, especially furniture and tableware, to be seen to better effect; they were often listed in probate inventories which, when they sur-vive, give a vivid insight into an increasingly consumerist material culture.[15] These developments helped transform the urban landscape. Rebuilding usu-ally occurred piecemeal, house by house, involving both the remodelling and the heightening of street frontages and the infill of back plots. Given the depopulation of most towns after the Black Death, there was little need, except in London, to expand significantly outside the medieval boundaries; even in Norwich, England's second largest city in the seventeenth century,[16] there was still plenty of open space within the walls. There was little overall aesthetic control by landlords or local authorities; their main contribution was to release, or refuse to release, land for development, and to impose regulations preventing fire. Streets therefore were, and usually still are, lined with houses of different, heights, widths, styles and sometimes building materials, adding in many ways to what we now see as their pictur-esque appeal.

Fire was a major scourge in many towns. 718 houses burned down in Norwich in 1507,[17] leading to an intermittently effective ban on thatch as a roofing material. A series of fires in Stratford-upon-Avon in 1594–5 and 1614 were likewise blamed on 'poore Tenements and Cottages which are thatched with Strawe, of which Sort very many have bin lately erected.'[18] But thatch did not disappear from many towns in the north and west until much later; it was only forbidden in Elgin in north-east Scotland, for instance, in 1735. Depending on the availability of other roofing materials, thatch eventually gave way either to clay tiles or pantiles fired in kilns, seen throughout eastern England and Scotland, or to locally quarried stone slabs or slates, ubiquitous in the English limestone belt and in the 'highland' zones of western Britain; the weight of the slabs necessitated lower roof pitches, as can be seen in many of the smaller Pennine towns of northern England.

Country gentry and noblemen increasingly sought urban *pieds à terre*. Stone-built aristocratic houses now lined Edinburgh's Canongate, the street leading east from the High Street to the royal palace of Holyroodhouse, and some can still be seen. There was also a strong aristocratic presence in Stirling, a second capital for the Scottish monarchy; 'Mar's Wark' (1570–2) and Argyll's Lodging, a sixteenth-century house enlarged by the Earls of Argyll in the 1630s and 1670s, both went up just outside the castle precinct.[19] 'Provost Skene's House' (now a museum) in Aberdeen is similar in character, originating in 1545 as a stone tower with prominent conical-capped turrets of a distinctively Scottish type, and enlarged in 1676–86 by a successful merchant, George Skene.[20] Plas Mawr, the largest house in Conwy in North Wales (Fig. 3.3), makes an equally impressive show. Begun *c*.1577, and subsequently enlarged by Robert Wynn, younger son of John Wynn of nearby Gwydir Castle and a former courtier, it was built of local rubble stone on a plot stretching back from the High Street as it slopes up from the quay to the market place.[21] The roofline is enriched with stepped gables (also a common feature in Scotland), and a panorama of *c*.1600 shows elaborate formal gardens behind the house.

Wealthy merchants usually had to rebuild their houses within the confines of their town-centre burgage plots. John Stow drew attention in his *Survey of London* (1598) to houses in Cheapside which 'in former times were but sheds or shops, with solers (upstairs rooms) over them...but by encroachments on the high street, are now largely built on both sides outward, and also upward, some three, four, and five stories high'.[22] A view of Cheapside in 1638 shows the north side of the street lined with four-or five-storeyed timber houses with shops or workshops on the ground floor, their upper floors jettied forward, the rooms lit by long continuously glazed windows.[23] And an engraving of 1643 by the Czech émigré artist Wenceslaus Hollar shows the shops projecting into the street, with wooden shutters on hinges, subsequently replaced by glazed windows.[24] A much-restored row of four-storeyed houses with attics on the south side of Holborn, outside the area devastated in the Great Fire of 1666, gives an idea of such once-ubiquitous

Fig. 3.3 The façade of Plas Mawr, the 'great house' of the Wynn family, stands on Conwy's High Street as it slopes up from the River Conwy to the market place. Built of local rubble stone, the symmetrical layout and classical detailing demonstrate the influence of Renaissance ideas circulated through pattern books; the stepped gables on the top floor help distinguish the building from the smaller and plainer houses nearby.

buildings (Fig. 3.4),[25] and others can be seen in many English provincial towns.[26]

Despite the risk of fire, domestic facades continued to be built of timber well into the late seventeenth century, or even longer; Daniel Defoe found that Coventry in the 1720s was still 'the very picture of the city of London...before the Great Fire'.[27] Timbers were sometimes arranged in geometrical patterns and were increasingly elaborately carved, as in the house that later became the Feathers Inn in Ludlow (Shropshire), a town that had grown up next to its medieval castle high above the River Teme, close to the Welsh border. The house was refashioned in 1619, with profusely carved beams and projecting bay windows, by Rees Jones, a lawyer whose business benefited from the town's position as the administrative centre for the Council of the Marches, responsible for the government of Wales.[28] Harvard House in the High Street at Stratford-upon-Avon (Fig. 3.5) is

Fig. 3.4 Staple Inn, High Holborn, London. These much-restored timber-framed houses were built in the 1580s as a speculation by the Principal of one of the Inns of Chancery, whose much-rebuilt Hall (1581) survives in a courtyard behind. The houses look out onto one of the main streets leading west out of London, just inside Holborn Bar, which marked the City's boundary; they are typical of the many houses destroyed in the Great Fire of 1666, which did not extend as far as this.

Fig. 3.5 Garrick Inn and Harvard House, Stratford. The ornate façade of Harvard House (right) dates from 1596, following a fire that devastated much of the town. The Garrick Inn (left), of similar date, was later refronted in brick, but its façade was reconstructed using some of the original timbers in 1912.

equally ostentatious. It was built in 1596, following a fire that had devastated much of the town, by Thomas Rogers, a grazier and butcher whose grandson founded Harvard University in the United States; it is adorned with lavish carving on the horizontal beams and corner posts, one of them displaying the bear and ragged staff, symbol of the earls of Warwick, together with Rogers's initials and those of his wife.[29]

In Newcastle, the six-storeyed 'Bessie Surtees house' (Nos. 44–46 Sandhill), one of the 'many shops and stately houses for Merchants' by the quayside recorded in 1649,[30] was similarly refronted in timber in the 1660s with continuous glazing on each floor to let the maximum light into the rooms. Sometimes, though, as at Nos. 4–6 Elm Hill, Norwich, built in or around 1619, timber framing was concealed by decorative plaster 'pargetting' contrived to look like stone. The inspiration here probably came from illustrations in Sebastiano Serlio's influential treatise, *Architettura*, an important influence on the decorative arts of the period, translated into English in 1611.

Stone was increasingly used for higher-status houses in towns with good quarries close at hand. Leland described early sixteenth-century Oundle (Northamptonshire) as 'all built of stone',[31] and several later buildings there, such as the Talbot Inn (1626), display date-stones recording their construction. There are houses with date stones of 1634 and 1694 in Elgin, in the north of Scotland, but in 1656 Richard Franck could remark that the houses in Aberdeen were still 'framed with stone and timber', and a subsequent visitor to Glasgow pointed out that 'the houses are only of wood, ornamented with carving'.[32] Brick was another substitute for timber, but it was rarely used for as the main constructional material before the seventeenth century. A relatively early example is the gabled Governor's House in Castle Street, Bridgnorth (c.1633), its symmetrical frontage flanked by chimneys at each end; another group of three brick houses for the schoolmaster, his assistant and the vicar, each with its own two-storeyed porch, went up at about the same time in St Leonard's churchyard at the other end of the town.

Most town houses of this period still had shops or workshops on the ground floor, with the main accommodation placed upstairs, and the service areas behind.[33] Many town-centre pubs still retain this arrangement, the main bar looking out onto the street and the other rooms placed behind it, reached by a passageway alongside the plot boundary. A surprising amount of accommodation could be crammed into a narrow burgage plot. The dull nineteenth-century stucco façade of No. 26 Westgate St, Gloucester, now an antique shop, conceals a very large house of 1617–22, possibly built by one of the city's aldermen, John Brown, with four storeys and an attic. It is flanked by an alley to the side, the light entering the rooms through bay windows; a lower range of 1586–7 takes up the rest of the hundred foot-long plot. At Totnes, a town that prospered through the marketing and export of cloth, some of the forty-seven surviving timber-framed houses of the sixteenth and seventeenth centuries—the most recent of them dated 1692—have open yards behind the street front, linked by upstairs galleries to what were originally detached blocks containing the kitchen.[34] Houses could be extended forwards as well as backwards; the upper floors of some of the houses on the main street of Totnes rest on colonnades or 'piazzas', first recorded in 1532 'for stondyngs on market days'. They can still be seen,

The Old Town of Edinburgh

In 1700 Edinburgh, including its suburbs and the port of Leith, had an estimated population of around 50,000, making it the second largest city in Britain.[35] Until the Union of 1707, it was the capital of an independent state, attracting gentry, nobility and professionals like London or any other European capital city; even after 1707 it remained the headquarters of the Scottish legal system and of the Church of Scotland. One of the 'four great towns' of medieval Scotland, it also prospered from its position on the main north-south route along the east coast, and above all from its proximity to the port of Leith on the Firth of Forth. Its topography, determined by the underlying physical geography, was unusual. Gordon of Rothiemay's map (really a birds-eye prospect) of 1647 (see Fig. 1.9) shows dense building on the plots to the north and south of the main street or 'Royal Mile' leading from the Castle through the Canongate to the Palace of Holyroodhouse, begun in 1529 and enlarged to its present size after 1672. David Buchanan wrote in his description accompanying the 1647 map that he was 'not sure that you will find anywhere so many dwellings and such a multitude in so small a space as in this city of ours',[36] though there were gardens to the south of Cowgate, which ran parallel to the main street, and there were more behind the frontages in Canongate, where several members of the aristocracy had their town houses.

The Royal Mile was, and still is, flanked by a 'wall of buildings', which encroached over time onto the public space between them.[37] The main public buildings—the church of St Giles, the Tolbooth or city hall, and the High Cross—were in the middle of the street, the Parliament House (rebuilt in 1637) to the south. The most prosperous inhabitants lived close to the market area, and as the population grew, especially from the time of King James VI (James I of England) onwards, the density increased. Before the seventeenth century few of the houses were more than three or, at the most, four storeys high. Some had thatched roofs till these were outlawed in 1621, and the Edinburgh city council insisted on the use of stone for new building there after a fire in 1652; existing timber fronts were finally outlawed in 1674. Smaller houses were laid out on the steep sites along the plot boundaries behind the main street; they were reached by alleys or 'wynds' approached from the street through narrow openings.

Street frontages began to be heightened from around 1600, with each floor occupied as a flat by a different family: something all but unknown in England before the nineteenth century. Rich and poor lived close to each other, often on different floors of the same building; William Maitland wrote in 1753 that it was not 'deemed mean, to dwell or lodge in the highest Apartments; for even Merchants and Bankers transact their affairs in the third or fourth stories [*sic*]; and many Persons of Distinction lodge higher'.[38] The earliest surviving houses along the Royal Mile had a 'foreland' facing the street and a 'backland' behind. Gladstone's Land, which still survives, was a four-storeyed sixteenth-century house with a timber façade to the street, but the 'foreland' was rebuilt in about 1620 by Thomas Gledstanes, an import-export merchant, and was extended forwards in stone over an arcade (Fig. 3.6), with two extra attic storeys behind gables; in 1635 Gledstanes was living in the top-floor flat, having leased out the rest of the building.[39] Later legislation forbade further encroachments onto the street, and by the end of the century groups of apartment houses were being built with plain, uniform stone facades. Milne's Court (1690s) with its smooth unbroken façade of six storeys and attics, is an early example, setting the pattern for the plain multi-storeyed blocks that line the Lawnmarket today, each with a courtyard on its steeply sloping 'backland'.

as can the arcaded front extensions of some Scottish town houses such 'Gladstone's Land' in Edinburgh (see Fig. 3.6) and the so-called Braco's House in Elgin (1694).

Building on back plots created dense townscapes, with houses looking out onto the narrow alleys that led off the main street. A merchant's house in King's Lynn in 1636 contained the usual rooms on the street front—hall, parlour, chambers, etc.—but there were also stables, malthouses, storerooms and a brewhouse on either side of the passageway behind it, which led to a wharf on the River Ouse:[40] a common arrangement in ports throughout the country. The effect of such infilling in Oxford can be seen by comparing the Agas/Whittelsey map of 1578—the first reasonably accurate map of the city—with another produced by David Loggan in 1675; the 1578 map shows little building behind the street facades, but by the middle of the seventeenth century the back plots along the main streets had been filled with houses (Fig. 3.7). The result can be experienced today by venturing into the narrow yard behind No. 130 High Street, where William Boswell, an alderman of the city, built himself a handsome timber-framed house ('Kemp Hall') in 1637, now a Thai restaurant; it looks out onto the brick wall of the adjoining plot, but still retains many of its elaborate internal fittings. But as merchants and professionals moved to new suburbs in the

Fig. 3.6 Gladstones Land, Edinburgh. Like most houses in Edinburgh's 'Royal Mile', this tall, narrow-fronted house accommodated several households, each living in a flat approached by an internal staircase. The frontage to the Lawnmarket replaced an earlier timber façade, and was built of local ashlar stone by a merchant, Thomas Gledstanes, who bought the property in 1617. There are two gables at roof level, and the building is approached from the street through a two-bay arcade.

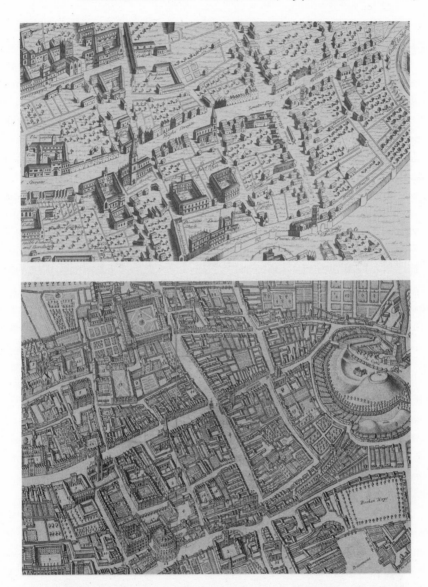

Fig. 3.7 These two birds'-eye views of the centre of Oxford (north is at the bottom), illustrate the process of infilling burgage plots to accommodate growing urban populations. In Ralph Agas's map of 1578 (above) there are long gardens behind the houses, but by 1675, when David Loggan made his map (below), most of them had been built over and the irregular frontages of the houses on the main streets straightened out. The Norman castle mound is seen to the right of Loggan's map.

nineteenth century, many back plots deteriorated into slum 'courts', often falling victim more recently to large stores or office blocks, or to car parks.

Most townspeople lived in much smaller houses. Many houses in late sixteenth-century Leicester still had only two rooms: a hall (sometimes called a shop) and a parlour, which could double up as a bedroom, or could contain a bed alcove in the roof space above, reached by a ladder. These rooms could be placed either next to each other or above one other on their tiny plots;[41] a timber-built house of the latter type, with a close-studded ground floor and a single upstairs room, survives facing the church-yard of St Leonard, Bridgnorth, (Fig. 3.8). A row of similar two-storeyed, stone-built cottages with a gabled roofline, was put up in 1571–6 on a site close to the parish church at Burford given by the clothier Simon Wisdom, who built up a small property empire in the town; some of his houses dis-play his initials over the doorways.[42] The same kind of layout was perpetu-ated in the rows of almshouses, often single-storeyed, that can be found in many towns. Less fortunate town-dwellers—poorer craftsmen, labourers and agricultural workers—were usually housed in cottages, many of them little better than hovels, alongside back plots or on the outer fringes of towns. The smaller houses in Carlisle, and probably elsewhere in the 'highland zone' of the far north and west of England, were still being built of cob, with thatched roofs, in the seventeenth century, but all have since vanished without trace.[43] Cob was usually replaced by rubble stone; an early nineteenth-century drawing of the market place at Dalton-in-Furness (Lancashire, now Cumbria) shows stone-built cottages with thatched roofs, none of which survived comprehensive rebuilding in better-quality stone later in the nineteenth century.[44]

The gradual replacement of subsistence farming by a market economy stimulated urban growth in the 'highland zones' of Wales, western Scotland and north-west England. Hawkshead, in the Cumbrian fells, and nowadays no larger than a village, began life as a chapelry of Dalton-in-Furness, the main entrepot for local wool until the closure of the Cistercian Furness Abbey. Hawkshead benefited from the ending of Scottish raids after the Union of Crowns in 1603, and in 1608 it obtained a charter, enabling the local 'statesmen' (yeoman farmers) to send their wool and cloth to the mar-ket there; there was also a school which the poet William Wordsworth attended as a boy.[45] Much of the wool was sent on to Kendal, a thoroughfare town situated at an important river crossing. Given the right to manage its own affairs in a charter of 1575, the town expanded in the seventeenth and

Fig. 3.8 Many of the smaller houses of 16th- and 17th-century towns have vanished, but a modest timber-framed cottage in Bridgnorth that was briefly occupied by the Puritan theologian and controversialist Richard Baxter (1615–91) has survived. Facing St Leonard's churchyard, and squeezed between two larger houses, it originally consisted of a single ground-floor room heated by a hearth in a side wall, and an upstairs room in the attic.

eighteenth centuries, due in large measure to the development of a special-ized cloth industry in the surrounding countryside. New buildings then went up on the boundaries of the long, narrow burgage plots or 'yards' behind the houses that line the single main street (Fig. 3.9); Daniel Fleming of Rydal, a few miles away, wrote in 1671 that the town was 'a place of excel-lent manufacture…the trade…makes it populous, and the people seem to be shaped out for trade, improving themselves not only in their old manu-factures of cottons, but of late in the making of drugget, serges, hats, worsted, stockins [sic], &c, whereby many of the poor are set on work, and the town much enriched'.[46]

King James VI/I gave charters to several new towns on the east coast of Scotland as part of a policy of stimulating the country's economy through trade along and across the North Sea. Culross, on the north side of the Firth of Forth, is a particularly well-preserved example. There was an abbey on

Fig. 3.9 Kendal's main street runs parallel to the River Kent, and the long, narrow burgage plots or 'yards' behind the street frontage are reached through inconspicuous doorways. Yard no. 83 (Dr Manning's Yard) lies behind a house built in the early 18th century by a George Braithwaite, a dyer and Quaker. It is lined with two-storeyed cottages of local rubble stone, probably dating from the late 17th or 18th centuries.

the hillside here in the Middle Ages, and, following the Dissolution, coal mines were opened in 1575 by the local landlord, Sir George Bruce. 89 per cent of Scottish sea salt also passed through the small town in the late sixteenth century, and it was given responsibility for managing its own affairs when it became a royal burgh in 1592, before shrinking after the coal pits flooded in 1625. Nowadays no larger than a village, with a population of some 500 people, it is made up for the most part of plain stone-built houses with red pantiled roofs, often with stepped gables surmounted by chimney-stacks, a common Scottish fashion; most of the houses are 'harled' (covered in roughcast plaster), their upper floors functioning as separate residences reached by external flights of steps. The two streets, one of them leading steeply down from the Abbey (now the parish kirk), with the (restored) Mercat (Market) Cross of 1588 at the top of a 'middle row' (Fig. 3.10), meet at the quay, which is overlooked by the Town House of 1626, with an ogee-topped central tower. It faces the Tron or weigh-house, and to the west is

Fig. 3.10 Culross flourished in the late 16th and early 17th centuries because of the coal and salt trade along the Firth of Forth. The Mercat Cross, seen here, dates from 1588. The houses behind it formed part of a 'middle row' of properties encroaching on the market place; the tower of the Town House, overlooking what was originally the quay, can be seen in the distance. By 1865 the small town had lost its industrial *raison d'etre*, but a restoration programme was begun by the National Trust for Scotland in the 1930s.

the 'Palace', put up by Bruce as his own residence in 1597 and extended by a tall three-storeyed addition in 1611.[47]

Growing civic pride could be expressed by the building of new town halls. Like their medieval predecessors, these buildings were usually built within, or overlooking, market places. Scottish town halls were nearly always built of stone, and contained prisons, council chambers, tax offices and court rooms. Many had towers that can easily be mistaken for church towers, like that of the Glasgow tollbooth (1625–7), close to the town's central cross-roads, though the rest of the building has gone. Most English and Welsh town halls were more modest, usually only two storeys high, with an open ground floor for market stalls and a meeting room or rooms above for civic business, including the regulation of markets. Timber-framed town halls still block the traffic through the streets of Llanidloes in Montgomeryshire

(1612–22) and Bridgnorth, the latter remodelled after Civil War damage in 1648. The market hall in the small town of Rothwell (Northamptonshire) is especially ambitious. The initiative here was taken in 1578 by the local landowner Sir Thomas Tresham of Rushton Hall, a Catholic recusant and builder of several eccentric structures on his estates. Intended as a tribute to 'his sweet fatherland and County of Northampton but chiefly to this town his near neighbour', it exemplifies the close links between small towns and their powerful landowning neighbours, its classical proportions and decoration proclaiming the growing allure of Renaissance-inspired architecture as transmitted to local master builders through prints and pattern-books.[48] Newly-fashionable Renaissance ideas also inspired the corporation at Exeter, the fourth largest provincial town in late sixteenth-century England, when it added a new classical façade to its medieval Guildhall in the High Street in 1592–4. The council chamber, lit by large mullioned and transomed windows, projects out into the city's main street and market place, and is supported on stumpy Doric columns, allowing pedestrians to pass underneath' a Renaissance-inspired balustrade that crowns the composition (Fig. 3.11).[49]

The Reformation diverted some of the resources formerly allocated to churches and chantries to charitable foundations. Some of the many newly-founded almshouses occupied the sites or even the buildings of suppressed medieval guilds, like the Lord Leycester Hospital in Warwick, which took over the premises of a former religious guild next to the town's west gate in 1571. Many of the grandest almshouses were built, like noblemens' country houses or the colleges of Oxford and Cambridge Universities, around closed courtyards, and were entered from the street through impressive gate towers. Abbot's Hospital in Guildford (Surrey) (Fig. 3.12) was founded in 1619 by the Archbishop of Canterbury 'out of love to the place of my birth',[50] the inmates serving as virtual members of the Archbishop's extended household, dining communally in the hall and attending regular services in the chapel. More often, almshouses were built as rows of cottages alongside a street, as at Chipping Campden, where the newly-rich cloth-merchant and money-lender Sir Baptist Hicks spent £1,000 in 1612 on providing housing for six elderly and impoverished men and six women next to the fifteenth-century parish church on the edge of the town. With their obelisk-topped gables, tall chimneystacks and smooth local ashlar facing, they complemented his magnificent house nearby. The house fell victim to Civil War damage, but the almshouses, along with the market house in the High Street—another of Hicks's benefactions—still stand as reminders of his gifts to the community.

Fig. 3.11 Exeter's Guildhall, first recorded on this site in the 14th century, was rebuilt in 1468–70. The council chamber, overlooking the High Street, was extended forward in 1592–4 over a classically-inspired ground floor or loggia, resulting a design described by Nikolaus Pevsner as 'as picturesque as it is barbarous'.

Fig. 3.12 Abbot's Hospital in Guildford was founded in 1619 by George Abbot, Archbishop of Canterbury, and is reached from the sloping High Street through a massive gate tower. The arched, classically-inspired doorway leads into a courtyard with accommodation for the twenty male and female residents, a dining hall, and a chapel where they attended services twice daily.

Endowed grammar schools also proliferated after the Reformation, some of them taking over existing premises like those of the former Carthusian monastery (Charterhouse) just to the north of the City of London; it became the town house of the Dukes of Norfolk before being re-founded as a school and almshouse by the immensely wealthy businessman Thomas Sutton in 1611. A mercantile fortune also accounted for the building of a new school in the small town of Market Harborough (Leicestershire) in 1614. Here the money was donated by a London merchant tailor, Robert Smyth, who stipulated in his will that it should stand, as it still does, 'upon posts or columns over a part of the market place to keep the market people dry in time of foul weather'. The school at Shrewsbury, the largest in Elizabethan England, resulted from a collective initiative by some of the leading townspeople. By the 1580s it had succeeded in attracting some 350 pupils, most of them boarders from outside the town. The new buildings of local sandstone went up in two phases between 1595 and 1630 on an L-shaped site facing one of the main streets, just outside the castle precinct.

They contained dormitories, a library, schoolrooms and accommodation for the schoolmaster (Fig. 3.13), and were designed in a hybrid style of architecture, part-Gothic and part-classical in inspiration, with large mullioned and transomed windows and a crenellated staircase tower at the junction of the two ranges.[51] A similar style of architecture was adopted at Oxford University's School's Quadrangle, built in 1613–19 to house lecture rooms on a site next to the University's medieval library. Largely funded by an ex-diplomat, Sir Thomas Bodley, whose generosity re-founded the library following post-Reformation depredations,[52] its construction initiated a process of rebuilding which ended in the eighteenth century with the creation of Radcliffe Square, one of the most impressive urban spaces in England. Yet from a purely architectural point of view even Oxford's Schools were out-classed by George Heriot's Hospital in Edinburgh, a boys' school begun in 1628 on an empty site on the southern edge of the city. Built out of a legacy from a rich goldsmith and banker, its architecture was almost certainly derived from one of Serlio's engravings. But the array of turrets projecting from the corner towers gives it a distinctively Scottish character, creating an effect that rivals that of the largest 'prodigy houses' of the late sixteenth and early seventeenth century landed aristocracy in both kingdoms.[53]

London: The Growth of a Metropolis

The most spectacular example of urban growth in the two centuries following the Reformation was London. In the middle of the sixteenth century most Londoners still lived within the boundaries of the medieval city on the north bank of the Thames (Fig. 3.14). Its street plan was, and to some extent still remains, roughly the same as it had been since the thirteenth century,[54] its skyline originally punctuated by the steeples of 106 parish churches, most of them very small, with the vast bulk of St Paul's Cathedral rising up above them. Timber-framed houses, most of them two or three storeys high, lined the streets, extending back onto the plots behind to create a townscape that was already densely packed by the time of the first accurate representations of the city.[55] Over the next century the city burst its boundaries, its population increasing five- or six-fold to over half a million by 1700; by the middle of the seventeenth century only Paris among European cities surpassed it. By then, half of all England's town-dwellers lived there, and already by 1600 seven eighths of the country's trade in manufactured goods

Fig. 3.13 Shrewsbury School was described by William Camden in 1586 as 'the largest school in all England', its buildings going up in two phases from 1595 to 1630 on a site next to the town wall. The former classrooms and dormitories for boarding pupils are lit by mullioned and transomed windows typical of their date; the Gothic-arched window on the top floor of the right-hand wing lit the chapel. The statues over the entrance doorway are of Philomathes ('he who loves to learn') and Polymathes ('he who has learnt much'). The school migrated to a more spacious site in 1882, and the old buildings were then turned into a public library.

(mainly cloth) passed through it, its economic importance increasing further with the massive growth of overseas trade that transformed Britain's economy as the seventeenth century progressed.

Panoramic views by Claes Visscher and Wenceslas Hollar show the densely built-up city as it appeared from the South Bank before the Great Fire of 1660 (Fig. 3.15), but they do not show its outward growth. Royal proclamations, and an Act of Parliament of 1593, sought to prohibit the expansion of the built-up area, but, with the walled City packed to capacity, most of the new immigrants had no option but to find accommodation outside the walls. Houndsditch, outside the north-eastern wall had been filled in and built up by the 1580s,[56] and John Stow, writing in 1598, mentioned that the Whitechapel Road, leading east out of Aldgate, was 'so encroached upon

Fig. 3.14 Braun and Hogenberg's map of London was first produced in 1572 as part on atlas of European city plans. It shows the city before its phenomenal expansion in the late 16th and early 17th centuries. Most of the inhabitants still lived within the walls and the 'bars' which marked the outer limits of the Corporations jurisdiction (see Fig. 3.4, above), and there is some ribbon development along the main roads leading north, east and west, and also at Southwark, south of London Bridge. The Strand, to the west, follows the bend of the river to Westminster.

Fig. 3.15 By 1647, when this panorama of London was published by the émigré Czech artist Wenceslas Hollar, the built-up area had expanded well beyond its medieval boundaries. The view was taken from the south bank at Southwark, slightly to the west of London Bridge, which is shown with tall, timber-framed houses built over the medieval arches. St Paul's Cathedral dominates the City, with its densely packed houses punctuated by the towers and spires of the hundred or more parish churches.

by the building of filthy cottages...that in some places it scarce remaineth a sufficient highway for the meeting of carriages and droves of cattle...which is no small blemish to so famous a city to have so unsavoury and unseemly an entrance or passage thereunto.'[57] The area to the east of the extramural market at Smithfield saw particularly intense development. Some 175 timber houses went up between 1598 and 1616 along newly-formed streets—Cloth Fair, Middle Street and New Street—laid out on the open ground that served as a venue for St Bartholomew's Fair;[58] Nos. 41–2 Cloth Fair, brick-built and probably dating from the early seventeenth century, though somewhat rebuilt, is a rare survival of a merchant's house of this period. Mingled with the suburban houses were some of London's earliest theatres—the Curtain in Shoreditch, the Globe and the Rose across the Thames in Southwark—together with inns, tanneries and other noxious trades. Here craftsmen and artisans could avoid guild regulations, and, as a result, the northern and eastern suburbs, and the parish of Southwark across the river, developed a workaday character which lasted until recent times, and to some extent still does.

By 1550 half of the English nobility owned houses in London. That proportion had risen by the 1630s, fuelling the development of the capital as a centre for conspicuous consumption and leading eventually, to the growth of what we now call the West End. The Strand, linking the City to Westminster, was already lined with large, detached town houses built for the most part for bishops and their entourages before passing into lay own-ership after the Reformation.[59] These 'private palaces' shared the street frontage with tall, narrow-fronted timber-framed houses of a type ubiqui-tous within the City; their plot widths still determine the dimensions of the mostly nineteenth-century buildings that now line the north side of the street between Aldwych and Trafalgar Square. Further south was the royal palace of Whitehall, and beyond it the Palace of Westminster, the centre of national government since the reign of Henry II. These magnets drew in the noblemen, gentry, professionals and their households which flocked to London, especially when Parliament was sitting, creating a demand for housing that eventually transformed the outskirts of the capital.

Covent Garden

Covent Garden (1629–37) was the first of the Renaissance-inspired squares that became the main defining feature of London's West End.[60] The development was laid out under special license from the King on former monastic land (the 'convent garden' of Westminster Abbey) to the north of the town house of the Earls of Bedford at the western end of the Strand. The aim— never fully realized—was to provide suitably impressive housing for aristocrats and courtiers; the original design included mews behind the main streets with stabling for horses and for the growing number of carriages (Fig. 3.16). Provision for wheeled traffic soon became a *sine qua non* for fashionable housing developments, and this helps explain the still-noticeable width of the streets, especially when compared with those of the City.

The idea of arranging buildings around an open space was not a new one. Many medieval towns in Britain had spacious market places, and some of the town (and country) houses of the Tudor and Stuart aristocracy, such as Somerset House in the Strand, were built around courtyards, as were the Royal Exchange in the City, first built in 1566–8, the Inns of Court, and the colleges of Oxford and Cambridge. The novelty of Covent Garden derived not so much from the shape of its central square as from the social and architectural character of the planned neighbourhood of which it formed a part. The houses were intended to form part of a coherent architectural whole, and the grid-like layout of the surrounding streets was clearly influenced by Italian Renaissance urban planning, with its implicit 'politeness'. The design was monitored by Inigo Jones, Surveyor of Works to King Charles I and architect of the Banqueting House of Whitehall Palace (1619), England's first example of 'pure' Renaissance-inspired classical architecture, and the only part of the sprawling palace to survive above ground. And it was Jones who designed the church of St Paul with its temple-like portico of the 'primitive' Tuscan order overlooking the western side of the new square. The uniformly detailed blocks of houses over arcades on the north and east sides showed the influence of Serlio's pattern-books, and they also bring to mind the recently-constructed piazza at Livorno in Italy, the Place des Vosges in Paris and the Plaza Mayor in Madrid: a clear visual statement of the sophisticated, cosmopolitan aspirations of the King and Court, and an exemplar for the future development of the western parts of London.

Already by the middle of the seventeenth century market stalls had begun to encroach on the square, and by the start of the following century the aristocratic tenants of the houses were beginning to move westwards as the surrounding neighbourhood became increasingly crowded and unruly. William Hogarth's 'Night' engraving from his 'Four Times of Day' series captures the transition, and the building of a covered wholesale market for fruit and vegetables inside the square by the Bedford Estate in 1828–31 (See Fig. 9.10) cemented the transformation of the area:[61] a development that was later to be paralleled in other major cities, as was its subsequent transformation into a tourist-orientated shopping district when the market moved to a new site in the 1970s.

Fig. 3.16 The new church of St Paul, Covent Garden, with its austere classical portico, dominates the square or 'piazza' in which fashionable residents are disporting themselves; there is even a four-wheeled carriage, a relative novelty. The row of brick houses to the right follow recent Continental precedent, but those along the streets to the left and right, with their rows of steep gables, are more typical of contemporary domestic architecture in London.

4

Classicism and Commerce,
1660–1760

When Charles II was restored to the throne in 1660 after the Civil War and the Interregnum that followed his father's execution, most British towns and cities still had an essentially medieval appearance. By the middle of the eighteenth century many of them had been transformed architecturally, and some had expanded significantly beyond their existing boundaries. These changes were driven partly by economics and partly by changes in fashion. Foreign trade increased on an unprecedented scale, fuelling the growth of London both as a port and as the centre of Britain's financial service sector. Bristol's population quadrupled between the 1530s and 1700, its growth encouraged by trade across the Atlantic. Newcastle grew because of its role in coastal trade and its coal mines. The continuing growth of a national market in England, and in the whole of Britain following the Union with Scotland in 1707, fuelled the growth of London; it also enabled towns like Norwich and Manchester to profit from an expanding demand for textiles. Provincial towns looked to London as the centre of national government and of elite culture. Smaller towns were affected too, both as markets for their rural hinterland and as centres of small-scale domestic industry as craftspeople and shopkeepers drew upon increasingly sophisticated networks of trade. Most of the suppliers for Abraham Dent, who marketed knitted stockings and had a grocer's shop in Kirkby Stephen (Westmorland, now Cumbria) from 1756–77, came from within a hundred-mile radius of the small Pennine town, but twelve of them were based in London, 270 miles away.[1] And architectural ideas emanating from London increasingly influenced the appearance of towns throughout the country.

London

London avoided large-scale destruction during the Civil War, but it suffered grievously from the Plague of 1665, the last of the major demographic crises that had repeatedly decimated the British population since the 1340s. Then in the following year the Great Fire destroyed an estimated 13,200 houses and laid waste to some four fifths of the area inside the medieval walls. Plans for radically changing the City's street plan along Renaissance-inspired lines foundered because of the resistance of the merchants, and in 1667 a decision was taken to retain the existing layout, save for the creation of a wharf running eastwards from London Bridge to the Tower and a new north-south thoroughfare (King Street and Queen Street) linking the Guildhall to the river. But while the lines of the existing streets remained essentially unchanged, their appearance was radically altered, making life easier for pedestrians and wheeled traffic: an increasingly important consideration. The more 'narrow and incommodious' streets and the 'straight [confined] and narrow passages' leading off them were widened, the main streets to 40 feet, the latter to at least fourteen. The projections and obstructions that hindered through traffic were removed, pedestrian pavements were created in front of the houses, street markets and 'noisome trades' prohibited, steep ascents levelled out or mitigated, and surface water removed by 'pitching' (cambering).[2] Despite a fall in the City's population,[3] these changes did little to change its densely-built up character. But they served as a template for urban improvement schemes carried out, albeit slowly and incrementally, both in the rest of London and in other towns and cities throughout Britain.

Recovery from the Fire was celebrated in the Monument (Fig. 4.1): a tall classical column placed within a small, newly-created square alongside New Fish Street, the main street leading north from old London Bridge.[4] St Paul's Cathedral and half the City's parish churches were rebuilt on their existing sites under the supervision, though not always to the design, of Sir Christopher Wren, one of the Commissioners for rebuilding the City, and from 1669 Surveyor of Works to King Charles II.[5] All but a handful were designed in a classical style influenced by the recent ecclesiastical architecture of Italy, the Low Countries and France, which Wren had visited in 1665, and they were fitted up internally for the worship of the Church of England, restored along with the monarchy in 1660. Their layout, whether centrally planned, as in the church of St Stephen Walbrook, or adapted from

Fig. 4.1 The Monument to the Great Fire of London of 1666. The massive Doric column is supported on a plinth with an allegorical carving celebrating the City's recovery from the Fire. It was built close to the place where the fire started, and it closed the view northward from the old London Bridge. The plain brick houses surrounding the square (all since rebuilt) are typical of those built throughout the City in the late 17th century.

the Roman basilica plan with nave and aisles, as in St Bride, Fleet Street, provided exemplars for new churches built in the expanding areas of London, and also in provincial towns, over the next 150 years. And their towers and spires, clustered around the mighty dome of St Paul's, gave the City a new and distinctive skyline that survived largely intact until the nineteenth century.

The 1667 and 1670 Rebuilding Acts gave the City a more uniform appearance. Heights of houses were standardized: four storeys plus attics over a basement for detached houses in the six 'high and principal streets,' three in the 'streets and lanes of note' and two in the 'by-lanes' that led off them.[6] Timber facades like those which had lined the streets before 1666 were now replaced by plainer frontages 'made of brick or stone, or of brick and stone together', the use of timber being limited to bressumers (load-bearing beams), door and window frames and shop fronts.[7] The resulting change in the appearance of houses can be seen in the small number of examples that have survived subsequent rebuilding; they include a pair of houses in Laurence Pountney Hill, one of the 'streets and lanes of note', with beautifully carved hoods over the doorways and sash windows in place of the formerly ubiquitous hinged casements (Fig. 4.2). Many City merchants still lived in courts and alleys leading off the main streets, and they continued to do so until the mass exodus to the suburbs that reached its climax in the mid-nineteenth century. Some of these enclaves still survive, such as Wardrobe Place, on the site of the medieval Great Wardrobe next to the former Blackfriars church; here the garden was converted shortly before 1720 'into a large and square court, with good houses'.[8]

By the time of the Great Fire three quarters of London's population already lived outside the City's boundaries. Development here was usually carried out speculatively, the buildings reflecting the influence of the City's Rebuilding Acts. The freehold of Essex House, just beyond Temple Bar, the western gateway into the City,[9] was bought in 1675 by Nicholas Barbon, son of a radical Puritan preacher and an expert manipulator of the financial market that flourished as London's commercial economy expanded. He borrowed the money needed to construct the roadway and the drainage, and then leased the land to twenty-six private individuals who included John Bland, a lawyer ('scrivenor') at the adjacent Middle Temple. The lessees then went ahead and constructed the houses themselves, either for their own occupation or, more commonly, for sub-letting;[10] some of them still

Fig. 4.2 Nos. 1–2 Lawrence Pountney Hill, in the City of London, were built in 1703. The semicircular wooden hoods over the doors are richly carved, and the sash windows are placed almost flush with the wall. The doors are reached by steep flights of stairs, allowing the basements to be given over to service quarters. Wrought iron railings demarcate the service area from the street.

survive, three-storeys high with sunken basements, a pattern that soon became ubiquitous. A larger-scale development occurred in Red Lion Fields, Holborn, where Barbon leased the land in 1687 in the teeth of opposition from the lawyers of the adjacent Grays Inn, who had treated it as a public open space; he then sublet the land to a bricklayer, who built three-storeyed brick houses around the open square which he reluctantly incorporated into the plan.[11] The building-lease system soon became almost universal for new developments around London's fringe, the length of the leases gradually extending to ninety-nine years, and the growing commercial and cultural prestige of the capital ensured that it was imitated in towns throughout Britain.

Following the Restoration, the owners of the land north of the Palace of Whitehall followed the example of the fourth Earl of Bedford at Covent Garden (see Chapter 3) by developing their estates for elite housing. These new developments, which continued incrementally until the end of the eighteenth century and beyond, satisfied the demands both of the growing political and administrative class, and of the rural gentry who were attracted to the capital for the pleasures of the 'London season'. It resulted in the growth of the new residential area that we now call the West End, and it cemented the already existing division between London's mercantile core (the City), the manufacturing districts to the north, east and south, and the more fashionable area to the west; for Daniel Defoe, writing in 1724–6, the City was the centre 'of commerce and wealth', the Court of 'gallantry and splendor [sic]', and the 'outparts... of its numbers and mechanicks'.[12]

The development of the West End began almost immediately after the Restoration on the rising ground to the north of St James's Park, a former royal hunting ground laid out by Charles II along formal, French-inspired lines and accessible to the public. An east-west thoroughfare, Pall Mall, was laid out to the north of St James's Park in 1661, linking St James's Palace— still a royal residence—to Charing Cross, at the western end of the Strand. The ground between it and Piccadilly, the main route leading south-west out of London, was then developed for housing by Henry Jermyn, Earl of St Albans, a former ambassador to France, his agents exerting strict control over the layout. The centrepiece was a large open space (St James's Square), enclosed, like Covent Garden before it, by wooden railings and flanked on three of its sides by 'great and good houses' intended for the 'Nobility and Gentry who were to attend upon his Majestie's Person, and in Parliament' (Fig. 4.3).[13] The houses, all of which have since been rebuilt or replaced,

Fig. 4.3 St James's Square was a speculative development between St James's Park and Piccadilly, seen at the top of this view of 1754. The facades of the houses are plain and almost uniform, and rows of low posts demarcate the footway in front; the carriages and sedan chairs give an indication of the high social status of the occupants. Wren's parish church of St James Piccadilly (1676–84) closes the northward vista from the square.

were designed with relatively uniform facades of three or four storeys plus attics; short wooden posts, like the metal posts that can still be seen along some of the streets in Amsterdam, separated the footway or pavement from the roadway used by carriages and tradesmens' carts. The rest of the site was laid out on rectilinear lines, with a church (St James, Piccadilly, designed by Wren) closing the northward vista from the square and a market occupying a rectangular space to the north-east. Housing also went up near the market for the artisans and tradespeople who provided the essential services without which cities could not function. Similar concentrations of smaller houses existed around the fringes of all the larger West End estates, explaining the sharp distinctions of appearance between adjacent areas that are still visible today; one example is Shepherd Market to the north of Piccadilly, still an enclave of what was once modest housing adjacent to the grander residences of the wealthy.

Spitalfields

Following the revocation of Edict of Nantes by King Louis XIV of France in 1685, Huguenot (French Protestant) silk-weavers settled in large numbers in the precincts of the former Priory of Spitalfields, north of the City, and in new housing developments carved out of the nearby common fields. One of these parcels of land was acquired by two lawyers, Charles Wood and Simon Michell, and they arranged for the existing buildings on the site to be razed, following an earlier levelling and heightening of the ground with rubble from fire-damaged City streets and buildings. A grid of streets was then laid out, starting in 1718, each street lined with handsome brick-fronted houses constructed, and in some cases inhabited, by their builders, many of whom were carpenters. Other houses were occupied by master-weavers, whose looms were housed on the top floor in wooden lofts lit by large windows, some of which still survive (Fig. 4.4).[14] The area was, and still is, dominated by its handsome new Anglican church, Christ Church (1714–29), designed by Wren's pupil and former draughtsman Nicholas Hawksmoor; it was financed by central government following the passing of the Fifty New Churches Act of 1711, intended to reassert the authority of the Church of England in the face of religious dissent, permitted under the Toleration Act of 1689. Many of the inhabitants nevertheless preferred to worship at a more modest Nonconformist church (subsequently a synagogue and now a mosque) built in 1743 at the corner of one of the new streets, Fournier Street, and the pre-existing Brick Lane, 'a long well pav'd street' that, according to Defoe, had originated as 'a deep, dirty road, frequented by carts fetching bricks that way into White-Chapel from Brick-Kilns in [the] fields'.[15]

The prosperity of Spitalfields rested on trade and manufacturing. A market was established on the site of 'a field of grass with cows feeding on it', and a brewery went up in Brick Lane in the 1660s, expanding in the 1730s and 1740s. Smaller houses meanwhile sprang up in Mile End New Town to the east and in the silk-weaving district of Bethnal Green to the north, most of them of two or three storeys and just one room deep. Many had elongated 'weavers' windows' on the top floor to give light to the looms, as can still be seen at Nos. 125–7 Brick Lane;[16] similar houses were built in the second half of the century in manufacturing towns in the north of England. But the silk industry declined in the early nineteenth century and, as London's population continued to increase, the houses of Spitalfields and Bethnal Green fell into multi-occupation. Other houses went up in insanitary courts and alleys behind the main streets, only to disappear as a

(continued)

Continued

result of successive slum-clearance programmes that culminated in the
1960s and 1970s, when they were replaced by blocks of flats. This process
was replicated in larger cities throughout the country, as was the renovation
and gentrification of the surviving larger houses that occurred from the
1970s onwards.

The pattern of development seen at St James's Square was repeated elsewhere, as landowners responded to the growing demand for fashionable
housing. There was no single overriding local authority outside the City,
and, as a result, the West End and the northern suburbs became a patchwork
of discrete housing developments: something that soon becomes obvious to
anyone trying to navigate his or her way through the side streets between
Piccadilly and Oxford Street today. The removal of surface water fell within
the purview of Commissions of Sewers, established under an Act of 1531.
Fire protection, and the selection of building materials, was regulated by a
succession of increasingly stringent Building Acts, culminating in 1774, and
street lighting began in 1685, though it was not very effective until the passing of an Act of Parliament in 1736 that allowed local rates (property taxes)
to be applied to the cost.[17] Some of the new developments failed to live up
to the expectations of their promoters. Seven Dials, north of Covent Garden,
was laid out in the 1690s by Thomas Neale, Master of the Mint and initiator
of London's first lottery, on an innovative and, for London, unique star-
shaped plan with a circular open space enclosing a Doric column embellished with sundials (rebuilt in 1988–9) at the centre. But it never attracted
wealthy residents, and the houses soon fell into multi-occupation. The area
adjoined what became one of London's most notorious slums, the St Giles
'Rookery', and when the slum houses were cleared in the second part of the
nineteenth century they were replaced by warehouses and industrial premises: a sequence of developments that was paralleled in cities throughout
Britain.

The design of London's houses remained fundamentally unchanged from
the late seventeenth to the mid-nineteenth centuries. They continued to be
narrow in plan, tall in elevation, and two rooms deep, with basements sunk
below the level of the streets, which were raised above ground level by spoil
and landfill. The main floors were reached by steps leading up to the front

Fig. 4.4 Fournier Street, Spitalfields, is named after one of the French Huguenot silk weavers who settled in the area, and forms part of a development laid out on a former market garden after 1718. The wooden lofts housing the weavers' looms can be seen at the top of the houses, many of which had been rescued from decrepitude shortly before this photograph was taken in the 1980s.

door, the servants working in the basements and sleeping in attics at the top of the houses; purpose-built blocks of flats, common on the Continent and in Scotland, did not catch on until the second half of the nineteenth century. Describing the typical London house in 1810, a French–American visitor, Louis Simond wrote: 'These narrow houses, three or four stories [sic] high...give the idea of a cage with its sticks and birds. The plan of these houses is very simple, two rooms on each story; one in the front with two or three windows looking on the street, the other on a yard behind, often very small; the stairs generally taken out of the breadth of the back-room. The ground-floor is usually elevated a few feet above the level of the street, and separated from it by an area, a sort of ditch, a few feet wide...enclosed by an iron railing. A bridge of stone or brick leads to the door of the house'.[18] This type of house plan spread rapidly to the larger provincial towns of England, and it eventually took root in the American colonies, in Ireland, and in Scotland, reaching its architectural apogee in Edinburgh's New Town (see pp. 149–151).

An important by-product of London's phenomenal growth was the foundation of new welfare and corrective institutions, most of which went up on the edge of the built-up area, where land was cheap. Royal patronage explains the spacious riverside layout and sophisticated architecture of Chelsea Hospital (1682–92), designed by Wren for retired soldiers on an open site well to the west of the built-up area. The even more lavish Royal Hospital at Greenwich, a Thames-side village to the east of the City, was begun in 1694, initially to Wren's designs, on the site of the former royal palace in which Queen Elizabeth had died. More typical was the Ironmongers' Almshouse (now the Geffrye Museum) for fourteen elderly inmates laid out in 1715 around an open courtyard on the eastern side of Kingsland Road, leading north from the City. Bedlam Hospital, a lunatic asylum, went up just outside the City wall, on the southern fringe of Moorfields, in 1675–6—it was moved in 1822 to Lambeth and is now the core of the Imperial War Museum. And in 1730–66 London's oldest hospital, St Bartholomew's, was rebuilt in a restrained classical manner around a spacious open courtyard to the south of Smithfield for sufferers from physical ailments (Fig. 4.5). Guys Hospital, on the South Bank, to the west of London Bridge, followed in 1738–41, and the London Hospital, on Whitechapel Road, in 1752.[19] These and other institutional buildings helped shape the landscape of the capital's periphery, and they were soon imitated in other towns and cities.

An East Prospect of S.ᵗ Bartholomew's Hospital. | *Vue de L'Hospital de S.ᵗ Barthelemi du Cote de l'Orient.*

Fig. 4.5 St Bartholomew's Hospital, London's oldest, was founded in 1123 on the north-western edge of the City. Its new buildings, designed by James Gibbs, and begun in 1720, were laid out around a spacious courtyard, with a central administrative block containing a magnificent Great Hall on the north side. It is flanked by the ward blocks, which are free-standing in order to reduce the risk of fire and infection.

Provincial Towns

When the intrepid and observant Celia Fiennes visited Gloucester in 1698 on one of her horseback tours of England, she mentioned the importance of the stocking and glove manufacturing and the trade in lampreys (eels) sent to London. She was also impressed by the clean streets and the 'very large good Key [quay] on the river', from which coal was unloaded and drawn on sledges through the streets.[20] Such activities supplemented the marketing of agricultural goods, always the staple of the economic life of small or medium-sized towns such as Farnham in Surrey and Ware in Hertfordshire, which prospered as entrepots for dealers who sent grain and other agricultural goods to the capital. River and coastal ports were enriched meanwhile by internal and foreign trade, leading to the erection of new public buildings whose design reflected architectural fashions emanating from London and the Continent. A handsome Custom House went up in 1681 on the quayside at Exeter after the navigation of the River Exe—first

Fig. 4.6 The Customs House at Kings Lynn (1683) overlooks the Purfleet stream, separating the original 11th-century town from the later extension laid out on land belonging to the Bishop of Norwich. The building served as a merchants' exchange, with accommodation for the Collector of Customs upstairs, and was financed by a local Member of Parliament. The design was supplied by Henry Bell, a merchant and amateur architect who was clearly familiar with the 17th-century architecture of the Low Countries.

initiated in 1564–6—was improved in order to cater for the expanding trade in serge cloth for the Continent.[21] Expanding overseas trade also explains the building of the Customs House at King's Lynn in 1683 to the designs of Henry Bell, the Cambridge-educated son of a Norfolk merchant (Fig. 4.6). Two-storeyed and stone-faced, with a cupola over the hipped roof, it dominates the wharf-side landscape of brick houses and warehouses, its profile and detailing echoing the seventeenth-century architecture of the Dutch towns with which the merchants of King's Lynn traded, and which Bell probably knew at first hand.

Streets are the veins and arteries of towns. The growth of wheeled traffic in the second half of the seventeenth century, and the subsequent building of turnpike (toll) roads linking towns and cities, gave rise to street-widening schemes, the removal of obstructions—especially projections onto the roadway—and the provision of channels for rainwater, as can still be seen in on either side of Trumpington Street, leading into Cambridge from the south. As in London, consumer goods began to be displayed and retailed in shops with glazed windows,[22] and streets to be lit by oil lamps, which first appeared in York in 1687 and in Norwich in 1692: an important precondition for the development of organized social activities after dark. Such provincial capitals seemed to the *Annual Observer* in 1761 to be 'universally inspired with the ambition of becoming little *Londons*.'[23] Efforts were also made to improve water supplies; in Cambridge a 'new river' had already been dug in 1610–14, and Hobson's Conduit (1614), since relocated to Trumpington Street from its original position in the market place, perpetuates the memory of the local carrier who contributed to the cost. Many provincial towns still had no piped water in the mid-seventeenth century, but that began to change in the 1690s, when reservoirs and pumping systems were provided in Newcastle, Leeds, Exeter and Derby (1692), and gradually elsewhere.[24]

Old timber-frontages now began to give way to plainer, classically-inspired facades of stone, brick or sometimes plaster. Thomas Baskerville, writing in 1681, described Nottingham, with its spacious medieval market place lined with new houses, as 'paradise restored', especially in comparison with York or Leicester, which he called 'an old stinking town, situated upon a dull river'.[25] At Bewdley, on the Severn, rebuilding in brick began in the 1670s, and continued well into the eighteenth century as trade expanded to and from the growing manufacturing centres of the west Midlands. Celia Fiennes, writing in 1698, enthused that Newcastle 'most resembles London of any place in England, its buildings lofty and large of brick mostly or stone; the streets are very broad and handsome and very well pitch'd and many of them with very fine Cunduits of water in each, allwayes running into a large stone Cistern for every bodyes use'.[26] Among the buildings that may have impressed her is the late seventeenth-century 'Alderman Fenwick's house' in Pilgrim Street,[27] with its symmetrical brick façade of four storeys over a basement. In Cirencester, described by Defoe in the 1720s as 'populous and rich, full of clothiers',[28] irregular gabled frontages of stone remained normal until around 1700, when symmetrical facades came into fashion, their upright, classically-proportioned window openings each divided by a single vertical mullion and horizontal transom. Several of these handsome houses survive intact, notably in Coxwell Street (Fig. 4.7), its name perpetuating the memory of a sixteenth-century wool merchant who had profited from the sale of land from the suppressed Abbey. The clothiers ran their businesses from their houses; the house now called Woolgatherers was built

Fig. 4.7 Cirencester owed its prosperity to the cloth trade, and the wealth of its clothiers is reflected in the handsome stone-built houses that flank Coxwell Street. The house on the left has a gabled roofline, but No. 51, opposite, is an early 18th-century rebuilding of an earlier house whose original roofline can be seen on the side wall to the right.

next to a large warehouse facing the adjacent Thomas Street, laid out along the line of the long-vanished town wall, and the detached office or counting-house still stands alongside its forecourt.

Sometimes, as in post-Restoration London, fire precipitated a thorough reshaping of the urban landscape, leading to the adoption of rigorously detailed classical facades and, more rarely, to the reconfiguration of public spaces. For John Aikin, writing about early eighteenth-century Manchester, brick-fronted, sash-windowed houses, with their 'new style of light and convenient rooms' represented an important change in social habits, allowing front parlours to be reserved for 'company' and the back rooms used for more everyday purposes.[29] Examples can be seen in provincial towns throughout the country, many of them built by successful professionals, tradesmen and businessmen such as the wine merchant Henry Peckham, builder of Pallant House at Chichester (now an art gallery), finished in 1713.

The Rebuilding of Northampton and Warwick

A large part of Northampton's town centre was destroyed by fire in 1675, and the commissioners for rebuilding entrusted responsibility for some of the more important new buildings to Edward Edwards and Henry Bell, described as 'two experience'd surveyors, now residing in the...Town'.[30] They supervised the rebuilding of the houses in the Market Square—a spacious rectangle like those of Cambridge, Norwich and other towns in eastern England—making it, despite some insensitive rebuilding in the 1960s, one of the most impressive ensembles of the period in the country. The surviving houses, some of them with classical pilasters on the upper floors, are similar to those built in London under the influence of Inigo Jones in the 1620s and 1630s; Defoe thought that Northampton was 'the handsomest and best built town in all this part of England...finely built with brick and stone and the streets made spacious and wide'.[31] The George Inn (since demolished), was 'more like a palace than an inn,' and the town's public buildings 'the finest in any county town in England, being all new built'. They included All Saints church (1676–80), whose tower and Ionic portico of 1701—clearly modelled on that added by Jones to Old St Paul's Cathedral in London—overlooks a widened central crossroads. Local gentry flocked to the Quarter Sessions at the new Sessions House (1676), where serious cases were tried by itinerant justices. The building was described by the local historian, John Bridges, as 'a very elegant structure and curiously ornamented';[32] the 'curious' ornamentation included the Corinthian half-columns and pilasters, and richly carved window-heads, on the main façade, matched by the elaborate plaster ceilings inside.

Fire, probably starting in a thatched house, also destroyed much of Warwick in 1694 (Fig. 4.8), and here too an Act of Parliament established a body of Commissioners to oversee the coherent rebuilding of the devastated parts of the town. Much of the impetus came from the local gentry and nobility, for whom the town was a social and service centre: a small-scale version of London's West End. The Commissioners imposed strict building controls for the new houses, specifying the use of brick or stone with slate or tiled roofs. Each house was expected to be ten feet wide and two storeys high, apart from the four houses at the central crossroads, which were of three storeys; the three surviving houses here were originally occupied by a mercer, a woolen draper and an apothecary. Upper-floor jetties were not allowed, and projecting shop counters were forbidden. The

(continued)

Continued

opportunity was also taken to widen some of the streets for wheeled traffic, part of an overall project 'for the better encouragement of gentlemen and others to build or reside in the same town'.[33] Two of their brick-built, hipped-roofed houses—Northgate House (1698) and Landor House, built for a physician in 1692 to the designs of a local builder, Roger Hurlbut—compare favourably with the gentlemen's country houses being built in large numbers in the west Midlands at the same time.

The nave of the parish church was destroyed in the 1694 fire, but the chancel and the elaborate late Gothic Beauchamp Chapel—the burial place of successive Earls of Warwick—survived. The rebuilding of the nave was carried out in a loosely Gothic style, albeit with an urn-capped classical balustrade, under the supervision of William Wilson, a sculptor from Leicester who rose socially after marrying a rich widow and acquiring a knighthood. His impressive, if somewhat fussily detailed, west tower projects into the roadway and faces a small square, one of the first to be newly laid out in an English provincial town. Finally, in 1725 a new Court House was designed on the site of an inn at the main crossroads. Designed by the local mason-architect Francis Smith, a former Mayor, it has a handsome *palazzo*-like façade of local sandstone, with a rusticated ground floor, Doric pilasters on the *piano nobile* above, and a figure of Justice in the central niche. The citizens, egged on by Whig politicians, objected to the cost of £2,500 and took the town's governing body to court for misappropriating charitable gifts in order to pay for 'stately buildings of no use to the...inhabitants' and used only for 'feasting and card-playing'.[34] They won the case, and the Corporation was expelled from the building, but it returned thirty years later, and Smith's portrait still hangs on the walls.

Like many houses of its type, it is set back from the street behind iron gates, with a façade beautified by carefully gauged and moulded brickwork, heavily emphasized quoins, and a carved wooden doorcase; the roof is hidden behind a parapet (Fig. 4.9). Most of the builders who designed houses of this kind were recruited locally, and, starting in the mid-1720s, they began to absorb the fashionable detailing promoted by metropolitan architects and disseminated in books such as James Gibbs's *Book of Architecture* (1728). Provincial builders could now follow detailed advice from pattern-books about the 'correct' proportioning of facades and the design of features such

Fig. 4.8 Church Street, Warwick, looking north to St Mary's church. The fire that destroyed much of the town in 1694 consumed the nave and west tower of the medieval church, which were rebuilt in a style loosely resembling that of the previous building. Church Street runs north from the town's central crossroads and is lined with buildings that echo the classical proportions of those in the rebuilt City of London, seen especially clearly in the house on the extreme left.

as doorcases, contributing to a growing aesthetic homogeneity that reflected the increasing integration of the national market.

The rebuilding, or re-fronting, of houses transformed the appearance of the more fashionable streets in towns throughout the country. Stamford, close to the Marquess of Exeter's country seat, Burghley House, prospered through the passing trade on the Great North Road and through the patronage of the local gentry,[35] Richmond (Yorkshire) from the local stocking trade and from the gentry and professionals who built new stone-built houses flanking two of the steep cobbled streets (Newbiggin and

Fig. 4.9 Pallant House, Chichester was built in 1712–13 by a wine merchant who traded with Portugal. It stands on the site of a malthouse in a densely packed area within the jurisdiction ('pale') of the Archbishop of Canterbury. Built of red brick, with strongly emphasized quoins, a classically-inspired wooden doorcase, and tall sash windows, it is set back from the street behind a low brick wall with iron railings. The gate piers are surmounted by carvings of ostriches, alluding to Peckham's coat of arms.

Framwellgate) outside the confined town centre. Brick was used instead where no good local stone was available, as at Wisbech (Cambridgeshire), a flourishing river port in the Fens where houses went up along the two 'brinks' or banks of the canalized River Nene, creating a landscape more typical of Holland than England.[36] Handsome brick houses also went up in Ludlow, an important market town with a prosperous commercial and professional middle class, though several timber houses survived. The main thoroughfare (Broad Street), was depicted by the 'English Canaletto', Samuel Scott, a local resident, in the mid-1760s, with its newly refronted houses, most of them still identifiable today, lining the street as it climbs the hill from the town gate to the Market Place, with its Butter Cross of 1743–4 closing the view.[37] Blandford, a thoroughfare town in Dorset, famous, according to Defoe, 'for making the finest bonelace in England', had to be rebuilt more quickly following a disastrous fire in 1731, after which two brothers, John and William Bastard, owners of a joinery yard, prepared a

Fig. 4.10 The market place at Blandford, Dorset. A fire destroyed much of the town in 1731, after which a survey was made by John and William Bastard. The new parish church was probably designed by John James. Sir James Thornhill, best known as a Baroque painter but also a local landowner, was responsible for the design of the pedimented stone-built town hall seen on the left of the picture.

survey for the rebuilding. A handsome new parish church, a new town hall and new brick-built inns in the market place are the main features of the refashioned, and still largely unaltered, townscape (Fig. 4.10); an inscription on a commemorative fountain of 1760, acknowledged the 'DIVINE MERCY that has since raised this Town, like the PHAENIX from it's [*sic*] Ashes to its present beautiful and flourishing State'.[38]

Eighteenth-century county towns had 'seasons', often coinciding with the assizes. The Worcester season lasted from early October to the middle of March,[39] many of the social events and assemblies (subscription dances) taking place in the Guildhall. It was begun in 1721, and was described by the local historian Valentine Green in the 1760s as 'the most magnificent [building] of the kind in the kingdom'.[40] Conceived and financed by the local Corporation, and jointly used by the county and city authorities, its architecture echoes that of many of the aristocratic country houses of the period;

the elaborate Baroque frontispiece was supplied by a local statuary, Thomas White, whose statue of Queen Anne over the doorway was said to have so pleased the civic authorities that they gave him an annuity of £30 a year for life.[41] Purpose-built assembly rooms meanwhile went up in York (1730–2), in Norwich (1754–5) and elsewhere.[42] They were financed by the local landed elite and by members of the aspirational middle class who strove to mingle with them and to imitate their manners; the organizers of assemblies in smaller towns usually had to make do with rooms in inns.

As the population of the larger towns grew, better-off inhabitants began to move out of the increasingly crowded central districts. Bristol was the third largest town in England in 1700, though still with an estimated population of only 21,000.[43] In 1650 the Corporation masterminded the building of a new street (King St) at the edge of the marsh to the south of the city wall (See Fig. 1.14), the lease forbidding 'noysome trades'. The first houses were built of timber, and some of them survive, including a group incorporating the Llandoger Trow inn, built c.1664: an inventory of No. 5, dated 1702, when it was occupied by Aaron Williams, a cooper, shows that it had two or three rooms on each floor, and that barrels were stored in the cellar.[44] Then, starting in 1699, a spacious new square—Queen Square—went up immediately to the south, with an equestrian statue of King William III in the middle and gravel walks for the elegant parading that was now seen as an essential part of polite social behavior (Fig. 4.11). The new houses here were built of brick, several of them double-fronted and held on leases that forbade trading,[45] the mercantile occupants storing their goods in warehouses nearby.[46] The city's Corporation also developed Orchard Street[47] in 1718–22 on land outside the walls close to the cathedral precinct and to the quayside where transatlantic shipping moored. Merchants' villas meanwhile began to be built at Clifton on the hillside to the west, well outside the city centre and over-looking the spectacular gorge of the River Avon (See Fig. 8.3).

Some towns, like Bristol, developed distinct industrial quarters on their periphery. Frome (Somerset) prospered from the expansion of the cloth trade in the second half of the seventeenth century, when its population quadrupled. An artisan suburb, now called the Trinity district, developed incrementally over some forty years from about 1685 on a hilltop site away from the town centre in the valley below. The streets were laid out on a loose grid plan, most of them following former field boundaries, and are lined with small two-or three-storeyed cottages for domestic cloth-workers, built of rubble stone and roofed with pantiles (Fig. 4.12): a pattern which

Fig. 4.11 Echoing the layout and design of the squares of London's West End, Queen Square was the centrepiece of Bristol's southward expansion in the early 18th century. The initiative came from the city's Corporation, and the surrounding houses, built by local builders over a period of about 30 years, provided spacious accommodation for merchants and professionals. The square, with its statue of King William III (1733-6) by the fashionable sculptor John Michael Rysbrack, provided a spacious setting for fashionable promenading.

anticipates the development of similar districts in later industrial towns.[48] The Rook Lane chapel (1707) nearby, with its handsome temple-like stone façade, catered for the inhabitants' spiritual needs and aspirations, such places of worship becoming the focal points of a Nonconformist subculture that played an important part in urban social and political life down to the twentieth century.

Whitehaven, on the coast of Cumbria, is sometimes seen as the quintessential new town of this period. It also originated as a planned expansion, albeit on an unusually large scale, of an existing settlement. A village had grown up in the early seventeenth century to service the local coal mines, and its subsequent development began in the 1680s on the initiative of the local landowner, Sir John Lowther. He laid out a grid plan—like that of the new suburban developments in London's West End—on an eighteen-acre site, with wide streets and houses of relatively uniform design required under the strict legal covenants (Fig. 4.13). In a court case of the 1690s he

Fig. 4.12 The Trinity district at Frome. The relatively wide streets of this planned hilltop expansion of the small Somerset town are lined with two- and three-storeyed cottages, built of local rubble stone and originally inhabited by domestic textile workers and their families.

stated that his 'chief care [was] to have the streets laid out regularly, and that the houses in each street should be made uniform so far as it could be . . . and for that end the builders were commonly obliged that they should not build their fronts under such a height, and that they should make their doors, windows, and other ornaments conformable to a rule that was given them'.[49] Starting as a coal port, by the middle of the eighteenth century the town had become a hub for the re-export trade in tobacco and slaves across the Atlantic, with an improved harbour and a population that had risen to 4,000.[50] Many of the streets, lined with plain, classically proportioned stucco-clad houses, still retain their early eighteenth-century character: a result of the town's isolated position to the west of the Lake District massif that inhibited subsequent expansion of the kind experienced by rival ports such as Glasgow and Liverpool.

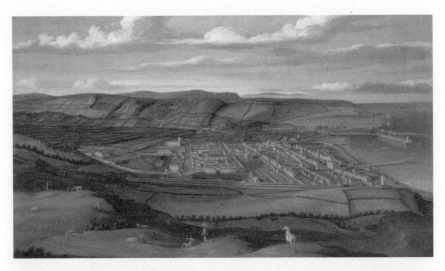

Fig. 4.13 A panorama of Whitehaven in the 1730s, by Matthias Read. The new town, on the coast of west Cumberland was laid out on classical lines on the initiative of the Lowther family, who profited from coal mines and later from the transatlantic trade in tobacco and slaves through the harbour, shown on the right. The townscape, defined by its wide, straight streets and relatively uniform houses, is still largely intact.

Liverpool

First mentioned at the end of the twelfth century, Liverpool started as a rudimentary grid of streets to the north of an inlet or 'pool' of the River Mersey. A charter was issued in 1207, and a castle went up later; it is shown, along with the riverside church of St Nicholas and a fortified house of the Stanley family, Earls of Derby, in a view of 1680. Leland mentioned that the town was 'much frequented' by Irish merchants, but further growth was hampered by sandbanks that hindered river traffic and by poor road access across the 'mosses and marshes' on the landward side.[51] The first transatlantic cargoes of sugar arrived in the middle of the seventeenth century, and, with the nearby port of Chester declining after the silting up of the River Dee, the population had risen by 1700 to around 6,000. For Celia Fiennes—who took fourteen hours to travel there from Wigan, only a few miles away, in the 1690s—it had already become 'London in miniature', its twenty-four streets lined with recently-built houses, many of them occupied by traders in serge, tobacco and the slaves on whose labour the flourishing West Indies sugar plantations depended. Defoe, writing in the 1720s, called the town

(continued)

Continued

'one of the wonders of Britain',[52] and drew attention to the creation of a 'basin or wet dock' within the Pool to the south of the town. Opened in 1715, and surrounded by a quay for the unloading of goods (and later by warehouses for storing them), it was the first enterprise of its kind outside London, and it set the scene for the creation of a novel urban landscape which was later to be replicated in other ports throughout Britain.

The initiative for building the dock was taken by the town's Corporation, which leased the Pool from the Molyneaux family, lords of the manor. Already by 1668 Lord Molyneaux had laid out a new street—Lord St— leading east from the castle, and, following the opening of the Dock, the Corporation planned other streets radiating from the eastern end of the Pool. Generally following the lines of the existing field boundaries,[53] they were soon lined with houses for the rapidly growing population, which had soared to an estimated 18,000 by 1750 and to more than 55,000 by 1790.[54] The marshy upper reaches of the Pool were drained, leading to the formation of new streets, now the core of the city's main shopping centre. The waterfront to the Mersey was meanwhile transformed by the construction of more docks (the present Canning Dock, opened 1737, and Salthouse Dock, 1753), and the dock system was later expanded to the north and south, growing from 3.5 to 28 acres between 1715 and 1796,[55] and cutting the rapidly expanding town off from the river behind a rampart of brick walls. Better roads and new canals, starting in 1755, improved the town's links with Manchester, only thirty-five miles away, and its nearby coalfields. By the end of the century Liverpool had overtaken Bristol as the largest port on the western side of England (Fig. 4.14),[56] its economy further buoyed by sugar refining, pottery manufacture, brewing and distilling.

The centre of Liverpool was so thoroughly rebuilt in the nineteenth century that only a handful of buildings survive to testify to the town's earlier prosperity. They include the former Bluecoat School (1717–25), now an arts centre, founded by Bryan Blundell, a retired sea-captain, on land belonging to the Corporation close to Church Street, then on the edge of the town. Its purpose was 'to teach poor children to read, write and cast accounts, and to instruct them in the principles and doctrines of the Established Church'; the brick buildings, originally housing some fifty children, who were clothed and fed by the charity, were disposed around three sides of an open courtyard, with residential accommodation in the wings and the schoolrooms and a chapel in the pedimented central block.[57] Then in 1749–54 an impressively classical Town Hall, designed by John Wood of Bath, one of the most fashionable architects of the time, went up at the far end of Castle Street. It was enlarged by James Wyatt in 1789–92, and is now at the heart of the Victorian business district, the residents having long moved away to residential suburbs.

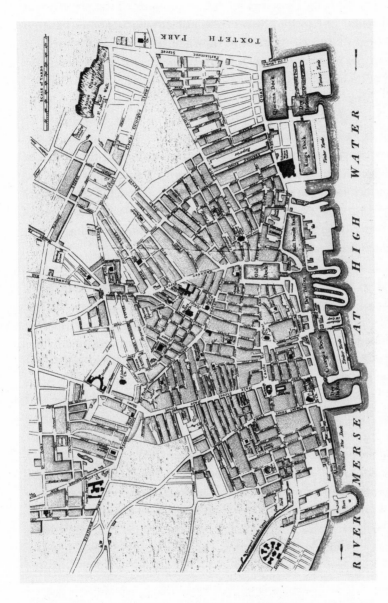

Fig. 4.14 By the end of the 18th century Liverpool had become the largest port on the west coast of England, and one of the largest cities in the country. The layout, shown in this 1795 map, was determined by the presence of quays and docks along the Mersey waterfront. The commercial area, centred on the new Town Hall, lay behind the docks, and, as the population expanded, new streets were laid out by local landowners and their agents on the rising ground to the east and south.

Rus in Urbe

Public promenading was already popular in early seventeenth-century Britain. A Royal Commission on Buildings in 1618 recommended the preservation and enhancement of Lincoln's Inn Fields, just outside London's built-up area, as 'a matter of greate ornament to the Citie, pleasure and freshnes [*sic*] for the health and recreation of the Inhabitants thereabout, and for the sight and delight of Embassadors and Strangers coming to our Court and Cittie':[58] a manifesto that anticipated the creation of the modern urban park. A 'public walk' at Northernhay, just outside the castle and northern walls of Exeter, was created as early as 1612,[59] and at Chester walks were laid out in the Grove by the River Dee, supplementing existing walks along the 'Rows' in the city centre and in the open on the city walls.[60] A 'gentlemen's walk' along the eastern side of the market place at Norwich attracted the approval of Thomas Baskerville when he visited the city in 1681; Barnstaple (Devon) went one better in 1708 when it built a covered arcade for promenading (Queen Anne's Walk) on the edge of the market place.

Large areas of 17th and 18th century towns were given over to private gardens and to bowling greens and tennis courts, to which respectably dressed citizens and travellers were admitted. They were also admitted at certain times to the gardens of Oxford and Cambridge colleges and to Oxford's Botanic Garden, established in 1621 on the marshy ground by the River Cherwell and open to visitors on payment of a fee. Celia Fiennes was impressed in 1698 by the Abbey Gardens on the far side of the River Severn at Shrewsbury, with its 'gravel walks set full of all sorts of greens orange and lemon trees.' Another set of walks was laid out in 1719 in the former Quarry just outside the town walls, still, despite changing fashions in landscape gardening, a public park.[61] By 1736 Richard Pococke could call Shrewsbury the 'paradise of England',[62] with a growing professional population catering to the local gentry who resorted there for entertainment, compensating to some extent for the decline of the cloth and leather trades that had formerly sustained much of the local economy. A similar process took place on a smaller scale in the market town of Ross-on-Wye (Herefordshire), where a garden and walk was created after 1696 by the philanthropically-minded John Kyrle, the 'Man of Ross', on land leased from the Marquess of Bath next to the church; it enabled residents and visitors to enjoy the view over the river, as they still can. Public walks could be also be created on under-used town-centre land, like the castle courtyard in Lewes, the assize town for East Sussex. And they could strike out into open countryside. New Walk, now a much-frequented public footpath alongside the River Ouse to the south of York, was begun in 1732,[63] and at Knaresborough in the same county a Long Walk was opened in about 1739 to give easy access to the famous petrifying well or Dropping Well, still a tourist attraction. Fashionable society was also attracted by race meetings, as happened at York, where a racecourse was established at Knavesmire, south of the city, in 1731. Such places of diversion were part of the *raison d'être* of resort settlements, and they played an important part in subsequent suburban development.

Specialized resort towns began to develop, often very slowly, close to medicinal springs. Tunbridge Wells (Kent), a small settlement at the meeting-point of three parishes, was already fashionable by 1638, when the first public walks were laid out through the traffic-free street now known as the Pantiles, adjoining a stretch of common land;[64] here, according to Celia Fiennes, 'all sorts of toys, silver, china' were bought and sold.[65] In contrast to places like Whitehaven, or to the big estates of London's West End, there was no single dominant landowner, and urban development, much of it in the form of lodging houses, was focused on two hills, re-named Mount Sion and Mount Ephraim, resulting in a scattered, diffuse urban landscape. The search for health cures intermingled with sybaritic relaxation—a potent combination then as now—also created a distinctive landscape in small spas such as Hotwells in the Avon valley to the west of Bristol, where a Pump Room went up in 1695, followed in 1721 by the building of Assembly Rooms (replaced in the 1760s) on the hillside above, and later by terraces and squares of new housing. Some of the houses served as lodgings for visitors, while others became the homes of permanent residents escaping the noisy and dirty city centre.[66] This pattern was repeated in other spa towns.

Bath

The greatest example of the commercialisation of leisure in early modern Britain was Bath, a fairly ordinary west country cloth-manufacturing town transformed into one of the most successful resort towns in the western world. John Leland gave a long description of the baths and their healing qualities in the 1530s, and in 1698 Celia Fiennes described the town as 'a pretty place full of good houses all for the accommodation of the Company that resort hither to drink or bathe in the summer'.[67] Trim Street, the first new street to be built outside the medieval walls, was laid out in 1707, following royal visits and the appointment of Richard 'Beau' Nash as the Master of Ceremonies who presided over entertainments for the visitors. Then came Kingsmead Square, laid out in 1727, and Beauford Square, with more modest two-storeyed houses built in the 1730s to the designs of a Bristol architect, John Strahan. His achievement was soon overshadowed by that of the Bath-born John Wood, who was responsible for introducing a grander style at Queen Square (1728–38). He had spent time in London and York, and had already rebuilt much of the former St John's Hospital in Bath to contain lodgings for the growing number of short-term visitors to the town.[68] The stately effect of his pedimented neo-Palladian terrace on the north side of Queen Square depends on the quality of the local stone, much of it coming from quarries on the far side of the river developed by the entrepreneurially-minded Ralph Allen, who had already established a regular postal service to London. Robert Gay, the landowner, was a London surgeon, and the development followed the usual London pattern of building leases; the obelisk in the centre of the square, promoted by Beau Nash, went up in 1738 to commemorate a royal visit. Wood went on in 1740–48 to build North and South Parades on open ground outside the city walls to the east of the Abbey and baths, and close to the old assembly rooms. The pavements here—still not yet a feature of some older towns—were unusually wide, allowing for fashionable promenading, and much earth-moving was needed to create the 18-foot-high substructure that compensated for the fall in the ground to the river, though, contrary to Wood's original wishes, the facades of the houses were remarkably plain.[69] Meanwhile the area inside the walls was comprehensively rebuilt, much of it with lodging-houses such as those in North Parade Buildings, a street of uniform houses promoted by a local apothecary and finished in 1750.

The growing popularity of the Bath 'season' led to the expansion of the city in all directions. Gay Street, leading uphill from the north-east corner of Queen Square, was begun in 1735–40, the cornices of the houses rising step-like as they climb the hill. The Circus, at the far end, followed in 1755–66. John Wood believed—or pretended to believe—that there had been a druidic temple here, with a stone circle like that at Stanton Drew, not far away, its circular form ordained by God and transmitted to the Jews and finally to the Druids, who counted among their number Bladud, the alleged founder of the city and son of the mythical King Lud and great-grandson of no less a person than Aeneas. Bladud was believed to have discovered Bath's springs after contracting leprosy, later becoming a swine-herd, infecting a herd of pigs and then following them to the springs where they were miraculously cured: hence the carvings of acorns on top of the cornice over the houses surrounding the Circus. The magnificent Royal Crescent followed in 1767–75 under the direction of Wood's son, John Wood the younger, 'bringing in the landscape' with its view over the undeveloped Avon valley: a pioneering and influential application of landscape-gardening ideas to urban design (Fig. 4.15). These developments shifted Bath's social centre of gravity northwards, a move epitomized by the building of new Assembly Rooms (1771) on a site to the east of the Circus to the designs of the younger Wood, modest externally but intern-ally lavish.

Bath continued to expand well into the nineteenth century. By 1800 it had spread uphill to Lansdowne Crescent (1789–93), west to Norfolk Crescent (1792) and also to the south, where a working-class area grew up by the river wharves. The River Avon had formed a barrier to eastward expansion, but it was crossed in 1769–74 by Pulteney Bridge, designed by the fashionable architect Robert Adam with rows of shops on either side of the thoroughfare. The land on the far side was then laid out, starting in 1788, with a hundred foot-wide street (Great Pulteney Street) leading to a pleasure garden (Sydney Gardens), originally lined with music boxes like those of the famous Vauxhall Gardens in London. Meanwhile the medieval walls were almost completely razed and the area around the Baths remod-elled by the city Corporation under an Act of Parliament passed in 1789. Its main feature was a new Pump Room (1790–5), designed by Thomas Baldwin, the city architect,[70] overlooking the remains of the Roman baths and facing a newly-created public square in front of the medieval Abbey. From here a new, colonnaded street, Bath St, leads to the Cross Bath, also rebuilt by Baldwin, and the Hot Bath (by the younger Wood 1775–7), cre-ating a planned townscape that alluded to the city's Roman origins and inspired similar improvements in other cities.

Fig. 4.15 Bath was a relatively small town built in a crook of the River Avon, but during the 18th century it expanded to the north and east, its layout and architecture reflecting its partly mythologized Roman and pre-Roman origins. The Circus, on the right of this air view, stands at the top of Gay Street, leading north from Queen Square. The upper Assembly Rooms are to the right of the Circus, and Brock St (left), leads to the Royal Crescent, 'commanding the prospect' over the southward view, with a uniform façade to the houses, designed by the younger John Wood.

5

Improvement and Industry,
1760–1830

Shortly before his death in 1789, James Spershott, co-pastor of the Baptist chapel in Chichester, wrote a memoir in which he described the changes that had taken place in his home town during his lifetime. It had, he recalled, 'a very mean appearance' in his youth, the buildings 'in general very low, very old, and their fronts fram'd with Timber which lay bare to the weather, and had a step down from the street to the Ground Floor...The Shops in General had Shutters to let up and down, and no other Inclosure, but were quite open in the daytime...There were very few Houses even in the main Streets that had solid Brick Fronts, except such as appear'd to have been Built a few years back', such as Pallant House (see Fig. 4.9). But, in recent years the town had been 'new built or new faced'. Brick frontages with sash windows brought more light into houses, 'a spirit of Emulation...having run through the whole, [so that] from its Beauty, Elegancey, and new taste in Buildings, Dress &c it would appear to an ancient inhabitant, if reviv'd, as if another Cissa [the legendary founder of the city] had been here'.[1] Obstacles had been removed from the streets, and trees planted alongside the public walks around the old castle site 'for the accommodation of the citizens and the ornament of the city'.[2] Then, two years after Spershott's death, an Act of Parliament was passed, allowing for better street lighting and drainage. Market stalls were removed from the streets, and in 1807 a new market building went up in North Street, designed by the fashionable London architect John Nash, for the sale of meat, fish, poultry, eggs and butter 'and such other things as are usually sold in public markets.'[3] Finally, starting in 1812, a planned 'New Town', including a church, was created in the south-eastern quarter of the city, on the undeveloped site of the former Dominican friary.[4]

Changes of this kind took place all over Britain. With a third of its population living in towns, Britain was already one of the most urbanized countries in the world by 1801.[5] The population had grown from an estimated six million in 1700 to ten and a half million, and that figure increased to over sixteen million over the next thirty years, precipitating a massive migration from the countryside to towns. London was still far and away the largest city, but provincial towns grew at an even faster rate. By 1801 Manchester, with a population of 94,000, was a tenth the size of the capital, easily outnumbering long-established cities such as Bristol, Norwich and York. The rate of urban growth was even more impressive in Scotland. Glasgow, with an estimated population of around 18,000 at the end of the seventeenth century, had quadrupled to 77,000 by 1801. Its population tripled over the next thirty years, giving rise to a planned westward expansion which permanently changed the city's character.[6]

Population growth and rapid economic change put a strain on existing town and city centres.[7] The main approach to Nottingham from the south was still so narrow in the 1740s that wagons had to go in single file; the streets between St Peter's church, close to the market place, and the River Leen were 'one continued swamp' and one of the markets a 'meer sink'.[8] Birmingham's first historian, William Hutton, complained in 1783 that encroachments had made the main streets between eight and ten feet narrower than they should have been, a problem exacerbated by the growth in wheeled traffic and the import of ever-increasing numbers of live animals and larger amounts of agricultural produce.[9] To remedy such problems, responsibility for new roads and other infrastructural improvements was increasingly taken out of the hands of existing local authorities and placed in the hands of street or paving commissioners—usually made up of members of the local middle-class elite—set up under private Acts of Parliament. This had already happened in Salisbury in 1736 and in Liverpool in 1748, and there were eventually four hundred such bodies in England.[10]

Town-centre improvements usually involved the removal of what were now seen as outdated features such as walls and gates, many of them fortunately recorded by diligent local antiquaries and artists before they were demolished. The walls of Hull were razed, starting in 1774, to make way for new docks, and in 1797-1801 Parliament Street, lined with handsome terraces of brick houses, was cut through under an Act of Parliament to link Whitefriargate, the town's main shopping street, and the dock (since filled in) to the north of the town.[11] Oxford's handsome new Magdalen Bridge was built in 1772–90 to the designs of John Gwynn, author of *London and Westminster Improved* (1766) in order to carry traffic to and from London over the marshy banks of the River Cherwell. It was followed by the rebuilding of houses along the eastern end of the High Street, the demolition of the remaining city gates and the removal of the market stalls at the central crossroads to a new Covered Market, designed by Gwynn behind a classical façade of 1773–4. Finally, in 1787 the seventeenth-century conduit house that blocked the road intersection at Carfax, the centre of the market area since Anglo-Saxon times, was pulled down and re-erected as a garden ornament by the second Lord Harcourt at his country seat, Nuneham Courtenay, a few miles away. And at Frome a completely new street—Bath Street, lined with stone-fronted, classically proportioned shops and houses—was cut through existing properties in 1810 as a by-pass to the steep and narrow, though picturesque, main street.[12]

Local Acts of Parliament also made it possible to improve street surfaces. The Westminster Paving Act of 1762 stipulated that kerbs and gutters should be made alongside the pavements of the main streets of London's West End, and stone slabs laid down to replace the pebbles formerly used for the road surfaces.[13] The steep gradients along the main routes leading into Shrewsbury from the north and east were eased in 1821–5 by lowering the surfaces, in some cases by as much as ten feet, as happened alongside the churchyard of St Julian in the High Street, now reached by steps from the pavement. Shrewsbury was on the main turnpike road from London to Holyhead, and thence to Ireland. Its approach from the east was marked in 1814–16 by the building of a 151 feet-high Doric column funded by subscriptions and designed by the local architect Edward Haycock; it commemorated a local hero, Lord Hill, one of the Duke of Wellington's generals in the wars against Napoleon. Then, as part of a scheme to reduce journey times for stage-coaches, the eastern approach road into the town was brutally realigned in 1836 through the south transept and cloister of the former Benedictine abbey, leaving the fourteenth-century refectory pulpit as an isolated survivor next to what is now a car park.[14]

Improved street lighting was another preoccupation. The lighting in Preston (Lancashire) came from carbonated hydrogen gas produced in a plant set up by a private company under the town's 1815 Improvement Act; a contemporary writer enthused that Preston was 'the first town in the British Empire... in which that beautiful light was generally used.'[15] By 1830 gas lighting in town-centre streets had become almost universal, and lamp-posts became a significant feature of the townscape.[16] The market cross at Richmond (Yorkshire) was replaced in 1771 by a curiously proportioned stone spire on top of an underground storage tank for water piped into the town. Meanwhile the 'middle rows' of many market places were removed as part of a process of widening and 'civilizing' streets, a process that sometimes involved the banning of cruel sports; bull-baiting in Birmingham was forbidden by the local Improvement Commissioners in the 1770s, though the name of the Bull Ring still lingers on in the busy central market area.[17]

The market in Bristol was removed from the central streets in 1741–3 and the old 'Tolzey' or market hall by the central crossroads replaced by the fashionably neo-Palladian Exchange built to the designs of John Wood of Bath; an open market was laid out in the courtyard behind it, surrounded by a tavern, coffee houses and 'houses for Insurance…or for tradespeople'.[18] The medieval High Cross at the crossroads fell victim to another drive for 'improvement' in 1764, and was exiled to Stourhead in Wiltshire, where it now forms a picturesque feature in the famous landscape garden. All but one of the city gates were also demolished, and banks and offices gradually took over houses in the city centre, the resident population moving away in ever-increasing numbers to suburbs on the surrounding hills.[19] Most important of all, the River Avon, on which the city's prosperity depended, was impounded in 1804–9 to create the 'Floating Harbour', allowing ships to remain in port when the tide rose and fell (See Fig. 1.14).

Urban improvement reflected, and also encouraged, social change. A report on Leeds in 1819 mentioned 'an evident alteration…in the character of the people…They are now putting off in some degree that rudeness which is peculiar to them, enlightened pursuits are more cultivated, and the elegancies and comforts of life are more sought after.'[20] Many towns acquired new theatres such as the well-preserved Theatre Royal of 1819, hidden away in a side street at Bury St Edmunds, or the more modest one built in Kendal in 1828 at the far end of an inn yard leading off the main street. Town-centre streets were increasingly lined with specialized shops with enticing frontages designed to attract a consumerist middle-class clientele. In Chester, which acquired its first street lamps in 1725, the shops were concentrated, as they still are, around the central crossroads, the main market area since medieval times, and especially on the southern side of Eastgate Street, the main approach from London.[21] Legislation passed in London in 1762 forbade hanging signs, and encouraged a fashion for fascia boards displaying the names of shops over the windows, which were sometimes rebuilt with curved bows to admit more daylight.[22] In Oxford, following the establishment of a Paving Commission in 1771, the diarist James Woodforde noted that 'The Streets...are much improved, all the signs taken down and put against the Houses, the Streets widened.'[23] Most of the owners and occupiers of the timber houses in the main streets now took the opportunity of giving them a face-lift in stucco, shaving off jettied projections, inserting sash windows and replacing gable-ends with straight parapets.[24]

The Rebuilding of Henley-on-Thames

35 miles north-west of London, Henley was depicted by the Flemish artist Jan Siberechts in a series of oil paintings dating from the 1690s. The wooden bridge over over the River Thames led past the fifteenth-century church into a main street lined with timber-framed houses, widening out into a market place. The river frontage was lined with wharves for the export of corn, malt, and timber from the surrounding Chiltern Hills; they helped to supply the growing needs of London, and formed the economic basis for the town's prosperity. Brick-fronted houses with sash windows began to be built at the beginning of the eighteenth century,[25] and by the middle of the century they could be found in all the main streets, their facades enlivened by the use of contrasting red and blue (vitrified) brickwork, and by different-coloured rubbed and gauged brickwork to emphasize details such as window surrounds and cornices.[26] The burgage plots behind some of these houses were occupied by workshops and malthouses; the Old Brewery House in New Street was built in about 1750 by Benjamin Sarney, a maltster and brewer, and the extensive late-eighteenth and nineteenth-century brewery buildings behind it have recently been turned into a hotel.[27] As the artisan and labouring population grew, new cottages were built and older buildings divided up, as at Nos. 17–33 Friday Street, where the carpenter and builder Benjamin Bradshaw (d.1738), a former mayor, created eight brick-fronted cottages out of two or three late-medieval timber houses.[28]

Henley's success depended on good communications, and the road from Henley towards London was turnpiked in 1718, the improvement of the road leading north-west towards Oxford following in 1735–6. Then in 1768 the London road was realigned by the building of a cutting to alleviate

(continued)

Continued

the steep ascent of the Chilterns on the far side of the wooden bridge. The bridge itself was replaced in 1781–6 by a handsome new stone structure of five arches designed by a Shrewsbury architect, William Hayward (Fig. 5.1), followed by the construction of a new embankment and wharf and the enlargement of some of the town's twenty-one inns, notably the Red Lion next to the bridge. Another important inn, the Bell Inn in Northfield End on the Oxford road, was extended and refronted in stucco in 1782 by the lord of the manor, Strickland Freeman, as part of an initiative to improve the northern approach to the town; it contained a 'spacious ballroom, comfortable sleeping rooms [and] four parlours' in 1794.[29] The *Universal British Directory* for 1790 recorded that Henley was linked to London by eight coaches per day, the streets having recently been 'widened, paved, and lighted'; tradespeople included three milliners, a peruke (wig) maker and two booksellers. The Middle Row in the market place was cleared in 1795–6 to provide a suitable setting for a new town hall with a double-height portico in front of a colonnaded space for the market stalls, surmounted by an assembly room. More street improvements followed in 1808 and 1829.[30] A theatre went up in New Street in 1805, and, as the population continued to expand, fashionably stucco-fronted houses with roofs of slate, imported from quarries in North Wales, were built along the northern approaches to the town.

Rebuilding transformed the appearance of towns throughout the country. Lancaster became England's fourth largest slaving port in the late eighteenth century—Arthur Young mentioned 100 ships there in 1771—and, as a result, new wharves and warehouses went up on reclaimed land by the River Lune. The houses of the town centre were meanwhile rebuilt in stone, the streets straightened and a new square (Dalton Square) laid out after 1783 to the south-east of the market place.[31] At Taunton, a workaday cloth-making town in Somerset, a group of 'sensible and public-spirited' citizens wrested control of the market from the Bishops of Winchester and secured an Act of Parliament in 1768 enabling them to clear the site, which had become, in the words of the town's historian, 'a spot of ground, so crowded with buildings .... [that] besides obstructing the free circulation of air, could not but be attended with many inconveniences and nuisances, by the filth lying in its narrow passages, and the receptacles for idleness and vice, which many

Fig. 5.1 The bridge at Henley-on-Thames was built in 1781-6, and carried the road from London to Oxford and South Wales into the small town. The parish church with its 15th-century tower is on the far side, with the Angel inn next to the bridge.

of its buildings, from their situation, became'.[32] The old market house was replaced in 1770–2 by a handsome new domestic-looking structure built of brick to the designs of a local gentleman-amateur architect, Coplestone Warre Bampfylde. Now turned into a restaurant, it looks out onto a triangular space originally serving, except on market days, as a Parade for the 'polite' section of the local population (and now as a roundabout for buses). More improvements followed on the initiative of Sir Benjamin Hammett, son of a local barber and serge manufacturer who made a fortune as an insurance broker, merchant banker and ship-owner. He leased and restored the castle as a meeting-place for the local assizes, and in 1788 he laid out a new street (Hammett Street), named after himself and aligned upon the magnificent west tower (c.1488–1514) of St. Mary Magdalene's church (Fig. 5.2). The street is lined with terraces of uniform and austerely detailed brick-fronted houses, each with its own pattern-book doorcase, supplying, in the words of the town's historian, 'what for many years [it] wanted, houses for the reception of genteel families out of trade'.[33]

Fig. 5.2 Hammett Street, Taunton, was laid out in 1788 and is lined with near-identical brick-fronted houses, aligned upon the Perpendicular Gothic tower of the 15th-century church of St Mary Magdalene.

The late eighteenth and early nineteenth centuries also saw a substantial resumption of church-building. The number of new Nonconformist places of worship rose especially dramatically; in the 1810s an average of five new chapels were being opened each week,[34] some of them built by the Methodists after they broke away from the Church of England in the 1790s. By the end of the 1840s Methodist membership had quadrupled to around 338,000, much of the growth taking place in manufacturing towns such as Sheffield, where the brick-built, pedimented Carver Street chapel of 1804, designed by the superintendent of the local Methodist circuit, seated 1,100 worshippers.[35] The chapel at Hanley in the Staffordshire Potteries, built in 1819, was even bigger, accommodating a mammoth 3,000 people in its vast amphitheatre-like interior. Prompted to some extent by a fear of social breakdown at a time of acute economic difficulty following the end of the Napoleonic Wars, the government responded with the New Churches Act of 1818, providing a million pounds-worth of funding for Anglican churches; it was followed by another half a million in 1824. Some of the churches, like Holy Trinity, Bordesley (1820–2), on what was then the edge of Birmingham, were Gothic in style, reflecting a growing fashion for romantic medievalism, but others, like the new church of St Pancras (1819–22), in a rapidly expanding part of London, were classical, their Grecian temple-like porticoes making an emphatic statement of institutional authority.

As urban populations grew, so too did the need for new administrative buildings. County authorities were responsible for providing court rooms and prisons for serious offenders, and many were rebuilt on a larger scale within the precincts of their medieval castles. This happened in York, where an imposing debtors' prison went up in the castle bailey in 1701-5 facing the medieval Clifford's Tower; it was followed in 1773–83 by the building of a female prison and a new assize court designed by the Yorkshire-born John Carr, one of the most successful provincial architects of the time (Fig. 5.3). The new county buildings at Lancaster were designed by another highly accomplished architect, Joseph Harrison, in a Gothic style that was deliberately chosen to match the surviving medieval buildings.[36] Prisons were now intended to punish and reform criminals, not simply to house debtors and people awaiting trial, and this was reflected in the design and layout of grim new correctional buildings like the prison at Hereford, designed by John Nash, its site now a bus station. In his *Hints for the Improvement of Prisons* (1817) the architect James Elmes urged that such buildings should be 'as

Fig. 5.3 The outer bailey of the former castle at York, seen from Clifford's Tower, the shell-keep on top of the Norman motte. The former Debtors' Prison is on the far side of the courtyard, flanked by the Assize Courts (right) and the former Female Prison, now part of the Castle Museum (left).

gloomy and melancholy as possible':[37] an apt description of the bastille-like gaol at Abingdon (1805–6), recently converted into flats.

Scotland

The most widespread and thorough rebuilding of older towns took place in Scotland. Scottish towns were enriched by a wave of agricultural improvement that gathered momentum in the second half of the eighteenth century, accompanied by industrial growth and an expansion of internal and external trade. Several new towns had already been established after the 1707 Union and the 1715 Jacobite rebellion; they included Crieff (Perthshire), an entrepot for cross-border cattle trade, laid out by George Drummond, Lord Provost of Edinburgh, in 1731, and Inveraray in the West Highlands, started in 1743 next to the Duke of Argyll's rebuilt Gothic castle. Older towns also expanded. A woollen factory was founded at Haddington (East Lothian), a

Fig. 5.4 Haddington was an important thoroughfare town on the main road leading to Edinburgh from the east. The Town House, in the centre of the market place, was begun in 1742 to the designs of William Adam, with a court room on the first floor and a prison below. The building was enlarged in 1788 to incorporate an Assembly Room, with a market for grain underneath, and the tower and spire were added by James Gillespie Graham in 1831. The houses on either side of the market place were rebuilt in stone in the 18th and 19th centuries.

thoroughfare town on one of the main routes leading west towards Edinburgh, in 1681, and a new Town House went up in 1742-5, to which a steeple was added in 1831, terminating the view along the wide main street from the Edinburgh direction (Fig. 5.4). Meanwhile the street frontages were gradually rebuilt in stone, creating a relatively uniform townscape of a type that can be matched across the whole country. Other towns improved their port facilities as overseas and coasting trade created new wealth.[38] Cromarty, a small fishing port on the northern tip of the Black Isle, north of Inverness, is one example among many. It prospered through the export of grain and the import of flax, and a new harbour was created in 1784 by the laird and local MP George Ross, a former army agent. Streets of stuccoed houses were then laid out to link the harbour to the now sleepy main street, with its Court House of 1773 (also funded by Ross) and fishermens' cottages close to the shore.

Polite society implied polite architecture. Thatch and heather were forbidden as roofing materials in Dumfries in 1722,[39] and in 1734 the town council at Montrose (Angus) removed the middle row that blocked the main street, going on in 1739 to mastermind the gradual imposition of a uniform street frontage; a painting of 1826 shows well-dressed, orderly citizens promenading in the well-drained, traffic-free street.[40] Kelso (Roxburghshire), close to the English border, was 'a place of great gaiety' in the words of one writer, and acquired a handsome new town hall facing its spacious market place in 1816.[41] The dominant feature of Elgin's town centre is the church of St Giles (1826–8), designed by the locally-born architect Archibald Simpson and presiding over the wide market place with its Greek Doric portico and steeple based on the Choragic Monument of Lysicrates in Athens. Perth, on the border between Scotland's highland and lowland zones, also flourished as the Highlands became increasingly integrated into a national economy following the second Jacobite rebellion of 1745. The population more than doubled (to about 20,000) between the 1750s and the 1790s, and, following the building of a new bridge over the Tay in 1765–71, the streets were widened, pavements laid and lighting improved. Another series of improvements was inaugurated at the beginning of the nineteenth century by Thomas Marshall, twice Provost of the town, involving the construction of an embankment on the site of the older wharves along the river. Now dominated by traffic, it was originally intended as an elegant parade, overlooked by a fashionably Greek Revival Court House of 1816–19.[42] Terraces of middle-class of houses were later built alongside the 'Inches' (stretches of common land) to the north and south of the town, and finally in 1830–2 a circular Pantheon-like waterworks (now an art gallery) with a cast iron dome went up close to the river, with a Doric column behind it hiding the chimney.[43]

A similar pattern of expansion took place in Aberdeen. Marischal Street, leading south from the old market place at Castlegate, was cut through to the quayside in 1766–7, and in 1801–3 two wide, new streets were laid out to the north and west of the city centre: King Street, leading northwards, and the mile-long Union Street (Fig. 5.5), leading west. Remorselessly straight, and lined eventually with handsome classical buildings in the local granite, Union Street bridges the deep gulley of the Denburn (later the site of the city's railway station), improving access from the rural hinterland and

Fig. 5.5 Union Street is one of the two new streets laid out in 1801–3 to link Aberdeen—the 'granite city' - to its northern and western hinterland. In the foreground is Castlegate, with the Mercat Cross of 1686. Beyond are the classical façades of the Union Buildings (1822–3: left) and the former North of Scotland Bank (1838), both designed by Archibald Simpson, and the Town House (1866-74) with its 'Scottish Baronial' tower beyond.

The New Town at Edinburgh

The most ambitious, and the most rigorously planned, town extension in Scotland occurred in the capital. In 1752, seven years after the defeat of the second Jacobite rebellion, the Corporation, encouraged by the Provost, George Drummond, framed proposals for a series of improvements to the notoriously crowded and filthy city centre. A new merchants' Exchange (now known as City Chambers), went up in the High Street in 1753–61 to the designs of John Adam, brother of the better-known Robert. It marked a decisive shift towards a new classically-inspired style of architecture which in time came to represent the public face of the Scottish Enlightenment. Then in 1753 an Act of Parliament ordered the removal of the 'forestairs and booths' that impeded passage along the street, which was newly paved;

(*continued*)

Continued

by the end of the century most of the buildings that lined it had also been remodelled with austere stone frontages. Rebuilding, though less extensive, also took place along Canongate to the east and Cowgate to the south, beyond which new squares lined with terraced houses sprang up; they included George Square, developed from 1765 by James Brown along the lines of the squares of London's West End and now much rebuilt by the University which has spread over the site.

The most important aspect of the 1752 proposals was the creation of a 'New Town' on the far side of the marshy North Loch. It was designed to provide comfortable housing for gentry and 'persons of considerable rank' whose presence, it was believed, would stimulate the economic growth of a city retarded, as was claimed by many, by the Union of 1707.[44] But before this could happen the City Corporation needed to improve communications with the Old Town: an aim achieved by the building of North Bridge (1765–72: since replaced), with the monumental, domed Register House, begun to the designs of Robert Adam in 1774, closing the vista at its northern end. The competition held in 1767 for planning the New Town was won by James Craig, whose scheme was the most rigorous restatement yet seen in Britain of Renaissance-inspired urban planning: a strict rectangle of streets bounded to the north and south by two long and unusually broad (80 feet-wide) east-west thoroughfares (Prince's Street and Queen Street) on either side of an even wider wide main street (George Street) with 10-feet wide pavements linking two spacious squares (Fig. 5.6).[45] The City Corporation acted as developer, laying out the streets and leasing the house plots to private builders. The side streets were filled with plain stone terraced houses, but Charlotte Square, the westernmost of the two squares, was designed in a grander style by Robert Adam, who died just before work started in 1792. The houses on the north side, of the locally-quarried grey Craigleith ashlar which became ubiquitous in Edinburgh, formed part of a unified *palazzo*-like design recalling that of the north side of Queen Square in Bath. Generously conceived and impeccably executed, they set a standard of monumental grandeur which was taken up, and elaborated upon, in a series of later extensions well into the nineteenth century. A South Bridge (1785–8), led meanwhile from the Old Town to a new set of buildings for the University, begun by Adam but finished by one of his most gifted successors, William Playfair. Then in 1817–22 Princes Street was extended east along Waterloo Place to Calton Hill, which was dotted with monumental buildings including a prison, an observatory and an unfinished Grecian-style memorial to Scottish soldiers killed in the

Napoleonic Wars. Taken together with the landscaping of the former North Loch and the Mound (see Chapter 7) linking the Old and New Towns, these improvements represent the most impressive contribution of the period to the urban landscape of Britain.

By providing more spacious housing for the prosperous middle classes, the creation of the New Town eventually destroyed the social character of the Old Town with its cheek-by-jowl juxtaposition of rich and poor. The Old Town remained the headquarters of Scotland's legal and ecclesiastical establishment, and with the rebuilding of the former Parliament Buildings (by Robert Reid) and the Signet Library (by Playfair, 1819–20) it acquired a set of classically-inspired public buildings matching those of the New Town. But the courts and wynds behind the houses along the Royal Mile, deserted by the social elite, became filled with sub-standard housing for the working-class immigrants who flocked into the city in growing numbers: a graphic illustration of the *de facto* social zoning which began to transform most of Britain's (and Europe's) larger cities in the first half of the nineteenth century.[46]

Fig. 5.6 An air view of the New Town in Edinburgh from the west. The rectilinear grid of James Craig's New Town (see p. 226), laid out after 1767, is at the top right of the picture. The streets and crescents in the foreground, lined with classically-inspired terraced housing, were built up on land belonging to the Heriot Trust in the second half of the 19th century.

encouraging the growth of suburbs in the years following the end of the
Napoleonic Wars, when middle-class housing began to go up on the far
side of the bridge.[47] But, as elsewhere throughout Britain, suburban
expansion of this kind was accompanied by a growing concentration of
the poor into crowded courts and alleys in the city centre. Their numbers
increased dramatically as the population grew in the early nineteenth
century, creating social and environmental problems that continued to
vex later generations.

London

London was the largest city in Europe at the end of the eighteenth century,
the size of its population rivalled among world cities only by Beijing, and
possibly by Edo/Tokyo. The 674,000 or so Londoners in 1700 had risen to
900,000 by 1801, and another half a million people were added between
then and 1831. Population growth of this magnitude was bound to result in
massive, if intermittent, rebuilding. All but one of the ancient gates of the
City were demolished in 1760–1, along with most of the long-redundant
medieval city wall. New bridges—Westminster (1739–51) and Blackfriars
(1760–9)—led to the laying out of new roads south of the river, precipitating massive suburban growth that continued well into the twentieth century (see p. 245). Following the building of Westminster Bridge, Parliament
Street was cut through to Whitehall, where the demolition of the sixteenth-
century gateways to the royal palace (abandoned after a fire in 1698) opened
up a handsome new thoroughfare lined with aristocratic town houses
and government buildings, including the Horse Guards—headquarters of
the Army—and the Admiralty. Then, starting in 1776, Somerset House in
the Strand was rebuilt by the Government to the designs of Sir William
Chambers, with a magnificent frontage to the river and accommodation
for Navy offices and for learned and scientific societies, including the
recently-established Royal Academy of Arts.

Steps were also taken to remove bottlenecks in the City. The remaining
portion of the Fleet River was paved over as a northern approach to the new
Blackfriars Bridge, and an Act of Parliament for paving and cleaning the rest
of the main streets was passed in 1766, incidentally involving the introduction of house numbering. The houses on London Bridge were demolished

in 1757–61, alleviating a notorious bottleneck,[48] and a new bridge was built slightly to the west in 1823–31. A new street—King William Street—was then pushed through the densely-packed townscape to the recently-enlarged Bank of England and the Royal Exchange, burned down for the second time and rebuilt in 1841–4.[49] The stage was now set for the subsequent redevelopment of the City as a central business district, denuded of its resident population, its central streets lined with banks, offices and the premises of insurance companies, its fringes and waterside redeveloped with warehouses.

London was not only Britain's capital city and the centre of its financial system; it was also Britain's largest port, and by 1800 its crowded quaysides were filled to capacity. The solution was to build docks on the low-lying land to the east of the City. The first docks had been established for shipbuilding and ship-repairing at Deptford, on the south bank of the Thames. The building of new and much larger dock basins on the north side of the river started in 1800 with the West India and London Docks, transforming the riverside landscape and creating enclosed, watery enclaves hidden behind high brick walls guarding massive brick-built bonded warehouses (see p. 181 and p. 297) grouped around large rectangular pools where ships could be moored. This was a landscape that remained fundamentally unchanged until the removal of the Port of London to new sites closer to the Thames estuary in the late twentieth century (see Chapter 9).

As London's wealth and population increased, so too did the demand for housing. By 1790 the West End had spread north to the 'New Road', Britain's first city-centre ring road or by-pass,[50] laid out in 1756 to take traffic around the fringe of the built-up area to and from the manufacturing districts to the north and east of the City. The new streets within this outer limit were lined with near-identical brick-fronted terraced houses with mews—rows of small houses and stables—lining alleyways on the lower ground behind the houses. The monotony of the resulting townscape was relieved by the provision of secluded open spaces, only accessible to keyholders, such as Bedford Square in Bloomsbury (1775–86) and Fitzroy Square further east, begun in 1798. They were landscaped with trees, shrubs and winding pathways,[51] creating a series of discrete miniature arcadias whose presence still helps shape the character of large portions of the capital.

Regent's Park and Regent Street

In his *London and Westminster Improved* John Gwynn proposed a comprehensive scheme of improvements designed to ease the passage of traffic through the built-up area of the rapidly expanding city. The fragmented nature of London's local government made this all but impossible to achieve at first, but in 1811 the lease of Marylebone Fields, a Crown property north of the New Road, long popular as a place of resort for Londoners, fell in, and John Nash, one of the architects for the Crown Estate, was asked to prepare a plan for developing the site for expensive housing set within and around a landscaped park.[52] Communications to Westminster and the City had to be improved before such a development could make a profit, and in 1813 Nash published his final plan for a new street. It followed the line of the existing Portland Place at its northern end before proceeding south to Carlton House in Pall Mall, home of the Prince Regent (from 1820 King George IV), creating new public spaces (Oxford Circus and Piccadilly Circus) where it crossed the existing east-west thoroughfares. The new street was curved at certain points in order to avoid expensive land purchases and was aligned so as to cut through Crown land wherever possible, creating, in Nash's words, a 'clear line of separation' between aristocratic Mayfair to the west and the more workaday Soho to the east (Fig. 5.7). Financed mainly by government-backed deficit spending, work began in 1815, the year of the Battle of Waterloo, and was finished in 1823. Nash acted as architect, arranging the acquisition of land, finding builders, supplying elevations of the stucco-fronted buildings lining the street, and sometimes, as in the Quadrant to the north-west of Piccadilly Circus, acting as developer. The buildings, in one of which Nash took up residence himself, had a superficial resemblance to the *palazzi* of Renaissance Italy or the *hôtels particuliers* of Paris, their gleaming stuccoed facades providing a sumptuous backdrop to what could be seen as a triumphal route from the Park to Carlton House. Nash's policy of 'hugging the coast', as he described it, between affluent and poorer districts paid off in the long run, and Regent Street became an integral and easily accessible part of a consumer-orientated district given over to shopping and entertainment (Fig. 5.8). Theatres had already migrated westwards in the late seventeenth century, and Nash himself was involved in the rebuilding of the long-established Royal Opera House in Haymarket and the building of a new Haymarket Theatre to his own designs, the former flanked by Britain's first covered shopping arcade (the Royal Opera Arcade, 1816–18).

With the new street completed, work began on the Marylebone (renamed Regent's) Park housing development, most of which was finished by 1830. Nash's original plan featured a lake and carefully placed clumps of trees, interspersed with detached villas. But in the end most of the housing took the form of terraces around the perimeter of the park, access to which was limited at first to residents but was later opened to the public. Regent's Park thus became a prototype of the picturesquely landscaped public parks which soon proliferated both in Britain and in the wider world (e.g. Central Park, New York). The terraces along the east, south, and western fringes, tenanted for the most part by wealthy City merchants and retired military officers, were given lavishly palatial stuccoed facades concealing what were in reality very ordinary brick structures. And on the Crown land to the east of the terraces Nash designed two other housing developments of a very different character. One (the Park Village) comprised stuccoed detached and semi-detached villas of a kind which were already becoming characteristic of middle-class suburbia; the other, to the south of Cumberland Basin—the termination of a branch of the Regent's Canal, of which Nash was a promoter—was an artisan community of small terraced houses grouped around squares, now replaced by blocks of flats.

King George IV, as he now was, decided in 1822 to abandon Carlton House in favour of a grandiose new palace to be built to Nash's designs around the mainly eighteenth-century Buckingham House—the former residence of his mother, Queen Charlotte—at the western end of St James's Park. This led to another spate of redevelopment master-minded by Nash himself. Carlton House was replaced by an open space (Waterloo Place) at the southern end of Regent Street, flanked on either side by gentlemen's club-houses designed in the newly fashionable Italianate *palazzo* manner. A Roman-inspired column surmounted by a statue of the King's brother the Duke of York, flanked by two magnificent stucco-fronted terraces of houses (Carlton House Terrace) overlooks St James's Park, newly laid out by Nash on Picturesque lines, with a curvaceous lake, clumps of trees and vistas of the Horse Guards in Whitehall at one end and the new Palace at the other. Finally, in 1826, legislation was passed to create another public space on the site of the Royal Mews at Charing Cross, with the eighteenth-century church of St Martin-in-the Fields opened up to view at its north-eastern corner. Nash's official career came to an end in 1830 amid Parliamentary criticisms of his handling of public finances, and the buildings around and within the new Trafalgar Square—notably the National Gallery and Nelson's Column, commemorating the naval hero of the Napoleonic Wars—were designed by other architects. But by then Nash had succeeded in transforming much of the western part of the rapidly expanding metropolis, and it is his vision that still shapes our perception of it today.

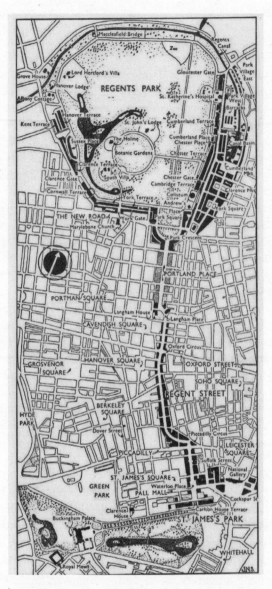

Fig. 5.7 A map of Regent's Park and Regent Street in London. Regents Park is at the top and St James's Park at the bottom, overlooked by Carlton House Terrace, with Buckingham Palace to the west (left) and Whitehall to the right. The new buildings surrounding the park, and along Regent Street, are shown in black.

HARMONIC INSTITUTION, REGENT STREET.

Fig. 5.8 A stretch of Regent Street, south of Oxford Circus, soon after completion. The nature of the clientele is indicated by the presence of wheeled vehicles and groups of well-dressed shoppers. The Argyll Rooms, a concert hall or 'Harmonic Institution' designed by John Nash, is on the left.

Resort Towns

Britain's economic success in the late eighteenth and early nineteenth centuries increased the demand for commercialized leisure. Dependent for their success on the pursuit of transient pleasure, resort towns had less settled populations than more conventional urban communities. The fashionable spa town of Cheltenham (Gloucestershire) is a case in point. The radical journalist William Cobbett denounced it in 1826 as 'a place to which East India plunderers, West India floggers, English tax-gorgers, together with gluttons, drunkards, and debauchees of all descriptions, female as well as male, resort, at the suggestion of silently laughing quacks, in the hope of getting rid of the bodily consequences of their manifold sins and iniquities.'[53] Before the eighteenth century it was an obscure market town, little more than a village, but springs were discovered at the south end of the main street,[54] and the first spa was inaugurated in 1738, reached by a public walk. People went there to drink the waters in the belief that they were good for internal disorders, but, as in many resort towns, it took a long time for large-scale urban development to get under way. The first master of ceremonies was not appointed until 1780, four years before the opening of Assembly Rooms in the High Street. A Paving (Improvement) Act followed in 1786, allowing the removal of the ramshackle old market house, the creation of pavements and the installation of 120 new street lamps.[55]

King George III visited the spa in 1788, when Fanny Burney was impressed by the 'long, clean and well-paved streets', but further development was held up by war with France. Another spring (Montpellier) was then discovered to the west of the main street, followed by a third (Sherbourne), approached by a public walk with a double row of trees which eventually became the Promenade.[56] The population quadrupled from 3,000 in 1801 to 13,000 in 1821: still relatively modest by the standards of Bath, but boosted by visits from the Prince Regent in 1806, and later by the Duke of Wellington. A tramway to import building materials (stone as well as stucco) was laid out in 1811, gas lighting was introduced in 1818, and piped water followed in 1824. There was no grand housing until the building of Royal Crescent in about 1806, but much more followed the passing of second Improvement Act in 1821, especially along the Promenade, which became the showpiece of the town, lined with stucco-fronted houses like those facing Regent's Park in London. It led to the Montpellier spa, which acquired a new pump room of its own in 1817, reached through an attractive row of shops with caryatids between the windows (Fig. 5.9). Meanwhile Joseph Pitt, a self-made lawyer and banker, employed the architect John Forbes to plan another residential development (Pittville) with its own Pump Room (1825–30) further north, flanked by villas for the growing number of permanent residents who soon supplanted the spa visitors as the main source of Cheltenham's wealth. Their life-style was supported by a service population inhabiting what Cobbett called 'very mean and shabby houses' that went up nearby. New churches proliferated, most of them Gothic in style and Evangelical in doctrine, together with boarding schools for such as the Ladies' College, founded in 1854 close to the first spa. This was a pattern of development followed by many spa towns, Bath included, as the nineteenth century went on.

Fig. 5.9 This row of shops in Montpellier Walk, Cheltenham, was begun in 1843 as part of the development of the land close to the adjacent Montpellier pump room, opened in 1819. Designed by the locally-based Jearrad brothers, the upper floor is faced in locally-quarried ashlar stone, but the shops have glazed frontages, separated by Grecian-style caryatids.

The growing popularity of sea bathing led to the growth of another type of resort town whose layout inevitably differed from that of inland towns like Cheltenham. The prototype British seaside resort was Scarborough, a medieval town that began to attract visitors to its recently discovered medicinal springs in the second half of the seventeenth century. But the most impressive example was Brighton.

Ports and Manufacturing Towns

The growth of overseas and coastal trade led to the rapid expansion of the ports on which the nation's growing commercial prosperity depended. Bristol and Glasgow profited from the exchange of goods and people across the Atlantic, Whitby, Hull and Great Yarmouth from the trade in coal and

Brighton

Before the eighteenth century Brighton was a small town on the English Channel contained within a rectangle of streets that housed some 4,000 people, many of whom made a living from fishing and seafaring activities. The population declined along with the fishing industry in the early years of the century, partly because of the lack of a harbour (the boats were launched from the pebbly beach). But in the 1730s the town began to profit from visitors, especially from London, attracted by easy access—by the 1750s the journey took less than a day by road—and also by the presence of a cross-channel ferry to Dieppe and, even more, by the bracing sea air. Brighton was already a flourishing resort town by 1752, when the Lewes physician Richard Russell published his famous treatise on the medicinal advantages of sea-bathing for diseases of the glands. The population, several of them lodging-house keepers, lived in narrow streets and alleys, now called the Lanes, bounded by West, North and East Streets; to the south was a 'cliff' overlooking the sea.[57] Medicinal baths, assembly rooms, theatres, circulating libraries, coffee houses and taverns went up around the periphery of the town, together with a racecourse on the Downs to the north. Then in 1786–7 the future Prince Regent took a house facing east onto the Steyne, an open space and public walk. By 1794 the population had risen to around 5,700, many of them involved in the service economy that supported the 10,000 or so annual visitors. By then pebble-built bow-fronted houses had already gone up in Pavilion Parade (c.1788), east of the Steyne,[58] and by 1808 a network of streets had been laid out on the rising ground still further east over what had been a common arable field called the Little Laine; it was divided into long, narrow strips of land or 'paul pieces' which determined the configuration of the streets.[59] They were lined with small houses built by developers, the sea-front sites being taken for larger houses, with a curved terrace row of fourteen houses (Royal Crescent) clad in 'mathematical tiles'—a Sussex speciality—going up between 1796 and 1805 overlooking the recently-created Marine Parade.[60]

In the years following the end of the Napoleonic Wars, when the town housed a large population of soldiers, Brighton grew faster than any other English town, doubling its numbers to nearly 25,000 between 1811 and 1821. The northern approach from London was improved under an Act of Parliament of 1810, and the Prince Regent's holiday home (the Pavilion) was transformed, both internally and externally, into a fantasy Oriental palace by that master architectural conjuror John Nash in 1815–22. It looked out onto the Steyne, which extended south to the sea front and the Chain Pier, built for ships crossing the Channel and immortalized in the paintings of John Constable—who came to stay in Brighton for the health of his consumptive wife[61]—and J. M. W. Turner. The Steyne was extended north in 1822–4, creating a linear garden in what soon became the centre of the town, with the Gothic St Peter's church, designed by the young

Charles Barry—one of the first of many impressive Anglican places of worship in the town—closing the vista to the north.

Brighton's growing popularity encouraged the lord of the manor, Thomas Read Kemp, and his architects Charles Busby and subsequently Amon and Henry Wilds, to lay out a large new housing development (Kemp Town) a mile or so to the east of Royal Crescent (Fig. 5.10). Work started in 1825 around a semicircular crescent of stuccoed houses overlooking a garden on the sea front, extended on either side by terraces facing the sea. Meanwhile in Hove, on the western edge of Brighton, the Rev. Thomas Scutt oversaw an equally grandiose, and equally successful, development (Brunswick Town) made up of long terraces, their display of classical columns and pilasters reminiscent of those in contemporary St Petersburg.[62] These developments gave Brighton a novel layout which in time came to characterize all British seaside resorts, with the grandest houses, most of them only occupied for some of the year, strung out along the sea front, service roads behind them, lined with smaller houses and shops, and middle-class villas on the hillside behind.

Fig. 5.10 Lewes Crescent is part of the Kemp Town development on the east side of Brighton, laid out by the Wild brothers and Charles Busby, starting in 1823. The stuccoed houses form part of a semicircle looking out onto a garden for the occupants of the houses, with the sea beyond. The furthest house was bought by the sixth Duke of Devonshire in 1829.

agricultural produce around the east coast of the British Isles, and to the Continent. In Liverpool, the leading transatlantic port, the straight, shop-lined Bold Street—'the Bond Street of the North'[63]—was laid out on the rising ground to the south-east of the town in the 1780s; it led to a burst of speculative house-building in what soon became an affluent hilltop suburb with long, wide streets of plain, well-proportioned terraced brick houses like those in Rodney Street, where the future Prime Minister William Ewart Gladstone, son of a Liverpool merchant, was born (at No. 62) in 1796. The early nineteenth-century boom in the cotton trade gave rise to further expansion of the docks, and to the construction of handsome new public buildings. By 1841 the population had risen to some 286,000, due in part to immigration from an increasingly impoverished Ireland, but this meant that some of the central area and, even more, its immediate periphery, degener-ated into slums, leaving a noxious legacy for future generations.

Britain's overseas trade ultimately rested on naval power. By 1800 Portsmouth and Devonport, a satellite of Plymouth, already had large work-shops and factories organized according to a strict division of labour; they were in many ways Britain's first modern factory towns. Devonport's dock-yard, on a sheltered, easily defensible site at the mouth of the River Tamar (or Hamoaze) was first planned during the reign of King William III in 1698, and an embryonic new settlement grew up to the north and east, around what Defoe called a 'very handsome street, spacious and large'.[64] The town was later developed in a grid-like fashion to fill the unoccupied space within the dockyard's fortifications. Further east, on a promontory between Devonport and Plymouth proper, was the village of Stonehouse, which grew behind its own defensive wall, with a north-south street (Durnford St) laid out in 1773 and lined with terraced houses, and the Royal Marine Barracks 1779–85 at the northern end.[65] Further north was the Royal Naval Hospital, built on an innovative 'pavilion' plan around a court-yard.[66] In 1812–20 the local architect John Foulston laid out Union Street to link Plymouth to Stonehouse and Devonport, where he went on in 1821–4 to design a civic centre of which the Grecian Guildhall, the neo-Egyptian Athenaeum and a commemorative Doric column are the sole survivors (Fig. 5.11). Finally, in 1825–33 the Royal William Victualling Yard went up to the designs of John Rennie next to the harbour at the southern end of the Stonehouse peninsula. One of the most impressive architectural ensembles of the time, for most of its life it was an enclosed town within a town, but now, following the decimation of Britain's armed forces, it has been turned over to housing, shops and restaurants.[67]

Fig. 5.11 The civic centre of Devonport featured a disparate group of buildings put up in 1821-4 to the designs of the local architect John Foulston, who also laid out Union Street, linking the dockyard town to Plymouth. The Town Hall is entered through an arcade of Greek Doric columns. To the right is a commemorative Doric column, a Gothic chapel (since demolished) and an Atheneum (meeting hall) in the Egyptian style. The area suffered badly from bombing in the Second World War, and subsequently fell into decrepitude from which it has slowly emerged in recent years.

Portsmouth is another city that developed as a group of distinct townships before coalescing in the early nineteenth century (Fig. 5.12). The Royal Dockyard grew up well to the north of the old town towards the end of the seventeenth century, enclosed at first by a wooden fence and in 1704-11 by a high brick wall; Daniel Defoe thought that the docks and yards were 'like a town by themselves'.[68] By then over 1,900 people worked there, their number doubling by 1814.[69] Housing was provided for the yard officials and senior officers, but most of the employees had to live outside the walls. That explains the growth of Portsea, developed from 1702 as 'a kind of suburb, or rather a new town', as Defoe described it, to the south and east of the yard. The parallel streets of small houses, erected piecemeal in twos or threes by builders on parcels of land sold by the original owners to local tradesmen, followed the lines of the strips in Old Dock Field, and there were no significant public buildings, save for the modest brick church of St George (1753-4).[70]

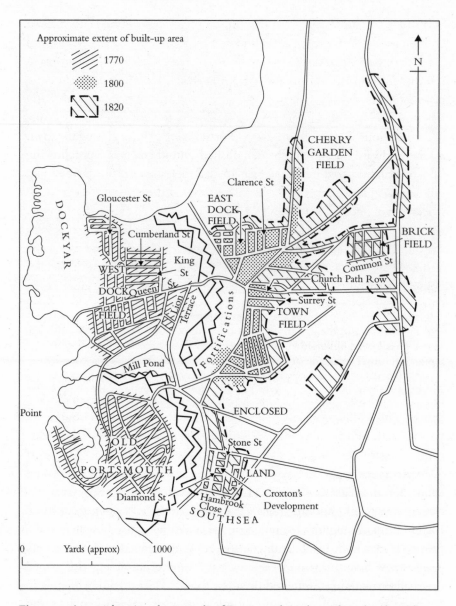

Fig. 5.12 A map showing the growth of Portsmouth in the 18th and early 19th centuries. A series of discrete townships grew up around the medieval town (Old Portsmouth) in response to the needs of the Royal Navy. Mill Pond separates the Old Town from the Royal Dockyard to the north. Portsea was built over the former West Dock Field in the 18th century, protected on the landward side by fortifications that were gradually strengthened. The present city centre, originally the township of Landport, grew up in the late 18th and early 19th centuries over East Dock Field and Town Field. Another township, Southsea, was begun in the 1820s on land further south belonging to Thomas Croxton, a local businessman.

By 1773 the streets had extended south over common land to the walled Gunwharf, an ordnance establishment on either side of the Mill Pond (later drained), north of the old harbour; the site has recently been turned into an ambitious housing and shopping development (p. 299), but the plain brick Ordnance Office of the 1770s and the impressive, and partly rebuilt, Storehouse, begun in 1811, were allowed to survive.[71] A second line of fortifications went up to the east of Portsea after 1770, enclosing the town on the landward side, only to be demolished a hundred years later following the construction of a new set of up-to-date defences on the surrounding hills and artificial islands out at sea. The site was then given over to open spaces and barracks, beyond which a third 'new town' (Landport) had begun to emerge by 1800, subsequently becoming Portsmouth's main administrative and commercial centre, with terraces of brick houses going up for the middle classes, in one of which Charles Dickens was born in 1812. Smaller houses were built for the working-class population, and shops lined Commercial Street, leading northwards. A fourth settlement, Southsea, grew up somewhat later to the east of the old town, beyond which was a stretch of common land, drained later in the nineteenth century, when it acquired a pier and other appurtenances of a seaside resort.

In 1700 Britain was already a major participant in a nascent globalized economy; by 1830 it had become the world's leading industrial and trading nation. This could not have happened without transport improvements, starting with improved river navigations and, from the middle of the eighteenth century, the digging of new canals. The small town of Stourport (Worcestershire) was created at the point where the Staffordshire and Worcestershire Canal, opened in 1771, disgorged into the River Severn, carrying goods to and from the rapidly industrializing Black Country, north of Birmingham, and killing off much of the trade of nearby Bewdley in the process. A distinctive watery townscape grew up here over the next forty years as new basins were created, lined with warehouses, along with a hotel originally containing a hundred beds; the town was described in 1813 as an 'emporium of river navigation'.[72] Rows of modest red-brick houses and shops went up meanwhile alongside the two wide main thoroughfares, and by 1810 the population had risen to 2,532.

Another distinctive type of industrial landscape grew up in the textile-manufacturing districts of the north of England and in Scotland. Textiles had always been an important part of the British urban economy, but the scale of production now increased hugely. Until the last years of the eighteenth

'City of a Thousand Trades'

The 'toyshop of Europe', as it was sometimes called, Birmingham was already the entrepot of a rapidly industrializing area by the beginning of the eighteenth century, when a middle-class suburb went up on a hilltop to the west of the old town centre, close to the new church of St Philip (now the Cathedral). The population doubled from the 1740s to the 1780s, but the further development of the economy was constrained by the lack of a navigable waterway. The first canal, from Wednesbury, to the north, was opened in 1770, and the system was subsequently extended by branches leading in all directions, creating a novel landscape of narrow waterways mounting hills on flights of locks. By the early twentieth century there were 159 miles of canal, with 216 locks.[73] Crossed by brick, stone and iron bridges, and interrupted by lock-gates, their impact on the landscape became even more distinctive with the establishment of steam-powered factories on their banks; a two-mile stretch of canal between Bordesley and Aston already had 124 wharves and works lining its bank before the first railway arrived in the city in the 1830s.

Birmingham owed its prosperity to the success of its metal industries. Its population doubled again from 1781 to 1801, when there were 73,670 inhabitants, and it had expanded to 101,532 by 1821, when it was the third largest provincial town in England. Expansion initially took place on the well-drained ground of the plateau which now forms the city centre, and by 1780 housing had spread north over a grid of streets on the Newhall estate, belonging to the Colmore family, and north-west to the Birmingham and Fazeley Canal, opened in 1783. At the centre is a square surrounding the church of St Paul, opened in 1779, and overlooked by substantial red-brick houses (Fig. 5.13). They were constructed on building leases, allowing a measure of control over facades and the width of streets, and building subsequently spread north and west beyond the canal. The resident middle-class population moved away during the nineteenth century, when the district was largely given over to the small factories and workshops of what became known as the Jewellery Quarter. Their premises occupied, or superseded, most of the houses, and extended over the former garden plots to create a dense industrial landscape that survives virtually intact.[74]

The low-lying alluvial soil to the west and south of the city-centre plateau was developed in a less organized fashion. The canals here, some of them now restored as places for pleasure-boating after years of commercial neglect, created a hidden landscape invisible from the main streets, though accessible to pedestrians following the towpaths. The landowners, including the Gooch family who owned much of the land to the south and east of the Gas Street canal basin, sold the land piecemeal to developers, who put up densely packed houses to accommodate the rapidly growing numbers of poor, badly paid immigrants who supplied the labour force for the town's workshops and service industries. Many were constructed back-to-back around narrow, fetid courts, and a handful still survive at the corner of Hurst and Inge Streets (Fig. 5.14) beyond the modern inner ring road just south of the city centre. A plot of land here was leased by the Gooch family in 1789 to a toymaker who built workshops on the site; the eleven brick houses, each of three storeys, and each one room deep, comprise what was known as Court 15—now restored and maintained by the National Trust—built between 1802 and 1830, and reached from the street through an arched tunnel.[75]

Fig. 5.13 St Paul's Square, Birmingham, formed part of the Newhall estate, laid out on a grid plan to the north of the existing town in the 18th century. St Paul's church was designed by a Wolverhampton architect, Roger Eykin in 1777-9; the tower and spire were added in 1822-3. The brick houses surrounding the open space were turned into workshops in the 19th century, their gardens gradually colonised by industrial buildings.

Fig. 5.14 Back-to-back housing was a way of accommodating England's rapidly expanding urban population on densely-packed inner-city sites. These brick houses in Birmingham were built in the early 19th century, each consisting of three rooms one above the other, the top room serving as a workshop for domestic industry (originally the manufacture of toys). The narrow archway leads to Court 15, with a communal water supply, toilet facilities and (originally) more houses.

century cloth was still produced on the domestic system, using yarn 'put out' by merchant clothiers and spun in the cottages of farm workers spread out over the countryside before being woven into cloth on looms within the homes of weavers in the larger villages and towns. This method of production, requiring relatively little capital investment, lay behind the prosperity of towns such as Norwich, Exeter and Leeds, where the leading merchants lived, and from which the cloth was marketed. Larger purpose-built markets were needed in the West Riding of Yorkshire when production increased in the second half of the century. They included the White Cloth Hall in Leeds, built in 1775–6 and containing no fewer than 1,210 stalls, and the Piece Hall in Halifax (Fig. 5.15), one of the most impressive structures

Fig. 5.15 Piece Hall, Halifax, is a monument to the West Riding woolen industry. The buildings around the courtyard were occupied by handloom weavers; the 'pieces' (lengths of cloth) were sold to buyers on Saturday mornings. Following the demise of handloom weaving, killed off by factory production from the 1820s onwards, the buildings became a wholesale food market, and, starting in 1976, they were restored. They now house art outlets, shops and cafes.

of its kind anywhere in Britain, constructed at a cost of £12,000 in 1775–8 around an open galleried enclosure with 315 separate rooms in which individual clothiers plied their trade.[76]

In the second half of eighteenth century spinning, formerly exclusively carried out in people's homes, began to be concentrated in factories driven by water power, one of the first of which was John and Thomas Lombe's silk mill at Derby (1717–18) since burned down and rebuilt. Most of these early factories were established in rural or semi-rural settings where fast-running streams could supply a sufficient head of water for the wheels that powered the spinning machines and later the weaving looms. In order to attract a workforce, factory villages developed, such Robert Owen's model settlement at New Lanark, 28 miles south-west of Glasgow, and Cromford in Derbyshire, which housed some of the two hundred workers at Richard Arkwright's pioneering cotton-spinning mill, begun in 1771. It was Arkwright who built the largely unaltered North Street at Cromford, one of the first streets of planned factory workers' houses, in 1771–6; three-storeys high and one room deep, they have continuous top-floor windows, like those of the weavers' houses in Spitalfields in London, to allow the maximum daylight for the looms.

Some water-powered factories were built on the edges of existing towns. They include the four-storeyed Park Green silk mill at Macclesfield (Cheshire), built in 1785, with a clock in the central pediment and large windows giving maximum lighting. But it was not until the application of steam power, starting in the 1790s, that factory production of textiles decisively shifted to towns, where the rapidly expanding populations supplied an easy reserve of cheap labour.

Cottonopolis

The new urban landscape of large steam-powered textile factories was first seen in Manchester, the 'centre of control' of the Lancashire cotton industry since the middle of the seventeenth century.[77] By 1800 it was already the second largest town in Britain, with a population of over 94,000, rising to over 300,000 by 1841.[78] Expansion took place through a series of housing developments to the south and east of the medieval core, landowners anticipating demand by selling off or leasing parcels of land on which streets were laid out, generally grid-fashion, by speculative builders: a pattern of development paralleling that in Liverpool and Birmingham, both of which had also grown rapidly from small and relatively unimportant beginnings. St Ann's Square was laid out to the south of the old town centre in 1720, and further development took place after the mid-century as waterborne communications improved, with the River Irwell navigation improving access to the River Mersey (1736) and the Bridgewater Canal (1759–65) providing a link to nearby coalfields;[79] its basin was at Castlefield, further south on the site of a Roman settlement. Plain brick merchants' houses went up along Deansgate, a long straight thoroughfare leading south from the town centre to Castlefield quay,[80] and also in Mosley Street, laid out in the 1780s on land belonging to the lords of the manor.[81] By the early nineteenth century some of the houses were being replaced by classically-inspired, stone-clad public buildings such as the Portico Library, designed by Thomas Harrison of Chester (1802–6), and Charles Barry's Royal Institution, now the City Art Gallery (1824–35), both of them in Mosley Street. Later, in 1836–9, Barry turned to the Italianate style of his London clubs for the adjacent Athenaeum, containing a lecture room, meeting rooms and a library (now an annexe to the art gallery). Together with the Exchange (since rebuilt) and banks and insurance offices, these buildings formed part of what later became the city's central business district, devoted largely to the financing and marketing of the raw materials and products of the cotton industry as it achieved worldwide supremacy. And as this happened growing numbers of the more prosperous residents moved to the suburbs.

At Ancoats meanwhile, a rural hamlet north of the town centre, a grid of streets was laid out at the end of the eighteenth century on open ground sold by the Legh family.[82] Canals to Rochdale and Ashton-under-Lyne, two of the textile towns within Manchester's economic orbit, were opened in 1799 and 1804, and their banks were soon lined by engineering works, glass foundries, warehouses and steam-powered cotton factories, the first of which dated from 1797 (Fig. 5.16). These massive structures were the main features of a novel urban landscape that both fascinated and appalled contemporaries, among them the German architect Karl von Schinkel, who made drawings of some of the mills when he visited Manchester in 1826.[83] Densely-packed back-to-back houses soon followed in order to house the workforce, many of them immigrants from Ireland (45 per cent of the total population by 1841); some had workshops on the top floor and many had cellars beneath, in which the poorest inhabitants were obliged to live for lack of other affordable accommodation. The small builders responsible for constructing these damp, gloomy dwellings used borrowed money, which they (ideally) paid back by selling the houses and investing what remained of the profit after paying off loans, in order to build more. Developments of this kind left a legacy that posed a seemingly insoluble problem for reformers and philanthropists for the rest of the nineteenth century and beyond.

Fig. 5.16 A cotton mill at Ancoats in inner Manchester. The new urban landscape of the Industrial Revolution first emerged with the building of steam-powered cotton factories in and around Manchester in the early 19th century. The buildings shown here went up alongside the Rochdale Canal, opened in 1799. They were built around iron frames, with brick frontages and tall chimneys for the smoke escaping from the steam engines that powered the looms.

6

Worktown

Alexis de Tocqueville was both fascinated and appalled by Manchester when he went there in 1835. 'Everything in the exterior appearance of the city', he declared, 'attests the individual powers of man; nothing the directing power of society. At every turn human liberty shows its capricious creative force. There is no trace of the slow continuous action of government'. He drew attention to the shocking environmental consequences of rapid industrialization: 'From this foul drain the greatest stream of human industry flows out to fertilize the whole world. From this filthy sewer pure gold flows. Here humanity attains its most complete development and its most brutish; here civilization works its miracles, and civilized man is turned back almost into a savage'.[1] His insights still resonate today as cities continue to expand worldwide.

The Industrial Landscape

Before the eighteenth century large-scale manufacturing made a relatively limited impact on the urban landscape. Most industrial production was small-scale by later standards, goods often being produced or finished in domestic workshops. Heavy industry, as we now understand it, arrived in Britain with the application of coke to iron-smelting, first in the rural setting of Coalbrookdale on the banks of the River Severn, where the small town of Ironbridge (Shropshire) grew up after the opening of the world's first iron bridge in 1780. By 1800 five ironworks had opened up at the head of the River Taf in the South Wales hills, and here a new town, Merthyr Tydfil, grew up virtually from nothing, its population expanding to 46,000 by the middle of the nineteenth century.[2] Then, starting in the 1790s, came

the application of steam power to cotton factories, enabling large-scale
production to move from the countryside to the fringes of Lancashire towns
(see pp. 170–2). Massive eight-or nine storeyed buildings now went up with
tall chimneys belching out smoke (Fig. 6.1): a sight that conjured up visions
of a man-made inferno to artists and writers. They included the young
Friedrich Engels, whose father owned cotton factories in Manchester; he
went on in 1845 to write *The Condition of the Working Class in England*, one
of the key texts both of Marxism and of British social history. Powered by
massive immigration from the countryside, and from Ireland, Manchester's
population grew more than fivefold in the first sixty years of the century. By
then over half the population of Britain was living in towns; by 1901 that
proportion had risen to four fifths, many of them living in conurbations
grouped around dominant centres such as Manchester, Birmingham,
Newcastle, Glasgow and—largest of all—London.[3]

Fig. 6.1 Bolton was a major centre of the Lancashire cotton industry, with a
population of over 82,000 by 1851. This panoramic view of 1848, by a local artist,
shows the effect of industrialization on the surroundings of the historic town.
Factories are interspersed with terraces of small houses, the smoke from their tall
chimneys polluting the atmosphere, as was it to do for the next century.

Textile factories grew ever larger, their environmental impact increasing as export markets expanded. By 1900 Oldham, north-east of Manchester, had 300 cotton mills, many of them built on a vast scale to the designs of specialist architects such as the Manchester-based Stott family; a survey taken in 1914–15 estimated that their smokestacks deposited an astonishing 960 tons of soot per square mile on the town.[4] Massive woollen mills went up in West Yorkshire towns like Bradford, Huddersfield and Halifax; in its heyday the Dean Clough Mills at Halifax, mostly dating from 1842–57, employed 5,000 people engaged in the manufacture of carpets.[5] Some of these leviathans, including the Dean Clough Mills, survived the near-collapse of the British textile industry in the later twentieth century and have been turned to new uses; others have been demolished, or lie derelict, their tall chimneys still towering above the surrounding housing or post-industrial wastelands.

Towns developed their own industrial specializations. Mid-nineteenth-century Dundee had the largest linen and jute mills in the world. Macclesfield—one of the first textile mill towns—specialized in silk, Leicester in hosiery, Nottingham in lace and Luton (Bedfordshire) in straw hats. Coventry, one of the most important towns in late medieval England, reinvented itself as a centre for ribbon-making, some of it carried out in 'cottage workshops' powered by central steam engines.[6] East London, with its vast and swelling population, remained for many years an outpost of domestic clothing (as opposed to cloth) manufacture, with legions of women employed to stitch garments on a piecework basis, like their modern counterparts in Bangladesh and China.[7] Most industrial production took place outside town and city centres. By the middle of the century large areas on the fringe of Birmingham and Sheffield had been colonised by workshops for the metal trades, usually built behind houses: Birmingham's Jewellery Quarter (see p. 166) is still a thriving centre of artisan production and marketing. Such areas were different in character from mill towns like Bolton (Lancashire)—the original 'Worktown' of the 1930s Mass Observation project—with their mammoth textile factories employing hundreds of people apiece. Yet even in Manchester, the cotton metropolis par excellence, only a minority of the labour force worked in large factories; most found employment in smaller workshops, or in the innumerable warehousing, marketing and service occupations found in all large towns both then and now.[8]

Industries became more highly capitalized as the nineteenth century went on, and, as they did, factories grew larger. In Sheffield, today the fifth largest city in England, the steel industry, devoted *inter alia* to the production of cutlery, edged tools and steel plating, had always been dominated by 'little mesters' (small masters). Some of their workshops were situated behind the street frontages of the town centre; others grew up to the south of the confluence of the Rivers Don and Sheaf, or outside the built-up area like the Abbeydale 'hamlet', now an industrial museum, on its riverside site. With the opening of the town's first canal in 1819, linking the River Don to the rest of the inland waterway network, larger firms expanded into new steam-powered factories. Many of them were built on the banks of the River Don, like the Globe cutlery works (1825) and the Green Lane Works for the manufacture of iron grates and fenders, its handsome classical façade of 1860 leading into a workshop courtyard.[9] Housing grew up meanwhile close to the factories, giving the city something of the character of a confederation of industrial villages. Its population tripled between 1810 and 1850, and it tripled again in the second half of the century as heavy industry, in the form of huge steel factories using the Bessemer process, spread east along the Don Valley, new complexes of housing growing up in their wake.

Domestic industries gradually became concentrated into factories in the second half of the nineteenth century. Workforces, especially from the 1870s onwards, were reinforced by immigrants fleeing an agricultural depression caused by cheap imports of foodstuffs from abroad: a delayed result of the Government's free trade policy enacted when the protectionist Corn Laws were repealed in 1846. Domestic workshops for the boot and shoe industry in Northampton and its surrounding small towns were gradually supplanted by three-storeyed brick factories located among streets of newly-built brick-built terraced houses on the fringe of town centres (Fig. 6.2).[10] As time went on, boot and shoe factories grew larger; the Co-operative Wholesale Society's Wheatsheaf shoe works in Leicester was the largest footwear factory in the world when it was opened in 1891, employing a workforce of 3000.[11] And, with the advent of electricity and motor transport, factories for consumer goods began to migrate from polluted inner cities to more salubrious industrial estates further away from town centres: a process that gathered momentum between the two World Wars (see pp. 272–3, 297).

Another distinctive landscape developed in the coal-mining valleys of South Wales from the 1860s onwards. Linear towns, with terraces of mainly two-storeyed houses put up piecemeal by small builders, grew up along the steep slopes of the valleys (Fig. 6.4), dotted with shops and Nonconformist

Fig. 6.2 These boot and shoe workshops, built in the 1870s and 80s, went up to the north-east of Northampton's town centre in response to a growing demand for ready-made shoes. The Hawkins factory, at the junction of St Michael's Road and Overstone Road, was built of brick in 1886 to the designs of a local architect, Charles Dorman, and is typical of many such buildings put up by small family-run businesses in Midland towns.

chapels, also an important feature of the Potteries towns. But their most distinctive feature was the metal winding gear for the lifts conveying the workers down to the underworld of the pits, and conical slag heaps for the waste, now all but vanished following the collapse of the industry in the late twentieth century. One ten-mile-long conurbation grew up in the Rhondda valley, with its fifty collieries and no fewer than 150 chapels; the number of houses, almost all occupied by miners and small shopkeepers, rose tenfold to 26,250 between 1871 and 1911.[12] Most of the coal from the valleys was taken by rail to Cardiff Bay, where a complex of docks was created, starting in the 1830s. A new industrial suburb, Bute Town, grew up here, a mile or so to the south of the existing town, servicing the docks from which coal from was dispatched across the world, supplying the power for, *inter alia*, railway loco-motives and steamships.[13]

The Potteries

One of the most distinctive urban landscapes emerged in the Potteries of north Staffordshire. Here the manufacture of ceramics expanded after the opening of the Trent and Mersey Canal in 1777, stimulated by a growing demand for high-quality tableware, seen as an essential accompaniment of polite living. The most striking feature of the new landscape was the proliferation of independent workshops with their brick-built, coal-fired, bottle-shaped ovens. They were grouped within and around six townships strung out along a coal formation to the east of the long-established market town of Newcastle-under-Lyme. Some of these settlements were newly formed, like Stoke, where a central square was laid out, starting in 1847, in front of the handsome Neo-Jacobean railway station; others, such as Burslem, were expanded villages or hamlets. Each retained its administrative independence until their amalgamation as the city of Stoke-on-Trent in 1910, and each retained its own distinctive identity afterwards.

At first the relatively small elite of successful factory owners lived close to their works; an elegant mid-eighteenth-century classical villa built by John and Thomas Wedgwood still survives close to the Market Place at Burslem. But, with the population of the six townships tripling to 63,000 in the first forty years of the nineteenth century (and expanding to 234,000 by 1900), such houses were swamped by speculative terraces of two-roomed, and latterly two-up and two-down, brick-built cottages. They went up within walking distance of the factories, some of which, like the Fountain Works in Burslem (1789: now flats), advertised their existence, and their wares, by their elegant classical facades. A writer in the *Monthly Magazine* (1823) drew attention to the contrast between 'meanness and magnificence... the humble hut of the artisan stands in immediate contrast with the palace of his employer, and splendid mansions rise their heads amid the sulphurous fumes and vapours of the reeking potworks'.[14] The works themselves were usually laid out around courtyards; a particularly impressive group of bottle-ovens has been preserved at the restored Gladstone Works in Longton, built in the 1850s and there is a largely-unaltered complex of workshops (save for the demolition of all but one of its bottle-ovens) at the still-functioning canal-side Middleport Pottery at Burslem (1889, Fig. 6.3).[15] By the end of the century most of the factory-owners had moved to more salubrious surroundings, but the distinctive townscape of potworks and terraced housing, often obscured by a pall of smoke, survived with relatively few changes until the second half of the twentieth century, when technological change led to the demolition of most of the workshops and bottle-ovens. Today the conurbation faces an uncertain post-industrial future.

Fig. 6.3 The Middleport works at Burslem, one of the six townships of the Potteries, were built after the Burgess and Leigh business, founded in 1851, moved to a new site alongside the Trent and Mersey Canal in 1889. The buildings survive largely intact and are still used for making pottery. They contain one of the original bottle-ovens and the chimney of the steam engine that powered the machinery in the workshops.

Exports of coal and manufactured goods were balanced by imports of food for a population that rose from sixteen to forty-three million between 1831 and 1911. New docks and granaries were needed for wheat imported in greater and greater quantities from the American and Canadian prairies. Few of the buildings were as idiosyncratic as the multi-storeyed granary designed on Welsh Back in Bristol for the firm of Wait, James & Co. in 1869–7, its brick façade, richly ornamented in an Italianate Gothic manner, framing the open grilles needed to allow the grain to dry. Starting in the 1880s, refrigerated steamships ensured that meat and dairy products could also flood into the country from South America and Australasia, fuelling the further expansion of ports. Some ports, especially on the east coast, specialized in the import and processing of fish, an increasingly important part of the diet for the growing population. At Grimsby (Lincolnshire), a town of medieval origin close to the mouth of the River Humber, a new dock was opened in 1857, followed in 1863 by an ice plant. The port was the fifth largest in Britain by 1865, its prestige marked by a 309 foot-high brick tower

Fig. 6.4 Terraces of houses at Ferndale in the Rhondda valley in South Wales. The houses were built of local stone for coal miners and their families, and are aligned along the steep valley slopes. They were interspersed with Nonconformist chapels, two of which can be seen in this photograph.

inspired by the campanile of the medieval Palazzo Pubblico in Siena; it was put up in 1851–2 as part of a hydraulic system designed to open lock gates. By the beginning of the twentieth century 165,000 tons of fish were being imported through the port each year,[16] and distributed by rail to retailers and fish-and-chip shops across the country.

The per capita consumption of alcoholic drinks peaked in the early twentieth century,[17] their production increasingly concentrated in large breweries. There were thirty breweries in Burton-on-Trent (Staffordshire) by 1880, supplying a quarter of all the beer sold in Britain; it was exported across the country by rail, and in bottled form across the British Empire. Breweries also made a significant impact on small towns like Tadcaster (Yorkshire) and Devizes (Wiltshire), both of them still functioning. Brakspear's brewery at Henley-on-Thames spread in the nineteenth century over a site between New Street, laid out in the thirteenth century, and the medieval parish church. Malt is essential for brewing, and the four-storeyed maltings at Henley, with their characteristic pyramidal roofline surmounted by tall air vents, went up in 1899 on the opposite site of the street: part of what was once a small-scale industrial quarter that could be matched in many country towns.[18]

Warehouses were an essential component of the new urban landscape. Shad Thames, on the south bank of the Thames in London, to the east of Tower Bridge, is lined with tall rows of brick-clad warehouses, originally for storing tea (and now turned into expensive flats), linked by iron bridges on either side of a narrow street. Albert Dock at Liverpool, laid out on reclaimed land by the port authority's engineer Jesse Hartley in 1843–7, is surrounded by bonded warehouses of brick, the floors resting on cast-iron beams (Fig. 6.5). Goods from overseas destined for re-export, such as coffee, tea, sugar and tobacco, could be stored in such places without paying customs duties; the goods themselves were manhandled by armies of casual labourers hired by the day at the dock gates, a system memorably described by Henry Mayhew in his *London Labour and the London Poor* (1851). Liverpool's docks

Fig. 6.5 Liverpool's Albert Dock was built on land reclaimed from the River Mersey. The arcades of the five iron-framed warehouses have arcades at ground level resting on hollow cast-iron Doric columns; the piers supporting the basement vaults rest upon wooden piles. The Anglican cathedral, designed by Giles Gilbert Scott and completed in 1978, can be seen between two warehouse blocks on the left. The dock was closed in 1972, and the buildings were later restored as an arts and retail complex by the Merseyside Development Corporation.

later spread north and south along what had been the sand dunes fronting the Mersey, cutting the city almost completely from its waterfront, an effect enhanced by the long-closed overhead railway which ran above the main north-south road. Stanley Dock, connected to the Leeds and Liverpool Canal, has a thirteen-storeyed tobacco warehouse of c.1897–1901, and massive bonded warehouses for tobacco were built likewise at Bristol in 1906–19 alongside a new cut of the River Avon.

Railways transformed urban landscapes everywhere, their cuttings carved through hillsides, their viaducts leaping over river valleys (Fig. 6.6), dwarfing homes and workplaces: an effect memorably evoked by the French artist Gustav Doré in his much-reproduced image 'Over London – by rail'.[19] Engine sheds, goods yards and warehouses created industrial enclaves close to railway termini on the fringes of built-up areas, such as that adjoining the

Fig. 6.6 The railway viaduct shown in this atmospheric photograph of the 1950s was built in 1839-40 to carry the Manchester and Birmingham Railway across the valley of the River Mersey at Stockport. The designer was George Watson Buck, whose career began with the design of canal aqueducts. Stockport grew rapidly as a cotton manufacturing town in the early 19th century, and the picture shows some of the mills with their tall chimneys.

Manchester terminus of the Liverpool and Manchester Railway (1830), the first line to link two major cities.[20]

New single-industry towns later grew up next to railway locomotive and carriage factories at Swindon (Wiltshire) and Crewe (Cheshire). Railway works also came to dominate large areas of older towns with important junctions or termini, such as Doncaster, York and Derby. This process gathered momentum in the second half of the century as companies, unrestrained by centralized State planning, competed for customers. The building of the Midland Railway's St Pancras terminus in London in 1866–76, just to the north of the eighteenth-century New Road (see p. 153), displaced an estimated 32,000 people from the working-class districts of Somers Town and Agar Town. Together with the Great Northern Railway's adjacent terminus at Kings Cross, it created a vast wedge of land entirely given over to goods and coal yards, sidings, warehouses and engine sheds (Fig. 6.7),[21] now (2021) being expensively redeveloped as a cultural and office quarter. And at Liverpool Street (1873–5, extended 1892–4) the eagerness of the Great Eastern Railway to deposit its commuting passengers as close as possible to the offices and banks of the City led to the building of a huge cutting through the existing urban fabric, displacing, along with the adjacent Broad Street station of the North London Railway, yet more people.[22] Countless others throughout the country lost their homes to railway building. As late as the 1890s, five hundred houses were demolished in Leicester to make way for the new London extension (since closed) of the Great Central Railway. Some of the inhabitants were rehoused in a new housing development begun in 1885 on former market-gardening land at Newfoundpool on the western side of the River Soar;[23] cut off from the city centre by railway yards, viaducts and the factories and workshops beside them, it was typical of many working-class suburbs that grew up at the end of the nineteenth century (see pp. 259–261).

As cities grew, so too did the need for better public services. Street lighting by gas was already common by 1830, and gas, produced from coal, later began to be supplied to homes for heating and cooking. Gasworks were usually situated close to rivers or canals; the railway landscape of Kings Cross and St Pancras in London was, and still is, overlooked by a group of gasholders for the Imperial Gas Light and Coke Company, first constructed in 1860–7 and recently adapted for an expensive housing scheme. Piped water, formerly available to only a minority of the urban population, now began to be supplied from reservoirs newly established on the edge of

Fig. 6.7 The building of railway termini and their associated engine sheds and warehouses transformed many areas around the fringes of 19th-century town and city centres. The Great Northern Railway's Kings Cross station (1851-2: right) and the Midland Railway's St Pancras (1866-8: centre) face the 'New Road', London's first by-pass road. The extravagantly Gothic Midland Hotel in front of St Pancras station was built in 1868-74 to the designs of George Gilbert Scott and conceals the functional train shed of iron and glass. Gasholders can be seen at the top of the picture, and to the left is the freight yard, site of the present British Library, opened in 1997.

built-up areas; by 1885 Oxford's waterworks were supplying two million gallons a day, and all the city's houses were supplied with mains water, a major precondition for improved living standards.[24] Another prerequisite was better sanitation. The need for improved drainage, sewerage and waste disposal was highlighted by well-publicized epidemics and, even more, by the discovery of the mortal danger posed by the siting of water pumps close to outdoor lavatories. The establishment of the Metropolitan Board of Works in London in 1855 made it possible to create a coherent system of outfall sewers pumped into purification beds before being disgorged into the Thames well to the east of the city, as at the Abbey Mills pumping station (1865–8), a lavishly decorated cathedral of sanitation. The northern and southern outfall sewers were constructed for much of their length on reclaimed land alongside the Thames, allowing for the creation of public gardens, opened in 1870, and a roadway (the Victoria Embankment) on the north side of the river between Westminster and Blackfriars Bridges. An underground railway, now part of the District and Circle Lines, was constructed beneath it as part of a scheme to ease congestion through the crowded streets and to cut journey times: a coherent system of infrastructural improvement which permanently changed the public face of the capital.

Housing the Workers

As the urban population grew, unprecedented numbers of often desperately poor people had to be housed quickly and cheaply in accommodation within walking distance from their workplaces. The demand was especially pressing in the 1820s and 1830s; in Manchester and Liverpool, where the population density was twice that of London, many of the newcomers were forced to live in attic rooms or cellars of existing houses.[25] Others moved into cheaply-built new housing on empty ground in town and city centres or in their immediate periphery. By 1832, according to Joseph Kay, the opulent merchants of Manchester had already moved away from the city centre, freeing it for commerce and leaving the surrounding area to the working class and the shopkeepers who catered for their needs:[26] a world that was later unsentimentally described in Robert Roberts's *The Classic Slum* (1971). The resulting social segregation became more marked as factories proliferated around the urban fringe. The notorious slum known as 'Little Ireland' to the south of Manchester grew up close to factories built on the low-lying ground within a loop of the River Medlock (Fig. 6.8). Cut off from the central commercial district by a railway line opened in 1849, it soon became a byword for urban squalor.[27] So too did Ancoats (see p. 171) where the streets remained unpaved and lacking sewerage until the 1840s; as late as 1865 nineteen per cent of families there were living in one room. A housing report of 1884 pointed out that 'With a population equal to that of a large city, [Ancoats] has not a single road or street enabling that vast population

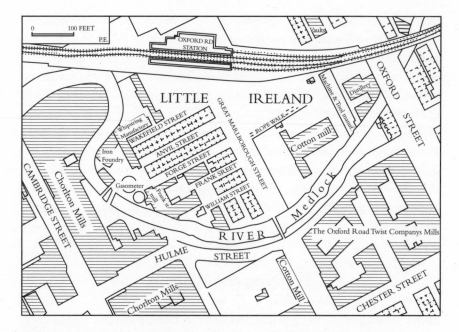

Fig. 6.8 A map of 'Little Ireland' in Manchester. Cotton mills, an iron works and a gasworks went up on the banks of the River Medlock, south of Manchester's commercial centre, in the early 19th century, and the opening of the Manchester, South Junction and Altrincham Railway's line cut the area off from the city centre in 1849. The terraces of back-to-back houses shown in the map have long gone, and some of the cotton mills have been turned into flats.

to communicate in a fairly straight line with the city with which its business chiefly lies'.[28] Developments of this kind can be paralleled in cities in the poorer countries of the world today, many of them likewise devoted to the production of cheap clothes.

New working-class housing was usually put up piecemeal, often in cramped courts and yards behind street frontages. There was nothing new about such developments; what was new was their sheer number, seen in Ordnance Survey maps of the late nineteenth century which show virtually every square yard of inner-city areas covered with housing, usually interspersed with factories and workshops. Courts, yards and alleys were often lined with 'blind-back' housing built against walls, or back-to-backs, where two sets of houses shared a back wall. Given the intense and growing demand for accommodation, the eagerness of landowners to sell their land, and the reluctance of public authorities to interfere with the working of the market, large numbers of people continued to live in this kind of environment well into the twentieth century. Back-to-backs continued to be built in Leeds and other towns in the West Riding of Yorkshire until the very end of the nineteenth century, when they were made illegal;[29] improved late nineteenth-century versions still survive in Bradford and elsewhere. Giving evidence in 1840 to a House of Commons Select Committee on the Health of Towns, Thomas Cubitt, one of the most successful builders in early Victorian London, described the purchasers of urban slum housing as 'the little shop-keeping class of persons' living on rentier incomes:[30] men like the oleaginous Mr Casby in Charles Dickens's *Little Dorrit*.[31] Many of them used the profits derived from the rents of slum properties to develop the outer residential suburbs, and in this way slums and the suburbs were symbiotically linked.[32]

From the 1820s onwards, it became increasingly common to build new housing in rows or terraces along streets rather than within courts. This allowed for the introduction of better street lighting and policing: an important consideration as the propertied classes took fright from the prospect of a growing and potentially dangerous urban working class, revealed in the Chartist movement of the late 1830s and 1840s.[33] New housing developments usually began with the sale of land to a speculator, after which streets were commonly laid out in parallel lines or grid-fashion. Most houses were of two storeys, entered directly from the street, with two rooms on each floor; a front parlour, back kitchen-cum-living room and upstairs bedrooms. A yard behind gave access to the scullery and outside toilet: a layout that was not very different from that found in the cottages of rural labourers that were going up at the same time. The Jericho suburb in Oxford,[34] to take one example, went up on low-lying ground on the banks of the Oxford Canal (1790) next to the new printing house of the Oxford University Press, opened in 1830. A grid of streets was then laid out on freehold land which had been sold five years earlier, and brick houses were put up piecemeal by small builders over the next twenty or so years, creating a superficially homogeneous townscape that has changed relatively little despite the exodus of the working-class population due to high property prices and subsequent gentrification. Housing of this kind can be seen, albeit modernized, in most English and Welsh towns; in parts of north-east England, and in Scotland, single-storeyed houses were also common, usually with upstairs rooms in the attic space.[35]

The relatively small number of completely new towns of the mid-century were developed along similar lines, At Swindon, following the completion of the Great Western Railway's main line between London and Bristol in 1841, a grid of streets of generous width was laid out to the south of the high stone wall of the company's locomotive works, some distance away from the existing small market town on its hilltop site. Over the next twenty years it was filled with terraces of stone-built cottages, each entered directly from the street and each with its own back yard. A Mechanics' Institute (1855) and a hospital occupied the central square, and there were Anglican and Methodist churches, but few shops and no public houses: a pattern common to most nineteenth-century planned communities. A similar, but larger, development took place at Barrow-in-Furness (Cumbria, formerly Lancashire), a new town laid out by the Furness Railway company following the discovery of iron ore on the bleak and isolated southern tip of the Furness peninsula in the 1850s. Shipbuilding, still the mainstay of the town's economy, began here in the 1870s,[36] and the first terraced houses, built of brick in parallel rows along parallel streets leading off the wide main thoroughfares, are overshadowed by the vast bulk of the shipyard on the neighbouring Barrow Island (Fig. 6.9).

Growing concern about the threat to public health posed by overcrowding and lack of effective sanitation led to national and local legislation that gradually put an end to the building of the worst kind of slum housing. Liverpool, where 86,000 people were crammed into city-centre courts, appointed its first Medical Officer of Health in 1846, and the standard of new housing slowly improved in the second half of the century, though this did nothing to improve the conditions of the existing court-dwellers. By the 1850s it was becoming common for new working-class terraced houses to be built with back extensions, allowing for an extra bedroom upstairs and a scullery for preparing food and washing clothes underneath; some even had front gardens. Philanthropically-minded mill-owners such as Titus Salt led the way by putting up improved accommodation for their workers in factory settlements like that at Saltaire, north-west of Bradford (1853–68), which survives virtually intact with its attractively detailed terraces of housing. Such developments recalled earlier rural estate villages and anticipated and the Garden Cities, Garden Suburbs and council estates of the early twentieth century.

In 1875, not long after the second Parliamentary Reform Act of 1867, which gave the vote for the first time to all urban working-class male

Fig. 6.9 An air view of Barrow-in-Furness in 1939. Barrow did not exist as a town until the 1850s, but it grew rapidly after shipbuilding began on Barrow Island, south of the town centre, in the 1870s. Shipyards and their associated sheds take up the whole of the island, interrupted only by a wide, straight street (right) with brick-built tenement flats of 1872-4 on its eastern side.

ratepayers, a Public Health Act was passed. It led to the adoption of model by-laws setting out minimum standards for new housing, and they became a foundation-stone of the modern planning system, creating a standard type of working-class housing that can be seem, with local variations, all over England and Wales. 'By-law' housing soon stretched further and further away from crowded city centres as migration from rural areas increased with the onset of the agricultural depression (see p. 259). For those who could afford the rent, a two-storeyed terraced house with a back yard and a rear passage to allow for the disposal of the rubbish (previously taken, *faute de mieux*, out of the front door), now became the norm.[37] Such housing is still sometimes the cheapest type of housing available for purchase by first-time buyers.

Mass housing took a different form in the larger Scottish cities. Here the 'feuing' system of virtually permanent leaseholds set a premium on fitting

Glasgow's Tenement Housing

Glasgow's prosperity in the late eighteenth century depended on the tobacco trade with America. New wharves were established along the Clyde after the flow of the river was regulated, and the first shipyard opened in 1818. By then textile manufacture had displaced tobacco as the dominant industry, and there were 107 cotton mills by 1830. Workshops for the industrial use of chemicals also grew up, including the soda works at St Rollox, north of the old city centre.[38] Heavy industry arrived from the 1840s onwards with the establishment of ironworks, engineering works and ever larger shipyards. Engineering and textile factories and their associated housing were concentrated to the east of the city centre, chemical and railway locomotive works to the north, and shipyards along the banks of the Clyde to the west. By the end of the century 820 acres had been given over to railway land—the equivalent of three quarters of the city's whole built-up area in 1840—of which 190 acres were accounted for by locomotive and other engineering works.[39] Even the handsome seventeenth-century University buildings in the High Street fell victim to the railway, their place being taken by a goods yard, though some fragments of the old buildings were re-erected in the new University built in 1864–70 in Kelvingrove Park in the affluent West End of the city (see p. 249). By then Glasgow's population had risen to half a million.

The new industrial districts attracted working-class housing that was often of an appallingly cramped and squalid character. By the 1870s the middle classes had fled the south bank of the river, originally overlooked by elegant terraces—two of which still survive south of the pretty Portland Street footbridge over the Clyde (1851–3)—to more salubrious settings in the western suburbs. By the 1880s Glasgow had the highest death rate and the highest number of persons per room in any British city. Some of the worst housing began to be replaced under a series of Police (Improvement) Acts which culminated in 1866, when new houses in alleys (wynds) were banned,[40] and the city council was given powers to demolish slum housing and to impose minimum standards of construction on the tenement blocks that replaced it. Some of these barrack-like buildings were put up by private developers or charitable bodies, others by the council's own City Improvement Trust.[41] Plain, even dour, externally, they were well built of local stone, and possessed basic amenities, though most of the flats still contained only one or two rooms; in 1886 a third of the city's families still lived in one-room dwellings, a higher proportion than in English cities.[42] But the new blocks, grim though they may appear from the outside, marked an improvement in living standards, however limited, over the slum courts that they superseded, and some of them still survive, despite the efforts of planners to demolish them and replace them with high-rise flats in the 1960s and 1970s.

Many members of Glasgow's expanding late Victorian and Edwardian middle class also lived in tenement blocks. Usually built of red Ayrshire sandstone, widely used from the 1880s onwards, and often architect-designed, these handsome buildings still line the streets in some of the western parts of the city, such as Garnethill, north of Sauchiehall Street, one of Glasgow's main shopping streets. Distinguished from the working-class blocks in less favoured areas by their ubiquitous bay windows and by their architect-designed external embellishments, their distinctive charac-ter can be seen at first hand in a three-roomed flat, restored by the National Trust for Scotland, in a four-storeyed block of this kind in Buccleuch Street, completed in 1892. It was tenanted for many years by the widow of a commercial traveller who made her living as a dressmaker.[43] For many Glaswegians of a similar socio-economic status, accommodation of this kind represented a satisfactory solution to the problem of finding com-fortable, inexpensive housing close to the city centre at a time of rapid population growth (Fig. 6.10).

the maximum number of people onto a site, and this led to the building of the large late nineteenth-century apartment blocks that can still be seen in the larger cities.[44]

Blocks of flats or 'model dwellings' also went up in London from the mid-century onwards, many of them built by charitable bodies like the Peabody Trust and the Improved Industrial Dwellings Company under slum clearance legislation enacted by central government in the 1870s.[45] Then in 1890 the Housing of the Working Classes Act enabled local author-ities in England to build housing for rental on their own initiative. Among the first results was the impressive Boundary Street complex put up in 1893–6 by the newly-established London County Council on the site of the notorious 'Jago' slum at Shoreditch in the East End. The five-storeyed flats, carefully detailed in red brick and terracotta, are arranged along wide streets radiating from a central open space with a mound, disguised by planting and topped by a pretty pavilion, made out of spoil from the demolished houses on the site.[46] Boundary Street, like the contemporary Millbank estate on the site of the Thames-side Millbank Penitentiary, next to the Tate Britain

Fig. 6.10 Glasgow's High Street, leading south from the medieval cathedral to the central crossroads, became increasingly run-down and shabby as the city's middle classes moved westwards in the 19th century. These blocks of flats, faced with local red sandstone, were part of a drive to improve the neighbourhood and provide a better standard of housing. Drawing on Scottish vernacular architecture, they were built by the City Improvement Trust in 1899-1902 to the designs of the local firm of Burnet, Boston and Carruthers.

art gallery,[47] became a citadel of the 'labour aristocracy'; the skilled workers who constituted the most prosperous ten per cent of the working class. But rents were set at a high level to help defray the cost of the development, and the less well-off, including those displaced by the new building, had to remain in the overcrowded streets nearby.

The building of council (local authority) flats in inner-city areas gathered momentum in the inter-war period, especially after the passing of a new Housing Act in 1930. Typically built of brick, and five storeys high, the new blocks were usually arranged around courtyards with internal staircases leading to balconies from which the individual flats were approached, as at Gerard Gardens in Liverpool (1937: demolished 1987), its design influenced by the monumental and much-admired Karl Marx Hof in Vienna (1926).[48] Impressive as developments of this kind sometimes are, or were, they still comprised only a relatively small proportion of the 1.1 million 'housing units' built by local authorities between the Wars, most of which went up in suburban 'cottage estates' far from city centres (see pp. 266–8).[49] The English middle classes also eschewed city-centre flats, except to some extent in London,[50] preferring the promise of a quiet suburban *rus in urbe* which still remains the ideal domestic environment for many, perhaps most, British people.

The Public Realm

For most of the urban working class, both men and women, social life centred around often overcrowded homes, workplaces and—to an extent that is almost inconceivable today—the neighbouring streets with their corner shops and pubs. Communal ties were strengthened by shared leisure activities and, for many, by religious practice. Church-building made a greater impact on the urban landscape in the nineteenth century than it had at any time since the Middle Ages. All religious denominations, including the Roman Catholics, newly assertive following Emancipation in 1829, saw the construction of churches in working-class districts as an essential component of their mission, rescuing the multitude from the alleged alienation and anomie of urban life. For many architects the Gothic style conveyed a unique sense of the numinous and transcendent; George Edmund Street, one of its leading exponents, believed, like many of his medieval predecessors, that height was 'of immense importance, and...to be attained at all costs'.[51] That aim is epitomized by the 309-ft spire of Joseph Aloysius Hansom's Catholic church of St Walburgh at Preston (1850–4), soaring over streets of terraced houses, many of them originally occupied by immigrants fleeing famine in Ireland, on the far side of railway tracks that separate them from the town centre, (Fig. 6.11).[52] James Brooks's sturdy brick-built Anglican churches of St Chad (1867–8) and St Columba (1867–71) at Haggerston in the East End of London make an equally emphatic statement of belief, reinforced for those who ventured inside by their spacious, numinous interiors. Such churches usually formed part of complexes of buildings that also contained schools and housing for the clergy, echoing the evangelizing minsters of Anglo-Saxon times.

Church-building was partially motivated by the fear of religious indifference, partly by inter-denominational rivalry; a census taken in 1851 revealed that only half the population of England and Wales attended any place of

St. Walburg's Church, Preston.

Fig. 6.11 St Walburgh's church, Preston. Despite persecution, Roman Catholicism flourished in much of Lancashire after the Reformation, and it acquired a more confident public face after Emancipation in 1829 and the influx of large numbers of Irish immigrants following the Great Famine of the 1840s. The church, designed by Joseph Hansom, was built in 1850-4 in a working-class suburb next to the main railway line linking London and Glasgow. The spire boldly proclaims the faith to the outside world, and the vast unaisled, 60 foot-wide, interior focuses the attention of worshippers to the richly ornate chancel.

worship on a given Sunday, of whom about half were Protestant Nonconformists. Usually loosely classical in inspiration, Nonconformist churches and chapels were especially prominent in recently urbanized industrial areas such as the Potteries, and in mining villages and small towns; the pedimented, granite-built Methodist churches in Redruth (1829) and Camborne (1839, refronted later) in the far west of Cornwall are still among the most significant elements of their workaday townscapes.[53] And in Scotland a series of schisms within the established church contributed to a further increase in church-building by breakaway congregations. This could have spectacular results, as it did in Glasgow, where the bold, uncompromising tower and portico of Alexander ('Greek') Thomson's Caledonia Road United Presbyterian church (1856–7) commands a street intersection in the Gorbals, an area now undergoing extensive rebuilding following the demolition not only of the surrounding tenement housing but also of the post-war blocks of flats that replaced it in the 1950s and 1960s.

Church-building continued into the twentieth century. Liverpool's Anglican cathedral, begun in 1904, occupies a hilltop site on the sandstone ridge to the south-east of the city centre, overlooking a former quarry which had served for some seventy years as a burial ground; completed in 1978 to the designs of Sir Giles Gilbert Scott, it ranks as one of the finest Gothic buildings of any date in Britain, its massive bulk towering over the city, especially when seen from the waterfront (Fig. 6.5). Equally impressive is the magnificent neo-Byzantine Roman Catholic cathedral at Westminster (J. F. Bentley, 1895–1903), squeezed into a confined site, formerly containing a women's' prison, close to Victoria railway station, its stripy Italian Romanesque exterior and tall campanile proclaiming the faith among the surrounding blocks of late nineteenth-century middle-class flats. Efforts were also made to evangelize the burgeoning urban population by the building of Nonconformist 'tabernacles' and 'central halls' offering inspiring preaching and organized community activities. The Victoria Hall in Sheffield, a stronghold of Methodism, was built in 1906–7 on the city-centre site of an earlier chapel in which John Wesley himself had preached; in 1909 the Trades Union Congress held its annual conference there. Its bold, eclectic façade and neo-Baroque tower point a sharp contrast to the nearby Congregational chapel and Catholic cathedral: a visual embodiment of the religious plurality that helped shape the landscape of nineteenth- and early twentieth-century towns and cities.

Religion and education had always been closely linked. The main providers of working-class education in England and Wales before 1870 were two church-based voluntary societies: The National Society (Anglican), founded in 1811, and the British Society (Nonconformist) in 1808. After 1833 these organizations became eligible for Government grants, subject to inspection; in Nottingham, where the population had more than doubled between over sixty years, there were thirty-six grant-aided elementary schools by 1870.[54] They set a precedent for the schools put up by the locally-elected School Boards established under the Education Act of 1870. Their purpose was to offer an elementary, non-denominational education in areas inadequately covered by existing schools; by 1902 there were ninety-four 'board schools' in Nottingham, along with another seventy-eight church schools, most of them Anglican. And after 1868 these schools were supplemented in the larger towns and cities by new 'higher grade' schools designed to offer a scientific or technical education to teenagers.

For E. R. Robson, architect to the London School Board, new schools were 'public buildings [that] should be planned and built in a manner befitting their new dignity'; in Conan Doyle's story 'The Naval Treaty' (1893), Sherlock Holmes, viewing one of them from a railway viaduct en route from Waterloo Station to the West Country, hailed 'those big isolated clumps of building rising above the slate' as 'lighthouses: beacons of the future, capsules with hundreds of bright little seeds in each'. Under rules established by the Government education department, the pupils were taught by age-group in classrooms lit by large windows; communal halls for assemblies and physical exercise also featured in most plans, as in the south London primary school, built in 1877, that I attended myself. Architects made use of a wide repertoire of styles. Some, including the talented local partnership of Chamberlain and Martin in Birmingham,[55] clung to a minimal form of Gothic, but the London School Board favoured an eclectic 'Queen Anne' style that later became popular elsewhere, gradually acquiring Arts-and-Crafts overtones, as in the Scarcroft Road school in York (1896) (Fig. 6.12).

Fig. 6.12 York spread south of its medieval walls in the second half of the 19th century. Scarcroft Road School went up in 1896 to the designs of the local architect Walter Brierley, whose large practice included the design of elementary schools built by the York School Board. As in many such schools, there were well-lit halls for communal assemblies in the central block, and classrooms in the wings.

It was built to the designs of the talented local architect Walter Brierley, and it still towers over an area of low-cost housing that had recently gone up just outside the southern city wall. Meanwhile many long-established grammar schools that had offered secondary education to the middle classes moved out from their cramped but potentially valuable city-centre sites to more spacious premises in the suburbs, the architecture of their new buildings sometimes evoking the schools' Tudor origins.

Terrified by the fear of crime and social breakdown, public authorities put up larger prisons incorporating ever stricter systems of surveillance. Prisoners had formerly been incarcerated in central sites, often within castle precincts, and this remained the case until relatively recently in places like Lancaster and Oxford. But the new prisons in the larger cities went up in the inner suburbs where security could be more effectively enforced, as in the Strangeways prison in Manchester (1866–8), built like many others on a radial panopticon-like plan that allowed central supervision of the inmates, each in his or her own solitary cell. The impact of such brutal-looking institutions on the surrounding landscape of working-class housing was deeply depressing.[56] Equally depressing, and equally intimidating, were the workhouses put up after the Poor Law Amendment Act of 1834, under which parishes were grouped together within Unions to tackle the problem of poverty more efficiently: a process that involved reducing the cost of relief by replacing handouts with a 'less eligibility' policy designed to deter the able-bodied poor from applying for relief and thereby becoming a burden on the more productive members of society. The application of the so-called 'workhouse test' led to the building of large barrack-like buildings which tangibly expressed the joyless, utilitarian philosophy of the framers of the legislation.[57] But workhouses failed to solve the problem of occasional poverty—much of it brought about by the prevalence of casual labour and by unanticipated trade depressions—and workhouses eventually became little more than sad homes for the elderly, the destitute and the infirm.

Workhouses were abolished in 1930, but some lingered on as hospitals. They include the massive Chorlton-on-Medlock institution in Manchester (now the Withington Hospital), built in 1856, to which an infirmary was added in 1865–6. Revelations about hygiene during the Crimean War (1853–6) led meanwhile to the building of new purpose-built 'pavilion-style' hospitals with the wards grouped in separate blocks, sometimes parallel, sometimes radial, in order to allow maximum light and air for the patients.[58] St Thomas's Hospital in London, opposite the Houses of Parliament, is one example of the type; others include the Leeds Infirmary, designed by George Gilbert Scott in 1864–8 and built of polychromatic brick in the Gothic style, with a central block linked by lower blocks to two wings containing wards (Fig. 6.13). Like the prisons and workhouses that they to some extent resembled, not least from their sheer size, such buildings helped shape the character of the fringe areas surrounding the centres of the larger cities. So too, but on a smaller scale, did public baths and wash-houses, first established in Liverpool and subsequently in other large cities. In Balsall Heath, a mainly working-class suburb south of Birmingham's city centre, to take one example, the baths, with their richly detailed neo-Jacobean façade of brick and terracotta, were built in 1905 next to a public branch library put up ten years earlier:[59] a tangible expression of a new civic idealism fostering the ideal of a healthy mind in a healthy body.

As the population increased, so too did the numbers of the dead. Already in the seventeenth century there were moves to relieve the pressure on town-centre churchyards by opening new graveyards outside the built-up

Fig. 6.13 Leeds's first hospital was built in the city centre, but the need for more spacious premises for the rapidly growing population dictated a move in 1864-8 to a new site in Great George Street. The architect of Leeds General Infirmary, George Gilbert Scott, adopted the pavilion plan of separate ward blocks linked by corridors, allowing maximum exposure of the patients to light and air, and chose an eclectic Continental-inspired Gothic style for the colourful red-brick exterior.

area. A non-denominational burial ground was opened at Bunhill Fields, just north of the City of London, as early as 1665, the year of the Great Plague, and in 1718 another was created at Calton Hill, to the north of Edinburgh's Old Town, later becoming one of the 'sights' of the city. New graveyards provided public spaces for reflective promenading by the citizens, while enabling the dead to be entombed away from the crowded and insanitary central areas. One of the most impressive of the fashionable new 'garden cemeteries' is that of St James in Liverpool, laid out in 1829 within a former stone quarry on what was then the south-eastern edge of the city. Landscaped in a lush, Romantic manner by the architect John Foster and his associate John Shepherd, it contains a memorial to the politician and local MP William Huskisson, run over by a train at the opening of the Liverpool and Manchester Railway in 1829. It is now overlooked by the massive bulk of Giles Gilbert Scott's Anglican Cathedral, resulting in a marriage of the Sublime and the Picturesque beyond the wildest imaginings of the cemetery's commercial promoters.[60] A similar privately-financed cemetery was established at Glasgow in 1832: a 'city of the dead' with an extraordinary array of classical temples, columns, obelisks and rotundas on a steep hillside overlooking the medieval Cathedral (Fig. 6.14).

Private graveyards proliferated in the 1840s, but they did little to solve the problem of how to dispose of the remains of the ever-increasing number of the urban poor. This was brought to the public's attention by the sanitary reformer Edwin Chadwick in a report of 1843, and, like his better-known report on the Health of Towns (1848), it led eventually to legislation. The Burials Acts of 1852–7 made it possible to close town-centre churchyards—541 were shut down in 1854–5[61]—and to establish local Burial Boards supported out of the rates. The resulting cemeteries were usually built well outside the boundaries of towns, like the City of London cemetery at Little Ilford, laid out in 1853–6 on 80-acre site seven miles from the capital,[62] their monotonous ranks of burial stones interrupted only by the Anglican and Nonconformist chapels from which the remains of the departed were committed to their final resting places.

Cemeteries were one way of supplying much-needed public open space in expanding cities; parks were another. Until the nineteenth century towndwellers, even in London, had been able to walk into the surrounding countryside for open air and relaxation, chiefly to fields or unenclosed common ground. The environs of London were dotted with spas, pleasure gardens, and more or less respectable inns.[63] Elsewhere there were 'public

Fig. 6.14 Glasgow's main cemetery, the Necropolis, was laid out on a hillside close to the city's medieval cathedral. The third 'hygienic cemetery' in Britain, it was opened in 1833, a year after the passing of a Act of Parliament designed to end the practice of burying the dead in crowded city-centre churchyards. The Doric column at the top of the hill (1825) predates the cemetery and is surmounted by a statue of the 16th-century religious reformer John Knox.

walks' such as the New Walk at Leicester, laid out by the Corporation in 1785 (see p. 247) and the circuits of the walls at Chester and Berwick. Such places of genteel recreation were supplemented in the 1830s by privately financed botanic gardens, strictly supervised and originally accessible only by payment of a fee, such as those opened on the edge of Birmingham in 1832 and at Sheffield in 1836. But the Arboretum at Derby (1839–40), on a site donated by the textile manufacturer Joseph Strutt, was open free of charge twice a week, allowing members of the 'respectable' working class to enjoy the central walkway and the sinuous paths leading through the dense, varied plantations around the undulating periphery.

The development of public parks grew out of both a demand for salubrious settings for middle-class housing and a perceived need for 'rational amusements for the poor', for which free admission was essential. Regent's Park in London (see pp. 154–5.) was a much-publicized precedent, and,

Birkenhead Park

Birkenhead (Cheshire) was a new town that grew up after the establishment of a steam ferry service across the Mersey from Liverpool in 1815. In 1824 William Laird, founder of a boiler factory (later expanded into a shipbuilding yard), employed a fellow-Scotsman, James Gillespie Graham, designer of the monumental Moray Place in Edinburgh, to lay out a grid of spacious streets, starting with Hamilton Square (completed in 1844), close to the ferry terminal and lined with handsome stone-fronted terraces. But ideas of developing Birkenhead as a prosperous twin town to Liverpool never came to fruition, and instead there was a large influx of shipyard workers who took up residence in closely-packed houses. With the population rising from 105 in 1811 to 24,285 in the first half of the century, the town's Improvement Commissioners secured an Act of Parliament in 1843 which enabled them to lay out a park on 125 acres of poor, low-lying grazing land to the north-west of the central area. It was intended to act as a *cordon sanitaire* separating the poorer areas of the town, within reach of the docks, from what was intended as an affluent villa suburb. Behaviour, as in most nineteenth-century public parks, was monitored by keepers, and alcohol was forbidden (or at least frowned upon):[64] part of an overriding project to control and 'civilise' what were perceived as the chaotic and potentially dangerous urban poor.

Opened in 1847, the park was designed by Joseph Paxton, formerly the Duke of Devonshire's head gardener at Chatsworth (Derbyshire), in which capacity he pioneered the building of glass-and-iron conservatories, the most celebrated of which was the Crystal Palace in London, built for the Great Exhibition of 1851 and later reassembled in a new privately-financed park at Sydenham in the southern suburbs.[65] Birkenhead Park did not have a conservatory at first, but it did, and still does, have a grand classical triumphal arch at the main entrance, and lodges in the Grecian, Italianate, Tudor and castellated styles. The extensive lawns are enclosed within a serpentine driveway and are punctuated with clumps of trees and flowerbeds; there is also a lake—an essential feature of all ambitious urban parks—crossed by an ornamental covered bridge (Fig. 6.15), with a boathouse surmounted by a classical pavilion. And, following a visit by the American landscape architect Frederick Law Olmsted in 1850, the park exerted an influence on New York's Central Park and, through it, urban parks throughout the world.

Fig. 6.15 Birkenhead Park was laid out to the designs of Sir Joseph Paxton in 1843-7 on the edge of the rapidly expanding town. The picturesque layout, featuring an artificial lake crossed by a covered 'Swiss' bridge, was strongly influenced by the landscaped gardens of the nobility and gentry; the purpose was to provide an attractive setting for the 'rational amusement' of the urban population within a strictly controlled environment.

not long after its completion, a House of Commons Select Committee on Public Walks (1833) recommended the provision of government-sponsored parks for the benefit of the inhabitants of London's East End and its burgeoning southern and northern suburbs.[66] It also encouraged the planning of new parks in provincial towns and cities.

Municipal parks could not be created or financed without the availability of cheap land around the fringes of towns and cities, the philanthropy of private individuals prepared to donate a site, and the capacity of local authorities to raise funds for maintenance through the rates. New national legislation was passed in 1859–60, and in 1864 local authorities were allowed to borrow money for purchasing land. Soon afterwards, following an Improvement Act of 1865, Liverpool successfully established a series of parks which, along with Prince's Park, already laid out 1842–4, formed a rudimentary green corridor around the crowded inner city.[67] Sefton Park, finished in 1872, was generously planned on a 375-acre site, 'barren but very undulating', and was financed in part by the sale of plots for large detached middle-class villas around the edge: a common practice. The layout was planned by the locally-based Lewis Hornblower—who had been involved in the layout of Birkenhead Park—and a Frenchman Édouard André. An important feature was an outer drive enclosing a series of separate tree-fringed enclosures set aside for different recreational purposes: a cricket ground, a deer park, rough grazing land and a lake. There were also flower beds, drinking fountains and a spectacular Palm House donated by Henry Yates Thompson, son of a rich banker. Such features came to be seen as essential components of public parks in most towns, and the parks themselves still help define the character of many inner-urban neighbourhoods today, enriching the lives of their inhabitants in a way that eludes quantification or precise definition.

7

Reshaping the Centre

Writing in 1909, the anonymous author of a guidebook to Leeds exclaimed: 'No city in England can boast of a more wonderful transformation than that witnessed in Leeds during the last two or three decades. The centre...has been practically re-carved and polished. Nearly the whole of the ramshackle property that skirted the east side of Briggate has been demolished, and on the site has been erected a class of shop property that would do credit to any city in the country.'[1] This was not an isolated case. As manufacturing industry took root around the fringe of British larger towns and cities, business, commerce and retailing strengthened its hold on the central areas. By the end of the nineteenth century land values had increased, doubling in each generation from 1830 to the First World War,[2] and commerce had driven out all but a handful of residents. George Macgregor, author of a history of Glasgow, wrote in 1881 that the city's central business district had recently spread over a greatly extended area, 'the resident population...being driven to the outskirts of the city; and what were once dwelling-houses...now turned into gigantic warehouses.'[3]

City centres were already densely built up by the beginning of the nineteenth century, their property divided among multiple owners, their main streets mostly following routes determined in the Middle Ages. Few local authorities or private landlords had the financial resources to embark on the complex process of buying land and compensating tenants in order to bulldoze streets through heavily built-up areas on the scale, and with the aesthetic flair, of John Nash's Regent Street or Baron Haussmann's Paris. Most relied on making piecemeal changes, rounding street corners to ease through traffic and removing bottlenecks by widening; Market Street in Manchester, only 15 feet wide at its narrowest point, was improved in this way under an Act of 1821.[4] More extensive changes were initiated in the second half of the century. The main achievement of London's Metropolitan Board of

Works, set up in 1855, was the building of the Victoria Embankment (see p. 185), but it also pushed new streets such as Charing Cross Road and Shaftesbury Avenue through the dingy eastern periphery of the West End. Horse-drawn trams began to make an impact on urban streets in the 1860s,[5] and that impact was increased in the 1890s by the adoption of electricity from overhead cables. Messy street surfaces were improved too; asphalt made its first appearance in Britain in Threadneedle Street in the City of London in 1869. And better street lighting, from increasingly intrusive lamp standards, helped transform the nocturnal townscape.

Railways made increasing inroads on town and city centres. Most of the first stations, like those at Huddersfield (1847), Chester (1848), Bristol and York, were built on the edge of the central area, where land was relatively cheap. The main railway station at Norwich was built on the far side of the River Wensum and was linked to the city centre by a new street (Prince of Wales Road), laid out in 1864. The need to attract more passengers led some railway companies to relocate their stations to more central sites. The first Birmingham terminus of the London and Birmingham Railway was in Curzon Street, in the city's industrial fringe, but it became a goods station after the building of a new passenger station (New Street) in 1849–54 closer to the commercial heart. The rival Great Western Railway responded in 1852 by tunnelling under the city centre to a new station of its own at Snow Hill.[6]

Newcastle

At the beginning of the nineteenth century Newcastle was a flourishing provincial capital with a wealthy and active mercantile and professional middle class, its economy fortified by the growth of industry along the steep banks of the River Tyne. An Improvement Act of 1783 led to the removal of the ancient town gates and to the building of new streets to ease communication between the riverside and the centre. With the building of Eldon Square (begun 1825–6) and the monumental Leazes Terrace (1829–34), the middle classes began to desert their timber-framed riverside residences for stone-fronted classical houses of a grandeur rarely seen in Britain outside Edinburgh and Bath. The purchase of a substantial house (Anderson Place) with its twelve-acre grounds on the site of a medieval nunnery just inside the walls enabled the town council, together with the

(continued)

Continued

builder and developer Richard Grainger, the Town Clerk (John Clayton), and a team of unusually talented locally-based architects, notably John Dobson, to lay out two spacious new streets—Grey Street and Grainger Street—linking the new residential quarter to the older centre. They were lined, like London's Regent Street, by *palazzo*-like classical buildings of a uniform height of three storeys and attics, with shops on the ground floor and 'chambers' above. The gently curving, 80-feet wide, Grey Street, is one of the finest urban ensembles of the time, with the portico of the Theatre Royal, opened in 1837, projecting over the pavement. The southern section of the street follows the line of the Lort Burn, an important feature of Newcastle's early topography, forced, like most urban watercourses, into a culvert.[7] A covered market went up in 1835 next to Grainger Street, with two gas-lit halls for the sale of meat and vegetables, the former containing 196 shops within four 'avenues'.[8] And the junction of the two streets was marked by a classical column commemorating the local hero Lord Grey, Prime Minister at the time of the 1832 Reform Act (Fig. 7.1): a provincial equivalent of Nelson's Column in London's Trafalgar Square.

In 1847, not long after the completion of Grey Street and Grainger Street, Newcastle was connected to London by rail. The steep-sided Tyne gorge was crossed by the double-layered High Level Bridge, a major piece of civil engineering designed by Robert Stephenson. He was the son of the steam-locomotive pioneer George Stephenson, who had established a locomotive works nearby in 1823; by 1860 the firm was the largest employer in the city. The bridge brought northbound trains into a station designed by Dobson on the high ground north of the river. Dobson believed that railway stations were 'public works—structures constantly seen by thousands and tens of thousands of persons, and might therefore do much towards improving the taste of the public'.[9] His station became the main point of entry for travellers into the city, its iron-and-glass roof covering the curving train-shed and a noble, arched carriage porch fronting a new public space overlooked by two hotels and a monument to Stephenson. The railway track continued northwards by cutting through the courtyard of the medieval castle, separating the keep tower from the main gateway (Black Gate) in the process, and crossing streets on handsome stone-arched bridges; in Dean Street, leading from the river front to the city centre, the bridge looms over a chasm flanked by tall stone buildings. But there was a human cost in the displacement of large numbers of the inhabitants, and a fire of 1854 further sealed the fate of most of the old, multi-occupied timber-framed houses adjoining the quayside; they were replaced in 1858–63 by handsome stone-fronted offices lining a grid of new streets planned by Dobson. Then in 1928 the quayside was transformed once more by the building of the Tyne road bridge, carrying traffic south across the river from the commercial and retail centre. Together with the High Level Bridge and the swing bridge built in 1876 on the site of the original river crossing, it forms part of one of the most dramatic urban landscapes in Britain (Fig. 7.2).

Fig. 7.1 Grey Street, Newcastle, looking north. The stone-fronted buildings on either side of the street contain shops at ground level and 'chambers' above. The projecting portico on the right marks the entrance to the Theatre Royal, built in 1836-7, and the Doric column in the distance (1838) commemorates Lord Grey, Prime Minister at the time of the Parliamentary Reform Act of 1832.

Fig. 7.2 Until 1763 Newcastle's medieval walls extended east along the quayside from the single bridge over the River Tyne to the Sandgate, leaving shipping to be pulled up onto the shore. The quay was widened over reclaimed land in the 1840s, and in 1868-76 the bridge was replaced by a new swing bridge, seen in the middle distance. The High Level Bridge, further west, was built in 1845-9 to carry the tracks of the main London to Edinburgh railway line into the Central station. The steel-arched Tyne Road Bridge, in the foreground, went up in 1925-8.

The Landscape of Commerce

Markets have always been central to urban life. Some had already been removed from town-centre streets by the 1830s to purpose-built covered complexes that were easy to control and regulate (see pp. 139, 143). This process continued throughout the nineteenth century. The Pannier Market at Tavistock (Devon), a large clerestoried aisled hall, went up in 1859–62 on a site behind the new neo-Tudor Town Hall (1860–4), built, together with the market, by the Duke of Bedford's estate surveyor, Edward Rundle, as part of a wholesale redevelopment of his property in the small town.[10] The most impressive new markets were in the north of England, many of them conceived in conjunction with street improvements. By 1893 Leeds was England's fourth largest city, with a population of 429,000, an eight-fold increase over that of 1811. The rebuilding of the Kirkgate Market (1901–4) formed part of a series of changes which transformed the whole of the

central area. It occupies a site at the junction of two streets, Kirkgate and
Vicar Lane, which were widened and their corners rounded. The market's
street frontages were rebuilt in a lavish, loosely French Renaissance, style,
with three storeys of chambers and an attic punctuated by gables, turrets and
domes over shops (Fig. 7.3); they enclose a spectacular interior divided at
ground level by rows of permanent stalls, with tall iron posts supporting a
glazed roof.[11] But these changes, like many others of a similar kind, entailed
a substantial human cost; some 40,000 inhabitants of central Leeds were
displaced by 'improvements' of one kind or another, and had to find accommodation in the already overcrowded inner suburbs.[12]

Fig. 7.3 Leeds City Markets. The glass-roofed market building of 1904, by the
local firm of Leeming and Leeming, replaced an earlier fruit and vegetable market
on this important city-centre site. The market hall is enveloped by an elaborate
'mixed Renaissance' building of brick and terracotta containing shops and,
originally, a hotel, a restaurant and coffee rooms, with 'chambers' above.

As railways facilitated the development of an increasingly integrated national market, larger and more pretentious shops proliferated along the main streets. By 1900, according to one observer, Birmingham was 'no longer "Brummagem" or the "Hardware Village"', but 'the Mecca of surrounding districts that attracts an increasing number of pilgrims who love life, pleasure and shopping'.[13] Town-centre streets are still defined for many people by their shop windows, and those windows became more enticing with the advent of plate glass, which made its first appearance in Manchester in Market Street in the 1820s.[14] Sir Robert Peel's government abolished excise duties (sales taxes) in 1845, and the window tax was axed in 1851, leading to the gradual substitution of plate glass for the small panes formerly used; the results that can be seen in virtually every High Street in the country. Shops grew larger in the late nineteenth and early twentieth centuries, and the advent of electricity in the 1880s enabled them to be better lit. London set an example with the opening in 1877 of the first, Parisian-inspired, department store, Bon Marché in the High Street at Brixton, then a prosperous middle-class suburb south of the Thames, linked by train both to the City and the West End. More centrally located establishments followed, including Harrod's, which gradually spread out from its relatively modest premises in the Brompton Road to reach its present size in 1902–3. Its showy exterior, richly detailed in terracotta, presented a sharp contract to the monumental classical Portland stone façade of the steel-framed Selfridges in Oxford Street, opened in 1909 and designed by the Chicago firm of Daniel Burnham. An advertisement proclaimed that Selfridge's was 'dedicated to Women's Service first of all', though some allowance was made for men, who were 'invited to use it as they would their club'.[15]

These massive structures found a more modest echo in provincial towns. By 1900 Reading was prospering through its position on the main road and railway line leading west from London to Bath, Bristol and beyond, and from its staple industries of 'beer, bulbs and biscuits.'[16] The population had grown threefold, to 59,000, over the previous fifty years, and a handbook of 1892 drew attention to the 'palatial trading establishments' springing up in the central streets, linked in 1903 by electric trams to the rapidly expanding suburbs.[17] Messrs. Heelas, founded as a drapery store in 1854, was employing between 300 and 400 people by 1909 in a 'large and well conducted emporium' on Broad Street, the main shopping street (Fig. 7.4);[18] its rivals included William McIlroy's drapery store in Oxford Street, distinguished

Fig. 7.4 Broad St Reading in 1905. Reading's main shopping street was rebuilt piecemeal in the late 19th and early 20th centuries. Most of the new buildings were taller than their predecessors, with shops at ground level and 'chambers' above. Shoppers and shop-workers came into the town centre by electric trams, which replaced horse-drawn trams in 1901.

from its neighbours by its exotically detailed roofline and its continuous row of plate-glass windows on the first floor. The local authority meanwhile employed the local firm of Stallwood and Smith to design a new street, Queen Victoria Street (completed 1904), lined with uniform shops and offices of brick and terracotta and linking the railway station to the central shopping area.[19]

Most larger towns, and some smaller ones, acquired at least one covered, glass-roofed shopping arcade, where purchasers could spend their money in a quiet, controlled environment away from the increasingly busy, noisy and—because of the droppings from innumerable horses—smelly main streets. The first arcade, inspired by those of Paris, was built by John Nash next to the Royal Opera House in London (see p. 154); others, such as the Burlington Arcade in Piccadilly (1818) and the Lower Arcade in the Broadmead district of Bristol (1824–5), followed soon afterwards. They reached their apogee in the second half of the nineteenth century, often in connection with redevelopment schemes designed to clear inner areas of poor housing and noisome trades. There are no fewer than nine arcades in

Cardiff, the first built in 1858, stretching back along the former burgage plots leading off St Mary's Street, the main north-south thoroughfare.[20] Leeds also boasts several arcades, the most impressive of which, the County Arcade (1900), was part of an ambitious redevelopment scheme for a large area between Briggate, the main shopping street, and Vicar Lane. It was carried out as a public/private partnership by the Leeds Estate Company, working in collaboration with the City Corporation, and involved the demolition of slum property around the former meat market. The architect was Frank Matcham, well-known for his theatres, and echoes of his lush style can be found in the richly decorated interior and in the terracotta street facades.[21]

Arcades could improve pedestrian transit through crowded city centres. The Great Western Arcade in Birmingham (1875–6), was built over the railway line leading to Snow Hill station, and in Norwich the Royal Arcade, designed by the talented local architect George Skipper in 1899 and extravagantly ornamented with terracotta tiles in an almost Art Nouveau taste (Fig. 7.5), went up on the site of a former inn yard built over one of the culverted streams or 'cockeys' that drained into the River Wensum.[22] It eased access from the Castle—the centre of Norfolk's county administration—to the main market place at a time when city's economy, depressed for much of the nineteenth century after the collapse of its textile industry, was enjoying a resurgence. Skipper went on in 1903–4 to design both the lavish Edwardian Baroque offices of the Norwich Union insurance company which occupied the site of the sixteenth-century Earl of Surrey's town house, and Jarrolds department store (1903) on the widened London Street, the city's main shopping street.

Shopping streets become more homogeneous after the First World War as chain stores such as Woolworth's, Marks and Spencer, Boots and W. H. Smith—names familiar to everyone in Britain—took over town- and city-centre streets, amalgamating pre-existing burgage plots in the process, and displacing smaller locally-owned shops.[23] Frontages became higher than those of their Victorian and Edwardian predecessors, but they also became blander and more uniform, save for occasional gestures designed to introduce a measure of local colour, such as the extravagantly neo-Tudor façade to Liberty's in Great Marlborough Street in London (1922–3); using timbers from two sailing ships, it was constructed behind the store's impeccably classical façade to Regent Street, part of the wholesale rebuilding of John Nash's street (see pp. 154–5) that followed the expiry of the original

Fig. 7.5 Royal Arcade, Norwich, was built in 1899 and designed by a local architect, George Skipper. The elaborate façade of glazed terracotta tiles leads into a covered arcade of shops, built over a culverted stream and leading from the medieval castle to the Market Place.

ninety-nine-year leases.[24] An equally monumental classical idiom was adopted in the comprehensive rebuilding of the northern side of the Headrow in Leeds, starting in 1927 to a plan devised by Reginald Blomfield, whose work can also be found in the Quadrant of the rebuilt Regent Street in London.[25]

Until the seventeenth century commercial transactions in towns were usually carried out in and around open markets and inns. London's first purpose-built exchange for business negotiations—the Royal Exchange— went up in the heart of the City in 1566–71 (aee Chapter 3), and specialized exchanges dealing in cotton were founded in Liverpool and Manchester in the eighteenth century. Corn Exchanges became a feature of most towns of any size after Sir Robert Peel's repeal of the Corn Laws in 1846, and the magnificent stone-faced oval of Cuthbert Brodrick's Corn Exchange in Leeds (1860–2: now shops) achieves something of the grandeur of the ancient Roman buildings that clearly inspired it. So too, on a much smaller scale, does the richly classical façade of the Exchange at Devizes (1857), surmounted by a figure of Ceres, goddess of grain. Architectural styles could have other symbolic connotations; the locally-based architects Lockwood and Mawson designed Bradford's Wool Exchange (1864–7: now a book-shop) in a spiky Gothic style clearly intended to evoke the civic and com-mercial buildings of late medieval Italy and Flanders.

As businessmen and their families moved out to the suburbs, banks, offices and warehouses moved in: a process most marked in the City of London, which lost nearly all its resident population in the mid-nineteenth century. The first banks were relatively small-scale enterprises, based initially in mer-chants' houses and later in purpose-built structures like Hoare's in London's Fleet Street (1829–30). An Act of Parliament of 1826 allowed the develop-ment of joint-stock banking in the provinces, and the Bank Charter Act of 1844 led to a spate of mergers. Purpose-built savings banks also went up in the early nineteenth century, especially in Scotland and the north of England,[26] followed later by insurance and building society offices.[27] Classical architecture conveyed the message of stability and reliability that was often deemed appropriate, and new Renaissance-inspired bank build-ings helped give a monumental public face to streets like Castle Street and Corn Street in the medieval heart of Bristol. The highly ornate façade of the former West of England and South Wales Bank (W. B. Gingell, 1854–7), opposite the city's eighteenth-century Exchange, was modelled on Sansovino's St Mark's Library in Venice, its richly carved frieze depicting putti stamping coins and holding scales.[28] Branches of the larger banks proliferated in the late nineteenth and early twentieth centuries, some of them on a monumental scale like the Midland in King Street, Manchester (1933–5), a steel-framed mini-skyscraper clad in Portland stone and designed by Edwin Lutyens.

Commercial offices were usually located in the early nineteenth century in converted houses or in 'chambers' above rows of shops. Purpose-built office blocks first appeared in the City of London in the middle of the cen-tury.[29] A large portion of the historic centre of Liverpool was almost com-pletely taken over by cotton-trading and shipping offices in the second half of the century, employing some 9,000 clerks in 1870, a number that grew substantially over the next forty years.[30] Four or five storeys high, the offices were much taller than the eighteenth-century brick-built houses that they replaced, contributing to an overall heightening of the built environment that was matched all the larger British cities. Their facades cover the stylistic gamut from Renaissance classicism through Gothic and the numerous variants of the 'free style' of the *fin-de-siècle* to a precocious modernism, seen in the largely glass-fronted facade of Oriel Chambers in Water Street, built in 1864 to the designs of a local architect, Peter Ellis, following the destruction of its predecessor by fire.[31] Finally, in the years just before the First World War, Liverpool's waterfront was transformed by the draining of George's Dock and the construction of the three monumental buildings which still define the image of the city when viewed from the River Mersey: the domed Mersey Docks and Harbour Board offices (1903–7); the ten-storeyed Royal Liver Building (1908–11), framed, like American skyscrapers of the time, in granite-clad concrete reinforced with steel, its height made possible by the advent of the electric lift; and the Cunard Building, a massive stone-fronted *palazzo* of 1914–16, also concrete-framed, its echoing, top-lit public hall serving as the passenger terminal for transatlantic liners.[32]

Wholesale and retail warehouses, like the offices that they often resembled, colonized large parts of city centres. Merchants had previously stored goods in, or adjacent to, their houses, but, as production increased, purpose-built structures were increasingly needed to house the growing quantities of goods. Town- and city-centre warehouses could be used to display furniture, like the glass-fronted Arighi Bianchi establishment at Macclesfield (1882). More commonly they housed factory-produced textiles for sampling by buyers. Elaborate facades were an essential component. Already in 1847 a writer in *The Builder* was comparing the recently-built warehouses in Mosley Street, Manchester, to the *palazzi* of Renaissance Italy, and even they were surpassed in bulk and in rich ornamentation by the mammoth Watts and Co. building in Portland St (1855–8: now a hotel), where 600 people were employed on the six floors.[33] Then, following the signing of a commercial treaty with France in 1860, Bradford's wool merchants, most of them of German origin, filled the hillside close to the fifteenth-century parish church (now the Cathedral) with densely packed stone-fronted warehouses for the storage and packing of worsted cloth, both for home consumption and for export. Each of five or six storeys, these handsome buildings still form the main component of a distinctive canyon-like streetscape which survives virtually intact despite the near-collapse of the industry that created it (Fig. 7.6).[34]

Exports of cotton goods from Lancashire soared after the opening of the Manchester Ship Canal in 1894. The advent of steel frames now enabled Manchester's warehouses to go up to seven or even eight storeys. India

Fig. 7.6 The Law, Russell & Co warehouse at Bradford was built in 1873-4 to the designs of Henry Francis Lockwood. It formed part of 'Little Germany', a district dominated by warehouses for locally-manufactured worsted cloth. The entrance, flanked by pairs of Corinthian columns, led into the counting house, a dining room for the directors of the firm, and the main staircase. The rest of the building was used for sorting and packing the cloth.

House in Whitworth Street, for Lloyd's Packing Warehouses (1905–7), and Lancaster House in Princess Street (1907–10), were both built to the designs of the Blackburn-based Harry Fairhurst, a specialist in this kind of structure. The goods were raised by hoists to the upper floors, where they were stored, the lower floors set aside for showrooms and offices.[35] With their elaborate facades of brick and terracotta—Lancaster House has a jaunty Baroque cupola over the corner of the building—these magnificent buildings helped redefine the character of the area between the Rochdale Canal and the River Medlock, just inside the city's commercial heart. Their looming presence was evoked in the impressionistic paintings of the Frenchman Adolphe Valette, whose pupils at the School of Art, a few minutes' walk away, included the artist L. S. Lowry; the works of both artists can now be seen in the city's Art Gallery, not far away.

Glasgow's Commercial Heart

Until the eighteenth century the centre of Glasgow was at the crossroads formed by the High Street, extending south from the medieval cathedral towards the Clyde, and Gallowgate and Trongate, continued to the west as Argyle Street (p. 22). The manufacture of linen and the import of tobacco brought prosperity to the city in the eighteenth century, and grids of streets with merchants' houses were laid out to the north of Trongate and Argyle Street, the area to the south (the Broomielaw) developing a more working-class character.[36] By 1800, when the population had reached 77,000, the built-up area extended as far west as Buchanan Street, now the city's main shopping street. The population doubled over the next twenty years, and it almost doubled again, to over a quarter of a million, by 1840. By then Glasgow's economic base had expanded (see p. 190), and in 1828 a Royal Exchange was established in the former town house of the tobacco merchant William Cunninghame at the western end of Ingram Street, laid out in the second half of the eighteenth century and now lined with nineteenth-century commercial premises (Fig. 7.7). The Exchange, with its impressive arcaded interior and portico of Corinthian columns and cupola (designed by David Hamilton), stands in the middle of a handsome square, one side of which is occupied by the Royal Bank of Scotland (1820–7), its Grecian portico of Ionic columns flanked by triumphal arches framing passageways to Buchanan Street, where the city's first covered shopping arcade went up in 1827.

(continued)

Continued

Rebuilding of the surrounding area began in the 1850s, with new *palazzo*-like banks lining the main streets, and retail warehouses—in some ways the ancestors of later department stores—taking the place of the more modest domestic buildings in the streets on either side of the 70 ft-wide Argyle Street.[37] Gardner's furniture warehouse of 1856 (now a pub) in Jamaica Street, running south to the river, has a many-windowed frontage of iron and glass, reminiscent of contemporary buildings in New York; the Ca' d'Oro (1872), another iron-fronted furniture warehouse in Gordon Street, named after a palace along the Grand Canal in Venice, is more richly detailed. Meanwhile Blythswood Hill, to the north and west of the commercial centre, was developed on a rigid grid plan that took no account of the steep hills, creating a dramatic townscape reminiscent in some respects of San Francisco, another boom town of the nineteenth century. The original terraced housing still survives in Blythswood Square, but elsewhere, as the inhabitants moved away to the west or further afield in the last decades of the century, houses gave way to blocks of offices or 'chambers'. Many went up on narrow sites and were exuberantly detailed in the local red sandstone; a particularly striking example is the so-called 'Hatrack' of 1899–1902 by the local firm of Salmon, Son and Gillespie, nine storeys high, copiously bay-windowed, and with Art Nouveau-like detailing. This was a time when Glasgow, venue of international exhibitions in 1888 and 1901, saw some of the most innovative new architecture and decorative art produced in any European city. It was exemplified above all by the work of Charles Rennie Mackintosh, whose Willow Tea Rooms (1903) still survive (though rebuilt) in Sauchiehall Street, a short distance from his masterpiece, the School of Art (1897–1909), tragically burned down in 2018.

The Public Face of Government

At the beginning of the nineteenth century most of Britain's older towns were still nominally governed by oligarchic corporations whose responsibilities were much more limited than those of today's local authorities, and their buildings were correspondingly small. Much of the essential work was entrusted to improvement commissioners operating under individual Acts of Parliament. The State did not begin to play an active role until after the Reform Act of 1832, and even then it saw itself as a facilitator of urban improvement and not as an active agent. The Burgh Police Act of 1833

Fig. 7.7 When Glasgow expanded to the west of its medieval core in the 18th century, a grid of streets was laid out which was occupied at first by houses for the city's mercantile elite and later, as the middle classes moved ever further westward, by commercial premises such as those shown in this picture. Ingram Street was opened in 1781 and terminates in the Corinthian portico and cupola of the Royal Exchange, begun in 1827.

established elected councils in Scottish burghs, and 178 new elected councils were set up in England under the 1835 Municipal Corporations Act, its provisions extending to previously unincorporated towns like Birmingham and Manchester. These new bodies took over some of the responsibilities of older authorities, and in 1848 the Public Health Act gave them permissive powers to improve sanitation. This initiated a more activist approach in cities such as Birmingham, which established their own gas and water companies, successive Acts of Parliament granting powers to provide other amenities such as public baths and libraries.[38] After the passing of the second Parliamentary Reform Act of 1867 permissive powers were gradually made mandatory, setting the scene for what some have seen in retrospect as a golden age of activist 'local self-government', proclaimed in the grand civic buildings that still help shape the landscape of most of our larger city centres.

Westminster, the seat of national government, was transformed meanwhile into a discrete administrative quarter peopled by a daytime population of civil servants and politicians. After the bulk of the Palace of Westminster was burned down in 1834 it was replaced by the new Houses of Parliament (1840–60),[39] permanently altering the river front with its superb array of neo-Gothic towers, spires and pinnacles. New Government offices followed after years of wrangling among the politicians, most of them loosely classical in inspiration, lining Whitehall and providing a backdrop to St James's Park (Fig. 7.8).[40] The larger provincial towns and cities followed suit.[41] One contemporary pundit, writing in *The Builder* in 1874, declared that new town halls could 'raise the character of the inhabitants'; Charles Barry, architect of the Houses of Parliament, wanted his richly Italianate Town Hall at Halifax (1859–63) to be 'the exponent of the life and soul' of the town. That sentiment seems to have been shared by the promoters of the handsome, classically-inspired Town Hall (1866–73) at Bolton, another textile-manufacturing town. It stands in the middle of the former market place,

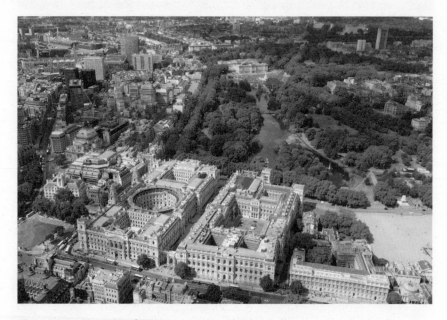

Fig. 7.8 An air view of St James's Park and Whitehall in London. In the foreground, looking out onto Whitehall, are the Treasury (formerly New Government Offices, 1899-1915) and the Foreign and Commonwealth Office (1862-75). To the right is the (Old) Treasury, formerly the Board of Trade, built in 1844-7. St James's Park is behind, with Buckingham Palace and Green Park in the distance.

vacated in 1851–5 when a new covered market was built on another site, and it now forms part of a handsome government quarter that also incorporates a semicircle of classically-inspired public buildings of the 1930s, including a Museum, Library, and council offices.[42]

Some civic authorities chose Gothic designs. The tower and spire of Manchester's Town Hall (Fig. 7.9), built in 1866–77 to the designs of Alfred Waterhouse, evoked the turreted exteriors of the medieval civic buildings on the Continent that had gone up while Manchester was still a small market town. The triangular site had formerly housed the Town Yard, bounded by factories and warehouses, and containing the city's fire-engine and weighing machine; the new building contained accommodation for the mayor and town clerk, a public hall, a council chamber, committee rooms for the Corporation and suites of offices for the city surveyor, the water board and the gas board.[43] The main façade looks out onto a newly-created

Fig. 7.9 Manchester Town Hall, Alfred Waterhouse's magnificent civic palace of 1866-77 looks out onto a newly-created square with a canopied monument to Queen Victoria's consort, Prince Albert, designed by Thomas Worthington, and inspired, like the Town Hall, by the Gothic architecture of medieval Europe.

Birmingham's Civic Forum

Birmingham's civic buildings (Fig. 7.10) went up piecemeal on a site close to the expanding commercial and banking district to the north-west of the old town centre. The first was a Town Hall, begun in 1832-4 on a site bought by the town's Street (Improvement) Commissioners. A free-standing temple-like structure on a podium, based on the Temple of Castor and Pollux in the Roman Forum, it contains a concert hall seating 4,000 people which saw the first performances of Mendelssohn's oratorio 'Elijah' in 1846 and Elgar's 'The Dream of Gerontius' in 1900, still two of the staples of Britain's thriving amateur choral tradition.[44] For one commentator, writing in 1835, the new building signified no less than 'a revival of the age of Pericles'; another, looking back fifty years later, saw it as 'the beginning of a new era. In this act we see the first steps towards the making of a city'.[45]

Birmingham's city council, set up under the 1835 Municipal Corporations Act, took over from the Street Commissioners as the main local authority in 1851, and, over the next forty years, buildings devoted to public administration and cultural pursuits went up close to the Town Hall. They included a Central Library (1855–7); a new Council House (1874–8, extended 1912) with offices for a greatly expanded municipal bureaucracy; a Museum and Art Gallery (1881–5), financed by the municipal gas company, which occupied offices underneath; Mason College (1875), the nucleus of what later became the University of Birmingham; and a central Post Office (1889). By 1881 the city's population had grown to more than 400,000, and, with Joseph Chamberlain as its mayor, it had become a byword for the 'civic gospel' or, as some called it, 'municipal socialism'. It had its own Medical Officer of Health (1872) and its own publicly-owned gasworks (1874) and waterworks (1875). When laying the foundation stone of the Council House, Chamberlain claimed that the local authority was 'endeavouring to show [its] respect for institutions upon which the welfare and happiness of the community very largely depend'. This sense of civic pride was underlined in 1880 when the Corporation laid out the sloping site surrounded by the new public buildings as a public open space with a Gothic memorial commemorating Joseph Chamberlain's mayoralty.[46] Other monuments commemorated the charismatic Baptist minister George Dawson; Josiah Mason, founder of the nascent university; the eighteenth-century scientist Joseph Priestley; and James Watt, whose business partnership with Matthew Boulton, builder of the Soho Works, north of the city, played an important part in stimulating the Industrial Revolution of which Birmingham was one of the main instigators and beneficiaries.

square whose construction involved the demolition of a hundred or so buildings, including workshops, back-to-back housing and a coal yard. Buildings were also needed to house Manchester's coercive and regulatory bodies. The police (magistrates') courts occupy a formidably turreted Gothic building of 1873 by the local architect Thomas Worthington,[47] and the mammoth central Fire Station of 1906, faced in orange terracotta and with a prominent tower, went up on a triangular site near Piccadilly railway station; it incorporated 38 flats for the firemen and their families, a laundry, gymnasium, billiard room, library and childrens' playroom.[48]

Expanding towns were especially eager to acquire the trappings of municipal prestige. At Croydon, a small market town engulfed by the spread of London's southern suburbs and experiencing a six-fold rise in population in the second half of the century, the modest town hall was demolished as part of a town-centre street improvement scheme; its replacement, built in

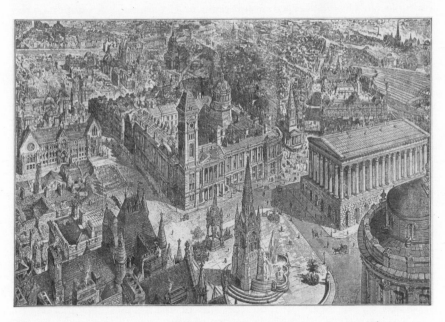

Fig. 7.10 A bird's-eye view of Birmingham's Civic Centre in 1885. The temple-like building on the right is the Town Hall, designed by J. A. Hansom and Edward Welch. To its left are the Council House, the headquarters of the city's administration, and the adjacent Museum and Art Gallery. Further left is the School of Art (1884-5). The Gothic Mason College, in the foreground has been demolished, along with the Central Library (bottom right), but the Gothic memorial to Joseph Chamberlain survives, together with a fountain of 1880 commemorating his mayoralty.

1892–6, has a massive clock tower inspired by the belfries of medieval Flemish towns.[49] The domed City Hall at Hull (1903–9), prospering from its flourishing fisheries and seaborne trade, faces a public square formed, like many similar public spaces throughout the country, by the clearance of slum housing. Like many other civic buildings of the turn of the century, it drew its stylistic inspiration from the architecture of Sir Christopher Wren. So too did the city's new Guildhall and Law Courts (1904–16), built on the site of the municipal gas works to the south of Queen's Dock; the dock was filled in in 1930, and a public park was created on the site.

An even more impressive civic complex was created at Cardiff, beginning in 1901. The city had recently developed as the main service centre for the South Wales coalfield (see p. 177),[50] and the buildings were laid out on a spacious open site in the former Cathays Park, belonging to the Marquess of Bute, owner of the recently-rebuilt castle, one of the most spectacular examples of Gothic Revival architecture in Britain, and developer of the docks from which the city ultimately derived most of its wealth. The City Hall, designed by E. A. Rickards, the most creative and exuberant architect of the 'Edwardian Baroque', shared the spacious site with an Art Gallery and Museum, buildings for the University of Wales and local government offices. Designed in the classical idiom, they are all set within a formal urban landscape which owed much to the Continental tradition of Beaux Arts planning. The wide streets are laid out on a rectilinear plan, and the copious provision of open space is reminiscent of contemporary ensembles of a similar kind in the United States and throughout the British diaspora, from Calcutta to Pretoria (Fig. 7.11).[51]

New civic buildings continued to go up between the Wars. Most, like the City Hall at Sheffield (1928–32) and the domed Council House in the Market Place at Nottingham (1927–9) were classical in inspiration. A more austere style was adopted in the new City Hall at Norwich; built 1937–9 of brick, with a 185-ft tower, it dominates the market place, from which it is separated by an open area on the site of the former fish market. At Southampton, a town that prospered following the Cunard company's removal of their transatlantic service from Liverpool in 1919 and the creation of new docks built on 460 acres of reclaimed mudflats, a new civic centre went up in 1927–33 on an undeveloped site in West Marlands, a surviving stretch of common land to the north of the city centre. Clad in Portland stone and comprising municipal offices, court rooms, an art gallery, a library and a tall clock tower, its symbolic intention was proclaimed by the

Fig. 7.11 Cardiff City Hall went up in 1901–5 in Cathays Park, a virgin site north of the city centre. Donated by the coal-owning Marquess of Bute, who profited from the development of the docks through which coal was exported throughout the world, it forms part of a purpose-built civic centre with monumental classical buildings, mostly of Portland stone, disposed along a grid of streets amid abundant open space. The City Hall is built around two courtyards, with a dome over the Council Chamber and a tower, inspired by the Baroque architecture of Spain and central Europe, to the left.

architect, E. Berry Webber, in 1938: 'The most important buildings of a city are its civic buildings and by them is the city labelled . . . the provision of our public buildings is something more than a mere job—its moral effect can be great and it deserves the finest efforts of us all. . . . Civic pride means good citizens, just as pride in a regiment produces good soldiers. The voices of all the cynics in the world cannot deny this fact.'[52]

Culture and Recreation

As Victorian city centres were tidied up, the wide, well-lit pavements of streets such as London's Regent Street and Edinburgh's Princes Street

Fig. 7.12 The Old Town of Edinburgh seen from Princes Street gardens. The Gardens were laid out in 1816-30 over the site of the North Loch, and the Old Town is seen in the distance, with the twin towers of the Free Church College to the left and the Castle to the right. The Greek-Revival National Gallery, in the foreground, stands on the Mound, an artificial hill linking the Old and New Towns.

attracted growing numbers of shoppers and *flâneurs*. Open-air promenading could also take place in public gardens like those laid out in 1816–30 in the valley of the former North Loch in Edinburgh, between Princes Street and the Old Town. From here the spectacular silhouette of the Old Town could be enjoyed as a picturesque landscape feature, its effect enhanced by the building of the Gothic memorial to Sir Walter Scott alongside Prince's Street in 1840–6. William Playfair's Grecian-inspired Royal Scottish Academy (1822–36), and his National Gallery of Scotland (1850–4) on the Mound (Fig. 7.12), created out of spoil from the building of the New Town, meanwhile proclaimed the city's self-image as the 'Athens of the North'. London's Embankment Gardens, opened in 1870 on reclaimed land above the new underground railway (see p. 185) fulfilled a similar civic and environmental function, as did, on a smaller scale, Reading's Forbury Gardens, on the site of the ruined Abbey's outer courtyard; it was rescued from dilapidation and laid out with gravelled paths and flower beds in 1861–2, and subsequently adorned with a bandstand and an over-life-size figure of a ferocious lion on a plinth, commemorating the deaths of 328 members of the Royal Berkshire Regiment during the second Anglo-Afghan War in 1879–80.[53]

The spaces around, and especially in front of, many Victorian and Edwardian public buildings became 'sites of memory', peopled by monuments to local and national heroes. The richly detailed façade of Glasgow's City Chambers (1881–9) overlooks George Square, first laid out in about 1782, and now punctuated by monuments to Queen Victoria, to Scottish heroes such as Walter Scott and James Watt, and to Prime Ministers including Robert Peel and W. E. Gladstone. The City Square at Leeds was likewise laid out in 1896 as a busy forecourt to the main railway station, following the demolition of the redundant Coloured Cloth Hall; statues of the Black Prince and assorted local worthies share the space with lamp standards modelled on the city mace and supported by lightly draped female figures representing Morning and Evening.[54] The aftermath of the First World War saw the building of countless memorials, most famously Edwin Lutyens's Cenotaph in Whitehall in London, but none is more moving than Charles Jagger's Royal Artillery memorial at Hyde Park Corner, unveiled in 1925 and featuring a huge Howitzer gun on a stone plinth carved with scenes of battle and flanked by bronze figures of mourning soldiers. A different approach was adopted by Ninian Comper for the Welsh National War Memorial (1924–8) in the gardens of Cardiff's new civic centre; here an open, circular colonnade of classical columns surrounds a plinth surmounted by a bronze figure representing Victory. Such memorials still serve as focal points for public commemoration, especially on the anniversary of Armistice Day on 11 November each year.

The emergence of a culturally active middle class in the nineteenth century created a growing demand for museums, libraries and concert halls. The plateau overlooking Liverpool's city centre, once a stretch of bare heathland dotted with lime kilns, is dominated by St George's Hall, built on the site of the City Infirmary to the designs of Harvey Lonsdale Elmes in 1841–56. One of the most impressive classically-inspired buildings in Britain, its majestic Roman-inspired façades, enriched with relief carvings by Alfred Stevens, enclose a huge, barrel-vaulted concert hall, used also for political meetings, along with court rooms and a smaller, apsidal concert room. The surrounding public space, dotted with monuments, is flanked on one side by an Art Gallery (1873–7), a Reading Room (1875–9) and the County Sessions House (1882–4), and on the other by the city's main railway terminus and a hotel. The former market square at Preston is likewise dominated by the noble Grecian-style temple front of the Harris Art Gallery (1882–93), financed by a local businessman and designed by one of the town's aldermen, James Hibbert.[55]

The most ambitious, and most impressive, collection of such buildings is at South Kensington, to the south of Hyde Park in London. The site, formerly market gardens, was purchased out of the profits of the Great Exhibition of 1851. Its wide, rectilinear streets are lined with educational and cultural institutions designed in a variety of architectural styles over a period of some sixty years: the Victoria and Albert Museum for the decorative arts—an offshoot of the Government- sponsored School of Design, begun in the 1860s; the Natural History Museum for the collections formerly housed in the overcrowded British Museum (1872–81); the Imperial Institute of 1887–93 (now Imperial College, a constituent part of the University of London); and the Royal Albert Hall (1867–71), a Roman-inspired amphitheatre for public meetings and concerts facing Gilbert Scott's Gothic memorial to the Prince Consort (1863–72) in Kensington Gardens. This was a novel urban landscape: spacious, monumental and stylistically highly diverse.

Public libraries, as distinct from subscription libraries such as the Portico Library in Manchester (1802–6), were first established under an Act of Parliament of 1850 that made it possible to fund them out of taxation and to open them free of charge.[56] Relatively few were built until the last decades of the nineteenth century, when increasing literacy and shorter working hours created a large potential clientele. At Wolverhampton, to take one example, the first public library was opened in 1869, but in 1900–2 a much larger building, of brick and terracotta, with a cheerfully eclectic exterior, was opened on the site of a former theatre in Garrick Street, south of the town centre (Fig. 7.13). The architect, H. T. Hare, one of the most gifted architects of the time, was a specialist in library design, and he made the most of the awkward obtuse-angled site, creating a strong sense of place and civic identity at what might otherwise have been an inchoate and characterless street intersection: an object-lesson both in rational planning and in successful urban design.[57]

Starting in the 1820s, Mechanics' Institutes began to offer evening classes on technical subjects to workers in full-time employment, especially in the industrial north of England. Some, like the handsome stone-built miniature *palazzo* put up at Wakefield (1825), contained libraries, reading rooms,

Fig. 7.13 Wolverhampton's first public library was housed in a former Mechanics' Institute and later in a disused police station and magistrates court. The present building, built in 1900-2 to celebrate Queen Victoria's Silver Jubilee, contained a Magazine Room and News Room on the ground floor, with reference and lending sections upstairs. They are reached by an internal staircase deftly fitted into the angle between the two wings, and surmounted by an elegant spire.

laboratories and museums.[58] The much larger Leeds Institute (now a museum) was designed 1865–8 by Cuthbert Brodrick, architect of the nearby Town Hall. It also housed an art school, supported in part by government funding designed to help improve the quality of British design, and following a curriculum established by the School of Design in South Kensington. By 1884 there were 177 such schools nationwide, some of them housed in handsome purpose-built premises, attended by 34,000 pupils. One of the finest is the Birmingham School of Art (Chamberlain and Martin, 1881–5), built of red brick, Gothic in style, and funded by local industrialists on a central site behind the city's Museum and Art Gallery; it was later expanded to include studios for craft workmanship, an important part of the local economy.[59]

Until the establishment of the Universities of London and Durham in the 1820s and 1830s it was only possible to take a degree at Oxford and Cambridge, or at one of the four long-established Scottish universities. The first universities in the England's manufacturing towns were founded in the second half of the nineteenth century, but at first they lacked the generous endowments of their older counterparts. Owens College, which became the University of Manchester, started modestly in the former home of Richard Cobden, apostle of free trade, in Quay Street, to which the businessman founder, John Owens, added a laboratory and lecture room on the site of the stables. It soon became inadequate, and, following the decision in 1859 to allow students to take examinations for University of London degrees, a new site was purchased in Oxford Road in the township of Chorlton-on-Medlock, south of 'Little Ireland' (see pp. 185–6). Here in 1869 Alfred Waterhouse, architect of the new Town Hall, and of London's Natural History Museum, designed an imposing group of structures, Gothic in style, with a ceremonial great hall, lecture rooms, laboratories and offices. Now the centre of an academic complex which includes a second university (Manchester Metropolitan) and other educational institutions,[60] it set the tone for other civic universities throughout Britain. The University of Bristol began on a suburban site in 1876, but in 1912–25 a Library and Great Hall, funded by the Wills tobacco firm, one of the city's main employers, went up on the site of an asylum for the blind next to the neo-Baroque Museum and Art Gallery at the top of Park Street (Fig. 7.14), leading uphill from the city centre to Clifton and the western suburbs. The architect, George Oatley, chose the Perpendicular Gothic style because it was, in his words, 'thoroughly English and suited to the climate and the temperament of the people', and his massive Wills Tower, closing the vista at the far end of the street, gave the city one of its most memorable landmarks.[61] The nineteen-storeyed central tower of Charles Holden's mammoth Senate House for the University of London (1932–7) is another landmark, but of a very different style and character. Steel-framed, and modernist in inspiration, though clad in Portland stone, it looms over the surviving early nineteenth-century houses of Bedford Estate in Bloomsbury (see p. 153), a substantial part of which was demolished to make way for it: a foretaste of later post-war academic developments.[62]

As more and more of the urban population moved into the suburbs, places of entertainment proliferated in city centres.[63] Private initiative lay behind a surge of theatre building in the second half of the nineteenth century. Some theatres, such as the Palace in Cambridge Circus in London (1889–91), looked out onto open spaces created by street improvements, allowing their elaborate facades to be seen from afar. Most, though, had to be fitted into existing streets, their auditoria and backstage facilities

Fig. 7.14 Park Street in Bristol, lined with early 19th-century stone-fronted houses and shops, climbs the hill leading from the city centre to the suburb of Clifton. The Wills Tower, built in 1912–25 at the top of the hill with funds from a local tobacco firm, was designed as a ceremonial entrance to the University's Great Hall and Library, its Perpendicular Gothic style alluding to the city's medieval origins.

occupying the back plots, invisible to the public. This did not prevent their promoters and architects from supplying eye-catching facades. The Grand Theatre at Leeds (1876–8) has a part-Romanesque, part Scottish Baronial façade to New Briggate, an extension of the city's main shopping and commercial street; it accommodated 3200 playgoers (including 200 standing), and the complex originally included a concert hall and 'Grand Saloon'.[64] Leeds, like other large towns, also had a smaller Music Hall (now the City Varieties theatre) offering less elevated drama to a predominantly working-class clientele in a building originally attached, like many of its kind, to an inn; it was reconstructed in 1865 by Charles Thornton, who later built the adjoining Thornton's Arcade (1877–8), leading off Briggate.[65] Cinemas made their first appearance before the First World War, many of them in suburban locations—there were already 111 in Manchester alone by 1913. But their heyday came in the inter-war period, when large and impressive buildings, often in an Art Deco-influenced modernist style, and with extravagantly exotic interiors, went up on central sites to the designs of specialist architects such as Harry Weedon (Fig. 7.15); he claimed in 1937 that his firm's buildings were 'objects of architectural beauty.... specially erected as the homes of the most progressive entertainment of the world today'.[66]

For many townspeople the main place of social interaction was the public house. Town-centre pubs offered a cheerful, warm and brightly-lit environment, with upstairs rooms over the bars that could be let out for meetings of the numerous clubs and mutual benefit societies that provided much of the cement of urban society. As real wages increased, and working hours were shortened, many pubs were lavishly rebuilt. Large breweries, such as Ind Coope's at Burton-on-Trent (see p. 180) bought up ever-greater numbers of them from the freeholders, rebuilding them to the specialised designs of architects who, in the words of a recent historian, 'knew their public and were more likely to be found in a saloon bar than an Arts Club'.[67] Often on street-corner sites, their extravagantly detailed exteriors were designed to entice the passing trade. The Philharmonic Hotel in Hope Street, Liverpool, one of the most lavish pubs in Britain, was designed in 1898–1900 in a very free version Neo-Jacobean style by Walter Thomas, a 'jovial man of large proportions, who was always immaculately dressed and wore spats'.[68] He worked with artists and craftsmen from the nearby School of Art to satisfy the brewer's aim 'to so beautify the public houses under his control that they would be an ornament to the town of his birth', and in

Fig. 7.15 Architectural modernism was slow to make an impact on Britain's town and city centres, and when it did so it was often in an Art Deco guise. Cinemas enjoyed enormous popularity in the 1920s and 30s, and their buildings were intended to convey a sense of slick, up-to-date glamour to their patrons, as seen here in Harry Weedon's Odeon, Leicester Square in London (1937), with its sans-serif lettering and the black marble cladding.

Fig. 7.16 The Vines occupies a corner site on Lime Street, leading to the Liverpool's main railway station and to St George's Hall, seen in the distance. The pub was built in 1907 to the designs of Walter Thomas, a specialist in this type of building, its extravagant façade appealing both to the brewers' need to lure customers and to the clients' desire for a lavish setting for their drinking.

doing so created one of the most successful fusions of architecture and craftsmanship of the period.[69] Thomas also designed the Vines (1907) at the corner of Lime Street, Liverpool (Fig. 7.16), close to the city's main railway station, announcing its presence with a riotous assemblage of loosely Baroque detailing, surmounted by curvy gables and crowned by a turret. The flashy exterior was no doubt intended to rival that of the Crown (1905), not far away in the same street, with its equally extravagant, almost Art Nouveau, façade displaying its own name, and that of its owners (Walker's brewery in Warrington) in bold, curvaceous lettering.

The larger town-centre pubs offered rooms for overnight visitors, but more accommodation was provided in the hotels that sprang up from the middle of the century onwards, often next to, or close to, railway stations. Hotel-owners needed to fit the maximum possible accommodation onto their sites. The seven-storeyed Midland Hotel in Manchester (1898–1903) occupies the whole of a two-acre block between four streets facing the Midland Railway's Central station (now the G-Mex centre) south of the Town Hall, its facades of granite, brick and terracotta complementing those of the nearby warehouses going up at about the same time. There were four hundred bedrooms, along with a luxurious restaurant, a thousand-seat theatre and a winter garden; a post office and a roof garden were also provided for the benefit of the 70,000 guests who stayed there in the year after its opening.[70] Similar levels of comfort were provided in the Adelphi Hotel in Liverpool, a steel-framed building of 1911–14 catering for passengers in transatlantic liners, its once-luxurious interiors concealed behind a bland facade of Portland stone.[71]

Hotels, like restaurants, which also multiplied in the late nineteenth century, went out of their way to provide an attractive environment for male customers and also for increasingly emancipated middle-class women, whose tastes and purchasing power did much to transform city centres. Less wealthy travellers had to make do with cheaper establishments, usually in converted houses or in institutions such as the Young Men's Christian Association, adjacent to the Midland Hotel in Peter Street, Manchester, 1911, built of reinforced concrete, and containing a swimming pool, running track, gymnasium and a 900-seat auditorium.[72] And for the destitute—then as now an inescapable component of the urban scene—there were night shelters or, at worst, the workhouse.

Resort Towns

Reporting in 1840, the Commons Select Committee on the Health of Towns made a useful distinction between different categories of English towns and cities: London, always *sui generis*; manufacturing towns; seaports; county towns; and watering places.[73] Seaside resorts had existed ever since the seventeenth century, and they proliferated from the 1840s onwards, when railway travel drastically cut journey times; one of the newer resorts, on the Wirral in Cheshire, was even called New Brighton. Seaside excursions and holidays came to play an ever greater part in the lives of the urban population in the second half of the century, especially after 1871, when new legislation limited the working week, allowing for Bank Holidays and holiday pay and creating further demand among the industrial working class.[74] Some existing resorts, like Tenby in South Wales and Whitby in Yorkshire, were developed on land alongside existing ports and harbours.[75] Others, like Torquay (Devon), Folkestone (Kent) and Eastbourne (Sussex), were newly laid out near villages or hamlets, or, like Southport (Lancashire) and Bournemouth (Hampshire), on virgin sites.[76] Most were linked by railways to particular cities for which they became in many respects detached adjuncts: places like Clacton-on-Sea (Essex) for east London, Weston-super-Mare (Somerset) for Birmingham, Llandudno and other resorts on the North Wales coast for Liverpool, Blackpool for the Lancashire cotton towns, Rothesay and Dunoon for Glasgow.

For any aspiring new resort town an essential precondition was the creation of an urban infrastructure enabling entrepreneurs and builders to build accommodation for both for visitors and for a resident population, many of them women, and most of them employed in service industries. This pattern of development was echoed to a greater or lesser extent in most seaside resorts. At Saltburn-by-Sea, on a cliff top on the North Yorkshire coast, the main promoters were the Pease family, prominent in the development of nearby Middlesbrough. They established an Improvement Company which laid out parallel terraces of small houses for service workers on either side of a branch railway line, with boarding-houses and hotels facing the sea. Detached villas and a 120-room hotel—the Zetland, named after the titled landowners of the site—face south over a picturesque public garden laid out on either side of stream running down to the sea; other attractions included a pier reached by a still-functioning funicular railway.[77]

Llandudno

Llandudno, on the North Wales coast, grew up around a north-facing bay with a sandy beach between two headlands—the Great and Little Orme—the first of which was dotted with copper mines. A small settlement, together with a handful of villas and a new church, grew up in the early years of the nineteenth century on the eastern slopes of the Great Orme, but large-scale development did not take place until the common land facing the bay was enclosed in 1848. Most of the land belonged to the Mostyn family, who soon set about draining the land along the sea front. They then commissioned a plan for laying out a 'New Town' on the neck of land between the seaside promenade and Conwy Bay, with a crescent raised up over the sand dunes, a broad, shop-lined street (Mostyn Street) on the land behind it, and a grid of parallel residential streets leading south, linked by narrower streets for the service population. An Improvement Act of 1854 established a body of commissioners, chaired by members of the Mostyn family, with powers to create an effective infrastructure, and to impose regulations which would 'ensure proper ventilation, sewerage and uniformity of frontage and elevation which bestow value upon property to the injury of none'.[78] The opening of a branch railway from the main Chester to Holyhead line in 1858 made the resort more accessible to holidaymakers, especially from the textile towns of the north of England. In this way Llandudno, like other resort towns, with their promise of fresh air, leisure and entertainment, provided—at least for those who could afford it—an escape from the rigours of modern urban life.

The building of Llandudno was left to the private market, with results that have determined its character down to the present day. Stuccoed hotels and boarding houses line the promenade along the sea front (Fig. 7.17), and the main shops went up along Mostyn Street, some of them sheltering behind attractive iron-framed walkways with glazed roofs and interspersed with churches and chapels. Hotels and boarding houses line the spacious streets leading south from the promenade, with smaller two-up and two-down terraced houses in the cross streets between them. Away from the beach, entertainment was focused on the pier, built in 1876–8 and lengthened in 1908, with its pavilion at the far end, and theatres and pleasure gardens offered further opportunities for recreation. And by the end of the century Llandudno, like most resort towns, was attracting a large middle-class residential population, many of whom lived in large brick houses fronting the streets leading south out of the town.

Fig. 7.17 Successful seaside resorts needed to attract visitors with the prospect of comfortable lodgings, ideally allowing views of the sea. This explains the linear layout of Llandudno, with its esplanade, seen here, hugging the shore. Laid out after 1854, the hotels and boarding houses catered for visitors arriving by train at the station, which is hidden away among commercial premises behind the sea-front hotels.

The resort's social character was neatly captured by a local newspaper in 1873: 'You don't run across the people you meet at a big hotel in Brighton, Wiesbaden or Ems, you are on the contrary drawn into a sort of big family party'.[79] For all its charm, Saltburn never attracted large numbers of visitors, and only half of the projected plan was ever completed. Blackpool, by contrast, the largest seaside resort of all, was attracting four million visitors by 1914, its development and promotion steered, unusually, by the local authority. At Cleethorpes (Lincolnshire) the Manchester, Sheffield and Lincolnshire Railway took the initiative following a hesitant start by the landowner, Sidney Sussex College in Cambridge; at Clacton-on-Sea a newly-established development company played the leading part.[80] These resorts, like Weston-super-Mare, Southend-on-Sea (Essex) and Margate (Kent) succeeded in luring day visitors as well as longer-term working-class

holidaymakers from London and the industrial towns, and their distinctive
seafront landscapes of funfairs and amusement parks presented, as to some
extent they still do, a sharp contrast to that of resorts like Eastbourne or
Frinton-on-Sea in Essex that catered for the more sedate tastes of the
middle class.

Inland resorts and spas also flourished in the late nineteenth and early
twentieth centuries, many them heavily dependent, like seaside resorts, on
railways. Bath, the oldest inland resort of all, enjoyed a renaissance with the
building of a large new hotel, the remodelling of the central baths complex
(1895–7) and the building of a new Museum and Art Gallery in 1897–1900.
A similar process took place at Harrogate (Yorkshire), an existing spa town
that became a genteel satellite of Leeds and Bradford after the arrival of the
first railway in 1848. Much of the development occurred at Low Harrogate,
close to the Royal Pump Room, built in 1841–2 over a sulphurous well by
Isaac Strutt, a member of an innkeeping family. New estates of substantial
houses for permanent residents went up along spacious streets at Victoria
Park, developed by a private company after 1860, and later, starting in 1889,
on a 54-acre estate belonging to the Duchy of Lancaster. This influx of
prosperous residents led in turn to the opening of new shops—of which
there were 800 by 1911—and new baths, theatres and a market, all catering
for the local resident population as well as for short term visitors. The *Daily
Graphic* exclaimed in 1892: 'One supreme advantage we have over many
holiday resorts— [Harrogate] enjoys an absolute immunity from the ordinary tripper'.[81] Something of this exclusiveness can be experienced in the
Valley Gardens, laid out as a private initiative—there is still an admission
fee—on low-lying swampy land dotted with springs, close to the Royal
Pump Room and opened in 1887. Here, as in other inland resorts such as
Tunbridge Wells and Cheltenham, the ideal of a health resort is fused with
that of the suburban *rus in urbe* to create an environment that still has the
power to captivate both residents and visitors.

8

The Suburban Landscape

The street where I live in Oxford does not figure in any of the tourist guides to that much-visited city. Fairly wide and dead straight, about a mile and a half south of the city centre, it is lined with terraced, semi-detached and detached houses built in the first half of the twentieth century, each with a front garden and many with long, narrow, leafy back gardens. There is a more recent housing development on the site of a small factory of the 1930s, demolished in 1993. An Anglican church and vicarage stand at one end, a Baptist church (currently shared with the Salvation Army) at the other and a bowls club at the end of a side street halfway along. The southern end of the street abuts onto a recreation ground next to a council estate of the 1920s. Shops, pubs, a car showroom, a tyre works and sundry bed and breakfast establishments are dotted along the Abingdon Road, an ancient highway which runs parallel to the east, now carrying a continuous procession of cars, buses and lorries into and out of the city. The population is a mixed one, increasingly ethnically diverse and of varied national origins, made up of professionals, managers, skilled and semi-skilled workers, students and retired people. Suburban streets like this can be found in every town and city in the British Isles, evading easy categorization or simplistic stereotyping.

The apparent similarity of most English suburbs masks a multitude of different, distinctive histories shaped by topography, the accidents of land ownership and the vagaries of taste. South Oxford, never as fashionable as the more affluent suburbs to the north of the city, is a narrow peninsula of housing laid out over a period of about a hundred years on the flood plain of the River Thames (see p. 29).[1] Save for one isolated farmhouse, few buildings are known to have existed alongside the main road until after 1844, when the Great Western Railway pushed a line through the parish of South Hinksey (then in Berkshire) to a terminus just south of the Thames;

by 1851 a hamlet called New Hinksey had grown up between it and the Abingdon Road. Like many settlements of its kind, it comprised terraces of small houses, some brick-built and others of stone, interspersed with shops and alehouses (Fig. 8.1). An elementary school, a church and a Wesleyan chapel served the small population, some of whom worked in Oxford's waterworks, established here in 1854, its reservoir occupying a lake formed by gravel-digging for the railway, whose main line was diverted to the west of the lake in 1852. After the closure of the waterworks in 1934 the site was turned into a park, with an outdoor swimming pool on the site of the filter bed; the handsome red-brick pumping station is now the local community centre.[2] The old railway branch lingered on as a goods line until 1872, and the northern part of the abandoned line soon became another street of terraced houses. Meanwhile speculative housing began to creep slowly southwards along the Abingdon Road, reaching New Hinksey by 1900. By then the hamlet had been absorbed into the city of Oxford; the development of my own street, further south, followed over the next forty years. This patchy pattern of development has been characteristic of most English suburbs since they first appeared in the Middle Ages.

Origins

Suburbs are residential districts attached to towns and economically dependent upon them. They have existed for as long as towns, but modern suburbia made its first appearance in London. Already in the sixteenth century some wealthy citizens were building houses well outside the walls. By the 1720s, according to Daniel Defoe, the road leading north from the City of London towards Enfield, some ten miles away, was like 'one continu'd street', lined with houses 'generally belonging to the middle sort of mankind, grown wealthy by trade, and who still taste of London; some of them live both in the city and in the country at the same time: yet many of these are immensely rich'.[3] Some of the houses were arranged in urban-style terraces, like a brick-built group of 1658 that survives at Newington Green, three miles or so north of the City.[4] Grander houses also began to cluster around existing agricultural villages. London merchants were already buying land and building houses at Hackney in the sixteenth century; the present Sutton House (now owned by the National Trust) is a much-altered survival of a house built in 1535 for Ralph Sadler, one of Thomas Cromwell's

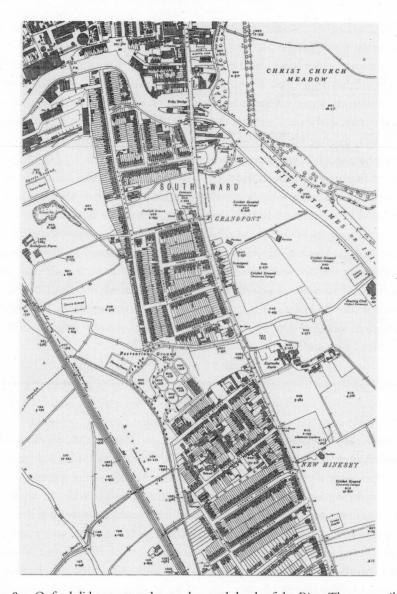

Fig. 8.1 Oxford did not expand onto the south bank of the River Thames until the second half of the 19th century, when housing was built piecemeal and incrementally on the low ground to the west of the Abingdon Road, originally an 11th-century causeway across the flood plain. The main line of the Great Western Railway is at the bottom left, and the reservoir next to it supplied the city with water; the filter beds next to the Recreation Ground shown between two lower blocks of housing were turned into a swimming pool in the 1930s.

henchmen.[5] The practice spread in the seventeenth and eighteenth centuries, especially to hilltop villages such as Hampstead, famous for its healing waters, and to places on the banks of the Thames such as Richmond and Twickenham, favoured by courtiers and politicians. Defoe pointed out that merchants moved out of London 'to draw their breath in clean air, and to divert themselves and their families in hot weather':[6] an equivalent of the Italian practice of *villeggiatura*, and an anticipation of the taste for second homes which has transformed much of rural England in modern times. The former presence of country estates of this kind influenced the development of several nineteenth- and twentieth-century London suburbs. Sometimes the houses have survived as museums or institutions, their gardens turned into public parks. Most commonly, both house and grounds fell victim to housing developments; at Leyton, a largely working-class suburb north-east of the City, nearly all of the fifty or so gentlemen's houses identified as having existed in the eighteenth century had vanished by 1900.[7]

Many Londoners escaping the crowded city built their houses alongside roads or beside greens and commons, where small parcels of land were easy to purchase. In 1779 the novelist Richard Graves deplored the fact that 'every little clerk in office must have his villa, and every tradesman his country-house. The cheesemonger retreats to his little pasteboard office on Turnham Green [at Chiswick, west of London], and when smoking his pipe under his codling hedge on his gravel walk... fancies himself a Scipio or Cincinnatus in his retreat; and returns with reluctance to town on Monday night (or Tuesday morning) regardless of his shop, and his inquisitive and disgusted customers'.[8] Some late seventeenth- and early eighteenth-century merchants' houses can still be seen at Stepney Green, a mile or so east of the City, in an area later swamped by working-class housing but now enjoying a measure of gentrification.[9] Houses also began to be built after 1700 in the area now called the Old Town on the north side of Clapham Common, four miles or so south of the river, and a few minutes' walk away from the existing village centre; they include a brick terrace of three houses (Nos. 39-43) put up as a speculation by a merchant-tailor in 1704 and another (Nos. 12-23) built by a carpenter in 1714.[10] By the end of the century all three sides of the triangular common were lined with houses,[11] most of them detached, and all containing the accommodation deemed necessary for prosperous middle-class domesticity: two or three reception rooms, four or five bedrooms, servants' quarters, and a garden (Fig. 8.2).

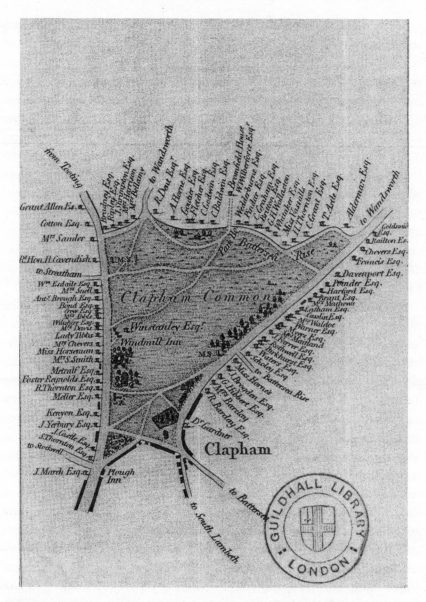

Fig. 8.2 A map of Clapham Common, London, in 1800. Clapham was one of the villages that attracted well-to-do Londoners in the 18th century by its well-drained ground and its easy riding distance along one of the main roads leading into the capital from the south. This map (north is at the bottom) shows the houses built around the Common, originally a tract of unenclosed land used by the villagers to pasture their animals.

A new church was built in 1774-6,[12] and, as the population continued to grow, shops opened to supply the new residents, some of which still survive; clusters of cottages were also built for the service population on which any urban community depended. Similar groups of houses went up in Kensington and Chelsea; to the north; in Islington, Hampstead and Highgate; and further out, at Maze Hill in Greenwich, Sion Row and Maids of Honour Row at Twickenham, and alongside Richmond Green.[13] The improvement of turnpike roads and the building of new bridges over the Thames after the end of the Napoleonic Wars encouraged ribbon developments of terraced houses, as in Kennington Road and Camberwell New Road. They linked the City and Westminster to semi-suburbanized villages like Clapham, But until the coming of the railway and the tram, when they were swamped by the spread of suburban housing, townships of this kind remained outliers of urban culture in what was still a hinterland of pastures and market gardens: *urbs in rure*, rather than the opposite.[14]

A similar pattern of development occurred on the outskirts of Bristol. St Michael's Hill, to the north of the city, become popular for 'garden houses'— the second homes of wealthy merchants—in the sixteenth and seventeenth centuries; Red Lodge (now a museum) was built in 1578-89 as a banqueting house by Sir John Young, collector of customs,[15] and nineteen such buildings existed by the 1660s. The area could be reached most easily from the city centre by Christmas Steps, 'steppered', according to a surviving commemorative plaque, 'done & finished September 1669 by and at the cost of Jonathan Blackwell, esq, formerly sheriff of this citty...and Sir Robert Yeamans when mayor'. Merchants' villas sprang up at Clifton, further west in the eighteenth century; Goldney House (now a students' hall of residence) was built by a Quaker banker in 1722 and was extended by his son, who imparted an air of classical sophistication by the construction of a grotto and a terrace walk overlooking the River Avon. One visitor exclaimed in 1777: 'What a different world you find yourself in after crossing [Bristol] and go on Clifton hill: I thought myself in a parallel situation with Aeneas, who after passing the abode of the unhappy, found himself in the Elysian fields'.[16] Terraces and squares followed soon after the expansion of hot springs in the 1780s (Fig. 8.3). Clifton's apogee as a middle-class suburb came in the post-Napoleonic years, when the Bristol's merchant classes began to flee the crowded and increasingly insalubrious city centre and to establish themselves in handsome stone-fronted classical terraces and villas.[17]

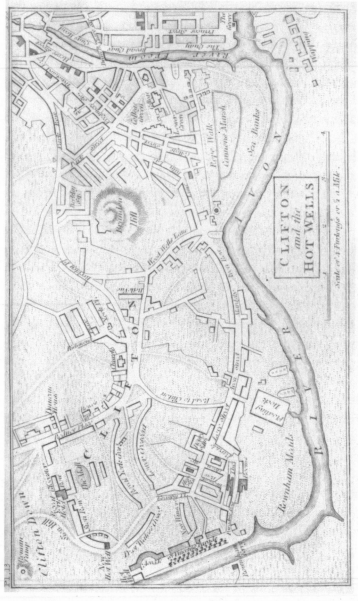

Fig. 8.3 Clifton grew up on the high ground to the east of Bristol, to which it was linked by Park Street (top right). The 'Hot Wells' (bottom left) were part of a spa on the banks of the Avon that enjoyed a brief popularity in the 18th century. Clifton's Parade and Assembly Rooms catered for fashionable visitors, but there were also terraces of housing for permanent residents, sited so as to command views over the river valley, with its shipping entering and leaving the city's docks and quays.

This process can be matched in all of Britain's larger towns. New Walk at Leicester is a tree-lined pedestrian thoroughfare laid out as a public walk by the town's Corporation in 1785, leading south out of the town through a still-rural landscape of common fields towards the town's racecourse. Following the enclosure of the fields, starting in 1824, it was gradually lined with middle-class villas and a proprietary (private) school, now the city's Museum and Art Gallery (Fig. 8.4).[18]

Exeter's merchants and professionals began to desert the densely packed city centre towards the end of the eighteenth century, moving into elegant houses outside the city walls such as those in Colleton Crescent (1802) and at Southernhay, begun in 1789 and laid out as a kind of garden suburb by the city authorities on the site of a former burial ground; the brick-built terraces, adorned with Coade stone detailing, overlook an open space which was later landscaped as a picturesque garden.[19] Some wealthy banking

Fig. 8.4 The tree-lined New Walk at Leicester was laid out through the common fields to the south of the city in 1785. Intended as a fashionable promenade for the wealthier citizens, it attracted housing, including the terraces on the right of the picture, after the fields were enclosed in 1824, and it still retains its leafy, semi-exclusive character.

families, like the Barings, preferred to live in detached villas, a good example of which can be seen at the end of Colleton Crescent; another (Rougemont House) was built for a surgeon, John Patch, next to the castle ruins. Suburbs later grew up further away, like Pennsylvania Park, built on Baring land with linked detached houses.[20] Developments of this kind implied a separation of home and workplace, encouraging a more secluded, privatized lifestyle for merchants, professionals and their families.

Places like Clifton grew by accretion; there was no overall planning of the kind that existed in upmarket urban extensions like those of London's aristocratic West End. Terraces stood cheek by jowl with detached houses. Most were classical in inspiration, but some had Gothic or castellated trimmings, like Hunter's Lodge (1808) in Belsize Lane, on the slopes of the hill leading from London to Hampstead. Others were designed in the self-consciously rustic *cottage orné* manner seen in the gabled, barge-boarded bungalow called The Hermitage at the top of Camberwell Grove.[21] By 1800, semi-detached houses were also appearing in large numbers around the fringes of London. The Paragon at Blackheath, on the southern edge of Greenwich Park, is an elegant development of six semi-detached pairs designed and built in 1793-1807 by a local carpenter and surveyor, Michael Searles; the houses are grouped around a shallow curve, linked by Doric colonnades.[22] Most early semi-detached houses were less architecturally ambitious; one of England's literary shrines, Keats House at Hampstead, was originally a semi-detached pair with a stuccoed facade and a low-pitched slate roof, in half of which the poet lived from 1818 to 1820.

By 1800, London's population was nearing a million. Writing in 1810-11, Louis Simond was appalled by the fact that, when approaching from the north, 'you travel between two rows of brick houses, to which new ones are added every day... London extends its great polypus-arms over the country around. The population is not increased by any means of production to these appearances—only transferred from the centre to the extremities. This centre is become a mere counting-house, or place of business. People live in the outskirts of the town in better air—larger houses and at a smaller rent— and stages [stage coaches] passing every half hour, facilitate communications.'[23] Much of this suburban growth took the form of small-scale extensions to existing villages and hamlets[24] and ribbon development along roads. But as the urban population continued to expand, and as city centres began to be transformed by commerce and industry, a new type of planned suburban landscape came into being, first in London and later in other towns and cities. Its character was determined by two related social changes: the urge to separate home and work, and the growing demand by middle-class people for socially differentiated urban areas. And its appearance depended increasingly on the application of the aesthetics of the Picturesque to the urban environment.

The first planned urban extensions for the middle classes were usually laid out, like the West End of London, on classical principles: rows of terraced housing aligned along wide, usually straight, streets, interspersed with squares and (sometimes) crescents, as in Belgravia and the Ladbroke estate in north Kensington.[25] The western extension of Edinburgh's New Town was also laid out in this fashion. Like most developments of this kind, it was built up slowly over a period of some fifty years, starting in the 1820s and culminating in the development of the Heriot Hospital Trust's land between the Haymarket and the Water of Leith in the 1860s and 1870s (Fig. 5.6); it provided a setting for new landmarks, notably St Mary's Episcopal Cathedral (by George Gilbert Scott, 1874-1917), which dramatically closes the vista at the western end of Melville Street.

Glasgow spread similarly in the second half of the century over the hills ('drumlins') to the north-west of the commercial centre. Here a wedge of land in multiple ownership began to be developed for middle-class housing after the opening in 1841 of the wide and relentlessly straight Great Western Road, formed under an Act of Parliament to provide a new route into the city. The building of terraces ('Dwelling-houses of a superior description'), got seriously under way in the 1850s (Fig. 8.5), and continued well into the 1870s. Developers and builders stressed the environmental attractions of the area.[26] Prospective buyers of a fourteen-roomed house of 1870 in Westbourne Terrace, south of the Great Western Road, were promised 'a landscape truly picturesque, seldom obtained in Suburban Dwellings'.[27] The prevailing westerly winds protected it from atmospheric pollution, and the natural beauties of the area were enhanced by the presence of a Botanic Garden, opened in 1842, and by Kelvingrove Park, laid on land acquired by the city council in 1851. Kelvingrove Park is overlooked from the east by the Woodlands Hill estate, made up of large terraced houses completed in 1855, and to the north by the University, removed in 1864-70 from its city centre site (see Chapter 6) to a magnificent Gothic palace designed by George Gilbert Scott. Taken as a whole, the area is one of the most impressive examples of urban domestic planning in nineteenth-century Britain.

Fig. 8.5 Great Western Terrace, Glasgow. This austere but impressive row of middle-class houses, flanking one of the main roads leading west out of the city, was designed by the Glasgow-based Alexander ('Greek') Thomson in 1869. The houses are faced in smooth local ashlar stone and are set back from the road. Mostly of two storeys over basements, they are entered through porches with columns of the Ionic order.

The Eyre estate at St John's Wood, to the north of the present Marylebone Road—London's first ring road—was developed on somewhat different principles. The first scheme, of 1794, envisaged a low-density layout of detached and semi-detached houses, each with a front as well as a back garden, lining gently curving streets.[28] It was never completed as originally intended, but the effect of a planned suburban *rus in urbe* can still be experienced not far away in the Park Village, laid out by George IV's favoured architect John Nash in 1824-38 on Crown land north-east of the new Regent's Park (see p. 155). Here, behind the stuccoed terraces fronting the Park, and on either side of a branch of the new Regent's Canal (of which Nash was a leading promoter), was a novel low-density townscape made up of curvaceous streets and houses designed in an engaging variety of architectural styles: a garden suburb in all but name.[29]

Neighbourhoods of this kind were products of the building lease system. Landlords and developers supplied the infrastructure of roads and drainage, and, by imposing restrictive covenants banning noxious trades and by stipulating large plot sizes and a low housing density, poorer inhabitants could be effectively excluded. This in turn created conditions for a suburban culture that celebrated domesticity. It also appealed to a growing cult of gardening, especially among middle-class women who were expected to stay at home when their husbands were at work. For John Claudius Loudon, writing in 1838, 'a suburban residence, with a very small portion of land attached, will contain all that is essential for happiness' for anyone with an annual income of £200-£300 or more.[30] This was the kind of salary that a successful shopkeeper might expect, and, as the numbers of such people increased, so too did the demand for suburban residences.

Victorian and Edwardian Suburbs

Starting in the 1830s, planned middle-class estates went up all over London's urban fringe, their inhabitants commuting into the City or West End either by short-stage coaches (replaced in time with horse buses) or, from the middle of the century, by train.[31] Some, like the Eton College estate to the north of Regent's Park, begun in the 1840s, aimed to attract 'opulent and industrious professional men and tradesmen' with annual salaries of around £500 or even more. Someone with this kind of income would be able to employ three living-in servants, and the houses on the Eton College estate, and comparable developments, were of three storeys, semi-detached, loosely Italianate in style, with servants' quarters in the basements (Fig. 8.6). Anglican churches, usually Gothic in style, were an essential part of such communities, but shops and pubs—essential for making cash payments to the builders—were relegated to the fringes, the residents depending for their supplies on horse-drawn delivery.[32] Such townscapes with their quiet, empty streets were later celebrated by artists such as Robert Bevan, and were imitated in the larger provincial cities of Britain and throughout the worldwide British diaspora.

A suburb, wrote one contributor to the *Builder* magazine in 1863, was not a closely-packed town but an agglomeration of semi-detached rural-looking villas within a moderate distance of town. That ideal still pervades Edgbaston, the fashionable suburb for Birmingham's manufacturers and merchant princes such as the Cadburys and Chamberlains. Edgbaston is two miles from the city centre, beyond the closely-packed streets of working-class houses that steadily encroached on the surrounding fields as the population

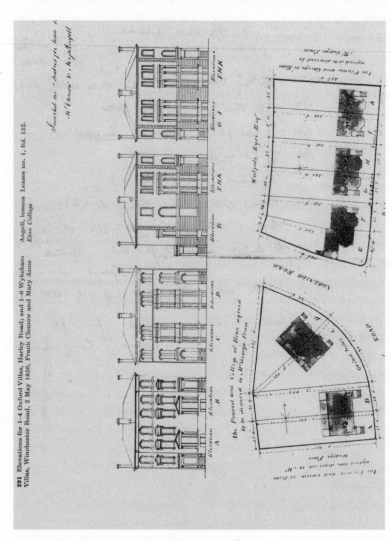

291 Elevations for 1–4 Oxford Villas, Harley Road; and 1–6 Wykeham Villas, Winchester Road, 2 May 1856, Frank Clemow and Mary Anne Angell, lessees. Leases no. 1, fol. 152. Eton College

Fig. 8.6 Eton College's Chalcots estate in north London was developed for middle-class housing, starting in the 1840s. With their three storeys and basements, the semi-detached houses shown in this plan of 1856 were large enough to accommodate businessmen and professionals, their families and their servants. Each house has a long back garden and a smaller front garden facing the street, resulting in a low housing density characteristic of newly developed middle-class districts throughout the country.

expanded. The first building leases were issued by the Gough family of Edgbaston Hall in 1811-13, and development went forward slowly and incrementally over the next forty years, with the detached villas of the merchant aristocracy in their spacious gardens occupying the heart of the estate and smaller houses on the lower ground.[33] A similar pattern of slow, carefully regulated development was followed at Victoria Park, roughly the same distance south of the centre of Manchester, from which it was originally separated by open country. Here a gated estate was laid out in 1837 on land acquired by eight promoters under an Act of Parliament and building continuing until the 1860s;[34] as at Edgbaston, the descendants of the city's merchant princes moved away when their protected enclave was surrounded by speculative housing in the twentieth century, and most of the villas that survive are now occupied by the University. Estates of this kind, with their gated entrances, were designed to create a sense of seclusion and protection for their affluent residents, solidifying already existing social divisions. Friedrich Engels, who later moved to Rusholme, another of Manchester's affluent middle-class suburbs, pointed out in 1844 that suburbanites commuting from places like Victoria Park to the centre of Manchester along shop-lined streets, or later by train, could remain unaware of the living conditions of the industrial workers on whose labour they depended.[35] Or, as an unknown Midlands poetaster wrote in 1851 of Edgbaston:

> 'The beauteous suburb swells with lofty pride;
> The vulgar poor are there forbid to hide'.[36]

Similar developments occurred in other towns all over the country, as successful merchants and professional people vacated their city-centre houses in search of more spacious, secluded environments. Ownership by a single individual or institution could lead to the development of desirable enclaves such as The Avenues, west of Pearson Park in Hull, opened in 1862, and Roath Park on the Marquess of Bute's estate in Cardiff, laid out in 1888-9.[37]

As the urban population continued to expand in the 1850s and 1860s there was a rise in building fuelled by the availability of cheap agricultural land and an abundance of capital which could be borrowed by builders at relatively low interest rates.[38] Much of this capital went into providing suburban housing for the affluent clerical and mercantile middle classes, and increasingly also for the much larger numbers of aspirational clerks, shopkeepers and tradespeople. The middle classes now made up roughly a fifth of the British population, and the expansion of suburbs echoed their

The Park Estate at Nottingham

The Park Estate was developed over a very long period on land belonging to the Duke of Newcastle, owner of the castle that looms over the site from the sandstone cliff on which it was built. The town's population nearly doubled, to over 50,000, in the first half of the nineteenth century, and in 1827 a plan was prepared by P. F. Robinson, author of several pattern books for picturesque villas and cottages. Rows of stuccoed, semi-detached houses soon went up close to the castle, but work stopped after it was burned down by rioters enraged by exclusion from the park and by the initial failure to pass the Parliamentary Reform Bill in 1832. Development resumed in the late 1830s, and in about 1840 a new plan was brought out. It envisaged a development of substantial detached villas laid out alongside gently curving streets in the chasm below the castle, with a Gothic church in the centre. But a nationwide slump in building then ensued, and building did not get going again until after the death of the unpopular fourth Duke in 1851 and the construction of a tunnel (finished in 1855), easing access to the road between Nottingham and Derby. Work started in 1854 under the supervision of the locally-based architect T. C. Hine, who brought out a new plan featuring wide streets arranged in concentric ovals around two 'circuses'. Classical elevations and stucco facings had now gone out of fashion, and the detached and semi-detached houses, many of them designed by Hine himself, were built of brick in a variety of styles which reflect the increasingly eclectic tastes of the second half of the century (Fig. 8.7). The site had been largely filled up by the 1880s, and the estate, with its 355 houses, many of them converted into flats, still retains its quiet, affluent character, zealously preserved by the private company that maintains it, and by an active residents' association.[39]

growing wealth.[40] For such people the possession of a house with a front garden became an essential mark of respectability. Charles Pooter, the fictional anti-hero of George and Weedon Grossmith's *Diary of a Nobody* (1892), lived at 'The Laurels', Brickfield Terrace, Holloway—never a fashionable suburb—in a six-roomed house with a 'front breakfast parlour' and a railway line at the back. The Frenchman Hippolyte Taine, writing thirty years earlier in 1862, observed that the English 'turn out houses as we turn out Paris fancy-goods... The most modest houses... are pretty by reason of their cleanness: the window panes are polished like mirrors, there is almost

Fig. 8.7 A street in the Park Estate, Nottingham, developed on land belonging to the Dukes of Newcastle. Park Drive was built up with substantial middle-class houses, starting in the 1850s. The estate is gated and through traffic is still not allowed.

always a small garden, green, and full of flowers, and the façade will be covered by a creeper or climbing plant'.[41]

Most suburbs did not grow in the slow, carefully controlled manner of places like the Park estate in Nottingham. More commonly, towns and cities expanded in a piecemeal and unco-ordinated fashion, their layout and appearance depending on the pattern of land ownership and increasingly on the availability of public transport, especially for places outside the two- or three-mile radius of city centres from which it made sense to walk to work. At Enfield, a small market town ten miles north of London, a branch of the Great Eastern Railway was opened in 1849, and soon afterwards a tract of agricultural land was bought up by the National Freehold Land Society with a view to creating 'forty-shilling freeholds' that carried with them the right to vote in Parliamentary elections; the estate, called Enfield New Town, was laid out on a rectilinear plan and was slowly filled up with detached, semi-detached and terraced houses.[42] The old market town had grown up on the edge of Enfield Chase, a large area of former royal hunting ground on higher ground enclosed in 1779, and in 1871 the Great Northern Railway opened a branch line of its own with a station on the former Chase land. An estate was laid out here in 1879 by a developer, A. Culloden Rowan, on the grounds of the nearby Bycullah House, built by a retired Indian army officer. With its spacious layout and winding streets, it was designed to attract wealthier residents, but development was slow, and many of the larger houses have now been demolished and replaced by blocks of flats. By the outbreak of the First World War Enfield's town centre had acquired new parades of shops interspersed with banks and large pubs of recognizably urban character. But the built-up areas that clustered around the old town and alongside roads remained separated from each other by agricultural, formerly open-field land and market gardens, and the intervening spaces were not filled with housing estates until the 1930s, many of them serving the industries which had grown up by then in the eastern part of the old parish, close to the River Lea (Fig. 8.8).

A similar pattern of piecemeal development can be found around the peripheries of all of Britain's larger towns. Bradford was one of the fastest-growing industrial towns in the second half of the nineteenth century, its inner districts gradually clogged with worsted mills, warehouses (see pp. 251–6) and back-to-back houses. Handsome stone-built terraces, interspersed with semi-detached villas, began to appear to the north of the centre in the 1840s, later expanding over the former open fields of Manningham, a village which had already attracted detached villas for the wealthier manufacturers (Fig. 8.9). The initiative for some of these developments came from the many building societies that sprang up all over England in the mid-century. Southfield Square, taking its name from one of the town's common fields, was built by a building society in 1853-65 and was lined with two-storeyed terraces grouped around three sides of an open space that was given over to allotments. The nearby Apsley Crescent (1854-5) was part of a similar planned development designed by a local surveyor, Joseph Smith and comprising thirteen linked two-storeyed houses, each with its front garden, pedimented doorcase and classical cornice.[43] Then in 1870-3 a massive silk mill (Manningham Mill) was built on higher ground to the west of Manningham Lane by Samuel Cunliffe Lister, and streets of back-to-back houses for the employees soon went up in its immediate vicinity. But the middle-class suburb, with its landscaped Lister Park, laid out after 1870 on

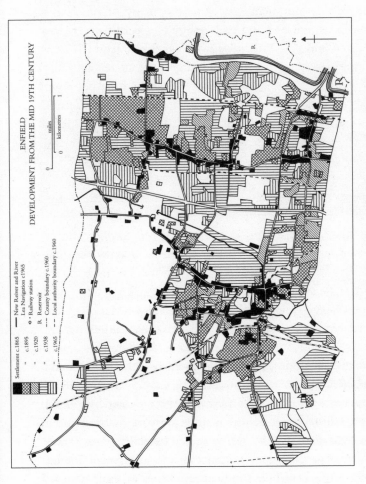

Fig. 8.8 A Map of the parish of Enfield, Middlesex, in the 1850s. Enfield, on the northern fringe of Greater London, is one of many outer suburban areas developed in a patchy, inchoate way over a long period. There was early ribbon development along the main north–south road leading out of London in the eastern half (right) and also around the old village (Enfield Town) in the centre. Later development, especially in the 20th century, was most intense in the eastern, more industrialised, half of the parish, stretching down to the River Lea. New railways encouraged some late 19th-century suburban growth in the western half, but large areas of the former Enfield Chase, former royal hunting ground, remained rural.

Fig. 8.9 St Paul's Road, Manningham, Bradford. This wide, straight street of middle-class brick-built terraced houses was laid out in about 1874, just after the building of the huge Manningham silk mills and Lister Park. It was deliberately aligned on the tower and spire of St Paul's church (1846–8), one of many Anglican churches in the Gothic style built in suburbs of large towns and cities in the second half of the 19th century.

the site of the former manor house, remained intact, and it still retains much of its original character.

H. J. Dyos's pioneering study of Camberwell showed that half of the 5,670 houses under construction in this rapidly growing South London suburb in the late 1870s were built by 380 firms,[44] most of them very small, and most relying on immediate sales to balance their books. Small builders usually put up only a few houses at a time, some of them three-storeyed over basements, but more commonly only two storeys high. Internal planning and layout usually followed patterns first laid down in the seventeenth century or even earlier, with the doorway leading into a passageway (hall) and staircase, flanked by two rooms on each floor and a back extension housing a kitchen and scullery.[45] Bay windows became increasingly common after 1850, allowing more light into the front rooms and distinguishing middle-class houses from those of the poor. Typical are the two-storeyed, bay-windowed houses in Fassett Square, built in the early 1860s close to the newly-opened North London Railway—now part of London Overground—in the rapidly growing parish of Hackney.[46] Attracting a quintessentially lower-middle-class clientele of shopkeepers and commercial travellers, their architectural detailing—notably the ornamental door surrounds with foliated capitals sometimes bought 'off the peg' by commercial suppliers—was borrowed from pattern books and builders' manuals, such as E. L. Tarbuck's *Builder's Practical Director* (1855). Set back from the street behind miniscule front gardens, such houses formed part of a recognizably suburban townscape which, with its accompanying public buildings—schools, churches, corner shops, pubs—enabled individuals and their families to lead their lives in more comfortable surroundings than their ancestors could have envisaged: an ideal which has fuelled the growth of suburbs ever since.

The demand for suburban houses continued to grow in the last third of the century. The agricultural depression that lasted from the 1870s until the Second World War brought about further migration from the countryside into towns and cities. Caused initially by cheap food imports from outside Europe, it led to a dramatic fall in food prices and a corresponding rise in real wages. This in turn made it possible for increasing numbers of better-off working-class people to move to suburbs. The Cheap Trains Act of 1883 obliged railway companies to run 'workmens' trains' from outer suburbs to city centres, and the coming of electric trams—sometimes dubbed 'gondolas of the people'—in the 1890s significantly cut the price of a daily journey to work. And, as working-class people started moving out of city centres, industries followed suit. These developments coincided with the first serious moves by central government to tackle the problems connected with inner-city slum housing, ensuring that new housing should conform to basic sanitary and environmental standards (see pp. 188–9). The model by-laws promulgated in 1877 enshrined planning principles that had been normal in middle-class housing developments ever since the eighteenth century: wide streets, decent sewerage and effective sanitation. The resulting townscape can be seen in a pristine form at Shaftesbury Park at Battersea in south London, a planned suburb of 1872. It was promoted by the Artisans', Labourers' and General Dwellings Company, founded in 1867, the year of the Second Reform Act, under the presidency of the philanthropic Earl of Shaftesbury, memorialized in the statue of Eros (1892–3) in Piccadilly Circus at the heart of London's West End. Built on former market-garden land just

south of the Thames, close to the recently-created Battersea Park but
also to Thames-side industries, and in the shadow of a labyrinth of railway
lines,[47] Shaftesbury Park housed 8,000 people—a larger population than
that of most medieval English towns—in rows of brick-built houses with
between five and seven rooms apiece, designed by an architect-surveyor,
Robert Austin. Some external decoration was supplied in the form of
Gothic doorways and octagonal turrets attached to the houses at the main
street intersections. No pub was allowed within the estate, but there was a
church, a co-operative shop and a school put up by the London School
Board following the Education Act of 1870: another piece of legislation that
helped transform the lives of the British people (see pp. 195–6).

Where the philanthropists led, speculative builders followed, swamping
former villages outside London and the larger provincial towns with rows
of two-storeyed 'by-law' housing usually containing two rooms on each
floor, with back extensions; some, easily recognizable by their pairs of adjacent front doors, contained separated self-contained flats on each floor.
By-law developments can be seen in almost every English town, and they
are omnipresent in fast-growing urban areas such as Walthamstow and East
Ham in outer London, in industrial and shipbuilding towns such as South
Shields on Tyneside and Smethwick in the Black Country north of
Birmingham; and on the edges of Manchester and Liverpool.[48] Liverpool
was the unhealthiest city in the country in the 1840s, with an overall life
expectancy of 26 and a large proportion of the population living in slum
courts or dark, damp cellars. By then better-off Liverpudlians had already
began moving out to surrounding villages and hamlets on higher ground
such as Everton and Toxteth, and in the middle of the century handsome
villa suburbs grew up around Prince's Park (1842-4) and Sefton Park (see
pp. 202–3). The hamlet of Anfield, beyond the existing suburb of Everton,
also experienced some desultory villa development of this kind, but large-
scale suburbanization did not occur until the last third of the century, when
new streets went up rapidly, the most important of them laid out by the
local authority along, or across, the lines of the strips in the medieval
common fields. They are lined with terraces of two- and sometimes three-
storeyed houses with bay windows, their facades rescued from monotony by
the differing patterns of brickwork adopted by the many small builders.
Schools and churches, both Catholic and Protestant, punctuate the main
roads, and shops and pubs occupy the street-corner sites (Fig. 8.10). But the
largest buildings are the football grounds of the two rival teams, Everton

Fig. 8.10 Streets of terraced housing at Anfield, Liverpool. The houses here, with their bay windows and tiny front and back gardens, are typical of those built all over the country to the standards laid down by local by-laws in the 1870s. The Liverpool and Everton football grounds loom large over the surrounding streets.

(Protestant) and Liverpool (Catholic), only a mile apart, testimony to the changing patterns of leisure that have continued to shape city centres and suburbs throughout the country.[49] Anfield's population was originally made up mainly of clerks and warehousemen employed in the flourishing port and its resulting financial services industry, whose magnificent office blocks transformed the centre and waterfront of Liverpool in the years leading up to the First World War (see pp. 181–2, 214–5); the city's poor remained in the crowded and insanitary city centre, from which they were not finally rescued until well into the twentieth century.

Garden Suburbs

For a growing number of late nineteenth- and early twentieth-century critics, by-law suburbs represented the nadir of urban planning. In an influential lecture given in Oxford in 1872, the influential cultural critic John Ruskin held up a different ideal of working-class housing: not 'a compartment of a model lodging-house, not the number so-and-so of Paradise Row; but a cottage all of our own, with its little garden, its pleasant view, its surrounding fields, its neighbouring stream, its healthy air, and clean kitchen, parlour, and bedrooms.'[50] This could be taken as a nostalgic call for the urban population to return to the land, at a time when increasing numbers of impoverished rural labourers were busy escaping it. But it also inspired the visionaries of the Garden City movement, and Bedford Park, a railway suburb on a 45-acre site at the boundary of Chiswick and Acton in west London, gave a foretaste of what a garden city or suburb might look like. It was conceived in 1875 by Jonathan Carr, a cloth merchant turned property developer, and was carefully marketed with the help of avant-garde architects, first E. W. Godwin and later Richard Norman Shaw. Mature trees from the grounds of the villa on the site were allowed to survive, and the brick houses, some tile-hung, others Dutch-gabled, were readily distinguishable from both the solemn Gothic and pattern-book Italianate of earlier middle-class suburban developments (Fig. 8.11).[51] The novelty of the architecture, together with the low housing density, the profuse planting and the care-fully contrived curving streets, appealed to artistically-inclined commuters and their wives seeking a home amongst like-minded neighbours; the poet W. B. Yeats, who lived for a time in Blenheim Road, wrote that 'We went to live in a house like those in pictures, and even met people dressed like people in the story books. The newness of everything, the empty houses where we played at hide-and-seek, and the strangeness of it all, made us feel that we were living among toys'.

Bedford Park was designed to appeal to prosperous members of the com-mercial and professional classes, and its houses were out of the financial reach of the growing number of clerks, still less the manual and service workers who made up four fifths or so of the English population. It was only with the building of Bournville, near Birmingham, after 1895, and Port Sunlight, Cheshire, begun in 1888, that the vernacular idiom of the English village and the cottage home began to be employed in low-density subur-ban working-class communities. Both were works villages situated some distance away from cities, though Bournville was eventually swallowed up by the spread of Birmingham. The cheapness of the land made it possible to adopt an unusually low housing density of between five and eight houses per acre, and to supply the cottages with large gardens designed to encour-age a degree of self-sufficiency; wide pavements or grassy borders hid the water pipes and other infrastructure, and copious amounts of open public

Fig. 8.11 Houses in Bedford Park, London. The houses shown here, among the first to be built in the estate, were designed by E. W. Godwin in or soon after 1875. The low-density environment is defined by wide streets and by the mature trees retained from the existing landscape by the developer, Jonathan Carr.

space were provided for healthy outdoor activities. Bournville even acquired a village green with a handful of shops and a central octagonal building (the Rest House) derived from the market house in the tiny town of Dunster in Somerset.[52]

The ideal of a planned low-density urban environment was promoted by Ebenezer Howard, a former Parliamentary reporter whose *Tomorrow: a Peaceful Path to Real Reform* (1898) first mooted the project of funding new towns of 30,000 or so inhabitants scattered across the depressed countryside.[53] Only two of the thousand or so self-contained garden cities originally mooted—Letchworth and Welwyn (both in Hertfordshire)—were ever built, but the principles of planning espoused by Barry Parker and Raymond Unwin, Howard's architects at Letchworth, were enshrined in several suburban communities of the early twentieth century. Many were set up on the co-partnership model of Letchworth, under which profits were distributed among the residents according to the rental value of their houses. Sixty such estates were in existence by 1913, among them the Moor Pool (originally Harborne Tenants') estate on the edge of Birmingham (1907-12). It was promoted by the local industrialist J. S. Nettlefold, chairman of the city's housing committee and author of *Practical Housing* (1908), and was laid out on a 56-acre site with 500 or so cottage-style houses of differing sizes and rental values.[54] The 'Garden Village' at Rhiwbina, on the northern edge of Cardiff, planned by Unwin in 1912 for the Cardiff Workers' Co-operative Garden Village Society, and containing 300 houses, is similar in character.[55]

Common to all such estates was a belief in the inherent virtue of open space, fresh air and healthy, high-minded activity, and a rejection of the monotony of by-law housing and the anti-social habits it allegedly encouraged. For Raymond Unwin, who had sat at Ruskin's feet at his Oxford lecture in 1872, 'the idea that a town consists of streets is to be very much avoided. Streets are not a virtue in themselves. In fact, the less area given over to streets, the more chance one has of planning a nice town'. Unwin was one of the main planners of Hampstead Garden Suburb in London, begun in 1906 under the inspiration of Henrietta Barnett, wife of an East End clergyman who believed in enlightened urban planning as an instrument of social reform. It was designed as a socially mixed community, close to the Golders Green terminus of the recently-opened Hampstead underground railway extension (now part of the Northern Line), and adjoining an expansion of Hampstead Heath that had been acquired as a means of saving the land from poorly planned speculative development.[56] Large houses went up next to the Heath Extension and smaller ones intended for working people further north, many of them grouped around closes or cul-de-sacs (Fig. 8.12), or in terraces. Some were designed by Unwin himself in a modest neo-vernacular style, with small front gardens, whitewashed, roughcast walls and steeply pitched tiled roofs; the back extensions, characteristic of by-law houses, were rigorously eschewed on the somewhat specious grounds that they reduced light and fresh air. The Arts and Crafts-inspired architect Mackay Baillie-Scott designed a courtyard of flats (Waterlow Court) for single working women, and Edwin Lutyens was responsible for the formal Beaux Arts-influenced civic centre at the highest point of the development, its two churches and neo-Georgian school punctuating the view from the Heath Extension. Shops were relegated to the edge of the estate; even today the air of well-meaning high-mindedness is inescapable.

HAMPSTEAD TENANTS, LIMITED, Nos. 29 to 41, Hampstead Way, N.W.

Fig. 8.12 A close of houses in Hampstead Garden Suburb. These houses, designed by Raymond Unwin and built in 1909, are not very large, and their almshouse-like layout around an open courtyard was intended to encourage a sense of community strongly advocated by Henrietta Barnett, the guiding spirit behind the estate.

Low density Garden City-style planning became enshrined in a flurry of books and pamphlets that appeared just before the First World War. Dispersal of urban populations from crowded city centres was advocated by influential social commentators like C. F. A. Masterman, author of *The Condition of England* (1909). Unwin's *Town Planning in Practice* came out in the same year, followed in 1912 by his *Nothing Gained by Overcrowding*; his ideas received official sanction in the Housing and Town Planning Act passed by the Liberal government in 1909, giving local authorities powers for the first time to make strategic plans for the whole of the areas under their control.[57] As a result of the Housing of the Working Classes Act (1890), local authorities already had the power to buy land for housing outside their own boundaries, and, starting at Totterdown Fields at Tooting (1903), the London County Council began to build 'cottage estates' of housing for 'respectable' members of the working class: those, in other words, who could afford to pay a regular rent, and not the desperately poor slum-dwellers. And, as time went on, estates such as the Old Oak estate at Acton on the western fringe of London (begun 1913) began to shake off the legacy of the by-law streets and to take on the character of contemporary co-partnership estates, with winding streets and cottage-style houses arranged in picturesque groups.[58]

Between the Wars

Cottage estates proliferated after the First World War. The cover of Richard Reiss's *The Home I Want* (1918) contrasted a dingy street of nineteenth-century terraced houses with a recently-built group of co-partnership cottages, each with its own large front garden. The subtitle is: 'You cannot expect to get an A.1. population out of C.3 homes' (Fig. 8.13). Inspired by its election promise of 'Homes fit for Heroes', David Lloyd George's post-war coalition government obtained an Act of Parliament (the Addison Act, named after the Minister of Health) allowing central government subsidies for local authority suburban housing schemes, and for much of the 1920s public authorities built more houses than private speculators.[59] Local authorities were expected to follow the guidelines laid down in the Tudor Walters Report, commissioned in 1917 and strongly influenced by Unwin. It stipulated that the street layout in the new estates, and the housing density of twelve per acre, should follow approved Garden City practice, including the ban on rear extensions. Later cuts in subsidies, enshrined in a series of Acts of Parliament, led to a reduction in the size of most council houses and to a simplification of external detailing, especially during the 1930s, when local authorities strove to rehouse many of the inhabitants of cleared slums in suburban council estates: a major change in policy.

Most council estates were fitted into relatively small pockets of land on the edges of towns and cities, where property prices were low. They merged easily into the existing suburban landscape, though they were, and still are, easily distinguishable from neighbouring private estates by the grouping of houses into short terraces set back from the road and the diagonal placing of groups of houses at street intersections.[60] Some estates were built on a much larger scale; in Scotland, and especially around Glasgow, which had a particularly acute housing problem, many were made up of low-rise tenement blocks without gardens.[61]

By 1939 a third of all houses in England and Wales had been built since 1918, three quarters of them privately, and most of them within the previous ten years. This return of large-scale speculative house-building, along with the building of council estates, often on adjacent land, created a new type of

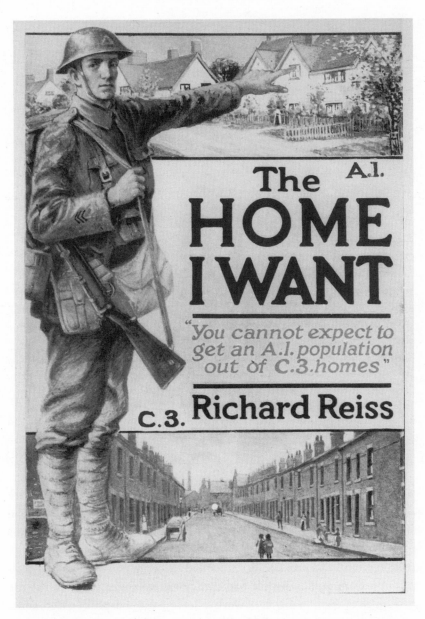

Fig. 8.13 The returning soldier in this pamphlet, produced in the final year of the First World War, rejects the monotonous terraces of late 19th-century houses found on the fringes of most cities. He points instead to a lower-density Garden City-type development of the kind that was already being pioneered by local authorities such as the London County Council for rented social housing. The picture implies that such houses were beneficial for public health and personal wellbeing.

Becontree and Wythenshawe

The Becontree council estate was begun in 1921 on a site nearly thirteen miles east of central London, and accommodated 116,000 people—the population of a substantial town—in 25,000 houses;[62] Wythenshawe, begun in 1928 and spreading over 3,547 acres on the edge of Manchester, housed a population exceeding that of the two pioneering garden cities of Letchworth and Welwyn combined (Fig. 8.14).[63] Both were made up almost exclusively of small two-storeyed houses, arranged in short terraces or in semi-detached pairs set back from the wide streets, or grouped around greens, closes and cul-de-sacs. They were designed for nuclear families with two or three children, increasingly the norm as working-class people began to limit the size of their families. Tenants could now enjoy the private domestic life-style formerly attainable only by the middle classes and skilled artisans, and there was ample open space in the large gardens, where the initially sparse planting has since come to fruition. Some of the first inhabitants missed the cosy communal life of the inner city, often romanticized in retrospect or in the minds of later middle-class pundits,[64] and others resented the lack of local employment and the inevitable long journey to work. The sparse provision of shops and public buildings certainly reinforced a sense of bleak monotony that, at least to outsiders, appeared to lack the virtues of either town or country. But for the working-class inhabitants escaping the cramped conditions of London's East End, or the squalid slums of central Manchester, they could offer for all their shortcomings, both a sense of release and an opportunity for a better life.

suburban landscape. Its most obvious manifestations could be found in south-east England. Here, following the inter-war Depression which blighted the industrial districts of South Wales and the North, there was an economic renaissance in the 1930s, fuelled by rising real wages and a consumer boom. A million people had already moved to the south-east in the 1920s, most of them in search of work following the collapse of older industries such as coal-mining, shipbuilding and textile manufacture. After the economic crisis of 1929–31, governments chose to stimulate the economy through low interest rates and tax relief on mortgages, making home ownership possible not only to the growing number of clerks and officials but also to skilled workers.[65] Mortgages, obtainable from the growing number of building societies, were available to people earning £3 10s. (£3.50) a

Fig. 8.14 This air view of the Becontree estate, thirteen miles east of London, brings out both the scale and the monotony of the larger 'cottage estates' built by local authorities for rental between the wars. Begun in 1921 and eventually housing 116,000 people—more than the total population of any provincial town at the beginning of the 19th century—Becontree was one of the largest of these estates.

week by the 1930s, enabling thousands of people to move out of city centres to the more salubrious environment of outer suburbs: an ideal vigorously promoted in London by railway companies which stood to profit from commuting. Underground Electric Railways, which extended the Hampstead tube line northwards from Golders Green into what remained of rural Middlesex in 1924, encouraged prospective house-owners to: 'Stake your Claim at Edgware. Omar Khayyam's recipe for turning the wilderness into paradise hardly fits an English climate, but provision has been made at Edgware of an alternative recipe which will at least convert pleasant, undulating fields into happy homes. The loaf of bread, the jug of wine and the book of verse may be got there cheaply and easily, and...a shelter which comprises all the latest labour-saving and sanitary conveniences. We moderns ask much more before we are content than the ancients, and Edgware is designed to give us that much more'.[66]

Large building firms such as New Ideal Homesteads, founded in 1932 and based in south-east London, took up the theme in their publicity, and estate agents jumped onto the bandwagon.[67] 400,000 people moved out of inner London between 1921 and 1937 (including those rehoused in council houses), most of them settling within the outer fringe of the metropolis. The rapid rise in the number of home-owners had a profound effect on national politics, through the creation of a 'property-owning democracy'. It also helped change English social mores, entrenching still further the already-existing tendency towards an inward-looking domestic life-style in which home improvement and gardening loomed large, though at the same time—contrary to the fears of many commentators—it promoted new forms of sociability in which interaction occurred not so much with immediate neighbours as with people across a wider area sharing similar interests and values.

Inter-war speculative suburbs have much in common with council estates. Both were built to low densities and in both the houses are laid out along wide, often curved, streets, or grouped together in closes and cul-de-sacs. But, in a society alert to the nuances of social status, speculative builders took care to make their houses look and feel different from council houses. Rooms and windows were generally larger, with bay windows on both floors, and the internal layout, dictated by the so-called 'universal plan', was lighter and more spacious, with two reception rooms and a kitchen downstairs and two or three bedrooms above.[68] External detailing was more eclectic, and often more lavish, sometimes alluding to a romanticized 'Old England' of half-timbered gables. Some speculative builders, like W. H. Knox and J. W. Moore in their Mayfield estate at Seven Kings, Ilford, developed between 1919 and 1934, specialized in detached bungalows, a fashion that first made its appearance in the late nineteenth-century seaside resorts; bungalows were rated the most popular type of house in Britain in an opinion poll of 2002.[69] Most speculative houses, though, were semi-detached or arranged in short terraces. The 88-acre estate of Blendon Hall, a eighteenth-century London merchant's villa at Bexley on the south-eastern edge of Greater London, just south of a new 'arterial' road of the 1920s, was bought in the early 1930s by a local builder, D. C. Bowyer, and soon filled with semi-detached houses in a variety of styles, mostly Neo-Tudor, some tamely Modernist. The low density—six to eight houses per acre—and the relatively high prices—between £700 and £1,000—guaranteed a solidly middle-class clientele. Further south, beyond a stream marking the southern boundary of the estate, a larger firm, New Ideal Homesteads, initiated

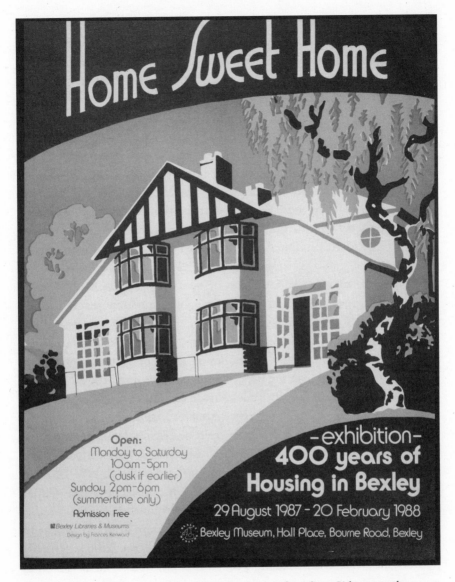

Fig. 8.15 An advertisement of c.1932–3 for houses for sale at Sidcup, on the south-eastern fringe of Greater London. These houses with their Neo-Tudor gables and bay windows were marketed for sale, with the help of cheap mortgages, to lower middle-class office employees and skilled workers eager to escape the inner city for more spacious surroundings on the suburban fringe.

another development, Albany Park (Fig. 8.15). Bricks were imported from Belgium, windows from Czechoslovakia, and by 1932–3 the 3,000 employees were putting up a hundred houses per month, each taking about three weeks to build.[70] The density of fifteen houses per acre, though still low by later standards, was double that of the Blendon Hall development (and double that recommended by the local authority), and the houses were marketed at half the price (between £395 and £580), putting them within the reach of less affluent clerks and skilled workers. The character of many of England's outer suburbs depended on such subtle distinctions of status and income.

Writing in 1934, J. B. Priestley, a native of Bradford, contrasted the England of the Industrial Revolution, in which he had grown up, with the new England of roads designed for motor traffic and sprawling low-density suburbs. 'After the familiar muddle of West London', he observed, 'the Great West Road looked very odd. Being new, it did not look English. We might have suddenly rolled into California.'[71] The widespread adoption of electricity now made it possible for factories to be located close to roads and railways on the suburban fringe. The former Hoover vacuum cleaner factory (1931–5), an icon of Art Deco design, is situated next to Western Avenue, a new road of the 1920s, close to a railway line (now part of London Underground's Central Line), and providing employment for the inhabitants of the surrounding housing estates (Fig. 8.16). Shopping parades, pubs and sometimes cinemas went up alongside roads, or around new railway stations.[72] At Southgate, on the Piccadilly Line's extension in north London, opened in 1933, a loosely Neo-Tudor parade of shops faces the forecourt of the station, another example of 1930s Art Deco modernism. Schools and churches were built along residential streets or near shopping centres. New public parks were created, some out of the existing grounds of country houses and villas, others out of formerly agricultural land, as at Florence Park in east Oxford, where the developer F. J. Moss laid out a low-density estate of mostly terraced brick houses for rental by employees—many of them migrants from the depressed coal-mining areas of South Wales—of the nearby Morris Motors plant at Cowley.[73] Here the park is the focal point of the estate, reached along a broad approach road with a with a pub and a handful of small shops: a democratized version of the vision which had inspired the creators of the first planned suburbs in the nineteenth century and the idealists of the Garden City movement. It is a vision that was to appeal to countless British people in the immediate post-War years (see Chapter 9), and it continues to do so today.

Fig. 8.16 The Hoover factory at Perivale, London. This factory, built in 1931–5 for the manufacture of vacuum cleaners, faces one of the main roads leading north-west out of London. By the inter-war period electricity had made dirty steam-powered factories redundant for new consumer-based industries, and the glitzy Art Deco-inspired exterior conveyed an image of cheerful up-to-date modernity.

9

The Way We Live Now,
1945–2021

In 1941, as British cities were still reeling from aerial attack, the architect Maxwell Fry wrote an article for the mass-circulation magazine *Picture Post* entitled 'The New Britain must be planned'. It contrasted views of 'a typical section of British land under our present haphazard development' with 'the same section reorganized under a coherent plan,' featuring parallel rows of eight-storey flats, wide, tree-lined roads, a new shopping centre, and factories expelled to the edge of the town. Fry's vision was shared by many other architects and members of the newly-influential planning profession, and it anticipated the way in which many towns and cities were remodelled in the second half of the twentieth century, shaping the urban world inhabited by four fifths of the British population today.

The Festival of Britain, held in 1951 on a redevelopment site of bomb-damaged former industrial buildings on the South Bank of the Thames in London, presented a seductive vision of modernist architecture and planning to a tired nation. Like the Great Exhibition of 1851 that inspired it, it was a popular success, visited by eight and half million people. The buildings, many of them of concrete and glass, were loosely scattered over the site, but only one—the Royal Festival Hall, a concert hall generously supplied with well-lit public space—was allowed to remain by the Conservative government elected in the same year; a tall office block (the Shell Building) still casts a blight over the southern part of the site.[1] The Festival also featured a 'live architecture exhibition.' It took the form of a new housing estate for 1,500 people on a war-damaged site at Poplar in the East End, and was named after the pre-war Labour Party leader George Lansbury. Its layout, by the London County Council, followed guidelines recommended in a housing manual brought out by central Government in 1949.[2] The unassertive mixture of brick council houses, low-rise blocks of flats and maisonettes, and pedestrianized shopping streets, interspersed with schools and churches, tangibly embodied a comforting Social Democratic vision of the Welfare State, best experienced today in the central square (1950-2) with its market, shops, pub and a jazzily detailed clock tower. Building continued into the 1960s, and by that time comparable developments had gone up throughout the country.

Wartime destruction made some degree of rebuilding essential; in London one in ten houses had been damaged. Many people still yearned for better living conditions; in 1951 a third of British homes still had no bath. But for nearly a decade after the War ended many towns and cities were still scarred by the empty sites of bombed buildings, some of them poetically recorded

Fig. 9.1 The bombing raid of 29 December 1940 left St Paul's Cathedral largely unscathed, but it devastated Paternoster Row, immediately to the north, well known for its bookshops and publishing firms. The dome of the Old Bailey, London's central criminal court, can be seen on the left and the tower of Sir Christopher Wren's Christ Church Newgate Street on the right. The gutted buildings in Paternoster Row were replaced by a modernist office development in in 1962-7, and this later gave way to another development completed in 2003 (see Fig. 9.12).

by photographers and artists such as John Piper. The creation of a new and more rationally planned urban environment entailed a major intervention by central government. The Town and Country Planning Act was passed in 1947 by the Labour government elected two years earlier, and imposed rigid land-use planning. It required local authorities to produce development plans, sometimes incorporating 'Comprehensive Development Areas' designated for *tabula rasa* rebuilding facilitated by the widespread use of compulsory purchase powers. Some sites were meanwhile filled with prefabricated houses ('prefabs'), usually single-storeyed and built on aluminium, steel or wooden frames.

Large-scale permanent rebuilding only began in 1954, following the removal of Government development controls, first imposed during the war and retained afterwards so as to channel scarce resources into the revival of export industries needed to pay off the massive war debt. Bristol's city architect had already called in 1941 for 'a good, simple and dignified architecture, cutting out all unnecessary "frills", and spending our money on good, sound hygienic ideas'.[3] This led in time to the building of such banal monuments of post-war public taste as the Broadmead Centre that went up in a heavily bombed area north of the medieval city centre between 1954 and 1960. Plymouth, with a population of a quarter of a million people in 1939, was one of the most bomb-damaged cities in the United Kingdom, and fared rather better. A plan, framed in 1943 by the City Engineer and the planning expert Patrick Abercrombie, recommended a rigid system of land-use zoning, with most of the former inhabitants of the central areas relocated to new suburbs, each organized as a 'neighbourhood unit' of between 6,000 and 10,000 people, and each with its own shopping precinct situated away from main traffic routes, following recommendations by H. Alker Tripp in his influential *Town Planning and Road Traffic* (1942).[4] The devastated city centre was replanned along Beaux Arts-inspired lines, with an east-west street (Royal Parade) bisected by a 200 foot-wide traffic-free route (Armada Way), 'enriched by the landscape architect's and gardener's art'; it leads south from the railway station towards Plymouth Hoe, overlooking the harbour. Bounded by its inner ring road—soon to be a feature of towns of any size throughout the country—the new city centre contained shops, a civic centre and hotels, faced with Portland stone in the 'stripped classical' style inherited from the pre-war period. The spacious, coherent, if somewhat bland, ensemble still survives largely intact.

Coventry

Coventry was the fastest-growing city in Britain from 1900 to 1940, and one of the country's most important centres of car manufacturing. Much of the existing city centre was already scheduled for obliteration before the War under plans framed in 1939–40 by the City Architect, Donald Gibson. After the first aerial Blitz, in November 1940, Gibson reiterated his planning philosophy, proclaiming that 'like a forest fire, the present evil might bring forth greater riches and beauty.'[5] Following another wave of devastating bombing in 1941, his revised scheme, based on a system of strict zoning, envisaged a new shopping centre arranged as a pedestrian precinct on two levels, loosely reminiscent of the medieval Rows at Chester. Completed in 1955, and aligned on the surviving fourteenth-century spire of the bombed cathedral (the former parish church of St Michael), the central open space—now unfortunately cluttered by later additions—is surrounded by low-rise brick buildings, reflecting the egalitarian and anti-monumental *Zeitgeist* of the immediate post-war era (Fig. 9.2). Other buildings soon followed, among them a new theatre (the Belgrade Theatre) and a new Cathedral (1951–62), both designed by Sir Basil Spence. Clad in red sandstone, the Cathedral was deftly sited at a right angle to the ruins of the old building, which serves as a forecourt and 'site of memory'. When completed, visitors queued to see the spectacular interior, and in 1999 it was voted Britain's favourite modern building.[6]

Gibson's understated, Scandinavian-influenced, style gave way under his successor, Arthur Ling, to a more overtly modernist idiom, seen in the lower precinct (1955–60), with its tower block of offices at the far end, intended to convey 'an intimate feeling of enclosure'[7] that is difficult to discern today. The city centre, like Plymouth's, was surrounded by a ring road, built in 1959–74, its construction entailing the demolition of many of the hundred or so surviving timber-framed buildings that had escaped the Blitz. Protected by iron railings designed to separate motorists from pedestrians, the road had the effect of cutting off the city centre, now almost entirely denuded of permanent residents, from the city's residential areas, which had to be reached through dank underpasses and narrow footbridges. Some of the surviving timber-framed houses were re-erected in Spon Street, a medieval extramural suburb that had largely escaped bombing, offering some compensation for the loss of what had been one of the most important, though least-appreciated, pre-industrial townscapes in the country.[8] The remaining city-centre residents were meanwhile rehoused in the burgeoning suburbs.

Fig. 9.2 The shopping precinct at Coventry in 1966. Much of Coventry's central shopping area was destroyed, along with the body of the Cathedral, in a German air raid on 14 November 1940. The new pedestrian precinct, of 1951-6, was aligned upon the Cathedral's magnificent 14th-century steeple, which survived the raid. Donald Gibson's layout was inspired by classical models, but the architecture of the lower precinct, in the foreground, was modernist in inspiration.

Housing

Given the lack of money available for private building in the immediate post-war years, the burden of housing the British people fell to the public authorities. Until the late 1970s there was a widespread conviction that central government had a duty to fund, and the local authorities to supply, housing for rent on a vast scale. Following the recommendations of the Dudley Report (1944), 'mixed developments' of low-density housing and flats were favoured. They were to be set within leafy environments, 'cosy rather than dignified', in the words of one writer, with groups of houses reached by pathways and artfully arranged within a carefully landscaped green setting.[9] That was the ideal, but much of the housing that initially went up around the fringes of towns and cities was cheaply and unimaginatively designed by local authority surveyors and engineers, who insisted on an inordinate amount of space for roads, and traffic intersections designed to improve sight-lines for motorists; a housing manual of 1949 recommended what now seems an absurdly over-generous street width, incorporating extensive grass verges and resulting in what some critics dubbed 'prairie planning'.[10] Higher standards were applied at Coventry and Plymouth, where the new suburbs were planned along low-density garden-city lines, with neighbourhood precincts and 'village greens' set within remnants of existing parkland and woodland. Prefabricated building, pioneered in the much-admired post-war local authority schools in Hertfordshire, was often employed for ease and speed of construction, and there was some variety in the types of housing, ranging from low-rise flats to terraces and semi-detached pairs. Mundane though they might appear today, suburbs of this kind represented a marked improvement in their residents' living conditions; Ernesettle, on the edge of Plymouth, was, according to one of its inhabitants, 'a marvellous place to grow up'.[11]

The unplanned suburban sprawl of the inter-war years was halted by the introduction of green belts, first proposed for London in 1935 and revived by Patrick Abercrombie in his Greater London Plan of 1944. Assuming that the urban population would fall, and inspired by the vision of Ebenezer Howard (see p. 263), Abercrombie advocated the relocation of both people and businesses from overcrowded cities into planned New Towns, laid out on garden-city lines on sites well away from existing urban agglomerations (Fig. 9.3). They were to have populations of some 60,000 apiece, each with a central civic and commercial area, and housing grouped within discrete 'neighbourhoods' of 10,000 people, each with its own school and shopping centre. Stevenage (Hertfordshire), one of the first of London's New Towns, has a pedestrianized square (1957–8) at the centre of the main shopping area, designed in a clean-cut Bauhaus-influenced modernist style and adorned with a clock tower, a fountain and abstract sculpture; industry, much of it deliberately relocated from inner London, was placed on the fringe. New Towns were also established in the north-east (e.g. Peterlee) and in Scotland (e.g. Glenrothes). But they accounted for only a small proportion of the houses built between 1945 and 1970, and they were expensive to build and prodigal of land. So existing market towns such as Basingstoke, Andover (Hampshire), Northampton, and Peterborough, were eventually chosen instead for large-scale planned expansion,[12] a process that is still continuing.

The first post-war council housing estates were not designed for mass car ownership, but that changed as prosperity rose in the late 1950s and 1960s, following the lifting of post-war austerity measures. The aim was now to

Fig. 9.3 The first new neighbourhoods in Stevenage New Town. were developed in the early 1950s, and the two-storeyed brick houses shown here are within walking distance of the newly-built town centre. They are grouped around an open space, their front gardens approached by footpaths, with vehicle access from the back.

group houses around cul-de-sacs with off-street garages behind them, as in the much-publicized inter-war development at Radburn, New Jersey (USA). This had the effect of freeing up the space in front of houses for landscaping, and doing away, as far as possible, with fenced-off front gardens— anathema to planning experts who saw them both as potentially untidy and as symbolic of bourgeois respectability.[13] 'Radburn'-type plans had already been employed in the private estates carried out by Span Developments, including an attractive group of 169 two-and three-storeyed blocks of tile-hung flats at Ham Common in south-west London (1953–6), designed by their consultant architect Eric Lyons at the relatively high density of 65 people per acre. Similar layouts soon appeared in council estates, like those that went up around the fringe of Coventry in the late 1950s and 1960s. Each had its own shopping centre, schools and churches; by 1970 no fewer than eleven secondary and fifty primary schools had been built in the city's suburbs.[14] Following the Government-sponsored Parker Morris report on housing (1961), the amount of land given over to roads and open spaces was reduced, resulting in denser layouts of houses linked by narrow alleys. Similar restrictions applied to the growing number of houses built for sale by private developers, many of them in terraces with narrow facades, tiny back gardens and an overall density of twenty or more houses per acre: twice that of the early New Towns. This tendency has continued to the present day as developers struggle to squeeze as many houses as possible onto the limited numbers of available sites.[15]

With large numbers of people still living in cramped and insanitary housing in inner-city areas, the Conservative party promised in its 1951 election manifesto to build 300,000 new housing 'units' per year; 357,000 went up in 1954, many of them on inner-city sites. Meanwhile the shabby, neglected districts of close-packed working-class housing from which the population was encouraged—and eventually forced—to migrate were left to fester until they were flattened as a result of slum clearance legislation, starting in the mid-1950s. As early as 1927 the Dutch architect Jacobus Oud had called for a future in which there would be 'No more little masterpieces for the individual but mass-production and standardization, with a view to provide decent dwellings for the masses . . . A house à la Ford, all light, air and colour'. The resumption of large-scale inner-city house building by local authorities in the 1950s presented an opportunity to realize this inter-war modernist vision. Reacting against the alleged tedium of the suburbs—a perception not necessarily shared by their inhabitants—and inspired by Le Corbusier's vision of the 'Radiant City', translated into English as *The City of Tomorrow* in 1929, as well as by recent Scandinavian developments, the inter-war architectural *avant-garde* soon became the new establishment. It found ample, and sometimes lucrative, employment in the public sector, and by 1948 local authorities were already employing four out of every ten British architects.

Pre-war blocks of council flats had usually been placed parallel to streets or around courtyards. Now, rows of parallel blocks placed at right or acute angles to the street came into vogue. An early example was Churchill Gardens, close to the River Thames at Pimlico in London (1947–52), with an initial density of 200 people per acre, housed in flat-roofed, eight-storeyed slabs. Elsewhere, there were 'mixed developments' of single high-rise slabs surrounded by low-rise blocks arranged around courtyards, or groups of tall 'point blocks' in open settings; the Ackroyden estate (1950–4), close to the edge of Wimbledon Common in south-west London, featured a group of eleven-storey blocks of this kind.[16] Tower blocks and parallel slabs were more expensive to build than high-density low-rise developments. But they seemed glamorous to planners, architects and local politicians, especially when contrasted with the depressingly drab and smoky inner-city environment of the post-war years. They also had the advantage of ease of construction, important at a time of full employment when labour was expensive and sometimes hard to find. Some fifty multi-storey blocks had gone up in Liverpool by 1963,[17] and many more were built in London, Sheffield, Glasgow and other large cities following the removal of a previous hundred-foot height limit that had been imposed by local authorities, allegedly determined by the length of firemen's ladders.

Many local authority architects of the 1950s and 1960s adopted the tough, Brutalist style of Corbusier's s famous Unité d'Habitation at Marseilles, finished in 1952. His vision inspired the architects of the Alton West estate at Roehampton in south-west London (1954–8), where slabs of flats faced in rough board-marked concrete, and resting on pillars or *pilotis*, as Corbusier called them, were aligned within the grounds of eighteenth-century villas overlooking Richmond Park: a ready-made landscape setting rarely matched in later developments of this kind. Park Hill (1957–61), by contrast, an estate of 995 dwellings arranged in slabs around an irregular-shaped courtyard, occupied a windy hilltop overlooking the centre of Sheffield, was intended to rehouse the local working-class population close to their former homes, most of which were swept away as slums (Fig. 9.4). The flats were approached along wide balconies, vainly intended to encourage something of the neighbourliness of the demolished streets, and the blocks were linked by bridges.[18]

The Barbican development (1962–82) was an even more ambitious example of inner-city place-making. It was designed to tempt residents back into the City of London, with housing for 6,500 people—more than the population of most medieval towns—many of whom worked in the thriving financial services industry. The architects, Chamberlin Powell and Bon, proclaimed: 'We strongly dislike the Garden City tradition with its low density, monotony and waste of good country, road, kerbs, borders, paths in endless strips everywhere. We like strong contrast between true town and true country ...The best views of towns are from high up'.[19] So, ignoring the pre-war street pattern of small houses and workshops, corner shops, pubs, churches and school buildings, already all but obliterated by the Luftwaffe, they placed the housing on a pedestrian-only deck raised above the street level, with car parking beneath 421 foot-tall towers rising up above lower, inward-looking courtyard blocks. With its

Fig. 9.4 The Park Hill estate at Sheffield, shown here as it was before renovation, was designed by a team of architects headed by J.L. Womersley and went up in 1957-61 on a hillside to the east of the city centre. The blocks, built of concrete and housing 3448 people, were reached by lifts which gave access to balconies. Much admired by architects, and later seen as an important monument of the Brutalist movement, the buildings fell into disrepair, but they have recently been refurbished as a mixed-use development of rented and private housing, and commercial premises.

ubiquitous raw concrete surfaces and its opaque, complicated circulation pattern, the Barbican, now much admired as a masterpiece of the Brutalist aesthetic and cherished by its often-affluent residents, represents one of the most radical changes to the British urban landscape since towns began.

The post-war baby boom—not anticipated by planning gurus like Abercrombie—added six million people to the British population between 1947 and 1971. Fear of a new housing crisis led Harold Wilson, who became Prime Minister in 1964, to demand half a million new 'housing units' per year, leading to an accelerated building programme. Under the Housing Subsidies Act of 1956, governments could now give extra subsidies for high-rise blocks, increasing according to height.[20] They were enthusiastically supported by local politicians who wanted to reduce waiting lists for existing council accommodation, while keeping their working-class voters in the inner city. 384 towers were built in 1965–7 by the Greater London Council, which replaced the London County Council, and many more by individual boroughs, most of them surrounded by hard landscaping interrupted only by children's' playgrounds and car parks.[21] Prefabrication was encouraged, and by the late 1960s forty per cent of new housing was in 'system-built' schemes.[22] Prefabrication economized on labour at a time of rising wages, and was used both for high-rises and for long monotonous blocks like those of the Aylesbury estate near the Elephant and Castle in south London (1963–77), housing 7,500 people and currently (2021) undergoing radical 'regeneration'. A more sympathetic, though aesthetically equally uncompromising, approach was adopted in the Foundling estate in Bloomsbury in central London, begun in 1968 and consisting of two parallel five-storeyed ranges of flats on either side of an open walkway, with car-parking underneath. Here the monumental external façades, punctuated by lift towers, offer a stark, but not unpleasing, contrast to the surrounding late-Georgian brick housing.[23]

High-rise flats had a particularly significant impact on the larger Scottish cities (Fig. 9.5), where there was a higher proportion of council tenants than in England. In some Glasgow estates the flats rose as high as 31 storeys, the city architect later admitting that 'It always came back to the target...as many [housing units] as could be constructed in the least possible time'.[24] Swathes of late nineteenth-century tenement housing were replaced by estates like Basil Spence's Hutchesontown (1961–6) in the Gorbals, one of the most deprived areas of the city.[25] But the two twenty-storeyed towers here only lasted until 1993 when they were blown up, the job architect having admitted that he and his colleagues had not realised the high cost of maintaining them.[26] Welcomed initially by many of the new residents, such blocks quickly became unpopular, though not primarily for their architecture. For one sheet-metal worker living in a twenty-storey tower in Edinburgh, 'It wasn't anything to do with the block...it was a change in the kind of people who lived there, and how people behaved...they were perfectly good houses, if only the council had bothered to look after them, rather than using them as a dumping ground'.[27] So, as the 'respectable' tenants left, what had been hailed as an urban utopia became in all too many cases a dystopia of malfunctioning buildings, vandalized public spaces and crime-ridden communities. The revulsion against high-rise building was exacerbated by a much-publicized gas explosion at Ronan Point in the East London borough of Newham in 1968; the blocks here were replaced by low-rise housing not dissimilar externally to that along the former streets

Fig. 9.5 The Wyndford estate in Glasgow, containing flats for 5000 people, is a 'mixed development' of high- and medium-rise flats and four-storeyed blocks of walk-up flats that went up in 1961-9 on the site of a barracks at Maryhill, north-west of the city centre. Designed by the chief technical officer of the Scottish Special Housing Association, at a density of 164 people per acre, it was intended to foster a community feeling among the tenants; in 1978 it was designated as a site of multiple deprivation.

on the site. The appalling fire of 2016 at Grenfell Tower in North Kensington, in which seventy-two people died, is a reminder of the problems that are still present in some of the blocks that have survived, exacerbated by the changing whims of the politicians and officials responsible for maintaining them.

High-rise flats had obvious drawbacks when lifts failed to work, or when local authorities placed families with young children, for whom they were not intended, on the upper floors. They were not even the most cost-effective way of housing large numbers of people on restricted inner-city sites.[28] By the early 1960s some local authorities had already begun to build 'high density, low rise' estates instead. Drawing on the influence of books like Gordon Cullen's influential *Townscape* (1961), the architects of such developments attempted to celebrate the virtues of variety, accident, surprise and sensitivity to the *genius loci*, long recognized by the theorists and practitioners of the Picturesque approach to architecture and planning. Low rise, high density housing pointed the way towards a more intimate, neighbourly form of layout, though it was by no means the social panacea that some of its advocates promised. It can be seen in Ralph Erskine's Byker estate in Newcastle (1969–81), where a minority of the inhabitants of the existing nineteenth-century inner suburb were rehoused on site. Some took up residence in an imaginatively designed wall of 620 flats, enjoying spectacular views over the Tyne valley from their balconies (Fig. 9.6). But most moved into the low-rise housing grouped along narrow streets and walkways,[29] and this type of layout soon became ubiquitous.

By 1975 1,165,000 dwellings had been demolished nationwide and some three million people rehoused.[30] Most of the remaining nineteenth-century slums had been levelled, but so too had whole neighbourhoods of run-down but potentially renewable housing. St Ebbes, a working-class district that grew up to the south of Oxford's medieval centre, was first proposed

Fig. 9.6 The 'Byker wall' at Newcastle. The much-applauded Byker estate, housing 9500 people, went up to the east of Newcastle's city centre. The sinuous block of housing shown here, completed in 1990, was built alongside a main road, but the residents could enjoy views from their balconies over the city. Low-rise housing takes up the remainder of the site.

for redevelopment in 1948,[31] and was re-zoned for shops under a 1953 development plan. This led to nearly twenty years of 'planning blight' before a new shopping centre (the Westgate) finally went up in 1970–2,[32] only to be demolished and rebuilt in 2017. The inhabitants meanwhile, two thirds of whom expressed a preference for remaining in the area, were moved to Blackbird Leys, a new council estate of 3,000 low-rise low-density dwellings on a 'greenfield' site on the edge of the city, later to become for a time a byword for anti-social behaviour. At Chelmsley Wood, on the outskirts of Birmingham, no fewer than 15,590 dwellings went up in 1966–70 for people displaced by inner-city clearance schemes. The estate was separated from the rest of the city, ghetto-fashion, by major roads. Some of the accommodation was in tower blocks, but most of the new residents were housed in small brick houses linked by labyrinthine paths to the new shopping centre: a world vividly described by the writer Lynsey Hanley, who grew up there.[33]

Redevelopment

Comprehensive redevelopment was not limited to depressed areas of inner-city housing; it also spread in the 1960s to the central districts of most towns and cities of any size. Under the 1947 Housing and Town Planning Act, local authorities could use compulsory purchase powers to acquire land before leasing it to private developers, resulting in the widespread destruction of existing buildings and their replacement by office blocks, shops and new roads.[34] The driving force came from local politicians, abetted by road engineers and businessmen, some of whom made fortunes by buying up land cheaply after 1945 and exploiting the 'plot ratio system' introduced in 1947 in order to control the density allowed on a given piece of land.[35] The property boom began in 1954 after the removal of a tax on 'betterment' (imposed in 1947), and it marked the culmination of a move away from often untidy mixed-use city centres towards zoned neighbourhoods devoted to shops and offices, permanently changing the urban fabric in the process.

London set the precedent. Actively encouraged by central government, which wanted to encourage businesses to move away from the centre, the capital's population plummeted from 8½ million in 1939 to just under seven million in 1991.[36] But the volume of office space tripled in the 1950s and early 1960s, with 50 million square feet being added: five times the amount destroyed by Second World War bombing. By 1969 there were over a hundred office blocks that topped the previous hundred-foot limit.[37] High-rise, steel or concrete-framed buildings, many of them with curtain walls of glass, brought a new, and at the time exciting, sense of scale and drama into drab nineteenth-century streetscapes. Some of the most striking, and intrusive, examples emerged from Richard Seifert, the 'wizard of the plot ratio'. His firm, employing some three hundred architects, was responsible for around a thousand projects between 1955 and 1972, including hotels, which proliferated after the Government introduced grants of £1,000 per room for such buildings. His 34-storey Centrepoint (1963–6) was the result of a partnership between the developer Harry Hyams and the London County Council, which at the time favoured tall buildings at road intersections.[38] It involved the redevelopment of an irregular site south of New Oxford Street, cut through the slums of the notorious 'Rookery' (see p. 114) in 1843–7. But, following a moratorium on new offices introduced by the Labour government in 1964, the building remained empty for ten years, by which time the rents had quadrupled; it has recently been turned over to flats.

Rebuilt town and city centres usually resulted from partnerships between local authorities, landowners and private developers. Croydon, ten miles south of central London, became a cut-price 'mini-Manhattan' in the 1960s, its development steered by a local authority eager to carry out an ambitious programme of road widening and encouraged by local property owners. Harold Macmillan, Prime Minister from 1957–1963, favoured this kind of development when he proclaimed that 'the people whom the [Conservative] Government must help are those who do things: the developers, the people who create wealth, be they humble or exalted'.[39] Armed with powers of compulsory purchase, local councils now tried to stimulate the economies of tired city centres by attracting office developments such as the concrete-and-glass headquarters of the Halifax Building Society (1968–74), which took up a whole block of the largely nineteenth-century Yorkshire mill town. Local authorities meanwhile endeavoured to tackle traffic problems by building inner ring roads and leasing the adjoining land to developers; they were expected to supply car-parking close to the shops for suburbanites who saw their real wages doubling from 1939 to the late 1960s. Developers and chain stores benefited from increased sales, local authorities from increased rateable value, consumers from a wider range of goods. But swathes of historic town and city centres were devastated in the process; the new market and shopping centre in Blackburn (Lancashire) involved clearing a fifteen-acre site and the demolition of 251 of the town's 388 shops.[40]

Covered shopping malls came into vogue, their fortress-like concrete exteriors, along with those of the multi-storey car parks that adjoined them, presenting an intimidating public face to passers-by and a sense of claustrophobia to those who entered their artificially lit, air-conditioned interiors. Among the more egregious examples was the Bull Ring Centre in Birmingham (1964: since demolished), built on the site of the city's nineteenth-century market and brutally separated from the city's commercial centre by an inner ring road (Fig. 9.7).[41]

With car ownership quadrupling from 1945 to 1964, the Government-sponsored Buchanan Report on *Traffic in Towns* (1963) recommended the large-scale segregation of people and vehicles.[42] This had the benefit of removing traffic from selected city-centre streets such as London Street in Norwich, one of the first examples (1967). But the building of ring roads

Fig. 9.7 The high-rise office towers in Birmingham's city centre went up inside Birmingham's inner ring road, seen in the foreground. First conceived by the City' Council's Chief Engineer, Sir Herbert Manzoni, in 1943, and involving the destruction of several major 19th-century buildings, the road was completed in 1971. The Bull Ring shopping centre is to the left, near the 24-storey Rotunda (1964-5), one of several high-rise buildings that transformed the city's skyline. Work on dismantling some sections of the road began in 1991, and it now survives only in a fragmentary form.

had disastrous results for the fabric of many towns and cities, blighting the areas alongside them, leading to the erection of metal barriers alongside pavements or, at worst, forcing people onto dark and sometimes litter-strewn underpasses or footbridges. Northampton, chosen for large-scale expansion in 1968, still has to recover from the assault on its town centre carried out under plans framed in 1969–70. A new inner by-pass cut the centre of Exeter off from the River Exe. And in Newcastle—touted as the 'Brasilia of the North' under the charismatic council leader T. Dan Smith (imprisoned for corruption in 1974)—a motorway sliced through Dobson's magnificent Royal Arcade, replacing it with an office block and isolating the seventeenth-century Holy Jesus Hospital on the far side of a roundabout.[43] Even Bath was not immune. Here scores of 'lesser' Georgian buildings were levelled in the 1960s, including many outside the southern boundary of the medieval city. They were destroyed to make way for a bus station and a covered shopping centre which went up in 1969–72;[44] the shopping centre lasted for less than forty years before being demolished in favour of a bland neo-Georgian replacement, laid out along pedestrian-only streets and completed in 2010.

The local authorities that encouraged 'comprehensive redevelopment' were not slow in commissioning new municipal palaces for their own growing staffs. The centre of Aylesbury, an expanding county town with over 60,000 inhabitants in 2019, is still dominated by its overweening twelve-storeyed Buckinghamshire City Council offices of 1963–6. The local government reforms introduced by Edward Heath's Conservative government in 1974 led to the building of yet more offices, both for the enlarged Greater London boroughs and for reconstituted counties like Oxfordshire, which put up a new administrative building of numbing banality in 1974 next to the site of Oxford's Norman castle. Berkshire meanwhile, following the loss of a third of the historic county to Oxfordshire in 1974, constructed an equally unmemorable set of offices next to the M4 motorway on the edge of Reading, the county town, only to sell it in 1998 after the rump of the county was split up into unitary authorities.

The Welfare State, a cornerstone of Government policy ever since the 1940s, demanded ever more ambitious buildings. Vast hospitals went up on the edge of towns and cities, like the Princess Margaret Hospital at Swindon (1957–9), close to a ring road and the M4 motorway. New cultural zones were created, none more striking than the South Bank Centre in London (1965–8), built by the London County Council on part of the Festival of Britain site; containing two concert halls and an art gallery, and reached by

Fig. 9.8 The South Bank Centre, London. This formidable assemblage of Brutalist-inspired buildings, designed by the Greater London Council's team of architects and built in 1965-8, contains two concert halls and an art gallery, originally approached by a pedestrian walkway. It forms part of a cultural enclave on the formerly industrial south bank of the River Thames, including the Royal Festival Hall, out of sight to the left, and the National Theatre on the east side of the approach to Waterloo Bridge.

raised pedestrian walkways of the kind recommended in the Buchanan Report, it achieved a genuine if brutal sculptural grandeur that epitomizes an important aspect of the Sixties *Zeitgeist* (Fig. 9.8).

New comprehensive schools and higher education institutions proliferated, and, following the Robbins Report of 1963, new university campuses went up on the fringes of provincial towns and cities such as York, Lancaster and Coventry (the University of Warwick). Like the American campus universities that they in some respects resemble, they were, and still are, miniature towns, with their own housing, social facilities and—to a limited extent—shops. Older higher-education institutions also expanded on or near their existing inner-city sites: a process that accelerated at the end of the century as former technical colleges such as Leeds Polytechnic became universities, commissioning new and sometimes architecturally innovative buildings as part of their quest to establish a new identity of their own (Fig. 9.9).

Fig. 9.9 New buildings for Leeds Beckett (formerly Leeds Metropolitan) University. The university traces its origin back to the city's Mechanics' Institute and other educational institutions which coalesced to become Leeds Polytechnic in 1970; by 2009 there were over 23,000 students on several sites. The former Friends' Meeting House in the foreground (1866-8), looks out onto the city's northern ring road, and was converted into broadcasting studios in the late 20th century. The University's angular 23-storey tower behind, designed by Fielden Clegg Bradley and built in 2008-9, is clad in weathered steel and forms part of a complex containing offices, teaching spaces and student rooms.

Decline and Regeneration

Comprehensive redevelopment began to lose favour in central Government circles in the late 1960s.[45] As inflation mounted in the following decade, following a sudden rise in the price of oil in 1973, the money for expensive road schemes began to dry up. A proposed ring of motorways around central London was dropped in 1973, leaving Westway and the East Cross Route as isolated fragments. Following the revelation, enshrined in the Housing Finance Act of 1969, that new 'housing units' cost on average twice what would be needed to renovate older ones, improvement grants gradually replaced clearance subsidies. They helped save some inner-city neighbourhoods that had been threatened with demolition, such as Jericho in Oxford (see p. 187). But they failed to revive housing markets in cities like Liverpool, where a quarter of the inhabitants had already moved away by 1976, following the closure of the docks and the collapse of their related industries. Their departure left a legacy of empty nineteenth-century terraced houses like those in the 'Welsh streets' next to Prince's Park, one of them the birthplace of the Beatle Ringo Starr.[46] Here 450 houses, built in the 1870s, were slated for demolition and replacement under the Government's 'Pathfinder' initiative of 2002–2011, only to be rescued by the withdrawal of the funding. The renovated houses are currently (2021) being offered for letting, but similar concentrations of badly maintained Victorian housing can still be found in many of our once-thriving ports and industrial cities.

Forgotten neighbourhoods that had escaped redevelopment slowly began to undergo gentrification, a process that has continued to the present day. Two thirds of the residents of the London Borough of Islington had already moved away by 1971, their places taken for the most part by middle-class professionals and, at least initially, by younger people who preferred inner-city life to that of the suburbs in which many of them had grown up. By the 1970s other inner-city areas, such as Handsworth in Birmingham, Brixton in London, and large parts of Leicester and Bradford, had been transformed by immigration from the countries of the former British Empire following the passing of the Commonwealth Immigration Act of 1962.[47] Mosques, and Hindu and Sikh temples, now went up in the areas in which the immigrants settled, most of them in nineteenth-century terraces abandoned by their owners and tenants as they moved into the outer suburbs or further away (see pp. 268–9). Neighbourhood shopping districts were transformed meanwhile by new food stores, street markets and restaurants. Brick Lane in

Spitalfields, an area with a large Bangladeshi population, had eight Indian or Bangladeshi restaurants in 1989; by 2002 the number had risen to 41,[48] and nowadays there are allegedly more Indian restaurants in London than in Delhi and Mumbai combined.

The survival of neglected inner-city areas like Spitalfields owed much to the conservation movement, which increasingly emphasized not just individual buildings—now 'listed' as worthy of preservation under the post-war Town and Country Planning Act—but also whole neighbourhoods designated as Conservation Areas under the Civic Amenities Act of 1967. The pioneering sociologist, geographer and town-planner Patrick Geddes had already inspired the preservation of 'Old Edinburgh' in the late nineteenth century, and the conservation of Scottish towns enjoyed a new impetus in the twentieth century, connected with a reviving sense of national identity; the results can be seen in the formerly run-down parts of Canongate in Edinburgh, where existing buildings like those in Chessels Court were sympathetically restored.[49] Then came the 'little houses' scheme of 1960, encouraging the refurbishment of dilapidated older housing in places like Fraserburgh (Aberdeenshire) and the small coastal towns of East Fife. In England the Civic Trust, founded in 1958, championed the sympathetic treatment of neglected town centres. Abetted by local pressure groups, it played an important part in the regeneration of Plymouth's run-down harbour area by Sutton Pool, sensitively-designed modern housing filling the gaps left by bombing and post-war demolition.[50] An even greater transformation of city centres nationwide resulted from passing of the Clean Air Act in 1956, banning coal emissions and leading to the cleaning of smoke-blackened buildings.

Urban conservation received further publicity from *causes célèbres* such as Covent Garden in London, earmarked for redevelopment following the decision to relocate its long-established fruit and vegetable market, which finally left in 1974. A development consortium produced a series of plans, starting in 1965, all of them involving the building of new roads and the construction of hotels and conference centres which would have entailed the destruction of an urban landscape that had grown up over 350 years (see pp. 103–4). They were discarded following a well-organized public campaign and a public enquiry of 1973, after which 250 buildings were listed (Fig. 9.10).[51] The area attracted crowds of visitors. But, as was often the case in such areas, there was a price to pay in the displacement of many of the residents, forced out by rising rents: a problem, already highlighted in

Fig. 9.10 Covent Garden market, London. The covered market building for fruit and vegetables was built in 1828–30 to the designs of Charles Fowler, and extends over the open space at the heart of Inigo Jones's residential development for the Earl of Bedford of 1629–37 (See Fig. 3:16). Following the removal of the market to Nine Elms in 1974, the building was restored by the Greater London Council's Historic Buildings Division, with individual units leased out as shops and restaurants catering for the city's growing tourist population.

Jane Jacob's influential *Death and Life of American Cities* (1961), that has not gone away.

While conservationists campaigned for the preservation of old urban landscapes, planners and architects changed their approach to the design of new ones. Architects in Essex were encouraged to follow the new county style guide of 1973, promoting a cosy neo-vernacular architectural style of pitched roofs and carefully chosen decorative details first employed at South Woodham Ferrers, a new town south-east of Chelmsford: the antithesis of modernism as conventionally understood.[52] Inspired by Camillo Sitte, the influential Austrian architect and author of *City Planning According to Artistic Principles* (1889) and, more recently, by Nicholas Taylor's *The Village in the City* (1973), the Essex recommendations were imitated in high-density housing developments elsewhere featuring narrow streets and intricate mazes of traffic-free cul-de-sacs or 'mews courts'. Some developments of this kind revived neglected areas of older towns such as Aldwark, just inside

Fig. 9.11 This 1970s housing at Bartle Garth in York was built on a decayed city-centre site in Aldwark, not far from the Minster, seen in the background. The houses and garages, arranged around a cul-de-sac, are picturesquely grouped on 'townscape' principles, using local materials and carefully chosen street surfaces.

the medieval walls of York. Here rebuilding started in 1980, under a scheme promoted by Lionel Brett (Lord Esher), with the aim of luring people back to live in the city centre. The new housing, of brick with pitched and pan-tiled roofs (Fig. 9.11), allowed, in the architect's words, 'precious little room for cars and minimal back gardens . . . To do all this the rules of density, street widths and sightlines, which create suburbia, had to be abrogated'.[53] Similar schemes soon followed in towns and cities across the country.[54] And in a bastardized form the new taste for traditional-looking brick or stone facades, pitched roofs and random turrets was taken up by supermarket chains such as Tesco, and have become part of the everyday urban landscape.

These developments occurred as the British economy was undergoing a fundamental change. Manufacturing jobs declined by a third from 1971 to 1984 as once-flourishing towns and cities faced the challenge of de-industrialization: a phenomenon experienced in 'rust belts' and single-industry towns across the western world. Staple industries such as shipbuilding, textiles and coal-mining collapsed. Containerization and mechanization put paid to the dock labour which had sustained many working-class families in port cities; in London the East India Docks closed in 1967 and St Katherine's in 1968, quickly followed by the remainder. Half of all London's manufacturing jobs had gone by 1985, including those in Ford's car works at Dagenham and Tate & Lyle's sugar refinery at Plaistow. Inner-city businesses were meanwhile decimated by local authority planners, inspired by what has been called a pervasive 'discourse of obsolescence'; 43,000 manufacturing jobs in Manchester had already been lost between 1965 and 1975, many of them from small firms that could not afford to relocate to new industrial estates on the urban fringe.[55] Processing and exchange, and financial and other services, increasingly took the place of manufacture as Britain's main sources of employment; service jobs accounted for nearly ninety per cent of London's employment by the end of the twentieth century. The departure of old staple industries freed up large swathes of urban land for new housing and office developments. Lightweight sheds for the storage and distribution of goods proliferated on the edges of towns, and on disused railway land. But many urban landscapes, especially outside the prosperous south-east, have still to recover from the collapse of the industries on which their inhabitants had long depended.

The election of Margaret Thatcher as Prime Minister in 1979 signalled the end of large-scale council-house building, already in decline during the cash-starved 1970s. The sale of existing council houses was inaugurated in 1980; it led, together with tax relief on mortgage payments, to a massive shift in emphasis from publicly-financed to private housing. Mrs Thatcher favoured a 'property-owning democracy'—the ideal of the 1930s in which she had grown up—and, in pursuit of that aim, large estates of private housing went up in places like Lower Earley, on the southern fringe of Reading, hailed in a 2014 survey as the fifth 'most desirable' postcode in England.[56] Development began here in 1977 with 6,500 houses for some 20,000 people (now in 2021, after further expansion, housing 85,000), almost all of them owner-occupied. At Poundbury, a suburban development on Duchy of Cornwall land on the edge of Dorchester (Dorset), the architects and planners opted for the neo-Georgian revivalism advocated by Léon Krier, a pupil of James Stirling, and the Prince of Wales, whose well-publicized interventions in architectural controversies enraged the modernist establishment. Begun in 1993, and intended to house some 6,000 people when completed,[57] the curvaceous streets are lined with classically-inspired

City of Towers

In 1981 London's Docklands, where 30,000 people had been employed until the 1960s, were designated an 'enterprise zone' by government fiat. Then in 1986 the 'Big Bang' of financial deregulation led to an influx of banks and financial enterprises. By 2013 there were over 100,000 employees in the American-style business zone that had grown up at Canary Wharf on the Isle of Dogs in the East End.[58] An 824-ft tower—twice the height of St Paul's Cathedral—went up there in 1988–92 to the designs of the Argentinian-American architect César Pelli, and 2,200 acres of derelict land had been reclaimed by 1998, some of it devoted to offices, the rest to new housing, most of which was out of the financial reach of the existing inhabitants of the area.[59] The City of London responded by inaugurating a new phase of building of its own. Half its office volume was replaced between 1985 and 1993,[60] a process marked most noticeably by the proliferation of high-rise towers such as Richard Rogers's eye-catching Lloyds building on Cornhill (1978–86), constructed around an internal atrium and externally fetishizing services like the lifts, seen as replaceable parts. At No.1 Poultry, facing the Bank of England and Royal Exchange—a site formerly occupied by a Victorian Gothic office development—the developer Peter Palumbo commissioned a sleek glass tower designed by the modernist pioneer Ludwig Mies van der Rohe, only to have the project rejected by the planning authority, which sanctioned in its place a stripy, low-rise, Post-Modernist office block of 1996–7 by the architectural maverick James Stirling: a case-study of changing taste in architecture and urbanism. More recently, some of the post-war behemoths that scarred the City have made way for new and more sensitively designed buildings, nowhere more so than at Paternoster Square (finished 2003), just to the north of St Paul's Cathedral (Fig. 9.12). Here an instant cityscape was created, reclaiming the ground level of a demolished 1960s deck-access development by the creation of a new open space entered from St Paul's Churchyard through the re-erected Temple Bar and surrounded by low-rise office blocks detailed in a fashionably Post-Modern manner. Elsewhere, new and sometimes bizarrely shaped office towers have continued to transform the City's skyline, a process that shows no sign of abating, despite the devastating impact of Coronavirus on employment patterns in 2020–21.

Fig. 9.12 The high-density Paternoster Square office development of 1996–2004 replaced an earlier development of 1962–7 on a badly bombed site to the north of St Paul's Cathedral (See Fig. 9.1). The plan, by William Whitfield, entailed the removal of the 1960s pedestrian deck at first-floor level and the creation of a public space entered from St Paul's Churchyard through the reconstructed Temple Bar (1670–2), seen at the bottom left. The Portland stone column in the middle of the square, designed by Whitfield's firm, conceals a ventilation shaft for an underground service road.

facades following design codes drawn up by the Prince's own Foundation, evoking the surrealist strangeness of a De Chirico painting. Elsewhere, abandoned factories, schools, hospitals, military establishments and even former workhouses were recycled for housing. The Gunwharf at Portsmouth, a naval site closed in 1985 (See p. 165), was reopened in 2001 with new flats, some of them fitted into in older buildings, a shopping centre containing ninety retail outlets, a cinema and a tall observation tower.[61] Such developments have multiplied recently, but the supply of housing for the growing population has still not matched the growing demand, especially in London and the prosperous south-east. And, with rising prices, exacerbated by rigidities in the market and in the planning system, the problem of supplying adequate housing for a growing population remains unsolved.

Milton Keynes

'Different by design', as its signposts have reminded motorists, the contemporary urban landscape can be experienced in unadulterated form at
Milton Keynes. With a population of over 250,000 people at the time of
writing—roughly that of Newcastle or Southampton—the city was begun
in 1967 on a generous site of 89 square kilometres in the deeply rural
countryside of north Buckinghamshire, roughly equidistant from London
and Birmingham and incorporating a handful of existing villages and three
small towns. Unlike the first New Towns, it was designed for mass car ownership (initially estimated at 1.5 per household), with wide well-landscaped
thoroughfares, more like North American parkways than English streets,
defining a chequer-board of 'grid squares' (Fig. 9.13).[62] The roads cross
each other at roundabouts, rather than multi-level intersections or junctions controlled by traffic lights, which are conspicuously absent, and
bicycle paths snake through the leafy landscape. Seen from the roads, much
of Milton Keynes looks like parkland dotted with small houses clustered
together: a modern restatement of the ideal that had inspired the Garden
City pioneers. Development was slow; the last of the grid squares was still
being filled with speculative housing at the time of writing.

The city centre occupies rising ground to the east of the railway station.
It is laid out on a rectilinear grid plan with a vast, low-rise, glass–clad
enclosed shopping centre in the middle, surrounded by car parking. Offices,
an ecumenical church, public buildings and a theatre line the wide and
rather featureless streets between it and the railway station. There is little
obvious manufacturing industry, but huge, windowless coloured boxes
containing warehouses for the storage of goods line the trunk road leading
east out of the city towards Bedford. Each of the grid squares contains
housing for approximately 5,000 people—the size of a substantial medieval
town—each with shops, schools and health centres grouped together,
many of them characterized by steeply pitched roofs and loosely neo-
vernacular detailing. Pre-existing villages, with their medieval churches
and vernacular housing, are incorporated into the plan, as are the small
towns of Stony Stratford, Wolverton and Bletchley, along with remnants of
open countryside, some of it forming a linear park dotted with recreational lakes.

The original intention was for half of the housing to be built for rent, at
an overall density of thirty people per acre; Beanhill (1973–7), one of the
first neighbourhoods to be completed, is largely made up of closely packed
single-storeyed houses to which, following complaints from the tenants,

pitched roofs were later added. But since the 1980s most of the housing has been built by private developers at a much lower density; a recent development at Tattenhoe Park offers a mixture of flats and houses of between one and five bedrooms apiece, some detached, some semi-detached and some terraced. Everywhere the houses are low-rise, most of them loosely neo-vernacular in character (Fig. 9.14), the houses lining wiggly roads or grouped in Radburn-style cul-de-sacs or around greens. There is no single aesthetic; though Milton Keynes is a planned city, its architecture has responded to the laissez-faire ethos that took root in the 1980s and 1990s, and is still changing as architectural fashions change. The result is an inward-looking, fragmented, unassertive and anti-monumental urban landscape that seems to embody the aspirations of its economically and increasingly ethnically diverse inhabitants.

By the end of the twentieth century council estates in some cities, once the homes of the aspirational working class, had become 'reservoirs of deprivation', their inhabitants including large numbers of impoverished individuals and families. By the 1990s the 'Crescents' at Hulme in Manchester, a massive council development of 1968–72, was being described as 'Europe's worst housing stock', from which a staggering 96.3 per cent of the inhabitants wanted to move.[63] Cut off by roads from the city centre, the estate was flattened in 1992–4 as part of central Government's 'City Challenge' programme and replaced by low-rise housing built along conventional-looking streets. Regeneration has been attempted in the once much-admired Park Hill estate at Sheffield (see pp. 282–3), and the remodelled flats there have recently been offered for sale, some of them as offices, some for rent by the design firm Urban Splash: part of a project to rebrand the city as the 'northern capital of cool'.[64] But much of the neighbouring Hyde Park development has been bulldozed. So too have many of the high-rise blocks of the 1960s and 1970s in Glasgow, following a shift in emphasis to the rehabilitation of the surviving nineteenth-century tenement blocks. Yet in October 2019 a development of 105 brick-fronted terraced houses in Goldsmith Street, Norwich, built for rent by the City Council, won the prestigious Stirling Prize for architecture: a portent perhaps of a more hopeful future for social housing and for sensitive urban design.

The centres of most of our larger cities, their permanent residents long decanted to the suburbs, have been refurbished over the past thirty years.

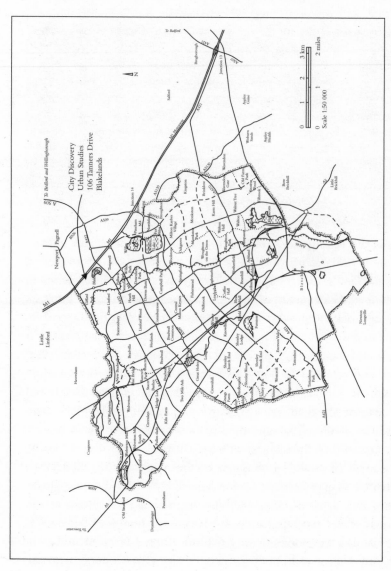

Fig. 9.13 A Map of Milton Keynes. Each of the 'grid squares' of the new city contains housing, schools, a neighbourhood shopping centre and open spaces within a framework of carefully-landscaped roads. The M1 motorway is close to the northern boundary, and the main railway line out of London's Euston station runs through the south of the city, with a station downhill from the central shopping area. The existing towns of Bletchley, Stony Stratford and Wolverton are incorporated within the plan.

Fig. 9.14 This low-density development of brick owner-occupied houses in Milton Keynes is set back from its curved approach road, protecting the residents from through traffic.

Older buildings have sometimes been dwarfed by brash newcomers, as at Bristol's Broadmead, where the glazed Galleries shopping centre (1991) incorporates and overwhelms the Merchant Taylors' almshouses of 1771 (Fig. 9.15). Birmingham's concrete-clad Bull Ring shopping centre has been replaced, and the former street pattern, obscured by the post-war Inner Ring Road, has been partially re-created, with a traffic-free open space created around the medieval parish church of St Martin, overlooked by the spectacular exterior of the Selfridges store (Amanda Levete and Future Systems, 1999–2003), its blobby exterior covered with anodized aluminium discs. Another civic focus has been created above New Street station, incorporating a new John Lewis store, opened in 2015 (and closed in 2020).[65] The Victorian civic centre (see pp. 222–3), tided up as Victoria Square in 1993, has been expanded westwards, leaping over the ring road to encompass a new Symphony Hall, a striking new public library (2013)[66] and a restored canal landscape overlooked by a Post-modernist office block. And a huge new educational area has recently grown up on abandoned railway land to the north of the former Curzon Street goods station, destined to be the terminus of the projected HS2 high-speed rail link to London.

Fig. 9.15 The Merchant Tailors' almshouses and the Galleries shopping centre at Bristol. The former almshouse was built in 1701 and now serves as the main entrance to a glass-fronted shopping centre of 1987–90. The building stands within the Broadmead area, east of the city centre, extensively redeveloped according to plans framed after the Second World War and zoned for retailing and offices.

The prosperity of the 1990s, however uneven, and the advent of funding from the National Lottery (1995), gave rise to the construction of new arts and leisure buildings in decayed post-industrial urban settings. The former Bankside power station on London's long-neglected South Bank was resurrected as the hugely successful Tate Modern art gallery, opened in 2000 and extended in 2016. Government funding was also directed towards new public galleries in struggling towns such as Walsall in the West Midlands (New Art Gallery, 1995–2000), Wakefield in Yorkshire (The Hepworth, 2007–11), and the decayed seaside resort of Margate in Kent (Tate Contemporary, 2008–11) (Fig. 9.16). Waterfronts have attracted a lot of attention, leading to the refurbishment and recycling of abandoned dock buildings and warehouses, as at Albert Dock in Liverpool (Fig. 6.5) and the Castlefield 'quarter' of Manchester. The depressed south bank of the Tyne at Gateshead was linked to Newcastle's city centre in 1997–2001 by the building of a new footbridge, followed in 2003 by the conversion of the Baltic Mill, dating from the 1930s, into an art gallery, and the building of the adjacent Sage

Fig. 9.16 The harbour and the Tate Contemporary gallery at Margate, Kent. The gallery, serving as an outstation for the Tate Gallery in London, was designed by David Chipperfield Architects and built in 2008-11. It occupies a site next to the harbour, allegedly that of a cottage occupied by the artist J.M.W. Turner when he visited the town. Margate, on the north coast of the Thanet peninsula, developed as a resort town in the 18th century. Droit House, in front of the gallery, was built as a Customs House in 1812 and was rebuilt after being bombed in the Second World War.

concert hall (2005). And, starting in 1994, the abandoned docks in Cardiff Bay, once the world's largest coal port (see p. 177), were transformed by the building of a barrage across the mudflats: a process that gave rise to the building of the Millennium Centre concert hall (2004) and Richard Rogers's innovative, glass-clad building for the newly-established Welsh Assembly (2006).[67]

The post-industrial peripheries of some city centres have been revived to accommodate the newly flourishing communications and entertainment industries. Trafford Park, an industrial estate established in 1896 next to the Manchester Ship Canal docks on the fringe of Salford, declined after the Second World War but was rescued by a development corporation in 1987; by 2006 there were 140 companies there, employing 40,000 people.[68]

The docks themselves, meanwhile, were newly marketed as Salford Quays and redeveloped as an 'enterprise zone', linked to Manchester's city centre in 1999 by a new tram line. Along with flats and offices, it contains the regional headquarters of the British Broadcasting Corporation and cultural magnets such as the Lowry arts centre, opened in 2000, and Imperial War Museum North, completed in 2002 to the deliberately jagged designs of Daniel Libeskind, influenced by Russian Constructivist architecture of the 1920s.[69] More recently, the handsome but abandoned furniture warehouses of Shoreditch, near the Old Street 'silicon roundabout' just to the north of the City of London, have been refurbished and put to new use since Microsoft moved there in 1999.[70] Similar developments are currently (2021) taking place on long-neglected former railway land at King's Cross, where surviving buildings have been imaginatively recycled among the new office towers.

The so-called nation of shopkeepers has mutated into a nation of shop-pers. Retail warehouses and shopping outlets have sprung up on abandoned industrial settings and alongside main roads on the fringes of towns and cities. A large portion of the former Great Western Railway works at Swindon was turned into a designer outlet centre in 1997, and there is an even larger establishment of a similar kind at Bicester Village, begun in 1995–7 on the edge of a small, unpretentious Oxfordshire town; it attracted more than six million visitors a year, more than the National Gallery in London, before the Coronavirus pandemic of 2020–21. The massive Trafford shopping centre, on a 150-acre site surrounded by main roads on the edge of Manchester, is even larger; built in 1995–8, until recently it employed some 7,000 people working in 280 stores. Surrounded by parking for 10,000 cars and described by its promoters as a 'powerful shopping machine', its rigidly controlled Las Vegas-like internal environment is organized around internal 'streets' extending out from a central domed area, embodying the strangely unreal world of modern consumerism.[71] But out-of-town shop-ping centres, superstores and, even more, internet purchasing come at a price, seen in the deterioration of central shopping streets and public spaces: a problem being faced in many British towns and cities at the time of writ-ing with no obvious sign of solution.

American-style business parks have also proliferated on the fringes of towns and cities. Most, like the Oxford Science Park, opened in 1991 on land belonging to Magdalen College, and housing over seventy companies employing, at least until recently, over 2,500 people, are made up of low-rise offices dotted around carefully landscaped and manicured sylvan landscapes. The office park at Merry Hill in the West Midlands, built in 1985-90 on the site of an abandoned steelworks near Dudley, is juxtaposed with a shopping centre, forming part of an 'edge city' of a kind that can be found on under-used or marginal land near most large centres of population, or close to airports and motorways.[72] As London has expanded eastwards towards the Thames estuary, the marshes of the Lea Valley to the east of London have also become ripe for this kind of development.[73] They were the home of the Queen Elizabeth Olympic Park at Stratford, created for the 2012 Olympic Games, held on formerly contaminated land dotted with the remains of derelict factories. The Olympic Village has recently been turned into private housing,[74] and some of the sports venues, including Zaha Hadid's 'Modernist Baroque' swimming pool, based on curvaceous forms made possible by new materials and computer-aided design, have become permanent features of a futuristic-looking urban landscape that it is hoped will flourish with the anticipated opening of the new Crossrail underground line in 2022.

Having increased relatively slowly for a generation after 1945, the population of the United Kingdom had grown by 2021 to an estimated 67.6 million—a ten million increase over thirty years—the vast majority of whom live in towns and cities. The urban environment has been trans-formed meanwhile by cumulative, and often little-noticed, changes carried out piecemeal by countless individuals: home improvements, such as loft conversions and back extensions into gardens; the addition of front porches and the replacement of windows; and the paving over of front gardens for car parking. Public authorities have also played a part through the prolifer-ation of street furniture: bigger lamp standards, traffic lights—first appearing at Piccadilly Circus in London in 1926—advertisement hoardings, and changes in road surfaces. Residential streets, used as late as the 1950s as infor-mal playgrounds for children, have been colonized by cars. The effect of these incremental changes has been alleviated to some extent by the sometimes-obsessive care taken by home-owners and tenants over their front, and even more over their back, gardens. As early as 1855 a witness to the Select Committee on Metropolitan Improvements could remark that 'The passion for country residence is increasing to an extent that it is almost impossible for persons who do not mix with the poor to know. You cannot find a broken teapot in which to stuff...some flower or something, to give them an idea of open fields and the country'.[75] This is an attitude that has persisted into modern times, as seen in the popularity of garden centres on the fringes of towns, and it shows no sign of diminishing.

For the contemporary architect David Chipperfield, architect of the Hepworth gallery at Wakefield and the Tate satellite at Margate, two of the most sensitively-designed public projects of recent years, the rapidly changing city centres of London, Birmingham and Manchester exhibit too many examples of 'slick and often thoughtless architecture put up at speed'. But another famous contemporary architect, Rem Koolhaas, has seen British 'fluidity' and responsiveness to the market as a virtue, and from the vantage point of 2021 it seems likely that his point of view will prevail in the immediate future.[76] As Spiro Kostof, one of the most perceptive recent writers on urban history, put it: 'Cities are never still; they resist efforts to make neat sense of them…In the end, urban truth is in the flow'.[77] Our towns and cities have changed in the past, they are changing now, and they will change even more in the years to come.[78] Change is built into their very identity, as the city fathers of Birmingham recognized when they chose the word 'FORWARD' as their motto. That should serve as both a challenge and an inspiration to us today.

Glossary

Aisle—a passageway flanking the central area of a building

Arcade—a row of arches resting on supports; a covered row of shops facing one another across a passage

Art Deco—a self-consciously modernist style of interior decoration that flourished between the two World Wars featuring bright colours and straight, sometimes jagged, lines

Art Nouveau—an innovative late 19th- and early 20th-century movement in architecture and the decorative arts, emphasizing sinuous lines and naturalistic forms

Arts and Crafts—a late 19th-century movement that encouraged the revival of manual craftsmanship, mainly in domestic buildings

Ashlar—large blocks of squared and carefully finished masonry

Assizes—see Quarter Sessions

Atrium—an inner, usually top-lit, courtyard of a multi-story building

Back-to-back—a row of houses sharing a common back wall

Bailey—the outer courtyard of a castle

Balustrade—a rail supported by bulbous supports (balusters), usually at the top of a building or alongside a staircase

Barbican—an outer fortification giving added protection to a gateway

Baronial—a style popular in 19th-century Scotland, influenced by Scottish Renaissance domestic architecture

Bartizan—a projection corbelled out from the top of a tower

Basilica—an aisled building with a heightened clerestory shedding light into the central aisle

Bastion—a projection designed to strengthen a castle or town wall

Bauhaus—a school of design in Weimar, and later at Dessau, in inter-war Germany that gave its name to a style of unornamented modernist architecture

Beaux Arts—the sometimes lavishly detailed Renaissance style promoted by the École des Beaux Arts in Paris in the mid and late 19th century

Borough—an independently governed (chartered) town

Brutalist—a style of modernist architecture popular in the late 1950s, 1960s and 1970s featuring raw concrete finishes

Building lease—a lease in which the lessee is expected to put up buildings in the first years

Burgage—a long, narrow plot of land in a town

Burgess—a freeman of a borough

Burh—a fortified settlement in Anglo-Saxon England, sometimes with urban characteristics

Buttress—a masonry projection at right angles to a wall designed to strengthen it against an outward thrust

By-law—laws relating to building and urban development promulgated by a local authority

Camber—a tilt in the middle of a road surface, sloping on each side

Campanile—bell tower

Canted—angled, usually at 45 degrees

Chancel—the eastern arm of a church, containing the main (high) altar

Chantry—an endowment supporting the provision of requiem masses for the souls of departed individuals or members of a group

Charter—a legal document giving rights or privileges to members of an institution

Cloister—a covered walkway around quadrangular space, usually attached to a cathedral or monastic church

Close—an area next to a cathedral originally surrounded by houses for the clergy and related buildings

Close studding—decorative upright posts on the outside of a timber-framed building

Coade stone—artificial stone patented by Eleanor Coade (1733-1831)

Cob—a walling material of earth, often strengthened with straw

College—an endowed institution serving as a residence for chantry priests, or with an educational function

Colonia—Roman military settlement

Colonnade—a row of columns

Common—a tract of unenclosed land over which villagers or townspeople had the right to pasture animals

Conduit—a channel for conveying water, sometimes supplied or dispensed from a conduit house

Cornice—a ledge, often ornamented, at the top of a classical façade or colonnade

Corporation—the governing body of a chartered borough

Cottage orné—a picturesque house in the late 18th or early 19th century displaying motifs taken from vernacular architecture

Court—a collection of closely packed small, and often slum, houses arranged around a courtyard behind a street front

Crenellation—an indented defensive or pseudo-defensive parapet

Cross-wing—a wing placed at a right angle to the main part of a building

Cruck—pairs of inclined timbers serving as a support for a building

Culvert—a covered channel for water underneath a street

Cupola—a small domed structure on a roof or surmounting a larger dome

Curtain wall—an outer, non-structural covering, often of glass, for a steel- or concrete-framed building

Flâneur—saunterer

Friary—a monastery for members of the mendicant orders (Franciscans, Dominicans, etc)

Gable—the end of a pitched roof, usually triangular-shaped but sometimes embellished and ornamented

Garden city/suburb—a town or residential suburb laid out in the first half of the 20th century at a low density with ample open space for the residents

Gauged brickwork—bricks sawn and rubbed to give a precise surface in higher-status buildings, especially around doorways and windows

Guild—an association of artisans and/or merchants devoted to organising the terms of trade. Their meeting places or guildhalls sometimes served as meeting places for the governing body (corporation) of a town

Harling—roughcast plaster for cladding a Scottish building

Hipped roof—a roof sloping up on four sides to a ridge

Italianate—the style of Italian Renaissance or vernacular buildings

Jacobean—the mixed style prevailing in the reign of King James 1 of England/VI of Scotland (1603-1625) and to some extent afterwards

Jetty—the projection of an upper over a lower storey in a timber-framed building

Keep—The central residential tower of a castle

Kirk—a Scottish church

Louvre—an opening in a roof to allow the escape of smoke from a hearth

Machicolation—openings in the projecting parapet of a medieval building from which projectiles could be dropped

Mathematical tiles—tiles applied to the front of a timber-framed building, especially in south-east England, giving an the impression of brickwork

Mercer—a dealer in high-quality textile fabrics

Mews—a long courtyard behind high-status terraces of urban houses, lined with rows of stables, often with accommodation above

Middle row—an area of a former market place filled with small, often closely- packed houses and shops

Minster—a large church, usually with a community of priests attached to serve communities scattered over a wide area in Anglo-Saxon times

Motte—a defensive mound in a medieval castle, often surmounted by a wooden tower

Mullion—a vertical post in a window

Murage—a tax levied to build or repair town walls

Nave—the westernmost arm of a church, often containing seating and (in Catholic churches) subsidiary altars

Nonconformist—(in England and Wales) Protestant churches whose congregations did not accept the authority of the established church

Oppidum—a fortified Iron Age settlement with some urban characteristics

Ordnance—mounted guns or artillery

Panopticon—a corrective building, often centrally planned with radiating wings, allowing for surveillance of the inmates from a central core

Pantile—a roof tile with a corrugated or S-shaped side

Pargetting—ornamental plasterwork

Parlour—a downstairs living room in a medieval or early modern house

Pattern book—a book of specimen designs for buildings, and details of buildings, usually in the 18th and 19th centuries

Pavement—raised sidewalk of an urban street

Pediment—the gable end of a classical temple

Pentice—a subsidiary structure with a lean-to roof, usually at the front of a building

Perpendicular—the style of Gothic architecture prevalent in England from c.1340 to the mid 16th century

Piano nobile—the main (upstairs) floor of a Renaissance *palazzo*, containing the most important rooms

Pilaster—a flat representation of a classical column applied as decoration to a building

Portico—the porch or entrance to a building designed after the fashion of a classical temple front

Post-modern—an architectural style popular in the 1990s and introducing motifs from earlier styles, sometimes in an exaggerated or ironical way

Postern—a subsidiary gateway in a medieval wall

Pump room—a room for drinking medicinal water in spas

Quarter Sessions—local law courts held in the larger English towns four times each year

'Queen Anne'—an eclectic, mainly domestic, style that flourished in the last quarter of the 19th century, characterized by the use of red brick with ornamental gables and white-painted window frames

Refectory—the dining hall of a monastery

Ribbon development—housing, often unco-ordinated, lining the roads leading into towns and cities

Rood screen—a stone or wooden screen in a medieval church surmounted by a representation of Christ's crucifixion

rus in urbe—'country in the town'. The phase was coined by Roman writer Martial in the first century CE

Scullery—the service area of a small house, used for washing dishes, clothes, etc

Shambles—a meat market

Solar—an upstairs room in a medieval house

Stucco—a smooth, lime-based plaster applied to a brick or stone building

System building—a method of construction using standardized prefabricated components

Tenement—an apartment or flat in a block of working-class dwellings

Terrace—a row of linked houses sharing common side walls with their neighbours

Terracotta—moulded and fired clay ornament

Tollbooth—a Scottish town hall

Transom—a horizontal bar in a medieval or early modern window

Transept—the cross-arm of a cruciform church, used in medieval times for subsidiary east-facing altars

Tudor—a loose stylistic term to describe the domestic architecture of the 16th and early 17th centuries, and its revival (Neo-Tudor) in the 19th and 20th centuries

Undercroft—the basement, usually vaulted, of a medieval building

Vault—an arched stone roof. A barrel vault is a continuous arch, usually over the central aisle of a building

Villa—a moderately-sized high-status house, often built close to a town or city, or in a suburb

Villegiatura—occasional residence in the countryside, sometimes in a second home

Wynd—an alleyway leading off a main street in a Scottish town

Yeoman—a prosperous farmer in medieval and early modern England

Zeitgeist—spirit of the age

Zoning—local laws regulating the development of land

Endnotes

CHAPTER I

1. P. Clark (ed.), *Oxford Handbook of Cities in World History* (Oxford, 2013), 49–57.
2. D. M. Palliser (ed.), *Cambridge Urban History of Britain* (*CUH*), vol. 1, 19–20; J. S. Wacher, *Towns of Roman Britain* (1995 edn.).
3. M. Aston and J. Bond, *The Landscape of Towns* (Stroud, 2000), 42–43.
4. Wacher, 101–37; Clark (ed.), 170.
5. W. G. Hoskins, *Two Thousand Years in Exeter* (1963), 2–10.
6. N. Pevsner and D. Neave, *The Buildings of England, Yorkshire: York and the East Riding* (1995), 116–8.
7. S. Reynolds, *An Introduction to the History of English Medieval Towns* (Oxford, 1977), 4–15; *CUH*, I, 21–24.
8. The remains of its theatre and the foundations of some of the houses have been unearthed and can be visited.
9. *CUH*, vol 1, 189–90; C. Ross and J. Clark, *London: The Illustrated History* (2008), 54–55.
10. P. Ottaway, *Archaeology in British Towns* (1992), 121.
11. D. M. Palliser, *Medieval York* (Oxford, 2014), 34–36.
12. S. Rees-Jones, *York: The Making of a City, 1068–1350* (Oxford, 2013), 10.
13. Palliser, *Medieval York*, esp. p. 70, and maps on p. 52; Ottaway, *Archaeology*, 47; J. Campbell (ed.), *The Anglo-Saxons* (1991), 166–67.
14. J. Blair, *Building Anglo-Saxon England* (Princeton and Oxford, 2018), 232–46; O. Creighton and R. Higham, *Medieval Town Walls* (Stroud, 2005), 35.
15. Campbell (ed.), *Anglo-Saxons*, 152–53; *CUH*, i., 41–42.
16. Ross and Clark, *London*, 56; Blair, *Building Anglo-Saxon England*, 270–71.
17. In the Burghal Hidage of *c.*914 it ranked among the largest burhs in the country.
18. M. W. Beresford and J. K. Joseph, *Medieval England: An Aerial Survey* (Cambridge, 2nd edn, 1979), 195–97. The bridge, which still has medieval masonry, was first mentioned in 1141.
19. The precise siting of the 'ford for oxen' which gave its name to the town has long been controversial, some modern scholars maintaining that it was to the west of the city and not—contrary to recent archaeological wisdom—on the site of the present Folly Bridge, to the south. See A. Crossley, *Oxoniensia* 83 (2018).
20. *CUH*, i., 256, 1–22.

21. Quoted in A. Brown, *et al.*, *The Rows of Chester* (English Heritage Archaeological Report 16, 1999), 9.

22. *Victoria County History* (hereafter *VCH*) *Cheshire*, vol. 5 (2003) 16–33; P. Carrington, *English Heritage Book of Chester* (1994), 56–57. Newgate (*sic*) Street was not made till after 1066.

23. B. Ayers, *English Heritage Book of Norwich* (1994), 26; M. D. Lobel *et al.*, *Atlas of Historic Towns*, vol. 2 (1975); Ottaway, *Archaeology*, 158, 166; Campbell (ed.), *Anglo-Saxons*, 174–75.

24. Royal Commission on Historic Monuments, *The Town of Stamford* (1977), xxxvi–xl.

25. T. Slater and G. Rosser, *The Church in the Medieval Town* (Aldershot, 1998), 155–76; T. Slater and N. Goose, *A County of Small Towns* (Hatfield, 2008), 301–26.

26. M. Freeman, *St Albans: A History* (Lancaster, 2008), 135–71.

27. *VCH Oxfordshire*, vol. 4 (1979), 10; A. Dodd (ed.), *Oxford. before the University* (Oxford, 2003), 35–41.

28. See for instance J. Blair, *Anglo-Saxon Oxfordshire* (Stroud, 1994), 150–1, 162–63.

29. Blair, *Building Anglo-Saxon England*, 84–85.

30. *CUH*, vol 1, 230–31. Cob buildings up to five ft high have been found under the bailey of Wallingford Castle (*ex.inf.* Trevor Rowley).

31. J. Blair, 'Frewin Hall', *Oxoniensia* 43 (1978), 48–99.

32. See Tatton-Brown on Canterbury in Slater and Rosser (eds), *Church in the Medieval Town*, 236–71.

33. J. Schofield and A. Vince, *Medieval Towns* (Leicester, 1994), 47.

34. T. Hassall *et al.*, *Oxford, the Buried City* (Oxford Archaeological Unit, 1987) 22–3.

35. R. Morris, *Churches in the Landscape* (1989), 192–14.

36. A. Taylor, *Cambridge: The Hidden History* (Stroud, 1999), 45–48.

37. Blair, *Anglo-Saxon England*, 275.

38. M. Biddle (ed.), *Winchester in the Middle Ages* (Oxford, 1976), 278.

39. *Wintanceaster: Saxon and Medieval Winchester* (Winchester Museums Service, 2001), 8.

40. D. Keene, *Survey of Medieval Winchester* (Oxford, 1985), vol. 2, 490–92.

41. C. Platt, *The English Medieval Town* (1979), 22; K. Lilley, *Urban Life in the Middle Ages* (Basingstoke, 2002), 154–55; Ottaway, *Archaeology*, p. 134.

42. The New Minster was re-founded on a new site as Hyde Abbey, outside the northern stretch of walls, in 1110.

43. See M. Biddle and D. Keene, *Winchester* (Historic Towns Atlas, 2017).

44. M. Biddle, *The Castle, Winchester* (Winchester; Hampshire County Council, 2000). A palace for King Charles II was begun on the site in 1682 but was never finished and in 1796 the shell was turned over to the Army, which later built barracks on the site (now turned into flats).

45. Biddle, *Winchester in the Middle Ages*, 283.

46. *CUH*, vol. 1, 83–84.

47. *CUH* vol. 1, 103.

48. *CUH*, vol. 1, 85; Lilley, *Urban Life*, 3.

49. *CUH* vol. 1,160; Schofield and Vince, *Medieval Towns*, 42.

50. *CUH* vol. 1, 60.

51. M. Lobel (ed.), *Historic Towns*, vol. 1 (Nottingham); Beresford and Joseph, *Medieval England*, 176–78.

52. Quoted in W. Makey, 'Edinburgh in the Mid-Seventeenth Century', in M. Lynch (ed.) *The Early Modern Town in Scotland* (1987), 192.

53. D. Bell, *Edinburgh Old Town* (Edinburgh, 2008), 7; Makey, in Lynch (ed.) *Early Modern Town in Scotland*, 202.

54. M. Lynch, *et al.* (eds), *The Scottish Medieval Town* (Edinburgh, 1988), 4–5; *CUH*, vol 1, 155–57. The others were Edinburgh and Aberdeen.

55. M. Lobel (ed.), *Historic Towns*, vol. 1 (Glasgow).

56. J. S. Smith (ed.), *Old Aberdeen* (Aberdeen, 1991), 1–13; E. P. Dennison, *et al.*, *Aberdeen before 1800* (East Linton, 2002), 14–18.

57. I. Soulsby, *Towns of Medieval Wales* (Chichester, 1983), 7.

58. Soulsby, *Towns of Medieval Wales*, 13–15.

59. Soulsby, *Towns of Medieval Wales*, 23. Cardiff declined after the Black Death in the mid-14th century, when it became half the size of Carmarthen: *Ibid.*, p. 26.

60. Soulsby, *Towns of Medieval Wales*, 18, 265–68.

61. M. Lobel (ed.), *Historic. Towns*, vol. 1 (Caernarfon, 1969).

62. Schofield and Vince, *Medieval Towns*, 77.

63. Beresford and Joseph, *Medieval England*, 215–17. 'Bury', a name commonly found in towns, is etymologically related to the Anglo-Saxon word *burh*, to the German word *Burg,* meaning a fortress, and to the words 'burgh', signifying an independent town in Scotland and 'borough' for an incorporated town in England.

64. M. Lobel (ed.), *Historic Towns*, vol. 1 (Reading).

65. D. O'Sullivan, 'Medieval Friaries', in P. S. Barnwell (ed.), *Places of Worship in Britain and Ireland 1150–1350* (Donington, 2018), 153–54. The Refectory and Guest House survive as outlying parts of the King's School.

66. S. Townley, *Henley-on-Thames: Town, Trade and River* (2009); *VCH Oxfordshire*, vol. 16.

67. Slater and Goose, *County of Small Towns*, 76–80.

68. A. Rosen and J. Cliffe, *The Making of Chipping Norton* (Stroud, 2017), 17. The small town of Clun in Shropshire was also established in the shadow of a Fitzalan castle.

69. W. G. Hoskins, *Local History in England* (1959) 106; N. Pevsner and E. Williamson, *Buildings of England: Nottinghamshire* (1979), 180–82.

70. J. Haslam, *Early Medieval Towns in Britain* (2010), 37–38; Schofield, *The Building of London* (1984), 25–27. Some of the piles can be seen in the Museum of London.

71. Schofield and Vince, *Medieval Towns*, 59–61; V. Parker, *The Making of King's Lynn* (Chichester, 1971), 1–3, 19–21. A third settlement, South Lynn, lay to the south of the Millfleet, and remained technically independent until the 16th century.

72. Beresford and Joseph, *Medieval England*, 208–209.

73. Beresford and Joseph, *Medieval England*, 206–207.

74. Beresford and Joseph, *Medieval England*, 238–41. Some of the gateways survive, as do the chancel of St Thomas, one of the town's three churches, and the Court House.

75. M. Beresford, *New Towns of the Middle Ages* (Gloucester, 1988), 106–107.

76. Beresford and Joseph, *Medieval England*, 182–83.

77. *VCH Gloucestershire*, vol. 8, 118–122.

78. In existence by *c.*1205; the Severn was not bridged till 1823.

79. *CUH* i, 170–71.

80. Hoskins, *Local History in England*, 72–3, pointing out that they only served part of the city. A Conduit was built in the High St in 1441: Portman, *Exeter Houses 1400–1700* (Exeter, 1966), 16. The bridge was demolished in 1770.

81. There was a 'Pixey or Fairy House' or public lavatory on the bridge: Portman, *Exeter Houses* 15.

82. Beresford and Joseph, *Medieval England*, 199.

83. Taylor, *Cambridge: The Hidden History*, 44; M. Lobel, *et al.* (eds) *Historic Towns*, vol. 2. It is shown in a map by William Smith of *c.*1588.

84. S. Kostof, *The City Shaped* (1991), 34.

85. J. Minnis and K. Carmichael, *Boston, Lincolnshire* (Swindon: Historic England, 2015), 1–10.

86. See Beresford, *New Towns*, 157 (plan)

87. M. R. G. Conzen, *Alnwick, Northumberland* (1960), 20–41.

88. J. Goodall, *The English Castle* (New Haven and London, 2011), 89.

89. M. Lobel (ed), *Historic Towns*, vol. 1 (Hereford).

90. M. Aston and J. Bond, *The Landscape of Towns* (Stroud, 2000), 96–97.

91. Schofield and Vince, *Medieval Towns*, p. 36.

92. M. Lobel (ed.), *Historic Towns*, vol. 1 (Salisbury).

93. *VCH Wiltshire*, vi, 87–90.

94. R. T. Rowley, *The Shropshire Landscape* (1972), 188–92; Lilley, *Urban Life*, 140–42.

95. Lynch *et al.*, *Scottish Medieval Town*, 42–59.

96. Lilley, *Urban Life*, 224.

97. M. Lobel, *et al.*, *Historic Towns*, vol. 2; Ottaway, *Archaeology*, 195–97; Schofield and Vince, *Medieval Towns*, 38; Lilley, *Urban Life*, 148, 172–3, 224.

98. Platt, *English Medieval Town*, 61.

99. F. Neale (ed.), *The Topography of Medieval Bristol* (Bristol Record Society 51, 2000), 81; Aston and Bond, *Landscape of Towns*, 97.

100. Haslam, *Early Medieval Towns*, 33.

101. Blair, *Building Anglo-Saxon England*, 165.

102. W. Urry, *Canterbury Under the Angevin Kings* (1967), 192.

103. Parker, *King's Lynn*, 34–36.

104. Beresford, *New Towns*, 163 (plan) and 524; Beresford in *Thoresby Society* 60–61 (Leeds, 1989), 86–87 (Turks Head Yard).

105. Platt, *English Medieval Town*, 65.

106. Rees-Jones, *York*, 208–209.

107. At Bala, a small town founded *c.*1310, with a regular street plan, they are 200 ft by 6 ft: Soulsby, *Towns of Medieval Wales*, 39–40.

108. Lobel, *Historic Towns*, vol. 1 (Banbury).

109. Hill, *Medieval Lincoln*, 171.

110. Schofield and Vince, *Medieval Towns*, 70; M. Lyle, *English Heritage book of Canterbury* (1994), 61.

111. *CUH*, vol. 1, 48, 185; *VCH Oxfordshire*, vol. 4, 312.

CHAPTER 2

1. A. Catchpole, D. Clark and R. Peberdy, *Burford: Buildings and People in a Cotswold Town* (Chichester, 2008), 15–22.

2. *CUH*, vol. 1, 103; Soulsby, *Towns of Medieval Wales*, 23.

3. *CUH*, vol. 1, 275–76.

4. *CUH*, vol. 1, 372.

5. A. Quiney, *Town Houses of Medieval Britain* (New Haven and London, 2003), 71.

6. M. Morris, R. Buckley and M. Codd, *Visions of Ancient Leicester* (University of Leicester, 2011), 50–51.

7. *CUH*, vol. 1, 453–54.

8. M. Lobel, *Historic Towns*, vol. 1 (Reading).

9. The University of Edinburgh was not founded until the 16th century

10. J. Chandler (ed.), *John Leland's Itinerary* (Stroud, 1993), 69–70.

11. Royal Commission on Historic Monuments (RCHM), *City of Salisbury*, vol. 1. (1980), xl.

12. Quiney, *Town* Houses, 71.

13. A. Betterton and D. Dymond, *Lavenham: Industrial Town* (Lavenham, 1989), 12.

14. *CUH*, vol. 1, 477.

15. *CUH*, vol. 1, 320, 449; Lynch (ed.), *Scottish Medieval Town*, 4, 10.

16. *John Leland's Itinerary*, ed. Chandler, 509 (modernized spelling); *CUH*, vol. 1, 376. The bridge was replaced by Thomas Telford in 1797–9.

17. E. de Mare, *Bridges of Britain* (1954), 48. Part of the structure still survives.

18. *John Leland's Itinerary*, ed. Chandler, 468.

19. M. Lobel, *et al., Historic Towns,* vol. 2 (Coventry); htpps://historiccoventry. co.uk. Only two of the gates survive: Cook St and Swanswell, the latter giving access to the cathedral priory, demolished after the Reformation.

20. O. Creighton and R. Higham, *Medieval Town Walls* (Stroud, 2005), 34.

21. Carrington, *English Heritage Book of Chester*, 68; H. Turner, *Town Defences in England and Wales* (1971), 202–203. The Water Tower in the north-west corner was built, according to a contract, in 1322–3: B. Harris, *Chester* (Edinburgh and London, 1979), 94–95.

22. Turner, *Town Defences*, 148–54; J. Newman, *The Buildings of England (B. of E.): North and East. Kent* (2013), 63.

23. Soulsby, *Towns of Medieval Wales*, 251–52; M. Davies, *The Story of Tenby* (Tenby, 1979), 10; T. Lloyd, *et al., The Buildings of Wales (B. of W.): Pembrokeshire*, 476–7. The walls enfolding the peninsula were demolished in the 18th and 19th centuries.

24. J. Gifford, *et al.*, *The Buildings of Scotland (B. of S.): Edinburgh* (1984), 84–85.

25. John Stow, quoted in *C.* Platt, *Medieval Southampton* (1973), 124.

26. K. Lilley, 'Urban Planning after the Black Death', *Urban History* 43/1 (Feb 2016): he discusses Coventry, Bewdley, Sutton Coldfield and Moorfields in London.

27. Platt, *Southampton*, 171.

28. *John Leland's Itinerary*, ed. Chandler, 205.

29. Parker, *King's Lynn*, 173–74.

30. *CUH*, vol. 1, 183; Quiney, *Town Houses,* 119. The first datable jettied house in London was erected in 1246: Schofield and Vince, *Medieval Towns*, 89.

31. Quiney, *Town Houses*, 95–109.

32. Quiney, *Town Houses*, 257–58; N. Pevsner and D. Neave, *B. of E: York and East Riding*, 233; RCHM, *City of York*, vol. 5 (1981) 220–236.

33. D. Clark, 'The Shop Within?', *Architectural History*, 43 (2000), 63–64.

34. e.g. No. 16 Edmund Street, Exeter (since moved to a site facing West Street); Portman, *Exeter Houses*, 3; B. Cherry and N. Pevsner, *B. of E.: Devon*, 424.

35. The timbers of the street front were felled in 1430–1: J. Newman and N. Pevsner, *B. of E.: Shropshire*, p. 572. The future King Henry VII was said to have lodged here before the Battle of Bosworth in 1485.

36. e.g. No. 77 North Street, Nos. 1 and 67–9 South Street.; J. Gifford, *B of S,: Fife,* 395, 400; Quiney, *Town Houses*, 283–84.

37. Gifford *et al., B. of S., Edinburgh*, 207–208.

38. Quiney, *Town Houses*, 88, 287–91.

39. RCHM, *Salisbury*, 103. According to Aubrey, he and another merchant called Webb bought 'all the wool from Salisbury Plain'. The mock-timber street frontage dates from the 20th century.

40. Quiney, *Town Houses*, 240. It was never a monastic property.

41. RCHM, *Salisbury*, 82, 68–69.

42. Catchpole, *et al.*, *Burford*, 42–3, 58–65, 178–9, 202–203. No. 109 has a narrow façade with a single gable; Nos. 111–3, adjoining it (later an inn and now a shop), and of similar date, has a wider timber frontage of three bays, each with its own gable.

43. S. Pearson, 'Rural and urban houses 1100–1500', in K. Giles and C. Dyer (eds), *Town and Country in the Middle Ages* (Leeds, 2005), 47.

44. Quiney, *Town Houses*, 244; M. Bullen, *et al.*, *B. of E. Hampshire: Winchester and the North*, 671.

45. Quiney, *Town Houses,* 150–51; A. Brown, *Rows of Chester*, especially pp. 55–62 for Nos. 38–42 Watergate St.

46. Lay subsidy 1523; Betterton and Dymond, *Lavenham*, 40–41 and *passim*.

47. It was subsequently used as a workhouse and is now a museum.

48. See Hoskins, *Provincial England*, 103.

49. Quiney, *Town Houses,* 214.

50. M. Girouard, *The English Town* (New Haven and London, 1990), 14.

51. G. Sheeran, *Medieval Yorkshire Towns* (Edinburgh, 1998), 124–26: see *Archaeological Journal* 137 (1980), 86–136.

52. S. Pearson in K. Giles and C. Dyer (eds), *Town and Country in the Middle Ages* (Leeds, 2005), 56. Some of the houses were re-erected here from other parts of the city that were redeveloped after the Second World War.

53. Nos. 60–72: see RCHM, *City of York* Fig. 86. The Statute of Mortmain (1297) forbade leaving money to the Church: Clark, 'Shops', p. 71. No traces of hearths or fireplaces have been found in these houses.

54. Quiney, *Town Houses,* 246. A building agreement of 1497 for a terrace of fifteen houses in Turnagain Lane, Canterbury, mentions staircases leading up to the chamber in each house.

55. Catchpole *et al.*, *Burford*, 60, 202–203. The wool store may have been in a rear wing.

56. W. A. Pantin in *Medieval Archaeology*, vols. 6–7, also Quiney, *Town Houses*, 209–10.

57. W. A. Pantin, 'The Development of Domestic Architecture in Oxford', *Antiquaries Journal*, 27 (1947), 121–39; J. Munby, *et al.*, 'Zacharias's: a 14ᵗʰ-century Oxford New Inn', *Oxoniensia*, 57 (1992), 245–309.

58. Quiney, *Town Houses*, 204; Lyle, *Canterbury*, 82–83.

59. G. Martin, *The Town* (1961), plate 13.

60. RCHM, *Salisbury*, xl.

61. RCHM, *City of York*, 212–20.

62. Sheeran, *Medieval Yorkshire Towns*, 141–43; Pearson, in Giles and Dyer, *Town and Country*, 50.

63. Bullen *et al.*, *B. of E. Hampshire: Winchester and the North*, 670–72; Quiney, *Town Houses*, 47.

64. It was replaced in 1826 by an Assembly Room (now the Northumberland Hall).

65. Pevsner and Wilson, *B of E, Norfolk 1*, 502–503.

66. Schofield, *Medieval London Houses*, 108–9, etc.: C. Barron, *The Medieval Guildhall of London* (1974).

67. G. Demidowicz, 'The Development of St Mary's Hall, Coventry', *British Archaeological Association Transactions* (2011), 164–82; Pickford and Pevsner, *B. of E., Warwickshire*, 247–50.

68. Parker, *Kings Lynn*, 143–48. Another hall, for the Guild of St George, established in 1408, also survives on a narrow plot between King Street and the river front, with an undercroft below.

69. RCHM, *City of York*, pls. 70–73; Pevsner and Neave, *B. of E. Yorkshire: York and East Riding*, 216–19.

70. Foyle and Pevsner, *B. of E. Somerset: North and Bristol*, 681.

71. It was shown in Warren's map of Bury (1776).

72. Lynch, *Scottish Medieval Town*, 64–66. The tower was influenced by that of St Nicolas (now the cathedral) in Newcastle (*c*.1474).

73. P. Barnwell, 'The universal church in the local community', in Barnwell (ed.), *Places of Worship in Britain and Ireland, 1150–1350* (Donington, 2018), 191–92.

74. A. E. Preston, *Christ's Hospital Abingdon* (Oxford, 1929).

75. The undercroft has been excavated and now forms part of an excellent museum.

76. T. Allen, *et al.*, *The Lost Abbey of Abingdon* (2012), 2–4.

77. Quiney, *Town Houses*, 222.

78. W. H. Godfrey, *The English Almshouse* (1955), 28–29.

79. Godfrey, *English Almshouse* 41–42; Pevsner, *et al.*, *B. of E. Lincolnshire*. 697–98.

80. W. Puddephat *et al.*, *The Guild Chapel* (Stratford, 1987); Pickford and Pevsner, *B. of E. Warwickshire*, 593–94. The school moved into the former Guildhall in 1553, following the suppression of the Guild.

81. P. Jeffrey, *Collegiate Churches of England and Wales* (2004), 377–79; Pickford and Pevsner, *B. of E. Warwickshire*, 266–67.

82. *John Leland's Itinerary*, ed. Chandler, 263.

83. C. Hartwell, *Manchester* (Pevsner Architectural Guide, 2001), 63–67.

84. M. Bullen, *et al.*, *B. of E. Hampshire: Winchester and the North*, 643–51.

85. See J. Buxton and P. Williams (eds), *New College Oxford* (Oxford, 1979), 147–92.

86. A. Taylor, *Cambridge: The Hidden History*, 86–97.

87. R. G. Cant, *The University of St Andrews: A Short History* (St Andrews, 1992), 26–45; J. Smith (ed), *Old Aberdeen* (Aberdeen, 1991), 91–93. The original buildings of Glasgow University were demolished in the 19th century and were replaced by the present University buildings, well to the west of the old city centre.

88. Lincoln's Inn, Gray's Inn and the Middle and Inner Temple.

89. J. H. Baker, quoted in J. Archer *et al.*, *The Intellectual and Cultural World of the Early Modern Inns of Court* (Manchester, 2011), 8–29.

CHAPTER 3

1. Gifford and Walker, *B. of S., Fife,* 357–67; R. Fawcett, *Scottish Cathedrals* (1997), 6–8, 96.

2. The Benedictine abbeys at Gloucester, Peterborough and Chester and what remained of the Augustinian Priory at Bristol and the former Priory of St Frideswide in Oxford.

3. See the 1692–94 map reproduced in W. Ison, *The Georgian Buildings of Bath* (1948), plate 1.

4. D. Gerhold, *London Plotted* (2016), 67–69.

5. Tyack, *et al.*, *B. of E. Berkshire*, 441–3, 453; P. Durrant and J. Painter, *Reading Abbey and the Abbey Quarter* (Reading, 2018).

6. C. O'Brien, *et al.*, *B. of E. Hampshire: South*, 439–40, 503–505; D. Lloyd, *Buildings of Portsmouth and its Environs* (1974), 5.

7. E. A. Menuge and C. Dewar, *Berwick-upon-Tweed* (English Heritage, 2009), 34–39. The medieval castle, outside the rebuilt western fortifications, was demolished to make way for the main railway line between London and Edinburgh in 1850.

8. M. J. Stoyle, 'Whole streets converted to ashes': property destruction in Exeter during the English Civil War, *Southern History*, 16 (1994), 62–81.

9. *CUH*, vol. 2., 462–63.

10. Norwich, Bristol, Newcastle, Exeter, York and Great Yarmouth: *CUH*, vol. 2, 384.

11. P. Corfield. Urban development, in England and Wales in the 16th and 17th centuries', in J. Barry (ed.), *The Tudor and Stuart Town* (1990), 45–49; *CUH*, vol. 2, 347, 352.

12. R. Harris and C. McKean, *The Scottish Town in the Age of Enlightenment* (Edinburgh, 2014), 17.

13. *CUH*, vol. 2, 316.

14. Quoted in Lyle, *Canterbury*, 85.

15. See, for instance, A. Buxton, 'Domestic Culture in Early Seventeenth-Century Thame', *Oxoniensia* 67 (2001), 79–115.

16. *CUH*, vol. 2, 473.

17. Ayers, *Norwich*, 92.

18. *VCH Warwickshire*, vol. 3, 229.

19. J. G. Dunbar, *The Historic Architecture of Scotland* (1966), 97–99; J. Gifford and F. A. Walker *B of S: Stirling and Central Scotland*, 717–28.

20. E. Dennison, *et al.*, *Aberdeen before 1800* (East Linton, 2002), 100–101.

21. R. Turner, *Plas Mawr, Conwy* (Cardiff: Cadw, 1997); R. Haslam, *et al.*, *B. of W., Gwynedd*, 336–39.

22. *Survey of London*, revised 1603 (Everyman ed., 1956), 240–41.

23. An engraving of 1547 and a painting based on it are reproduced in J. Schofield, *Medieval London Houses* (New Haven and London, 2nd edn), 151.

24. Gerhold, *London Plotted*, 24–25.

25. Schofield, *Medieval London Houses*, 189–90.

26. e.g. Nos. 224–27 High Street: Portman, *Exeter Houses*, 4–6.

27. Everyman ed. (1928), vol. 2, 83.

28. Newman and Pevsner, *B. of E.: Shropshire*, 75.

29. The adjacent house, later the Garrick Inn, was built by a mercer (dealer in fine textiles).

30. William Grey, *Chorographia* (1649), 16; D. Heslop, *et al.*, 'Bessie Surtees House', *Archaeologia Aeliana*, 5th series 22 (1994), 1–27.

31. *Itinerary*, ed. Chandler, 322.

32. Dunbar, *Architecture of Scotland*, 95; Dennison, *et al.*, *Aberdeen before 1800*, 100–101.

33. See for instance R. H. Leech, *The Town House in Medieval and Early Modern Bristol* (Swindon, 2014), 117–20.

34. M. Laithwaite, 'Totnes Houses 1500–1800', in P. Clark (ed.), *The Transformation of English Provincial Towns* (1984), 62–92.

35. *CUH*, vol. 2, 473. The population of the Old Town was about 25,000: *Ibid.*, 419.

36. Quoted in Makey, 'Edinburgh in the Mid-Seventeenth Century', in M. Lynch (ed.), *The Early Modern Town in Scotland* (Edinburgh, 1987), 216.

37. D. Bell, *Edinburgh Old Town* (Edinburgh, 2008), 14.

38. W. Maitland, *History of Edinburgh* (1753): see Bell, *Edinburgh Old Town*, 99; T. C. Smout, *A History of the Scottish People, 1560–1830* (1969), 346.

39. Makey, in Lynch (ed.), *Early Modern Town in Scotland*, 204–209; Royal Commission on the Ancient and Historical Monuments of Scotland, *Edinburgh*.

40. Parker, *King's Lynn*, 46.

41. Hoskins, *Provincial England* (1963), 104–107.

42. Catchpole *et al.*, *Burford: Buildings and People*, 165, 181.

43. M. Brennand and K. J. Stringer (eds), *The Making of Carlisle* (Kendal: Cumberland and Westmoreland Antiquarian and Archaeological Soc., 2011), 147–48.

44. Barrow-in-Furness Libraries, reprod. G. Martin, *The Town*, p. 12.

45. R. Millward, 'The Cumbrian Town between 1600 and 1800', in C. Chalklin and M. Havinden (eds), *Rural Change and Urban Growth 1500–1800* (1974), 210–12.

46. *Description of the County of Westmorland* (Cumberland and Westmorland Antiquarian and Archaeological Society tract series, vol. 1, 1882).

47. Gifford and Walker, *B. of S: Fife*, 143–57.

48. The stonemason was a local quarry-owner, William Grumbold, whose kinsman went on to build several of the most important university buildings in 17th-and early 18th-century Cambridge: H. M. Colvin, *Biographical Dictionary of British Architects 1600–1840* (New Haven and London, 2008), 454–55.

49. R. Tittler, *Architecture and Power* (Oxford, 1991), 41.

50. Godfrey, *English Almshouse*, 59–60.

51. M. Seaborne, *The English School* (1971), 51–55; M. de Saulles, *The Story of Shrewsbury* (Logaston Press, Herefordshire, 2012), 70–72; Newman and Pevsner, *B. of E. Shropshire*, 538.

52. G. Tyack, 'The Schools Quadrangle at Oxford: function and rhetoric', in P. S. Barnwell and P. Henderson (eds), *Architect, Patron and Craftsmen on Tudor and early Stuart England* (Donington, 2017), 115–33.

53. Gifford, *et al.*, *B. of S., Edinburgh*, 179–82; A. Rowan, 'George Heriot's Hospital, Edinburgh', *Country Life*, 6, 13 March 1975, 554–7, 634–37.

54. C. Barron, *A Map of Medieval London* (Historic Towns Trust, 2019).

55. H.M. Colvin and S. Foster (eds), *Wyngaerde's Panorama of London* (London Topographical Society, 1996); P. Barber, *London: A History in Maps* (2012), 28–29; Schofield, *Medieval London Houses*, 67, illustrates a late 16th-century map of Bishopsgate.

56. Gerhold, *London Plotted*, 115–17.

57. F. Sheppard (ed.), *Survey of London*, vol. 36 (1970); D. Duggan, 'New Light on Covent Garden', *Architectural History* 43 (2000), 140–61.

58. R. Thorne, *Covent Garden Market* (1980), 12–22.

59. J. Stow, *A Survey of London*, Everyman ed. (1956), 375–76.

60. P. Guillery, *The Small House in Eighteenth Century London* (New Haven and London, 2004), 41.

61. Schofield, *Medieval London Houses*, 35–43.

CHAPTER 4

1. T. S. Willan, *An Eighteenth-century Shopkeeper: Abraham Dent of Kirkby Stephen* (1970), quoted in F. Braudel, *The Wheels of Commerce* (1982), 64–67.

2. 19 CII, *c.* 3, section 20–24; CII 22, c.11, sections 1–12; T. F. Reddaway, *The Rebuilding of London after the Great Fire* (1940), 55, 291, 296–98.

3. Bradley and Pevsner, *B. of E., London 1: The City of London*, 69.

4. C. Stevenson, *The City and the King* (New Haven and London, 2013), 223–39.

5. See P. Jeffrey, *The City Churches of Sir Christopher Wren* (1996); Reddaway, 123–30.

6. 19 CII, *c.* 3, section 5: see also Gerhold, *London Plotted*, 23.

7. 19 CII, c. 3, section 7; Reddaway, *Rebuilding of London,* 80.

8. Stow, *Survey of London*, ed. Strype (1720); Nos. 1–5 are a surviving example of the original houses.

9. Rebuilt in 1670–2 after the Great Fire, exiled to Theobalds Park in Hertfordshire as a result of a street-widening scheme in 1880, and re-erected at the entrance to the new Paternoster Square in 2004. See p. 299.

10. E. McKellar, *The Birth of Modern London* (Manchester 1999), 39–40, 66–67.

11. McKellar, *Birth of Modern London*, 62–3, 204.

12. *Tour through England and Wales* (1928 edn), vol 1, 335.

13. National Archives, PRO SP/44/13, quoted in T. Longstaffe-Gowan, *The London Square* (New Haven and London, 2012), 30. See also F. Sheppard (ed.) *Survey of London*, vol. 29, (1960), 56–76.

14. D. Cruikshank and N. Burton, *Life in the Georgian City* (1990), 5–6.

15. Cruikshank, *Spitalfields* (2016), 115–7, 201–11; Cruikshank and Burton, *Life in the Georgian City*, 209–35; A. Byrne, *London's Georgian Houses* (1986), 64–67.

16. *Tour through England and Wales* (1928 edn), vol 1, 327.

17. P. Guillery, *The Small House in 18th-Century London*, 83–87, 100–15.

18. C. Hibbert (ed.) *An American in Regency England* (1968), 36–37.

19. A. Smith, 'What the doctors ordered: the early history of the London Hospital', *Georgian Group Journal* 25 (2017), 131–50.

20. *Journeys of Celia Fiennes*, ed. C. Morris (1947), 234. She called it 'a low, moist place'.

21. Hoskins, *Exeter*, 79; *Journeys of Celia Fiennes*, 245.

22. K. Morrison, *English Shops and Shopping* (New Haven and London, 2003), 29.

23. M. Falkus, 'Lighting in the Dark Ages', in D. C. Coleman and A. H. John (eds), *Trade, Government and Economy in Pre-Industrial England* (1976), 259.

24. P. Borsay, *The English Urban Renaissance* (Oxford, 1989), 68–74; J. Ellis, *The Georgian Town, 1680–1840* (Basingstoke, 2001), 102; F. Williamson, 'George Sorocold of Derby: a pioneer of water supply', *Derbyshire Archaeological and Natural History Society Journal* 57 (1936), 48–86.

25. 'Thomas Baskerville's Journeys in England', Historical Manuscripts Commission, *Portland* (1893), vol 2, 308, 310.

26. *Journeys of Celia Fiennes*, 208.

27. D. H. Heslop, *et al.*, *Alderman Fenwick's House* (Newcastle, 2001).

28. *Tour through England and Wales* (1928 edn), vol. 2, 33.

29. J. Aiken, *Description of . . . the Thirty and Forty Miles Round Manchester* (1795), 186, referring to the houses built in and around St Ann's Square in the early 18th century.

30. H. M. Colvin, *Biographical Dictionary of British Architects 1600–1840*, 116.

31. *Tour through England and Wales* (1928 edn), vol 2, 86.

32. *History and Antiquities of Northamptonshire* (Oxford, 1791) 328.

33. M. Farr, *The Great Fire of Warwick* (Dugdale Society, 36, 1992); Borsay, *Provincial Towns*, 153–63; Borsay, 'The landed elite and provincial towns in Britain 1660-1800', *Georgian Group Journal* 13 (2003), 283.

34. *VCH Warwickshire*, vol. 8, ??.

35. A. Rogers, *The Making of Stamford* (Leicester, 1965), 83–86; RCHM, *The Town of Stamford* (1977).

36. A. Oswald *Old Towns Revisited* (1952), 97–120, 163–84.

37. D. Lloyd, *Broad Street* (Birmingham, 1979); Girouard, *English Town*, 101–107. The Butter Cross was designed by William Baker, an architect and surveyor from Audlem in Cheshire.

38. H. M. Colvin, 'The Bastards of Blandford', *Archaeological Journal* 104 (1948); RCHM, *Dorset*, vol. 3.

39. J. Stobart, A. Hann and V. Morgan, *Spaces of Consumption* (Abingdon, 2007), 45.

40. R. Morriss and K. Hoverd, *The Buildings of Worcester* (Stroud, 1994), 65.

41. Girouard, *English Town*, 51–53.

42. Girouard, *English Town*, 131–44. The York assembly rooms were designed by the Earl of Burlington, a local landowner and one of the leading arbiters of taste in early Georgian England.

43. *CUH*, Vol. 2, 352.

44. Leech, *Town House in . . . Bristol*, 389.

45. Borsay, *Urban Renaissance*, 294–95.

46. Girouard, *English Town*, 39–40, 121, 158–59.

47. W. Ison, *The Georgian Buildings of Bristol* (1952), 152–56.

48. R. Leech, *Early Industrial Housing: The Trinity Area of Frome* (London: RCHM, 1981); Defoe, *Tour Through England and Wales* (1928 edn), vol 1, 280.

49. C. Chalklin, 'The Making of some New Towns c.1660-1720', in C. Chalklin and M. Havinden (eds), *Rural Change and Urban Growth 1500–1800* (1974), 231, 239–40.

50. E. Sigsworth, 'Ports and resorts in the regions' (typescript conference papers, Hull, 1980) 13–23.

51. *John Leland's Itinerary*, ed. Chandler, p. 269; Sigsworth (ed.), in 'Ports and Resorts' (1980), 24–25.

52. *Tour Through England and Wales* (1928 edn), vol 2, 259.

53. J. Sharples, *Liverpool* (Pevsner Architectural Guides, 2004), 5–6; E. Moore, *Liverpool in King Charles II's time* (ed. W. F. Irvine, Liverpool, 1899), 27.

54. Sharples, *Liverpool*, 10.

55. Girouard, *English Town*, 38–39.

56. J. Stobart, *The First Industrial Region* (Manchester, 2008), 147–48.

57. Seaborne, *English School*, 111–2, 115–16.

58. Quoted in Longstaffe-Gowan, *London Square*, 20. See also S. E. Rasmussen, *London: The Unique City* (1967 edn, Cambridge, Mass), 76–88.

59. Hoskins, *Exeter*, 64–65. It is shown in a 1792 map.

60. Stobart, *First Industrial Region*, 152.

61. *Journeys of Celia Fiennes*, 227.

62. A. McInnes, 'The emergence of a leisure town: Shrewsbury 1660-1760', *Past and Present* 120/1 (1988), 67–68.

63. Hist MSS Comm, *Verulam*, 1906. A well-head, designed by the local architect John Carr in 1752, still survives alongside it.

64. Chalklin, 'Making of some New Towns'. 233–4, 243–44.

65. *Journeys of Celia Fiennes*, 133.

66. P. Borsay and J. Walton, *Resorts and Ports* (Bristol, 2011), 50–57.

67. Leland, *Itinerary*, ed. Chandler, 405–408; *Journeys of Celia Fiennes*, 236.

68. T. Mowl, ed., *Obsession: John Wood and the Creation of Georgian Bath* (Bath: Building of Bath Museum, 2004). See also Wood's own *Essay towards a Description of Bath* (2nd edn, 1749).

69. M. Forsyth, *Bath* (Pevsner Architectural Guides, 2003), 209.

70. He had already designed the Guildhall (1775–8) as part of an improved northern approach to the city centre.

CHAPTER 5

1. 'Spershott's Memoirs of Chichester in the 18th Century', *Sussex Arch. Collections*, 29 (1879), 222; 30 (1880), 159.

2. A. Hay, *The History of Chichester* (1804) 364.

3. Quoted in C. Chalklin, *English Counties and Public Buildings, 1650–30* (1998), 19; A. J. Green, *The Building of Georgian Chichester* (Chichester, 2007), 35–38.

4. Green, *Chichester*, 134–146.

5. Clark, *Transformation of English Provincial Towns*, 13.

6. *CUH*, vol. 2, 473.

7. Borsay, *English Urban Renaissance*, 62–68.

8. G. C. Deering, *Nottingham Vetus et Nova* (1751), quoted in Ellis, *Georgian Town*, 88.

9. *History of Birmingham*, cited in Ellis, *Georgian Town*, 90.

10. *CUH*, vol. 2, 625.

11. I. and E. Hall, *Georgian Hull* (York, 1979), 17, 80–81.

12. Girouard, *English Town*, 171–73.

13. Cruikshank and Burton, *Life in the Georgian City*, 13–14.

14. M. de Saulles, *Story of Shrewsbury*, 134–5, 148–48.

15. *Brief Description of the Borrough and Town of Preston* (ed. J. Taylor, 1818), 91.

16. *CUH*, vol. 2, 626.

17. Stobart *et al.*, *Spaces of Consumption* (Abingdon, 2007), 107.

18. Leech, *Town House in . . . Bristol*, 36, 138. The courtyard was later glazed over and is now filled with permanent stalls.

19. Leech, *Town House in . . . Bristol*, 142. One of the first of the city's banks was built behind No. 35 Corn St, in 1790.

20. K. Grady, *The Georgian Public Buildings of Leeds and the West Riding* (Leeds: Thoresby Society 62, 1989), 93–94.

21. Stobart, *First Industrial Region*, 155; Stobart et al., *Spaces of Consumption*, 154–55. Chester's local historian Joseph Hemingway (*History of the City of Chester*, 1831) thought that the town was a desirable place of residence for the middle classes because of its lack of dirty manufacturing industry.

22. Morrison, *Shops and Shopping*, 42.

23. *The Diary of a Country Parson*, ed. J. Beresford (Oxford 1949), 77.

24. *VCH Oxfordshire*, vol. 4, 188–191; A. Crossley, et al., *Shopping in Oxford: A Brief History* (Oxford: Oxford Preservation Trust, 1983).

25. Examples include the Old Rectory, with dates 1701 and 1714 on bricks; No. 55 New Street with 1715 on a rainwater head.

26. See for instance No. 20 Market Place, of *c.*1750, occupied by a surgeon in the early 19th century. The facades of 15th-century timber-framed houses in Bell Street and Northfield End were also stuccoed over: *Henley-on-Thames Archaeological and Historical Group Journal* 31 (April 2018).

27. Francis Sheppard, *Brakspear's Brewery* (Henley, 1979). New Street derived its name from a medieval expansion of the original town.

28. There is also a row of five formerly one-up, one-down cottages behind Nos. 58–78 New Street: see *VCH Oxfordshire* 16.

29. Townley, *Henley-on-Thames: Town, Trade and River*, 102.

30. G. Tyack, 'The Rebuilding of Henley-on-Thames, 1780–1914', *Oxfordshire Local History* 3/2 (1989), 67–89. The present town hall was built on the same site in 1899–1901.

31. A. White (ed.), *A History of Lancaster* (Edinburgh, 2001), 119–121, 128–29; White, *The Buildings of Georgian Lancaster*, 23–26.

32. J. Toulmin, *History of the Town of Taunton* (1791), quoted in Girouard, *English Town*, 174.

33. Girouard, *English Town*, 176.

34. C. Wakeling, *Chapels of England* (Swindon, 2017), 67, 73.

35. D. Baker (ed.), *The Church in Town and Countryside* (1979); G. W. Dolby, *The Architectural Expression of Methodism* (1964), 118.

36. Chalklin, *English Counties and Public Building*, 140; A. White, *Buildings of Georgian Lancaster* (Lancaster, 1992), 32.

37. R. Evans, *The Fabrication of Virtue* (1982), 251.

38. T. C. Smout, *History of the Scottish People* (1969), 340–42.

39. Harris and McKean, *The Scottish Town in the Age of Enlightenment* (Edinburgh, 2014), 82.

40. Harris and McKean, *Scottish Town in the Age of Enlightenment*, plate 8.

41. Harris and McKean, *Scottish Town in the Age of Enlightenment*, 36.

42. Harris and McKean, *Scottish Town in the Age of Enlightenment*, 243–264 and Appendix 22.

43. J. Gifford, *B. of S.: Perth and Kinross* (2007), 605.

44. D. Bell, *Edinburgh Old Town*, 112; A. J. Youngson, *The Making of Classical Edinburgh* (Edinburgh, 1966), 11.

45. Gifford, *et al., B. of S. Edinburgh*, 271–273.

46. C. McKean, *Edinburgh: An Illustrated Architectural Guide* (Edinburgh, 1992), 4.

47. Examples include Golden Square, begun in 1817 and Bon Accord Crescent and Square (1823): Dennison, *Aberdeen Before 1800*, 42–43; W. H. Fraser and C. H. Lee (eds), *Aberdeen, 1800–2000: A New History* (2000), 22–25.

48. The roadway was only about fifteen feet wide at its widest: D. Gerhold, *London Bridge and its Houses* (London Topographical Society, 2019), 11–12.

49. The Bank was begun on its present site in 1734 and was progressively enlarged, first by Sir Robert Taylor and then by Sir John Soane: D. M. Abramson, *Building the Bank of England* (New Haven and London, 2003); D. Keene in A. Saunders (ed.), *The Royal Exchange* (1997), 253–275.

50. Now Marylebone Road, Euston Road and City Road; Rasmussen, *London: The Unique City*, 129–30; Barber, *London: A History in Maps*, 174–75.

51. D. J. Olsen, *Town Planning in London* (New Haven and London, 1982), 43–48. For Fitzroy Square, see A. Rowan, *Vaulting Ambition: The Adam Brothers, Contractors to the Metropolis* (Sir John Soane's Museum, 2007), 2–5.

52. See A. Saunders, *Regent's Park* (1981); H. Hobhouse, *Regent Street* (Chichester, 2008); James Anderson, 'Marylebone Park and the New Street' (unpubl. thesis, University of London, 1998); J. Summerson, *Life and Work of John Nash* (1980); G. Tyack (ed.), *John Nash: Architect of the Picturesque* (Swindon: English Heritage, 2013), 101–124.

53. W. Cobbett, *Rural Rides* (Everyman edn, 1953), 126 (30 September 1826).

54. B. Little, *Cheltenham* (1952), 28.

55. G. Hart, *A History of Cheltenham* (Leicester, 1965), 136.

56. The pump room was on the site of the later Queen's Hotel, built in 1837–8.

57. S. Berry, *Sussex Archaeological Collections* 140 (2002), 97–112; Berry, *Georgian Brighton* (Chichester, 2005), 7–18.

58. N. Antram and R. Morrice, *Brighton and Hove* (Pevsner Architectural Guides, 2008), 93–94.

59. Berry, *Georgian Brighton*, 97–110.

60. Berry, 'Royal Crescent, Brighton', *Georgian Group Journal* 25 (2017), 237–246.

61. S. Lancaster (ed.), *Constable and Brighton* (2017).

62. A. Dale, *Fashionable Brighton 1820–1860* (1947), 49–148; Berry, 'Thomas Read Kemp and the Shaping of Regency Brighton', *Georgian Group Journal* 17 (2009), 125–140.

63. Stobart *et al., Spaces of Consumption*, 80.

64. *Tour through England and Wales* (1928 edn), vol 1, 231. S. and N. Buck published a panoramic view of the town in 1736.

65. Cherry and Pevsner, *B of E, Devon*, 671.

66. A-M. Akehurst, 'St Bartholomew's Hospital and Gibbs's role in hospital pavilion planning', *Georgian Group Journal* 27 (2019), 103–104.

67. C. Miele, 'Bold, well-defined masses: Sir John Rennie and the Royal William Yard', *Architectural History* 49 (2006), 149–178.

68. *Tour through England and Wales* (1928 edn), vol. 1, 137.

69. J. Coad, *The Royal Dockyards* (Aldershot, 1989), 3.

70. Chalklin, *The Provincial Towns of Georgian England* (1974), 123–4, 218–19; Chalklin and Havinden, *Rural Change and Urban Growth*, 236–7, 245.

71. Coad, *Royal Dockyards*, 257–59; C. O'Brien, *et al.*, *B. of E. Hampshire: South.* 484–496.

72. C. Giles, *Stourport-on-Severn: Pioneer Town of the Canal Age* (Swindon: English Heritage, 2007), 24.

73. M. Palmer and P. Neaverson, *Industry in the Landscape* (1994), 174–75.

74. The buildings are described in J. Cattell and R. Hawkins, *The Birmingham Jewellery Quarter* (Swindon: English Heritage, 2000).

75. Chalklin, *Provincial Towns*, 81–89; Chris Upton, *Living Back-to-Back* (2005) and Upton, *Back to Backs* (National Trust guidebook, 2004), 12–13.

76. Grady, *Georgian Public Buildings of Leeds and the West Riding*, 76, 87.

77. Stobart, *First Industrial Region*, 96.

78. *CUH*, vol. 2, 474.

79. Hartwell, *Manchester* (Pevsner City Guide), 9–13.

80. Chalklin, *Provincial Towns*, 89–98.

81. J. Parkinson-Bailey, *Manchester: An Architectural History* (Manchester, 2000), 4–11; Hartwell, *Manchester*, 12. Mosley Street was already shown in a map of *c.*1773.

82. M. Rose, *et al.*, *Ancoats, Cradle of Industrialisation* (Swindon: English Heritage, 2011), 67.

83. *The English Journey*, ed. D. Bindman and G. Riemann (New Haven and London, 1993), 175–79.

CHAPTER 6

1. *Journeys to England and Ireland*, ed. J. P. Mavor (1958), 105–107.

2. J. Hilling, *Cardiff and the Valleys* (1973), 38–40.

3. Teesside, the Nottinghamshire and South Yorkshire coalfields, the South Wales valleys and the London suburbs were among the places that experienced especially rapid growth in the second half of the century: *CUH*, vol. 3, 71; P. Waller, *Town, City and Nation* (Oxford, 1983), 68–126; R. Dennis, *English Industrial Cities of the Nineteenth Century* (Cambridge, 1984), 38–40.

4. M. Palmer and P. Neaverson, *Industry in the Landscape* (1994), 107; M. Williams and D. A. Farnie, *Cotton Mills in Greater Manchester* (Preston, 1992); C. Giles and I.H. Goodall, *Yorkshire Textile Mills 1770–1930* (Royal Commission on Historical Monuments, 1992); *CUH*, vol. 3, 642.

5. A. Betteridge, *et al.*, *Calderdale: Architecture and History* (Halifax, 1988), Fig. 58 and caption.

6. Palmer and Neaverson, *Industry in the Landscape*, 109.

7. P. Johnson, 'Economic Development and Industrial Dynamism in Victorian London', *London Journal* 21 (1996), 27–37.

8. R. J. Morris, 'Urbanization', in R. J. Morris and R. Rodger (eds), *The Victorian City*, 48–50.

9. R. Harman and J. Minnis, *Sheffield* (Pevsner City Guide, 2004), 165–175.

10. K. Morrison and A. Bond, *Built to Last?* (Swindon: English Heritage, 2004).

11. Palmer and Neaverson, *Industry in the Landscape*, 114, 136.

12. Palmer and Neaverson, *Industry in the Landscape*, 62; Hilling, *Cardiff and the Valleys*, 102–111; [J. B. Lowe], *Welsh Industrial Workers' Housing* (Cardiff: National Museum of Wales, 1977).

13. M. Daunton, *Coal Metropolis* (Leicester, 1977), 9, 17–21, 74–75.

14. D. Baker, *Potworks* (1991), 38–39.

15. Baker, *Potworks*, 54–6, 68–70. Many of the buildings are described and illustrated in www.thepotteries.org.

16. Palmer and Neaverson, *Industry in the Landscape*, 31.

17. See B. Harrison, *Drink and the Victorians* (1994). For breweries, L. Pearson, *Built to Brew* (Swindon: English Heritage, 2014)

18. F. Sheppard, *Brakspear's Brewery* (Henley, 1979). The brewery is now a hotel and the maltings have been turned into flats.

19. G. Doré and B. Jerrold, *London: A Pilgrimage* (1872), facing p. 120.

20. S. Taylor, *et al.*, *Manchester: The Warehouse Legacy* (Swindon: English Heritage, 2002), 14–18. The railway's impact on Liverpool in 1830 was memorably conveyed in John Cooke Bourne's engraving of the Olive Mount cutting, leading to the terminus in Lime Street.

21. J. Simmons, *St Pancras Station* (2003 edn), 28: M. Hunter and R. Thorne (eds), *Change at King's Cross* (1990), 91–123.

22. J. R. Kellett, *Impact of Railways on Victorian Cities* (1969), 327; R. Thorne, *Liverpool Street Station* (1978), p. 27.

23. Palmer and Neaverson, *Industry in the Landscape*, 169–70; *VCH Leicestershire*, vol. 4.

24. Liz Woolley, *Oxford's Working Past* (Oxford, 2012), 9–31; see Chapter 8.

25. R. Rodger, 'Slums and Suburbs', in P. Waller (ed.), *The English Urban Landscape* (Oxford, 2000), 236–7, 240.

26. See also William Cooke Taylor, *Notes on a Tour of the Manufacturing Districts of Lancashire* (1842), quoted in Dennis, *Industrial Cities*, 53–54.

27. Kellett, *Impact of Railways*, 16–17. It was subsequently redeveloped as part of a warehouse district.

28. John Leigh, quoted in J. R. Kellett, *The Impact of Railways*, 343.

29. M. Beresford, 'The Back-to-Back House in Leeds' in S. D. Chapman (ed.), *The History of Working Class Housing* (Newton Abbot, 1971), 95–132; 'The making of a townscape', in Chalklin and Havinden, *Rural Change and Urban Growth*, 281–320; Muthesius, *English Terraced House*, 106–107.

30. W. Ashworth, *The Genesis of Modern British Town Planning* (1954), 21.

31. Charles Dickens, *Little Dorrit*, (1855–7).

32. H. J. Dyos and D. A. Reeder, 'Slums and Suburbs', in Dyos and Woolf (eds), *The Victorian City*, vol. 2 (1973), 359–386.

33. M. Daunton, *House and Home in the Victorian City* (1983), 12.

34. A. Whitehead, 'The history of working class housing in Jericho' (1977), htpps://www.andrewwhitehead.net/working-class-housing-in-jericho-oxford.html. The name seems to derive from the New Testament parable of the Good Samaritan, in which a man went down from Jerusalem to Jericho and was set upon by thieves.

35. Muthesius, *Terraced Houses*, 103–104.

36. Bell, *City Fathers*, pp. 173–194; J. D. Marshall, *Furness and the Industrial Revolution* (Barrow, 1958), 228–232.

37. Muthesius, *English Terraced House*, 123–30; A Quiney, *The House and Home* (1986), 101–125.

38. E. Williamson *et al., B of S., Glasgow*, 85–93. See also A. H. Gomme and D. Walker, *The Architecture of Glasgow* (1987 edn).

39. Kellett in Morris and Rodger (eds), *Victorian City*, 186.

40. G. Best, 'Another part of the island', in Dyos and Woolf (eds), *The Victorian City*, vol. 2, 396–411; S. D. Chapman (ed.), *Working Class Housing*, 57–85; M. Daunton, *House and Home*, 51–4, 68–9, 88.

41. Chapman (ed.), *Working Class Housing*, 57–85; W. H. Fraser and I. Maver (eds), *Glasgow 1830–1912* (Manchester and New York, 1996), 20–31.

42. Smout, *Century of the Scottish People*, 33–35. Fifty per cent still lived in one- or two-room dwellings in 1951, compared with 5.5 per cent in London.

43. L. Hepburn, *The Tenement House* (National Trust for Scotland, 1999).

44. T. C. Smout, *A Century of the Scottish People* (1986), 37; *CUH*, vol. 3, 496.

45. For model dwellings, see J. N. Tarn, *Five per Cent Philanthropy* (c.1973).

46. S. Beattie, *A Revolution in London Housing* (1980), 17–69. See also J. Boughton, *Municipal Dreams* (2018), 21–23.

47. It was funded by a philanthropically-minded sugar manufacturer who also paid for new public libraries in South London.

48. S. Pepper, 'Ossulston Street: early LCC experiments in housing, 1925–29' *London Journal* 7/1 (1981), 45–64. For Gerard Gardens, *CUH*, vol. 3, 462–64 and E. Harwood and A. Powers, *Housing the Twentieth Century Nation* (London: Twentieth Century Society, 2008), 38–50.

49. Boughton, *Municipal Dreams*, 31.

50. Some blocks of well-serviced flats, such as Albert Hall Mansions, South Kensington (designed 1879), went up in London in the late 19th century. Many more were built in the inter-war period; they include Dolphin Square, Pimlico (1935–7), which contained 1236 flats.

51. Quoted in S. Kostof, *The City Shaped* (1991), 295.

52. B. Little, *Catholic Churches Since 1623* (1966), 132.

53. J. Lake, *et al., Diversity and Vitality: the Methodist and Nonconformist Chapels of Cornwall* (Truro, 2011), 80, 89. See also A. Jones, *Welsh Chapels* (Cardiff, 1984); Wakeling, *Chapels of England*, 93–216.

54. A. Rogers, *Approaches to Local History* (1977), 198–207; Seaborne, *English School*. See also D. Baker, *Schools in the Potteries* (1984).

55. A good example is Oozels Street School (1877–8), now the Ikon Gallery.

56. Evans, *Fabrication of Virtue*, 346–378.

57. For examples, see www.workhouses.org.uk

58. For hospital design in general, see J. Taylor, *The Architect and the Pavilion Hospital* (1997).

59. It was designed by the local firm of Cossins and Peacock: P. Ballard (ed.), *Birmingham's Victorian and Edwardian Architects* (2009), pp. 236–37.

60. C. Brooks, *Mortal Remains*, 9–10. By 1830 the cemetery was paying an eight per cent dividend to investors.

61. H. Conway, *People's Parks* (Cambridge, 1991), 215.

62. S. Rutherford, *The Victorian Cemetery* (Oxford: Shire Library, 2008), 34–36.

63. E. McKellar, *Landscapes of London* (New Haven and London, 2013), 111–143.

64. Conway, *People's Parks*, 48–49. See also G. F. Chadwick, *The Park and the Town* (1966).

65. Hartwell, *et al.*, *B. of E, Cheshire*, 144–46. See also G. F. Chadwick, *The Works of Sir Joseph Paxton* (1961), 53–61.

66. Initially Victoria Park and Battersea Park: G. Tyack, *Sir James Pennethorne and the Making of Victorian London* (Cambridge, 1992), 87–118.

67. Q. Hughes, *Seaport* (1964), 147–157.

CHAPTER 7

1. *Shopping in Leeds* (1909), quoted in S. Gunn, *Public Culture of the Victorian City* (Manchester, 2000), 48.

2. Gunn, *Public Culture*, 43.

3. G. MacGregor, *History of Glasgow* (Glasgow and London, 1881), 506.

4. Waller (ed.), *Urban Landscape*, 154; Parkinson-Bailey, *Manchester*, 59.

5. Waller (ed.), *Urban Landscape*, 219.

6. A. Foster, *Birmingham* (Pevsner Architectural Guide, 2005), 100, 110.

7. I. Ayris, *A City of Palaces* (Newcastle, 1997), 40–58; see also L. Wilkes and G. Dodds, *Tyneside Classical* (1964).

8. J. Schmiechen and K. Carls, *The British Market Hall* (New Haven and London 1999), 2–4, 282.

9. *Yorkshire Gazette*, 6 January 1849, quoted in L. Wilkes, *John Dobson* (Stocksfield, 1980), 67.

10. Cherry and Pevsner, *B. of E., Devon*, 783–85; www.tavistock.gov.uk, design and access statement 2012/16.

11. Schmiechen and Carls, *British Market Hall*, 118–19; D. Linstrum, *West Yorkshire: Architects and Architecture* (1978), 331, 325.

12. Gunn, *Public Culture*, 5–6.

13. T. Anderton, *A Tale of One City*, quoted in Gunn, *Public Culture*, 37.

14. Parkinson-Bailey, *Manchester*, 57; Morrison, *Shops and Shopping*, 49.

15. Morrison, *Shops and Shopping*, 134–6, 159–66; *CUH*, vol. 3, Plate 26.

16. Simmonds brewery, Sutton's seed and bulb establishment and Huntley and Palmer's biscuit factory.

17. D. Phillips, *The Story of Reading* (Newbury, 2004), 140–43.

18. www.berkshirehistory.com/businesses/heelas.html.

19. Tyack, *et al.*, *B of E: Berkshire*, 468.

20. Daunton, *Coal Metropolis*, 53.

21. J. F. Geist, *Arcades* (Cambridge, Mass, 1983), 290–97; Morrison, *Shops and Shopping*, 118–19; Leach and Pevsner, *B. of E., Yorkshire West Riding: Leeds, Bradford and the North*, 444–45.

22. Ayers, *Norwich*, 101.

23. Morrison, *Shops and Shopping*, 193–247; Waller (ed.), *Urban Landscape*, 167–70.

24. H. Hobhouse, *Regent Street* (Chichester, 2008), 120–22.

25. Leach and Pevsner, *B. of E., Yorkshire West Riding; Leeds, Bradford and the North*, 449.

26. J. Booker, *Temples of Mammon: The Architecture of Banking* (Edinburgh, 1990), 89–126; I. Beesley and A. Caveney, *Calderdale: Architecture and History* (Halifax, 1988), Plate 97.

27. Beesley and Caveney, *Calderdale*, Plate 99.

28. Booker, *Temples of Mammon*, 84–87.

29. J. Summerson, *The Unromantic Castle* (1990), 196–212.

30. D. K. Stenhouse, 'Liverpool's Office District, 1875–1905', *Transactions of the Historical Society of Lancashire and Cheshire* 133 (1983), 72; J. Sharples, '"The visible embodiment of modern commerce": speculative office buildings in Liverpool, c.1780–1870', *Architectural History*, 61 (2018), 131–73.

31. Hughes, *Seaport*, 58–63; C. Withall, 'Liverpool's pioneering role on commercial architecture', *Liverpool History Society Journal* (2011), 74–81.

32. R. Fellowes, *Edwardian Architecture: Style and Technology* (1995), 108–14.

33. Parkinson-Bailey, *Manchester*, 79.

34. Girouard, *English Town*, 39–242; Linstrum, *West Yorkshire*, 299–304; S. Duxbury-Neumann, *Little Germany* (Stroud, 2015).

35. Taylor, *et al.*, *Manchester: The Warehouse Legacy*, 28–40.

36. Fraser and Maver, *Glasgow 1830–1912*, 488–510.

37. For details, see E. Williamson *et al.*, *B of S., Glasgow*, 67–72.

38. *CUH*, vol. 3, 22–23; Waller (ed.), *Urban Landscape*, 299–303.

39. See M. H. Port, *The Houses of Parliament* (New Haven and London, 1976); C. Shenton, *Mr Barry's War* (Oxford, 2016).

40. See M. H. Port, *Imperial London* (New Haven and London, 1995).

41. See C. Cunningham, *Victorian and Edwardian Town Halls* (1981).

42. Girouard, *English Town*, 215.

43. Cunningham, *Town Halls*, 22–23; J. Archer (ed.), *Art and Architecture in Victorian Manchester* (Manchester, 1985), 128–61; Parkinson-Bailey, *Manchester*, 106.

44. See A. Peers, *Birmingham Town Hall* (Farnham, 2012) 124–5, 155.

45. For municipal reform in Birmingham, E. P. Hennock, *Fit and Proper Persons* (1973) 17–176.

46. It was designed by a local architect J. H. Chamberlain (no relation of the politician), who was responsible for many of the city's schools and other public buildings.

47. Hartwell, *Manchester*, 172–73; Archer (ed.), *Art and Architecture in Victorian Manchester*, 81–110.

48. Figueirido and Beesley, *Victorian and Edwardian Manchester,* Plate 83.

49. R. C. W. Cox, 'The Old Centre of Croydon; Victorian Decay and Redevelopment', in A. Everitt, *Perspectives in English Urban History* (1973), 184–212.

50. Daunton, *Coal Metropolis*, 53.

51. Hilling, *Cardiff and the Valleys*, 145–60; Newman, *B. of W: Glamorgan*, 220–37; Hilling, *History and Architecture of Cardiff Civic Centre* (Cardiff, 2016).

52. N. E. Shasore, 'Southampton Civic Centre', in E. Harwood and A. Powers (eds), *The Architecture of Public Service* (Twentieth Century Society, 2018), 47 and *passim*.

53. Phillips, *Reading*, 130–2, 135–36.

54. Hennock, *Fit and Proper Persons*), 282.

55. G. Waterfield, *The People's Galleries* (New Haven and London, 2015), 148–50.

56. A. Black, S. Pepper and K. Bagshawe, *Books, Buildings and Social Engineering* (Farnham, 2009), 73–161.

57. Fellows, *Edwardian Architecture*, 128–34.

58. I. Beesley and P. de Figueiredo, *Victorian and Edwardian Manchester*, plate 44; M. P. Tylecote, *Mechanics Institutes of Lancashire and Yorkshire Before 1851* (Manchester, 1957).

59. R. Lawrence, 'The Evolution of the Victorian Art school', *Journal of Architecture*, 19/1 (2014), 81–107; G. Tyack, 'The architecture of art education', in E. Gillin and H. Joyce (eds), *Experiencing Architecture in the Nineteenth Century* (2018), 61–74.

60. W. Whyte, *Redbrick* (Oxford, 2015), 107–109; Parkinson-Bailey, *Manchester*, 112–14.

61. S. Whittingham, *Wills Memorial Building* (Bristol, 2003), 10.

62. N. Harte, *The University of London 1836–1986* (1986), 219–30.

63. Gunn, *Public Culture*, p. 26.

64. C. Webster (ed.), *Building a Great Victorian City* (Leeds, 2011), 252–53; V. Glasstone, *Victorian and Edwardian Theatres* (1975), 62–65; J. Earl and M. Stell, (eds), *Theatres Trust Guide to British Theatres* (2000), 87–88.

65. www.arthurlloyd.co.uk.

66. D. Sharp, *The Picture Palace* (1969), 52, 55–9, 140.

67. Girouard, *Victorian Pubs* (1984), 110.

68. Hughes, *Seaport*, 90–93.

69. J. Sharples, *Liverpool* (Pevsner Architectural Guide), 234–35.

70. Parkinson-Bailey, *Manchester*, 133–34.

71. It occupies the site of two earlier hotels fronting the former Ranelagh garden, the city's first public open space, laid out in 1722.

72. Beesley and Figueredo, *Victorian and Edwardian Manchester*, Plate 70.

73. Ashworth, *Planning*, 15.

74. See R. Walton, *The English Seaside Resort* (1983).

75. P. Borsay and J. Walton, *Resorts and Ports* (Bristol, 2011), 86–106, 126–43.

76. Bell, *City Fathers*, 137–40.

77. Sigsworth, 'Ports and Resorts', 191–00.

78. Quoted in H. Carter and W. K. D. Davies (eds), *Urban Essays* (1970), 74.

79. *Middlesborough Gazette*, 12 August 1873, quoted in Sigsworth, 'Ports and Resorts', 197.

80. For Cleethorpes, see Sigsworth, 'Ports and Resorts', 179–90; for Clacton, *VCH Essex*, vol. 11.

81. Quoted in B. Jennings (ed.), *A History of Harrogate and Knaresborough* (Huddersfield, 1970), 433.

CHAPTER 8

1. See M. Graham, 'On Foot in Oxford: Folly Bridge and South Oxford' (Oxford Central Library, Local History Collections, n.d.); C. Newbigging, *The Changing Faces of South Oxford and South Hinksey*, 2 vols (Witney, 1998–99).

2. Liz Woolley, *Oxford's Working Past* (Oxford, 2012), 28–31.

3. *Tour through England and Wales* (1928 edn), vol. 2, 2.

4. Cherry and Pevsner, *B. of E., London 4: North*, 694–95.

5. A. Saint, *London Suburbs* (1999), 31–33. Sadler sold it in 1550, having built a much larger house in Hertfordshire.

6. *Tour*, vol. 2, 170.

7. *VCH Essex*, vol. 6, 179.

8. Quoted in P. Langford, *A Polite and Commercial People* (Oxford, 1989), 422.

9. C. O'Brien and N. Pevsner, *B. of E., London 5: East* (2005), 456–59; see the 1703 map on p. 457.

10. E. F. Smith, *Clapham* (London: Clapham Society, n.d.), 26–8, 34–37; Byrne, *London's Georgian Houses*, 14, 60–61.

11. 'Map of Country Twelve Miles Round London' (1811), reproduced in P. Barber, *London: A History in Maps*, 138.

12. The old church survived to be rebuilt as a chapel of ease in 1815.

13. McKellar, *Landscapes of London*, 145–167; S. Jeffery, 'The Building of Maids of Honour Row', *Georgian Group Journal* 18 (2010), 65–76.

14. See McKellar, *Landscapes of London*, 169–203. The effect was memorably conveyed in Ford Madox Brown's painting 'An English Autumn Afternoon' (1852–53: Birmingham Museums and Art Gallery).

15. Leech, *The Town House in Medieval and Early Modern Bristol*, 231–2, quoting 1662 Hearth Tax returns.

16. Borsay, *English Urban Renaissance*, 296.

17. A. Foyle, *Bristol* (Pevsner Architectural Guides, 2004), 208–10.

18. Girouard, *English Town*, 150, 154.

19. R. Yallop, 'Matthew Nosworthy,: A builder in Georgian Exeter', *Georgian Group Journal* 26 (2018), 157–78.

20. www.exetercivicsociety.org.uk. See also M. S. Simpson and T. H. Lloyd, *Middle Class Housing in Britain* (Newton Abbot, 1977), 34–43.

21. J. Summerson, *Georgian London* (New Haven and London, 2003 edn), 325, 327. For Camberwell Grove, see J. Bullman, *et al.*, *The Secret History of Our Streets* (2013).

22. M. Bonwitt, *Michael Searles: A Georgian Architect and Surveyor* (1987); Saint, *London Suburbs*, 49.

23. *An American in Regency England*, ed. C. Hibbert, 142–43.

24. As at Kentish Town: see G. Tindall, *The Fields Beneath* (1977).

25. See H. Hobhouse, *Thomas Cubitt: Master Builder* (1971); F. Sheppard (ed.), *Survey of London,* vol. 37: North Kensington (1973).

26. *B. of S., Glasgow*, 51–2, 307–13; Simpson and Lloyd, *Middle Class Housing*, 45–47.

27. Simpson and Lloyd, *Middle Class Housing*, 51.

28. M. Galinou, *Cottages and Villas: The Birth of the Garden* Suburb (New Haven and London, 2010), 67–83.

29. J. Mordaunt Crook in Tyack (ed.), *John Nash*, 90–94.

30. *The Suburban Gardener and Villa Companion*, quoted in L. Davidoff and C. Hall, *Family Fortunes* (1987), 189.

31. H. J. Dyos, *Victorian Suburb: A Study of the Growth of Camberwell* (1961), 60–80.

32. D.J. Olson, 'House Upon House', in Dyos and Woolf, *Victorian City*, vol. 2 (1973), 333–57. See also F. M. L. Thompson, *Hampstead: Building a Borough* (1974).

33. See D. Cannadine, *Lords and Landlords* (1980).

34. M. Spiers, *Victoria Park, Manchester* (Manchester: Chetham Society, 1976), 1–6.

35. *Conditions of the Working Class in England*, ed. W. O. Henderson and W. H. Chaloner (1958), 54–56.

36. Quoted in Davidoff and Hall, *Family Fortunes*, 368.

37. Pevsner and Neave, *B. of E. Yorkshire: York and East Riding*, 554–55; Newman, *B. of W. Glamorgan*, 310; Daunton, *Coal Metropolis*, 74–75.

38. See J. P. Lewis, *Building Cycles and Britain's Growth* (1965), 194–97 and *passim*.

39. K. Brand, *The Park Estate, Nottingham* (Nottingham Civic Society, n.d.).

40. G. Best, *Mid Victorian Britain 1851–75* (revised edn, St Albans, 1973), 35–37.

41. E. Hyams (ed.), *Taine's Notes on England* (1957), 14.

42. *VCH Middlesex* vol. 5., 218.

43. S. Taylor and K. Gibson, *Manningham: Character and Diversity in a Bradford Suburb* (Swindon: English Heritage, 2010), 40–44.

44. *Victorian Suburb*, 125.

45. Muthesius, *English Terraced House*, 88–97.

46. M. Hunter, *Victorian Villas of Hackney* (Hackney Society, 1981), 24–28. It was allegedly the model for Albert Square in the TV drama series 'East Enders'.

47. B. Cherry and A. Robey (eds.), *Rediscovered Utopias: Saving London's Suburbs* (London: Save Britain's Heritage, 2010), 27–37.

48. Waller, *Town, City and Nation*, 2–4.

49. A. Menuge, *Ordinary Landscapes, Special Places* (Swindon: English Heritage, 2008).

50. *Works of John Ruskin*, Library Edition, vol. 22, 263.

51. W. L. Creese, *The Search for Environment* (1966), 87–107; T. A. Greeves, 'London's First Garden Suburb', *Country Life*, 7, 14 December 1967, 1524–9, 1600–02.

52. Creese, *Search for Environment*, 108–43.

53. S. Meacham, *Regaining Paradise* (Yale, 1999), 44–54; M. Miller, *English Garden Cities: An Introduction* (Swindon: English Heritage, 2010), 2–5.

54. P. Ballard (ed.), *Birmingham's Victorian and Edwardian Architects* (Wetherby, 2009), 352–57. The architect was Frederick Martin.

55. Newman, *B. of W, Glamorgan*, 295–96.

56. See M. Miller and A. S. Gray, *Hampstead Garden Suburb* (Chichester, 1992)

57. A. Sutcliffe (ed.), *British Town Planning: The Formative Years* (Leicester, 1981), 41–42.

58. S. Beattie, *A Revolution in London Housing* (London, 1980), 85–119.

59. See M. Swenarton, *Homes fit for Heroes* (1981).

60. A. Ravetz and R. Turkington, *The Place of Home* (1995), 24–26; A. Ravetz, *Council Housing and Culture* (2001), chs. 6–7.

61. Smout, *Century of the Scottish People*, 52–56.

62. See A. Olechnowicz, *Working Class Housing in England Between the Wars: The Becontree Estate* (Oxford, 1997).

63. See D. Deakin, *Wythenshawe: The Story of a Garden City* (Chichester, 1989).

64. R. Roberts, *The Classic Slum* (Harmondsworth, 1973) provides a corrective. See also R. Durant, *Watling* (1939)—a study of the Burnt Oak estate in north-west London—and M. Young and P. Willmott, *Family and Kinship in East London* (Harmondsworth, 1961).

65. The number of salaried workers grew by a million, to 2.7 m, between 1911 and 1931.

66. Quoted in A. Jackson, *Semi-Detached London* (1973), 258.

67. See for instance P. Oliver et al., *Dunroamin* (1981); D. Edwards and R. Pigram, *London's Underground Suburbs* (1986).

68. Quiney, *House and Home*, 148–65.

69. *Rediscovered Utopias*, 122–30.

70. Thompson, *The Rise of Suburbia* (Leicester, 1982), 212–67.

71. *English Journey* (1937 edn), 4. See also *CUH*, vol. 3, 512–14.

72. M. J. Law, *The Experience of Suburban Modernity* (2014), 197.

73. C. Paine et al., *The Worker's Home* (Oxfordshire Museums Service, 1979), 31; S. Tree, *Changing Faces of Florence Park* (Witney, 2001).

CHAPTER 9

1. C. Mullins, *A Festival on the River* (2007); E. Harwood and A. Powers (eds), *Festival of Britain* (Twentieth Century Society, 2001).

2. Harwood and Powers, *Festival of Britain*, 141–54; A. Ravetz, *The Place of Home* (1995), 30.

3. J. V. Punter, *Design Control in Bristol 1940–1980* (1990), 24–33.

4. J. Gould, *Plymouth: Vision of a Modern City* (Swindon: English Heritage, 2010), 5.

5. T. Mason and N. Tiratsoo, 'People, Politics and Planning in Coventry', in J. M. Diefendorf (ed.), *Rebuilding Europe's Bombed Cities* (1990), 97.

6. J and C. Gould, *Coventry: The Making of a Modern City* (Swindon: English Heritage, 2016), 122–24.

7. Gould, *Coventry*, 40.

8. E. Harwood and A. Powers (eds), *The Heroic Period of Conservation* (London: Twentieth Century Society, 2004), 65–86.

9. J. M. Edwards, *The Design of Suburbia* (1981), 165.

10. Edwards, *Suburbia*, 159–61.

11. Gould, *Plymouth*, 46–49.

12. L. Esher, *A Broken Wave* (1981), 250–51; Boughton, *Municipal Dreams*, 85.

13. A. Ravetz, *Council Housing and Culture* (2001), 102; S. Ward, *Planning and Urban Change* (2004), 50–51.

14. Gould, *Coventry*, 93–99, 115. One of Coventry's post-war estates, Tile Hill, has been memorably immortalised in the hyper-realist paintings of the contemporary artist George Shaw, who grew up there.

15. Edwards, *Suburbia*, 166–70; Ravetz, *Place of Home*, 32, 183–4, 192–93.

16. For LCC housing of this period, see E. Harwood and A. Powers (eds), *Housing the Twentieth Century Nation* (London: Twentieth Century Society, 2008), 99–120.

17. E. Harwood, 'White Light/White Heat: Rebuilding England's provincial towns and cities on the Sixties', in Harwood and Powers (eds.), *The Sixties* (London: Twentieth Century Society, 2004), 66.

18. M. Glendinning and S. Muthesius, *Tower Block* (New Haven and London 1994), 125–31.

19. *Architects' Journal*, 15 Jan 1963.

20. Harwood and Powers (eds), *Sixties*, 70; Glendinning and Muthesius, *Tower Block*, 154–55.

21. R. T. Rowley, *The English Landscape in the Twentieth Century* (2006), 111; *Home Sweet Home* (London Architectural Monographs, 1976), 62–71.

22. Boughton, *Municipal Dreams*, 128–30.

23. *Architectural Review*, Oct 1972; P. Hodgkinson, 'Brunswick Centre, Bloomsbury', in Harwood and Powers (eds), *Sixties*, 83–90.

24. Glendinning and Muthesius, *Tower Block*, 168.

25. M. Glendinning, R. MacInnes and A. MacKechnie, *History of Scottish Architecture*, (Edinburgh 1996), 452–54.

26. A. Powers, *Britain: Modern Architectures in History* (2007), 133.

27. Glendinning and Muthesius, *Tower Block*, 322–23. See also L. Hanley, *Estates* (2007), 124.

28. Ravetz, *Place of Home*, 44–8, 54–55.

29. Harwood and Powers (eds), *Housing*, 149–62.

30. Ravetz, *Place of Home*, 73; S. Ward, *Planning and Urban Change* (2004), 40.

31. T. Sharp, *Oxford Replanned* (1948).

32. R. J. Morris, 'The Friars and Paradise', *Oxoniensia*, 36 (1971), 72–98; J. Simmie, *Power, Property and Corporatism* (1981).

33. L. Hanley, *Estates: An Intimate History* (2007).

34. For individual case studies, see C. Amery and D. Cruikshank, *The Rape of Britain* (1975).
35. *CUH*, vol. 3, 517–20.
36. By 2021 it had risen again to almost 9 ½ million.
37. Rowley, *English Landscape in the Twentieth Century*, 108–109.
38. O. Marriott, *The Property Boom* (1967, reissued 1989), 111–12.
39. Marriott, *Property Boom*, 15.
40. O. Saumarez Smith, *Boom Cities* (Oxford, 2019), 83; Morrison, *English Shops and Shopping*, 259.
41. Morrison, *Shops and Shopping*, 261; Harwood and Powers (eds), *Sixties*, 66–67; Marriott, *Property Boom*, 223.
42. O. Saumarez Smith, 'Central Government and Town-Centre Redevelopment in Britain 1959–1966', *Historical Journal*, 58/1 (2015), 222–23.
43. Harwood and Powers (eds), *Sixties*, 69; Harwood and Powers (eds), *Conservation*, 101–10; Esher, *Broken Wave*, 176–78.
44. See A. Fergusson, *The Sack of Bath* (1973).
45. See S. Gunn, 'Ring Road: Birmingham and the collapse of the motor city ideal in 1970s Britain', *Historical Journal*, 60/1 (2018).
46. http://www.welshstreets.co.uk; Boughton, *Municipal Dreams*, 239–40.
47. For Bradford, see S. Gunn, 'The Rise and Fall of British Urban Modernism: Planning Bradford, circa 1945–1970', *Journal of British Studies* 49/4 (2010), 865–69.
48. S. Humphries and J. Taylor, *The Making of Modern London 1945–85* (1986), 110–37.
49. Glendinning *et al.*, *Scottish Architecture*, 349, 355, 423–25.
50. Harwood and Powers (eds), *Conservation*, 47–48.
51. R. Thorne, *Covent Garden Market: Its History and Restoration* (1980), 106–108; Harwood and Powers (eds), *The Seventies* (London: Twentieth Century Society, 2012), 13–14.
52. Harwood and Powers (eds), *Seventies*, 22–24: Edwards, *Design of Suburbia*, 250–54.
53. Harwood and Powers (eds), *Conservation*, 94.
54. e.g. the Weller Streets Housing Co-operative in Liverpool: A. Quiney, *House and Home* (1986), 166–89.
55. A. Kefford, 'Disruption, Destruction and the Creation of the "inner cities": the Impact of Urban Renewal on Industry', *Urban History*, 44/3 (2017), 502–13.
56. Ravetz, *Place of Home*, 33; http://www.bbc.co.uk/news/business-28918709.
57. *Guardian*, 26 Oct 2016; Powers, *Britain*, 244; Hill, Newman and Pevsner, *B. of E., Dorset*, 258–60.
58. *Financial Times*, 18 August 2013.
59. J. White, *London in the Twentieth Century* (2001), 75–82; Rowley, *English Landscape in the Twentieth Century*, 114–17.
60. E. Harwood and A. Powers (eds), *Building for Business* (London: Twentieth Century Society, 2020), 21.
61. Bullen, *et al.*, *B. of E., Hampshire: South*, 505–508.
62. See T. Bendixson and C. Platt, *Milton Keynes: Image and Reality* (Cambridge, 1992); Harwood and Powers (eds), *Seventies*, 103–17.

63. Powers, *Britain*, p. 240; Ravetz, *Council Housing*, 229–33; Parkinson-Bailey, *Manchester*, 193–98.

64. *Sunday Times*, 4 November 2018.

65. http://www.benflatman.com/BullRing/BullRing.html; *Financial Times*, 28 September 2015.

66. It followed the demolition of John Madin's concrete behemoth of 1974, which in turn replaced the Victorian library.

67. Powers, *Britain*, 237, 271–72; L. Goberman, 'The State and Post-Industrial Urban Regeneration: The Reinvention of South Cardiff', *Urban History*, 45/3 (2018), 503–23.

68. Parkinson-Bailey, *Manchester*, 127–9, 230; Rowley, *English Landscape in the Twentieth Century*, 158–59.

69. Parkinson-Bailey, *Manchester*, 219, 276–77.

70. *Economist* special report, 30 June 2012.

71. Parkinson-Bailey, *Manchester*, 272–73; Morrison, *Shops and Shopping*, 301–303.

72. For American examples of this phenomenon, see J. Garreau, *Edge City* (New York, 1991). Other British examples include Cribbs Causeway, next to the M4 and M5 motorways on the edge of Bristol.

73. Ross and Clark, *London: The Illustrated History*, 334–35.

74. *Evening Standard* 16 May 2014; *Guardian*, 3 Aug 2017.

75. *Parliamentary Papers*, 1854–5, vol. 10, p. 158.

76. Powers, *Britain*, 275.

77. S. Kostof, *The City Assembled* (1992), 305.

78. Not least because of the effects of the 2020–2021 Coronavirus pandemic, the long-term effects of which are still uncertain at the time of writing.

Further Reading

This list contains a selection of the books that I have found especially useful in preparing this book. It does not pretend to be a complete bibliography of British urban history, and readers in search of information about specific towns and cities are recommended to consult the titles listed in the footnotes to each chapter, and also, where relevant, the volumes of the Victoria County History (for English towns)–https://www.history.ac.uk/research/victoria-county-history, the most recent editions of the Pevsner Architectural Guides for England, Scotland and Wales (Yale University Press), and the Historic Towns Atlas–http://www.historictownsatlas.org.uk/atlases.

Ashworth, W, *The Genesis of Modern British Town Planning* (1954)

Aston, M. and Bond, J., *The Landscape of Towns* (Stroud, 2000)

Barley, M. W. (ed.), *Plans and Topography of Medieval Towns* (Council for British Archaeology, 1976)

Bell, C. and R., *City Fathers: the Early History of Town Planning in Britain* (1969)

Bell, D., *Edinburgh Old Town* (Edinburgh, 2008)

Beresford, M. W., *New Towns of the Middle Ages* (Gloucester, 1988)

Beresford, M. W., and Joseph, J. K.) *Medieval England: an Aerial Survey* (Cambridge, 1979)

Blair, J., *Building Anglo-Saxon England* (Princeton and Oxford, 2018)

Borsay, P., *The English Urban Renaissance: Culture and Society in the Provincial Town 1660–1770* (Oxford, 1989)

Borsay, P. and Walton, J., *Resorts and Ports: European Seaside Towns Since 1700* (Bristol, 2011)

Boughton, J., *Municipal Dreams: The Rise and Fall of Council Housing* (2018)

Briggs, A., *Victorian Cities* (1970)

Burnett, J., *A Social History of Housing 1815–1970* (1986)

Chalklin, C., *The Provincial Towns of Georgian England* (1974)

Chapman, S. D. (ed.), *The History of Working-class Housing: A Symposium* (Newton Abbot, 1971)

Clark, P. (ed.), *The Transformation of English Provincial Towns, 1600–1800* (1984)

Clark, P. (ed.), *The Cambridge Urban History of Britain: Volume II, 1540–1840* (Cambridge, 2008)

Clark, P. and Slack, P., *English Towns in Transition 1500–1700* (Oxford, 1976)

Corfield, P., *The Impact of English Towns 1700–1800* (1982)

Creighton, O. and Higham, R., *Medieval Town Walls: An Archaeology and Social History of Urban Defence* (Stroud, 2005)

Daunton, M., *House and Home in the Victorian City* (1983)

Daunton, M. (ed.), *The Cambridge Urban History of Britain: Volume III, 1840–1950* (Cambridge, 2008)

Dennis, R., *English Industrial Cities of the Nineteenth Century* (Cambridge, 1984)

Dyos, H.J., and Wolff, M (eds.), *The Victorian City, Image and Reality* (1973)

Edwards, J. M., *The Design of Suburbia* (1981)

Ellis, J., *The Georgian Town, 1680–1840* (Basingstoke, 2001)

Esher, L., *A Broken Wave: The Rebuilding of England, 1940–1980* (1981)

Everitt, A. (ed.), *Perspectives in English Urban History* (1973)

Fraser, W. and Mayer, I., *Glasgow: Volume II 1830 to 1912* (1996)

Giles, K. and Dyer, C. (eds)., *Town and Country in the Middle Ages* (Leeds, 2005)

Girouard, M., *The English Town* (New Haven and London, 1990)

Glendinning, M. and Muthesius, S., *Tower Block: Modern Public Housing in England, Scotland, Wales, and Northern Ireland* (New Haven and London 1994)

Gomme, A. and Walker, D, *Architecture of Glasgow* (1968)

Gunn, S., *The Public Culture of the Victorian City* (Manchester, 2000)

Hanley, L., *Estates: An Intimate History* (2007)

Harris, R. and McKean, C., *The Scottish Town in the Age of Enlightenment 1740–1820* (Edinburgh, 2014)

Haslam, J., *Early Medieval Towns in Britain* (2010)

Hilling, J. B., *Cardiff and the Valleys* (Cardiff, 1973)

Hoskins, W. G., *The Making of the English Landscape* (1955)

Hoskins, W. G., *Local History in England* (1959)

Hughes, Q., *Seaport: Architecture and Townscape of Liverpool* (1984)

Kain, R.J.P. and Oliver, R.R, *British Town Maps: a History* (2015)

Kellett, J. R., *The Impact of Railways on Victorian Cities* (1969)

Kostof, S., *The City Assembled* (1992)

Lilley, K., *Urban Life in the Middle Ages: 1000–1450* (Basingstoke, 2002)

Linstrum, D., *West Yorkshire: Architects and Architecture* (1978)

Lobel, M. D. (ed.), *The Atlas of Historic Towns, Vols. 1 and 2* (London, 1969, 1975)

Lynch, M. (ed.), *The Early Modern Town in Scotland* (Edinburgh, 1987)

Lynch, M., *et al.* (eds), *The Scottish Medieval Town* (Edinburgh, 1988)

Marriott, O., *The Property Boom* (1967, reissued 1989)

Martin, G., *The Town* (1961)

McKellar, E., *Landscapes of London: The City, the Country and the Suburbs 1660–1840* (New Haven & London, 2013)

McWilliam, C, *Scottish Townscape* (1975)

Meacham, S., *Regaining Paradise: Englishness and the Early Garden City Movement* (Yale, 1999)

Morris, R. J. and Rodger, R. (eds), *The Victorian City: A Reader in British Urban History, 1820–1914* (1993)

Morrison, K., *English Shops and Shopping: An Architectural History* (New Haven and London, 2003)

Muthesius, S., *The English Terraced House* (1984)

Nairn, I. ed. Hatherley, O., *Nairn's Towns* (2013)

Oswald, A., *Old Towns Revisited* (1952)

Ottaway, P., *Archaeology in British Towns: From the Emperor Claudius to the Black Death* (Oxford, 1992)

Palliser, D. M. (ed.), *The Cambridge Urban History of Britain: Volume 1, 600–1540* Cambridge, 2008)

Palmer, M. and Neaverson, P., *Industry in the Landscape, 1700–1900* (1994)

Parkinson-Bailey, J., *Manchester: An Architectural History* (Manchester, 2000)

Platt, C., *The English Medieval Town* (1979)

Porter, R, *London: a Social History* (1994)

Powers, A., *Britain: Modern Architectures in History* (2007)

Quiney, A., *Town Houses of Medieval Britain* (New Haven and London, 2003)

Ravetz, A., *Council Housing and Culture* (2001)

Ravetz, A. and Turkington, R, *The Place of Home English Domestic Environments, 1914–2000* (1995)

Reynolds, S., *An Introduction to the History of English Medieval Towns* (Oxford, 1977)

Rogers, A., *Approaches to Local History* (1977)

Ross, C. and Clark, J., *London: The Illustrated History* (London: 2008)

Rowley, R. T., *The English Landscape in the Twentieth Century* (2006)

Saint, A., *London Suburbs* (1999)

Saumarez Smith, O., *Boom Cities* (2019)

Schofield, J., *The Building of London: From the Conquest to the Great Fire* (1984)

Schofield, J. and Vince, A. *Medieval Towns* (Leicester, 1994)

Sigsworth, E. M. (ed.), *Ports and Resorts in the Regions* (Hull, 1982)

Simpson, M., and Lloyd, T. H., *Middle Class Housing in Britain* (1977)

Skipp, V., *Greater Birmingham* (Birmingham, 1980) and *The Making of Victorian Birmingham* (Birmingham, 1983)

Slater, T. and Goose, N., *A County of Small Towns: The Development of Hertfordshire's Urban Landscape to 1800* (Hatfield, 2008)

Slater, T. and Rosser, G., *The Church in the Medieval Town* (Aldershot, 1998)

Soulsby, I., *The Towns of Medieval Wales* (Chichester, 1983)

Stobart, J. *et al.*, *Spaces of Consumption: Leisure and Shopping in the English Town, c.1680–1830* (Abingdon, 2007)

Summerson, J., *Georgian London* (New Haven & London, 2003 edn)

Thompson, F.M.L. (ed.), *The Rise of Suburbia* (Leicester, 1982)

Turmer, H., *Town Defences in England and Wales* (1971)

Upton, C., *Living Back-to-Back* (2010)

Wacher, J. S., *The Towns of Roman Britain* (London, 1995)

Waller, P., *Town, City and Nation: England 1850–1914* (1983)

Waller, P. (ed.), *The English Urban Landscape* (Oxford, 2000)

Walton, J.K., *The English Seaside Resort* (1983)

Ward, S., *Planning and Urban Change* (2004)

Youngson, A.J., *The Making of Classical Edinburgh* (Edinburgh, 1966)

Credits

Topographical Collection / Alamy Stock Photo: 1.1; © Geoffrey Tyack: 1.2; 1.10; 1.16; 1.17; 2.3; 2.7; 2.8; 2.9; 2.12; 2.13; 2.14; 2.15; 2.16; 3.3; 3.4; 3.7; 3.8; 3.10; 3.13; 4.2; 4.4; 4.6; 4.7; 4.8; 4.9; 4.10; 4.11; 4.12; 5.2; 5.3; 5.9; 5.10; 5.14; 6.2; 6.12; 6.13; 6.14; 7.1; 7.2; 7.5; 7.6; 7.7; 7.11; 7.12; 7.13; 7.16; 7.17; 8.4; 8.5; 8.7; 8.9; 8.11; 9.3; 9.6; 9.8; 9.9; 9.10; 9.11; 9.14; 9.15; 9.16; De Agostini / G. Wright: 1.5; JLImages / Alamy Stock Photo: 1.6; Paul White Aerial views / Alamy Stock Photo: 1.8; Antiqua Print Gallery / Alamy Stock Photo: 1.9; 2.6; 8.3; KGPA Ltd / Alamy Stock Photo: 2.1; 2.11; 5.5; PURPLE MARBLES YORKSHIRE / Alamy Stock Photo: 2.2; Greg Balfour Evans / Alamy Stock Photo: 2.5; 3.11; Pictures Now / Alamy Stock Photo: 2.10; Ian Dagnall / Alamy Stock Photo: 3.10; Border Image / Alamy Stock Photo: 3.2; Britain – cities and towns / Alamy Stock Photo: 3.5; The Bodleian : 3.6; Angela Serena Gilmour / Alamy Stock Photo: 3.9; Travel Pictures / Alamy Stock Photo: 3.12; British Library: 3.14; 4.1; 5.8; Wikipedia Commons: 3.15; 5.11; 7.10; Harris Brisbane Dick Fund, 1917: 3.16; Heritage Image Partnership Ltd / Alamy Stock Photo: 4.3; 5.13; 6.9; Wellcome Collection. Attribution 4.0 International (CC BY 4.0): 4.5; Yale Center for British Art, Paul Mellon Collection, USA/ The Bridgeman Art Library: 4.13; Granger Historical Picture Archive / Alamy Stock Photo: 4.14; Richard Cooke / Alamy Stock Photo: 4.15; Graham Mulrooney / Alamy Stock Photo: 5.1; Iain Masterton / Alamy Stock Photo: 5.4; By kind permission of the National Churches Trust: 5.7; CC/ Tim Green: 5.15; 7.3; lowefoto / Alamy Stock Photo: 5.16; © Bolton Museum and Art Gallery / Bridgeman Images: 6.1; John Keates / Alamy Stock Photo: 6.3; Matt Botwood / Alamy Stock Photo: 6.4; Arcaid Images / Alamy Stock Photo: 6.6; © Historic England / Mary Evans Picture Library: 6.7; 9.2; travellinglight / Alamy Stock Photo: 6.10; Rodhullandemu: 6.15; Chronicle / Alamy Stock Photo: 7.4; Mike Hughes / Alamy Stock Photo: 7.8; The Print Collector / Alamy Stock Photo: 7.9; WhiskyBottle / Alamy Stock Photo: 7.14; Mark Beton/London / Alamy Stock Photo: 7.15; A.P.S. (UK) /

Alamy Stock Photo: 8.10; Mary Evans Picture Library/Town & Country Planning: 8.13; Tony Ray-Jones / RIBA Collections: 8.14; © The Bexley Archive Image Collection, The London Borough of Bexley / Mary Evans Picture Library: 8.15; Angelo Hornak / Alamy Stock Photo: 8.16; By Kind Permission of The Commissioner of the City of London Police. ID no. IN7106: 9.1; © CSG CIC Glasgow Museums and Libraries Collection: The Mitchell Library, Special Collections: 9.5; Mirrorpix / Contributor: 9.7; CC / Grenavitar: 9.12; Jane Tregelles / Alamy Stock Photo: 9.15

The publisher and author apologize for any errors or omissions in the above list. If contacted they will be pleased to rectify these at the earliest opportunity.

Index